God, Man, and the Thinker

God, Man, and the Thinker

---◆---

Philosophies of Religion

---◆---

D O N A L D   A.   W E L L S

A DELTA BOOK

To June, Miriam, & Michael

Preface

THE ENDEAVOR to think critically about the subject of religion raises problems of a peculiar sort. Not only is this an area in which many persons are only partially informed, but it is one to which these same persons are seriously committed. This situation poses a double task for the reader who wishes to approach the field with critical objectivity. On the one hand, the partial information needs to be seen in the larger context of the history of comparative religions, and on the other hand, the religious issues to which both personal and cosmic significance are already attached need to be investigated with impartial scrutiny. Philosophy of religion is no substitute for religion, nor, therefore, should it be considered as opposed to religion.

This book presents a panorama of many philosophies of religion. Indeed, the question, "What is philosophy of religion?" is in itself a problem. There have always been two general areas of concern in the philosophical study of religion. One is the question of the truth or falsity of religious claims. The other is the question of the value, the ultimate significance or meaning of religion. The answers to these questions fall into two general positions. There are those who maintain

that the determination of the true and the false religious assertions affects, or ought to affect, the commitments we make
to religion. On the other hand, there are those who insist
either that religious claims lie outside the question of truth
or that the determination of truth or falsity does not influence
the decision for religion. This book investigates the meaning,
consistency, and implications of both views.

It is not my intention to decide where the reader should
stand. It will be assumed, further, that awareness of what
philosophers of religion have said entails no defense of either
theism or atheism. Thinking about religion may, however, enable the religious person to see both the grounds and the limits
of the religious claims. This book intends no bias toward one
religion or against another. If the question of the superiority
of a particular religious faith is to be answered at all, it should
be answered by religion, not by philosophy. Because our society is based on the Judeo-Christian traditions, the ideas and
problems discussed are rooted in this position, but since East
and West share common religious concerns, Hinduism, Jainism, and Buddhism are discussed at some length. The primary
emphasis, however, is on the major classical formulations in
the traditions of Judaism, Catholicism, and Protestantism.

The average person studies the philosophies of religion
for one or more of the following reasons. He wants not only to
study what the term "god" has meant, but also to investigate
what grounds there are for the existence of a god. He is troubled by the relation of contemporary psychology to religion and
he wishes to know what implications, if any, current data provide for the possibility of immortality. There are some who
wish to know at what points their own religion differs from
certain other religions. Although no attempt is made to discuss
denominations within Christianity, the general positions which
Catholic and Protestant thinkers have held are discussed. I do
not intend to indicate preference for any particular tradition.
The point is rather that awareness of a position and of its implications may assist the reader in making up his own mind.

The varied views are presented with as much affirmative

conviction as their staunchest supporters will permit. In all matters involving claims of truth three positions will be explicated. In the first place, I will present and discuss some representative supporters of the truth of the idea in question. Second, I will, where possible, present the views of some who assert the falsity of the idea. Finally, I will explain the positions of those who deny both truth and falsity to religious claims. The reader will be expected to draw his own conclusions.

Less than one hundred years ago John Stuart Mill observed: "There is no subject on which men's practical belief is more incorrectly indicated by the words they use to express it, than religion." With this observation in mind the reader will be advised to apply four questions to each religious issue before he draws his own conclusions.

1. What does the statement in question mean?
2. Does the statement contain a self-contradiction?
3. Are there data to support the truth of the statement?
4. Is the inference a valid one?

While these questions load the religious problems by presuming that religious statements should be given precise meanings and should be amenable to the rules of logic, this seems to be a preferable starting point to any alternatives. Since the book does investigate those claims which argue for the basic mystery of religious meanings and for the non-logical character of genuine religious concerns, the reader will still be able to choose whether he wishes religion to be cognitive or non-cognitive.

It is a pleasure to have an opportunity to express my appreciation for both the assistance and encouragement which I received in the writing of this book: to Mrs. Beverly Puterbaugh for typing the entire manuscript and to Mr. and Mrs. John Nunemaker for technical assistance; to Mr. Charles Lieber and Mrs. Leonore Hauck of Random House for their encouraging suggestions; and finally to Miss Katherine Stechmann of Random House for her imaginative queries and wise

Preface

recommendations. I also wish to thank the many publishers who have given permission for the use of their material. Special acknowledgment is given in each case in the footnotes.

D.A.W.

Pullman, Washington

Contents

PREFACE   vii

I.   *What Is Philosophy of Religion?*   3

IS PHILOSOPHY OF RELIGION A QUEST FOR TRUTH?   7
DOES PHILOSOPHY DISCOVER RELIGIOUS VALUES?   9
PHILOSOPHY OF RELIGION AND THE SCIENCES OF
   RELIGION   15
PHILOSOPHY VERSUS PHILOSOPHIES OF RELIGION   20

II.   *The Definition of Religion*   22

WHAT DOES A DEFINITION GIVE US?   23
IS RELIGION A MATTER OF BELIEF?   27
IS RELIGION A MATTER OF FEELING?   29
IS RELIGION A KIND OF ETHICS?   33
RELIGION NOMINALLY DEFINED   38

Contents

III.   *Why Do We Have Religion?*   41

IS RELIGION INHERITED?   42
WAS RELIGION INVENTED BECAUSE THE WORLD WAS
   SO GRIM?   43
WAS RELIGION DESIGNED BY POLITICAL SCHEMERS?   45
IS RELIGION PSYCHOLOGICALLY DEMANDED?   51
IS THE ORIGIN OF RELIGION IMPORTANT TO
   PHILOSOPHY?   60

IV.   *The Idea of God: to What Does the Term
            Refer?*   63

A MULTIVERSE REQUIRES MANY GODS   65
A UNIVERSE MEANS ONE GOD   69
   PANTHEISM: EVERYTHING IS GOD   69
   DEISTIC SUPERNATURALISM: THE FAR-OFF GOD   72
   NATURALISM: THE PROCESS GOD   73
   NEO-ORTHODOXY: THE GROUND OF BEING   74
   PERSONALISM: THE SENSITIVE GOD   77

V.   *Arguments for the Existence of God*   83

THE ONTOLOGICAL ARGUMENT   84
THE TELEOLOGICAL ARGUMENT   91
THE COSMOLOGICAL ARGUMENT   97
THE MORAL ARGUMENT   103
IS ANY ARGUMENT FOR GOD POSSIBLE?   105

VI.   *The Problems of Religious Knowledge*   115

THE DEFINITION OF "TRUTH"   121
THE TESTS OF TRUTH   125
THE METHODS: INDUCTION AND DEDUCTION   129

Contents

VII. *The Problem of Natural Evil* *138*

MAN'S FREEDOM REQUIRES NATURAL EVIL 141
NATURAL EVILS ARE PUNISHMENT FOR MORAL EVIL 145
NATURAL EVIL BUILDS CHARACTER 149
NATURAL GOODS NECESSITATE NATURAL EVILS 152
THERE IS NO EVIL 155
THE ANSWER OF BLIND FAITH 158
GOD IS FINITE 160

VIII. *The Problem of Immortality* *166*

WHAT DOES IMMORTALITY MEAN? 167
THE PRAGMATIC ARGUMENT 177
THE METAPHYSICAL ARGUMENT 182
THE APPEAL TO THE PSYCHIC 188
IS ANY ARGUMENT POSSIBLE? 190

IX. *Is Religion a Matter of Knowledge?* *194*

REASON AND FAITH DO NOT CONFLICT: THE MEDIEVAL
   VIEW 195
FAITH IS NONSENSE: .THE POSITIVIST VIEW 204
FAITH IS BEYOND KNOWLEDGE: THE EXISTENTIAL
   VIEW 207
FAITH IS AN ILLUSION: FREUD 217
THE LIMITATION OF RELIGION BY REASON: KANT 219

X. *The Problem of Inerrant Scripture* *226*

THE OLD TESTAMENT CLAIMS 230
WHO CANONIZED THE SCRIPTURE? THE OLD
   TESTAMENT 233
WHO CANONIZED THE SCRIPTURE? THE NEW
   TESTAMENT 237

Contents

THE BIBLE MUST BE INERRANT: SAINT AUGUSTINE   240

INERRANCY IS INVINDICABLE AND FUNCTIONLESS   243

XI.   *The Problem of Fixed or Evolving Religions*   250

HAS JUDAISM EVOLVED?   252

HAS CHRISTIANITY EVOLVED?   262

IS CHRISTIANITY UNIQUE?   270

IS CHRISTIANITY A RELIGION AMONG RELIGIONS?   277

IS CHRISTIANITY FINAL?   282

XII.   *The Problem of Fundamentalism*   286

THE ATTACK ON ROMAN AUTHORITY: MARTIN LUTHER   289

THE RISE OF BIBLIOCRACY: JOHN CALVIN   296

THE FUNDAMENTALIST PLATFORM: 16TH CENTURY   299

THE FUNDAMENTALIST CONTROVERSY: 20TH CENTURY   302

PERSISTENT PROBLEMS OF FUNDAMENTALISM   304

XIII.   *The Problem of Modernism*   309

THE SPIRIT OF MODERNISM: CATHOLIC AND PROTESTANT   312

THE QUEST FOR BIBLICAL TRUTH   319

MYTH AND CHRISTIANITY   322

XIV.   *The Problem of Humanism*   329

HUMANISM IN GENETIC BUDDHISM   330

HUMANISM IN GENETIC JAINISM   337

THE PIONEERS OF HUMANISM   343

WHAT DO HUMANISTS BELIEVE?   346

SUMMARY   353

xiv

Contents

XV. *Psychology and Religion*   354

IS RELIGION NORMAL?   354
IS RELIGION NEUROTIC?   362
IS RELIGION A MIXED BLESSING?   368
DOES PSYCHOLOGY THREATEN RELIGION?   373

XVI. *The Church and the State*   381

THE PENDULUM OF HISTORY   382
MARTIN LUTHER AND THE STATE CHURCH   387
JOHN CALVIN AND THE CHURCH STATE   389
IS THERE AN AMERICAN TRADITION?   392
IS THERE A ROMAN CATHOLIC TRADITION?   398
THE CURRENT CONTROVERSY   404

XVII. *Religion and Science*   417

THE LOCI OF THE CONTROVERSY   418
MUST RELIGION BE THREATENED BY SCIENCE?   427
RELIGIOUS MEANING AND SCIENTIFIC TRUTH   436

SUMMARY QUESTIONS   445
NOTES   463
BIBLIOGRAPHY   483
INDEX   495

God, Man, and the Thinker

I

What Is Philosophy *of* Religion?

THE SUBJECT of religion stands unrivaled in the area of human speculation in terms of the sheer numbers of persons who believe themselves to be qualified both to expound and to analyze it. While politics may appear to be a close second, there is nowhere near the seriousness or the depth of concern associated with the topic. While both politics and religion are expressions of human value concerns, both the range and the emotive urgency of the values associated with religion exceed, for the mass of men, those in any other area. The phenomenon of religious education, with a day set apart for its special use, has had no counterpart in human history.

We have all been exposed to religious ideas, religious emotions, and all the subtle nuances of religious liturgy ever since childhood. This has been true even for those who have never been formally associated with any denomination. The religious atmosphere has touched us all. Long before we were in a position to think critically or to understand the meaning

3

of what was said, we were exposed to ideas claimed to be of eternal and religious significance. The student who approaches the subject of religion has already spent many years of serious questioning concerning the matters of God, sin, and immortality. If a person has been exposed to a more fundamentalist vein in Christianity, for example, he may already have known the pangs of guilt through the commission of putative sins. The average adult has heard a good many sermons, and may even have witnessed on the modern medium of television what are declared to be acts of healing. In addition, most homes possess a copy of the Judeo-Christian scriptures which, though they may be covered with dust, still occupy a visibly prominent place. In "bull sessions" on college campuses probably no subject rivals that of religion for popularity, unless it be that of sex. But even on that subject the differences of opinion are nowhere near so tinged with emotional involvement, nor do they engender such heated debate. As a consequence of all this, it can usually be assumed that the person who approaches the subject of philosophy of religion comes to it already more or less "involved." Although he may not have accurate factual information, he has at least very real emotional concerns.

In view of this state of affairs, it may seem unnecessary to spend any time explaining what philosophy of religion is all about. Isn't this what most of us have already been engaged in? The fact is, however, that interest in religion has reflected a wide range of different concerns. There are many persons whose interest in religion reflects an elementary curiosity about the question of truth. They may wonder, for example, whether there really is a God. Or perhaps they are uncertain about the idea of immortality; they may suspect that immortality is a fiction created out of human wishes to escape death. Perhaps they suspect that the increase in human knowledge casts suspicion upon the Christian claim to an "inerrant" scripture. Most of us have already sampled a variety of Christian denominations, and we may now wonder what grounds there are, if any, for preferring a particular one. Those who contemplate marriage may wish to know what would be involved if they were to marry someone of a different religion.

Perhaps the student has already encountered, through courses in other academic disciplines, an attitude of suspicion toward religion—a belief that there has been too much undisciplined emotion and not enough dispassionate examination. Exposure to courses in psychology of religion, sociology of religion, or history of religion may provoke curiosity as to what the information gained in these areas has to contribute to both an understanding and an evaluation of religion. If the data of sociology are true, what logical bearing will they have on the truth or falsity of religious claims? If the student has read Sigmund Freud's *The Future of an Illusion* or *Totem and Taboo*, he may understandably wonder whether religion really is an expression of infantile neuroses. At any rate, it can be assumed that all who approach religion have already been exposed to a wide variety of judgments, both favorable and unfavorable. It is highly unlikely, therefore, that a student can approach religion as a disinterested bystander. There has been too great an expenditure of thought and emotion for dispassionate objectivity. There is evidence, however, to support the observation that large numbers of students who take a course in such a field as this believe themselves to be agnostics, skeptics, or at any rate doubters of some variety. As a consequence, they may approach the subject with their defenses up. Perhaps they suspect that philosophy of religion has the same purpose as the average clergyman—namely, to persuade, to convert, or to win followers for some particular point of view.

This text, however, has no such aim. It is our intention to study the field of religion philosophically. To make clear precisely what this means is the function of the first chapter. It will not be the purpose of this book to attempt to proselyte for any particular position. What we shall do is to present the various religious views from the standpoint of their staunchest defenders. After we have set forth this affirmative information, we shall survey the rebuttals of some of the serious opponents. While our illustrations will be drawn from both

5

Occidental and Oriental religions, the emphasis will be upon the Judeo-Christian traditions. This seems defensible in view of the simple fact that most students in American universities have been reared in a Judeo-Christian culture. If, on the other hand, we were natives of Cairo, Egypt, it would be equally reasonable to draw more heavily from the religion of Islam. The fact that the primary emphasis will be on Judeo-Christianity ought not to be interpreted as a special pleading for these points of view, nor as an indication that it is an accepted fact that a preponderance of either truth or value lies there. A study of philosophies of religion is not equivalent to Christian apologetics.

It has been traditional for the philosopher to approach his task with a degree of impartiality and a lack of prior commitment that have distinguished him from the theologian or apologist. It may be assumed that the theologian begins his task with his conclusions already in hand. Whatever demonstrations or proofs he may give are more of the order of systematics. The dogmas of the faith are never in doubt, although the particular mode of explication or justification may be. From the philosophic perspective the theologian's approach is question-begging, since the truth or falsity of the doctrines is never seriously in question. The philosopher, on the other hand, utilizes an approach which requires intellectual open-mindedness and emotional tolerance. It is not justifiable to imagine that all religion is simply fraud and superstition, and it is equally indefensible to maintain that everything asserted in the name of religion is true or even of moral worth. It will not be easy for the student to approach this subject with the necessary degree of impartiality if he is already committed on these very issues. Nevertheless, we shall attempt to approach religion from what may seem to some readers to be an excessively neutral position.

Since the problems of philosophy of religion are neither simple nor commonly agreed upon, let us consider some of the views which have appeared in the long history of the Judeo-Christian tradition as to what philosophic speculation about religion really means.

What Is Philosophy *of* Religion?

One of the perennial philosophies of religion has insisted that the question of truth or falsity of religious claims are what philosophy is concerned to investigate. This position was held by the late E. S. Brightman in his text, *A Philosophy of Religion*. According to Brightman, the essential problem in the philosophical analysis of religion is, "Are any religious beliefs true? If so, which ones, and why? Are any religious value-claims truly objective? If so, which ones, and why? The best possible answer to these questions is the best possible philosophy of religion." [1] In his answers to these questions he concluded that the truth will be determined "simply by the fact that they are beliefs which form a system consistent with itself and consistent, as far as we know, with every phase and type of experience." [2] The basic problem is one of truth, and the basic criterion for determining truth is coherence with experience. Not only do religious statements become true, but religious experiences become real, precisely insofar as they hang together with the rest of experience. His assumption, consistent with that of Hegel, was that only truth could be fitted into a coherent picture. Brightman further assumed that an equally coherent pattern of falsehoods was impossible.

This approach uses epistemology as the basic philosophic tool. By tradition the epistemological questions have been: "What can be known to be true?" and "How can we prove it?" On this basis, therefore, the fundamental religious problem is an intellectual one. The cognitive problem is to determine which, if any, religious claims are true, and to specify the appropriate strategy for proof.

Now the preference of Brightman for the criterion of coherence as the proper mode of demonstration has not been universally accepted—although, as Brightman intends to show, all other methods for the demonstration of truth or falsity as applied to religious statements may in fact be reduced to the basic elements of the coherence position. He argues that the task of science is not merely to show that

7

certain events occurred, but to indicate further that the statements and complex theories concerning these events hang together in a coherent pattern. The very dream of a grand unified science seems to support this thesis that coherence is an acceptable criterion of truth. Although there are many methods which may be used to determine that some states of affairs do exist, or that some statements concerning these states of affairs are true, Brightman held that everyone assumed that the interlocking system of such statements would be coherent with the rest of human knowledge. This assumption of the coalescence of experiences has been apparent even for those religious attempts to predicate that there is a God who is radically different from the world, or that this God occasionally intervenes with miracles. Even where the possibility of the miraculous was maintained, attempts were still put forth to account for these otherwise inexplicable occurrences in some coherent fashion.

If this were to be our approach in philosophy of religion, then it would be clear that we would need to accept certain basic assumptions concerning not only the nature of logical consistency, but also the supposed implications which follow from this consistency. Perhaps the assumed premises involved are no more complex than those in any field of empirical science. We would be assuming that logical consistency is preferable to inconsistency, and that order is a truer report of what exists than is chaos. In addition we would be presupposing that the data of religion are available for public inspection. While our emotions might be psychologically involved, and while some moral actions might be inferred to follow from our investigations, our basic task would be intellectual.

The approach of the medieval theologian, Saint Thomas Aquinas, has something in common with this notion that philosophy of religion is an affair of the mind. Saint Thomas began his analyses with certain basic postulates borrowed from Aristotle regarding the nature of logic, and with certain assumptions as to what it is legitimate to infer from sheer logical consistency. Thomas's speculations constitute perhaps the grandest system ever constructed upon the basis of consistency and coherence. Unlike Brightman's approach, however, there may appear to be in the Thomistic plan less reference to everyday human experience and more dependence upon certain metaphysical assumptions. For example, the coherence of Saint Thomas's theoretical hypotheses is more obvious than the coherence between these hypotheses and the world of experience. In spite of this, both Brightman and Thomas did believe that there were certain experiences which served as the starting points in the data-gathering process. When these experiences were put in conjunction with appropriate axioms, truth could be inferred. Part of the problem of the modern thinker is to determine whether the axioms satisfy the requirements of truth in the same way that those statements which report experience do. In any case, the Thomistic system is a marvel of internal consistency and is, at least, a noncontradictory theoretical possibility. The truth of the conclusions which Saint Thomas draws, although they will appear to be open to some doubt, at least indicates that he is in the tradition of those philosophers who see philosophy of religion to be a cognitive affair.

The history of Roman Catholic theology in the Middle Ages suggests, however, that the search for truth, even in the sense of coherence, was not assumed to be the primary theological task. There is an underlying assumption that the basic dogmas of the religion are true without proof, and consequently these medieval systems are more apologetic than philosophical. While medieval thinkers seriously attempt to unravel alternative speculative possibilities, their endeavors are primarily concerned with the meaning of the Christian faith, rather than with determining the truth or falsity of the Christian dogmas. This whole approach is, nonetheless, one of the continuing intellectual options available to modern students who are looking for a philosophy of religion.

DOES PHILOSOPHY DISCOVER RELIGIOUS VALUES?

Some of the major thinkers of the nineteenth century viewed philosophy of religion as the search for religious values. William James's analysis of the philosophical task applied to religion serves as a link between the truth hypothesis and this new one. While James recognized that truth was a philosophical problem of religion, he doubted that the term "truth" ought to have the exclusively intellectual meaning which medieval thinkers had given it. In his explication of the pragmatic theory of truth, which had a specific meaning for ethics, aesthetics, and religion, he insisted that the emotional reaction of the believer was a necessary component. No statement in these areas could be considered true if the emotional response of the believer was one of either misery or indifference. Our passional nature has a role to play in deciding which type of religious knowledge we want. In the area of religion, in particular, the problem is to find an explanation that will be emotionally satisfying. While no religious explanation ought to be empirically too incredible, factual plausibility alone will never suffice. There are, after all, a great many religious propositions which have been asserted to be cognitively true. A good many of these propositions leave religious persons emotionally unmoved. This has meant that while some dogmas are given a certain amount of lip service, they get no serious emotional support. It was this state of affairs which concerned William James. Religion cannot afford to have mere logical consistency as the criterion of its correctness. To do so is to admit into the body of religion dull, uninspiring, and emotionally dead truths. Unless a religious belief moves human beings to act, it ought not to be considered as religiously true.

If we accept James's position, then philosophy of religion will not be merely a matter of intellectual or empirical proofs. There is a proper function of the human will, both in the discovery and in the justification of what is significant in religion. There are, James contended, cases where "faith in a fact can help create the fact." [3] What is even more important is that there are instances, specifically those in which no inductive or deductive inferences can be made, where the options before us are live, forced, and momentous. In these cases, the "will to believe" [4] becomes not merely a mode of discovery but a mode of religious justification. In situations where truth requires a willing act on our part, it would be absurd to imagine that intellectual assent is sufficient. Religion, like ethics, involves not so much what is the case as what we would be willing to have the case. The problem is not description but prescription, and hence the will is the monitor of religious truth.

W. E. Hocking formulated a second version of the thesis that the human will is crucial in religion. In objecting to the Brightman approach, Hocking said that it supposes "that the objects of religious interest are all made up in advance, and that our wills have no part to play in determining what is. . . ." [5] The overemphasis upon the intellectual element ignores the meaning and the reality of religious ideas and experiences. Mere logical coherence is not adequate to determine what is true in religion, for many coherent theories will always be possible. A coherent theory which includes God will have to be confronted with an equally coherent theory which excludes God. The property of sacredness, which the God thesis conveys, is bestowed upon the world by human wills; it is not discovered by human intellect. Hocking doubted, for example, "whether immortality is any such predetermined reality that exists for any person apart from that person's will to make it real." [6] Like James, Hocking saw the important philosophical problem of religion as entailed in the question, "What is the meaning of religion in human experience?" rather than in the question, "Which religious statements are true?"

This will mean that the task of the philosopher is to determine what has happened in the lives of human beings when they have committed themselves to religious beliefs, and what these beliefs have meant in the whole social enterprise of forming moral convictions. The question as to the value of religious statements must precede any question as to the truth of religious statements. If religion is one of the great normative enterprises of mankind, no analysis which intends to come to grips with its essentials can afford to remain at the level of logic alone. According to Hocking's thesis, the data of religion are found by our experiences of willing and feeling, but the establishment of true statements about these experiences is a matter of reason. For James the will both discovers and certifies religious data; for Hocking the will functions only in the former role. Hocking remarked, "The question, 'What kind of world would best satisfy the requirements of our wills?' can never finally determine what kind of world we, in reality, have. But such questions may go far toward clearing our minds about those requirements themselves; they may give some not-unimportant hints of what we have to expect of reality." [7]

Both Ludwig Feuerbach and Friedrich Schleiermacher shared this view that religion is not a matter of determining objective reality or logical proof. It is, rather, a matter of the heart. It deals with the internal assurances and hopes which men express. Even though it may be claimed that these religious expectations are derived from experience, the essentially religious element remains subjective. Now, if it is assumed that religion is not a question of determining objective matters, but is indeed subjective, then it is clear that the conventional quest for truth is not adequate to discover either the essential properties of religion or, what is more important, the basic worth of religion. On this assumption, Feuerbach concluded that religion was humanistic; that is, that its only referent was human. Schleiermacher, on the other hand, saw the humanistic feelings of man as pointing to something greater than man.

George Santayana, a philosopher whose religious attachments were to the Roman Catholic tradition, shared with James, Hocking, Feuerbach, and Schleiermacher the preoccupation with the emotive element in religion. Not only is religion not a matter of determining objective truth, but there is no cognitive element in religion whatsoever. Religion is an expression of man's imagination, and in the formulation of religion the statements must always be considered as fictions or myths. It is not of religious concern to investigate the truth of fictions, nor the reality of the referents of myths. On the contrary, what is important is to discover, if possible, the moral worth of these religious fictions. As a consequence, the question, "Which religion is the most true?" is out of order. Religions are not true or false, and consequently no one religion is more true than another. In addition, it becomes equally improper, in Santayana's view, to ask, "But what religion is the most valuable?" Religion is an exceedingly personal affair, and what may be of value for one person may be completely unmoving to another. Religious preference is much like a man's choice of a mate. It is a reflection of his personal psyche and a report of his own emotional reaction to the world in which he lives. Religion is in no sense an attempt to describe.

Santayana explains that his own personal attachment to Roman Catholicism is to be interpreted in this light. His preference for the Roman Catholic church was not a function of either logical consistency or the supposed truth of the basic dogmas. Nor, on the other hand, was his preference to be interpreted as an indication of his conviction that the liturgy, rites, and sacraments of Roman Catholicism were somehow superior even from a utilitarian point of view. Fundamentally, the choice of religion is aesthetic, and Santayana developed in his *Reason in Religion* a glowing defense of Roman Catholicism, for him, on aesthetic grounds. He appreciated the beauty of the ceremonies even though he found no cognitive truth in them. He appreciated some of the grand fictions, although he did not imagine that what they asserted did, in fact, exist.

While the position reflected by Santayana may seem to be extreme, few Roman Catholic and Protestant theologians have seriously expected religion to stand or fall on the issue of truth. The only persons we can find during the nineteenth century who thought that religion was essentially a matter of knowledge were those secularists who attacked religion as being false or nonsensical. Most of the opponents of religion in the history of the Christian church have presupposed that philosophers of religion intended to give logical justification for religion. These opponents of religious arguments assumed that religious thinkers had claimed either empirical support for dogma, or at least deductive validity for the inferences which established doctrines. From the point of view of the persons whom we have been considering, such attacks question only the form of religious arguments, and leave quite untouched the meanings of religious arguments. While it might be disturbing to epistemologically minded theologians to be informed that their arguments were all invalid, it would not be of serious concern to either James or Santayana. If religion is not a matter of knowledge, and if its content does not claim to be descriptive of any reality, if religion is essentially a report of an internal state, then it follows that the long history of opposition to religion has been directed to the wrong point. If this is so, then, even if the opponents of religion are correct in their judgments of the invalidity of religious argument, the religion of Santayana and James is still untouched, and its essential worth remains in spite of these logical objections.

In view of this, it will be necessary to keep in mind that there are two distinct views with regard to what philosophy of religion is all about. On the one hand, there will be those who maintain that religion is basically a matter of truth and the existence of religious referents. On the basis of this position, it will be assumed that religious arguments are both possible and necessary. Much of our discussion presupposes this point of view. We shall analyze some of the classical arguments for the existence of God, for immortality, and for the resolution of the problem of natural evil. In these investigations we shall be concerned with the validity of inferences and with the question of the evidential support of religious claims. There is an advantage in discussing religion from this viewpoint, since it is familiar to those who have already investigated cognitive problems in empirical science. Religion will thus appear to be one more academic discipline in which the search for truth may be involved.

On the other hand, there will be those who insist that long after the issue of truth or falsity has been resolved, the essential property of religion still remains untouched by all these investigations. In part, this second view will appear as a form of objection not only to religious arguments, but to the possibility of any logical explanation of religion whatsoever. In this sense it will be the task of each person to prescribe the meaning of religion.

In the light of these two distinct approaches to the meaning of philosophy of religion it will be the problem of each person to determine which way he intends to investigate religion, and, more important, what he thinks religion basically is. For example, for every argument which has ever been proposed for the existence of God, there has been a counterargument which claims to demonstrate its invalidity. And for every counterargument, there have been religious thinkers who were able to put forth a new argument against the old objection to the first argument. Now this sort of procedure could go on in an infinite progression in which it does not seem fruitful to become involved. Perhaps the student will conclude, after all the discussion is over, that religion is not simply a matter of intellect or of empirical proof. Even if it is decided that religion does involve logical considerations, one may conclude that philosophy of religion does not involve everything that there is of importance in religion. Whether this is so or not will be part of our problem. Indeed, the variety of religious speculations reveals that there is no general agreement either as to the results or as to the questions which produced these results.

PHILOSOPHY OF RELIGION AND THE SCIENCES OF RELIGION

Another way of approaching the philosophies of religion historically is to determine how the various philosophical approaches have differed from those of sociologists, historians, or psychologists. There are, after all, many ways of studying religion, and philosophy is only one of them.

History of religion, for example, is a comparatively recent discipline in the study of religion. Plato, to be sure, wrote about religious matters, but he was more concerned with the truth or falsity of religion and the political and social usefulness of religion than with the historical development of religion. Even during the Middle Ages, when religion was of such universal significance, histories of religion were not produced. Theology was so dominant and so subjective that the impartiality needed for a historical approach was lacking. In addition to this, the neutrality of the historian's position exposed him to the risk of a charge of heresy. Those who were interested in religion were so personally involved in their own particular brand of dogma that the incentive to study its development was lacking. Furthermore, there may have been the feeling that to explain religion as a historically evolving movement somehow detracted from its purported miraculous and spontaneous origins. It takes a special kind of dispassionate calm to investigate the history of one's own religion.

Part of the difficulty with the historical approach stems from the fact that when other institutions are studied in this fashion, we see that the later developments are more complex, more reasonable, more true, and, what is of particular importance, more to the point of contemporary interests. For example, the history of medicine begins in a mist of witchcraft, and only after centuries of serious intellectual labor does predictably useful medicine emerge. The history of astronomy shows that astrology and observation were at first confusedly mixed. Ancient clan and tribal structures have, in general, little practical relevance to contemporary problems. Yet these are the contexts in which early religions are to be found, and it was for such social organizations that many of the religious practices were developed. To portray religion as having grown out of naïve and intellectually confused thinking conflicts with the usual serious attitude toward religious dogmas. While the nineteenth-century phenomena of biblical criticism show that scholars have been able to look historically at religions other than their own, it has not been easy to expose the religion of our choice to what appears to be an unfavorable analysis.

Among the early classics in the field of history of religion were David Hume's *The Natural History of Religion* (1755) and G. W. F. Hegel's *Lectures on the Philosophy of Religion* (1832). The chief academic obstacle to writing a history of religion was lack of information. This void was not adequately filled until the late nineteenth and early twentieth centuries.[8]

While the history of religion supplies data for philosophical analysis, there has been a difference between the two approaches. It is important for the historian to know that it was true that a certain statement was made, but it is not important for the historian to know that what was said was true. Indeed, if one were interested in religion only hypothetically, which probably no one has ever been, it could be stated that the philosopher is not concerned with whether it is true that a statement was made, but only with whether the statement is true, even if it has not been historically asserted. In addition to this epistemological distinction, philosophers have been distinguished from historians of religion in that the former have been essentially concerned with the evaluation of what Hocking called "the meaning of God in human experience." The historian may report such meanings, but unless he is writing a philosophy of history, he does not judge them. While what religions have said or done are historical issues, both the truth and the value of religious claims are philosophical problems.

A second way in which religion has been studied has been in the field of sociology of religion. Here the scholar has been concerned with the effect of religion on other social institutions, as well as the influence of these institutions upon religion. Once again, the historian and the sociologist are distinguished from the philosopher in their indifference to religion's claims to truth. The sociologist wants to know what difference religious ideas have made independently of the question of whether these ideas were true or false. While the sociologist may express judgments about the utilitarian consequences of religion, they are not of the normative order which we find in the religious claims of ultimate significance.

The sociological study of religion is likewise relatively recent. Auguste Comte (1798–1857), credited with being the father of sociology, was one of the first to direct attention to what may be called the sociological problems of religion. Some scholars in this field did, however, allude to religious beliefs as myths, and hence wrote as if the truth or falsity of religious statements were of sociological concern. This was the case with Richard H. Tawney's book, *Religion and the Rise of Capitalism*. He saw the Protestant church, in particular, as having uncritically and unfortunately advanced the cause of capitalism. The conclusions reached in his study do make value judgments about religion. The question, however, is whether he wrote as a sociologist or a moralist. A similar question may .be raised with regard to Max Weber's *The Protestant Ethic and the Spirit of Capitalism*. There seems to be little doubt that Weber was unsympathetic toward many of the allegiances which Protestants had demonstrated. Are such expressions of antipathy sociological conclusions, or philosophical conclusions, or are they simply part of Weber's autobiography?

Many of the principles of sociology of religion have been of particular interest to the philosopher of religion who expresses the temper of a James or a Hocking. This has been particularly true where the data seem to indicate that religion has had socially disastrous consequences. A pragmatically inclined philosopher of religion might have to decide whether a truth which had harmful social consequences was better or worse than a fiction which had beneficial results. Of course, he could avoid this dilemma by defining religious truth solely in terms of favorable results, but this leads to confusions which present him with new dilemmas. After all, social adjustment or civic order may be purchased at a wide variety of prices, which indicates that the ends may not be sufficient as criteria. In any case, a religious theorist who wants to claim superiority for his sect on the grounds of its utilitarian value may find sociology of religion quite useful as a source of evidence.

A final approach which may be contrasted with the methods of philosophies of religion is that of psychology of religion. The source data for this approach are ancient, but the major psychological works did not appear before the late nineteenth century. While the account of the Great Awakening (1734–1739), given by Jonathan Edwards, provided source data for psychology of religion similar in value to the *Confessions* of Saint Augustine, neither of these could be considered to have been psychologies of religion. The most important early work in the field was William James's *Varieties of Religious Experience* (1902). Apart from the psychological insights which this work presented, it endeavored to show that religious experience was not the special province of neurotics. The foes against whom James was directing his work were not, however, psychologists so much as religious persons themselves. One of his chief implied points was that religious experience could be studied in the same fashion as were other types of experience. The phenomena of religion were not unique or isolated from the rest of human striving, and they were not, as a consequence, exempt from scientific investigation. From the viewpoint of psychology, mystical encounters, conversions, and liturgic ceremonies could all be fruitfully studied. James contributed to the psychological study of religion both objectivity and sympathy.

In the writings of Sigmund Freud, however, at least the sympathy seemed to be removed, from the point of view of the religiously devout. Religion now appeared to be a basic sign of human neurosis. Although nothing that Freud had to say affected the truth or falsity of religious claims, the stigma of neurosis created an antagonism toward psychology on the part of most religious persons. This mutual distrust prevented, for many years, any widespread attempt to show any possible amicable relations between these two areas.

The psychologist of religion, like the historian and the sociologist, differed from the philosopher at the same epistemological point. The truth of religious claims was not of psychological concern. To be sure, the psychologist did need to know that it was true, for example, that a given patient made a given remark, but the clinician did not need to worry over whether the religious dogmas of his patient were true or false. The motivation of the patient to assert them and the influence they had on the psyche of the patient were far more important than any logical issues of truth.

PHILOSOPHY VERSUS PHILOSOPHIES OF RELIGION

In view of the foregoing, there are two options which may be explored. On the one hand, we can attempt to construct an epistemology to defend a particular set of religious doctrines. This procedure would be question-begging, for it would presuppose the truth of the doctrines at the outset, and would hence be indistinguishable from theology. Coherent systems of truths accepted without proof have always been possible. At most, the construction of such an ordered pattern might demonstrate the logical possibility of what the system entails. To move from mere logical possibility to factual existence, however, would be an infeasible leap. If truth is our problem, then we can ill afford to solve it by such a naïve procedure.

Since the search for truth has been one of the ways in which philosophers of religion have conceived their task, it will be less presumptuous if we simply accept the attempts at argument of various religious persons, and see whether the inferences as given are valid and whether the premises from which conclusions are drawn are supportable by evidence. This is one of the two primary approaches which we shall use. If a particular philosophical approach asserts that the existence of the referents of its dogmas is the heart of the problem, then we will take this as our problem and see whether the inferences in question actually make their case. If it turns out that the initial presumptions were unfounded and unprovable, we still have two alternatives. Either we can move on to another putative epistemological defense in the hope that it will be able to do a better job of proof, or we may decide that, after all the analyses are made, this was not really the philosophical problem of religion. We can then turn to our second option.

In this case our problem will be essentially normative; namely, to determine whether any particular religion can make a case for its moral worth or for the ultimacy of its values. In those instances where this claim to worthiness rests upon its claimed utilitarian function, our problem will

What Is Philosophy *of* Religion?

be at least in part empirical. We shall need to determine whether some religion has some consequences which would support its claim to significance. If, for example, it is claimed that Christian persons are happier, freer from anxiety, better adjusted to their world, and more responsible citizens, then our task will be twofold. The first is the simpler of the two— namely, to see whether the evidence supports these pragmatic claims. The second task requires both empathy and imagination, for we need to conjure with the question, "Are these ends really worth the effort?" It is in considering the value claims of religion that the student will need to exercise more open-mindedness in order to understand, if not to appreciate, what other persons have found to be of value for them.

This second approach involves us in ethical and moral questions. The truth or falsity of the claim that a particular religion has insights of appreciable significance is not determined by any simple logical argument. In part, our problem will be to determine whether the imaginative insights, expressed perhaps in myths and fictions, are indeed expressive of those things which we find worth while. When we are investigating the value claims of cultures and ages radically different from our own, appreciation may turn out to be impossible, and we shall have to rest content with understanding. If we find some value in religion, we still need to determine whether the world in which we live is of such a sort that values of this kind could ever be fulfilled. If what is religiously of moral worth is impossible to practice, as many religious thinkers have freely admitted, then apparently even the failure to defend a religion on the grounds of its feasibility does not constitute the last word. If we discover some truth in a religion, we still need to determine its value. Consequently, the failure to establish claims to religious truth may still leave untouched the issue of the ultimate worth of religion.

As a consequence we shall not assume that there is *a* philosophy of religion, but rather that there have been widely divergent philosophies of religion. The investigation of their truth, value, and meaning will be our aim.

2 I

II

The Definition *of* Religion

IT SEEMS APPROPRIATE in studying philosophies of religion to have some reasonably precise notion as to the area to be investigated. The normal procedure in academic circles is to do this by means of a definition. While for most areas of discussion this is a fairly simple matter, there seems to be something about religion which makes even the task of defining a contentious problem in itself. In *A Psychological Study of Religion* by James Leuba, the author lists forty-eight definitions of religion, and then, after some qualifications, he adds a forty-ninth definition of his own. The mere fact that there are some 265 religious sects in the United States listed in the 1960 *Yearbook of American Churches* would seem to indicate that there must be the same number of definitions of religion in use also. In virtually no other area of human concern is there found such a chaotic situation with regard to what the subject means, although there appears to be an inverse correlation of conviction on precise meanings as we move from the physical sciences to the biological sciences, to the social sciences, and finally to the humanities. In religion, as in few other areas, even the definition of the subject is a matter of serious and enthusiastic commitment. Since a part of our problem stems from the semantic nature of definitions, we shall begin our investigation by seeking for a definition of definition, before we attempt to define religion.

WHAT DOES A DEFINITION GIVE US?

We may infer from the history of definition making that definitions intend one of two objectives. On the one hand, they may purport to describe how a given word has actually been used. This is the case with dictionary definitions. They report that such-and-such a word has in fact certain assigned meanings, and as a consequence, it is not within the proper province of the author of a dictionary to decide that a given word really ought not to mean what in fact it is used to mean; if common usage changes, the change in meaning will be reported in the next edition. This element of conforming to usage underlies all dictionary definitions. On the other hand, a definition may propose to assert how a word ought to be defined. In this instance common usage may be irrelevant. It may be that a given word has such a variety of assigned meanings that there is no "common usage," and the definer intends to bring order out of this chaos, for one reason or another, by prescribing that a certain term should be assumed to have some stated meaning.

The motives lying behind such prescriptive attempts may be quite varied. Indeed, the failure of the listener to understand why a certain definition has been prescribed accounts partially for the furor of discussion which usually ensues. The listener asks, "Why should we define this word in this particular way?" He suspects that some trick is plotted and that the definition is a covert way of proving some implicit factual issue. When we consider the medieval usage of the expression "real definition," the suspicion appears to be well founded. During many centuries medieval thinkers sought for definitions which had a ground in the metaphysical nature of things, such that the acceptance of a prescriptive definition carried with it acceptance of views about the nature of reality. The assumption was that if the world is such-and-such, then certain terms ought to have appropriate defined meanings. It will not be our intent to investigate such putative "real definitions," even though there still exists some interest in this medieval enterprise. Indeed, contemporary usage would suggest that such an effort involves us in matters of truth and falsity more compatible with the problem of descriptions than that of definitions.

In contemporary discussions concerning definitions there are certain terms which we may well report as having a bearing on our problem of defining religion. In modern usage, the expression "real definition" commonly means one which reports what a word actually is used to mean in common usage. In this sense all dictionary definitions are "real." On the other hand, the expression "nominal definition" refers to one which reports only what the speaker wishes a word to mean. Such definitions would be prefaced by the qualification, "When I say 'X,' I mean . . ." Nominal definitions may be prompted by many motives. There may be some reason why the real definition is too ambiguous or undiscriminating, and hence a nominal definition is called for to provide clarity in discussion. Or a speaker may wish the range of meaning of a term to be extended, so that some honorific word may have a broader intent. On the other hand, this nominal approach may be an attempt to clarify a real definition. We may say, "When Mr. X uses the term 'religion,' I believe that what he really means is . . ." It is, in part, over attempts of this sort that much religious discussion has been generated, for Mr. X may have friends present who are sure that they have a better idea of what he intended by the use of the term "religion" than our interpreter. While matters of this sort are concerned with definitions, they will not be resolved by definitions.[1]

It will be much safer, in a field like religion, with all of the emotional overtones which it possesses, to consider that any attempted definition has the properties usually assigned to what is known as a stipulative definition. As a point of departure this will enable us at the outset to avoid heated disputation on matters which are really not crucial, for strictly speaking, the way in which religion is defined does not affect religious truth. Now stipulative definitions have the following properties, by definition, and hence, what follows may be considered as a nominal definition of definition.

1. Their aim is to clarify the meanings of terms by means of verbal equivalents. Given some term "X," it is asserted that some other term "Y" has the same meaning. Given, for example, the term "bachelor," it is asserted that the term "unmarried male" has the same meaning. In such a function it is clear that definitions are prerequisites to unambiguous communication.

2. Stipulative definitions do not intend to describe the world outside of words. Such definitions do not claim to have referents which they intend to describe. No state of affairs outside the sentence of the definition itself is being referred to. As a consequence, no state of affairs in the world can affect the correctness or incorrectness of a definition. "All bachelors are unmarried males" is correct if the meaning of "bachelors" is the same as the meaning of "unmarried males." The condition of men in the world is irrelevant to the definition. If there were no bachelors in society, or if there were a cancellation of the institution of marriage, "all bachelors are unmarried males" would remain as a consistent expression of verbal meaning. This would mean specifically that the definition "Religion means belief in God" would be unaffected by the discovery that there was no God.

3. There is an element of arbitrariness in all stipulative definitions at the point of their formulation. We are familiar with the fact that general dictionaries may not have the same definitions as those found in technical dictionaries. We are also aware that this is simply due to the fact that each dictionary has a frame of reference for the determination of what is "common usage." The former dictionaries pay attention to what the man in the street

says, while the latter consider only the trained specialist. Even in the case of general dictionaries there will be alternative meanings, but this merely means that the word in question has had several meanings in its history. A brief consultation of a dictionary of religion will indicate how much more varied the actually used meanings are in this field. The definitions of the word "God" may occupy a full page, and if one wishes to know which definition he ought to use, the dictionary does not give much information. Nonetheless, if we wish to be understood within some limited domain, and to communicate without unnecessary confusion, there will usually be a practical limit to the choice of a definition.

4. It follows from the preceding, and particularly from No. 2, that stipulative definitions are neither true nor false. If it is assumed that by "truth" we mean to refer to that property which a sentence has when what it talks about exists as described, then it is clear that such definitions are neither true nor false. They have no reference to any state of affairs in the world whose existence or non-existence could certify truth or falsity.

5. There is a corollary which follows from the neutrality of definitions with regard to truth and falsity. No definition ought ever to be used as a premise in an argument, the conclusion of which is claimed to be true. Indeed, where definitions do appear as premises, it must be inferred that the conclusion is at most validly drawn and formally correct with respect to the premises, but never true.

To consider definitions in terms of these five properties will enable us to avoid a type of argument which has never proved logically or practically fruitful in religion—namely, "What is religion really?" This question is covertly a request for a definition which is true; and as we have seen, this is an impossible request. This type of issue was involved in a debate held within the confines of the late Federal Council of Churches of Christ in America. It was held by some of the constituent denominations that to be a Christian required belief in the divinity of Christ. Unitarians would not make this assertion of trinitarianism. It was held, therefore, that Unitarians were not Christians, and, thus, not proper members of the Federal Council. While the question as to who is or is not a Christian may be of religious interest, it is not of philosophic interest. The historian of religion, confronted as he is with a welter of conflicting ideas of Christianity, is in no better position to answer the question, "Who is really a Christian?" than the most narrow-minded sectarian. While it was certainly within the province of the Federal Council to determine whom they wished to admit, it ought not to be imagined that this type of definitional inference determined the true beliefs of Christianity. The most that was determined was that it was then true that those who do not accept the Trinity do not get into the Federal Council. Every religious sect faces problems of this type when the issue of membership arises. Who should be admitted is always decided by a stipulative definition, and admission is the most that is decided.

If there are common properties to definitions of religion in use, it should be possible to give a definition that is in accord with the way in which the term "religion" is actually used. Such a definition, if it can be found, would then have the properties which any specialized dictionary definitions have; namely, it would report what the word means in use. Let us consider some of the attempts to discover a generally approvable definition of religion.

IS RELIGION A MATTER OF BELIEF?

The Nicene Creed (325 A.D.) is a good example of a definition of religion which is equated with beliefs. Here it is claimed that belief in a single God of certain specifiable attributes, of a Messiah who was divine, of a church which would play some function in the world, of divine judgment, and of an immortal life constitute the essence proper to the Christian religion. The fate of this definition illustrates the thesis that overly specific definitions shut out many who wish to be called religious, and in addition, soon lead to arguments over meanings at the definitional level which are neither logically reasonable nor religiously productive. Nonetheless, this manner of assigning meaning to the terms "Christian religion" has had wide vogue.

The multiplicity of Christian sects is primarily due to this penchant of Christians to define religion in terms of belief. The sheer divisiveness which has resulted would indicate that efforts of this sort become exceedingly nominal as each group stipulates, "Religion means, to us, belief in . . ." There has been an advantage in having sects stipulate what they mean by religion. This makes it clear to the initiate what kind of a sect he is joining, and they make it clear to the dissident what it is that he opposes. To imagine, however, that a definition based upon belief could ever be more than subjective and nominal is to be unaware of the history of the Christian religion, let alone of other religions. If we were to stipulate that religion means belief in a God of certain Judeo-Christian properties, then we would omit from "religion" Hinayana Buddhists, Jainists, probably most Hindus, Confucianists, and humanists. If we insist that religion means belief in immortality of a personal kind, then we omit the Hindus, Buddhists, and Jainists, not to mention those "Christians" who insist that immortality is an expendable idea. Anyone who sets down a definition of religion based on the beliefs it is supposed to entail can almost be assured that within a few years he will have invented a new sect. Beliefs associated with the Messiah of the movement become even more chauvinistic and divisive than beliefs associated with the idea of a deity. The honorific role assigned to Christ is unacceptable to non-Christians, the same role when assigned to Buddha is unacceptable to non-Buddhists, and only Moslems can appreciate the importance of such beliefs when they are associated with Mohammed.

The difficulties which emerge in defining religion in terms of belief may be summarized as follows:

1. What seems to be of greatest importance to a particular religious group will not be universally accepted as such. Indeed, beliefs are what divide religions, and thus cannot be

used as defining properties of religion. While it is clear that general acceptability is not a criterion of truth, it is a criterion of adequacy as far as definitions are concerned. When religion is defined by the use of what are claimed to be significant beliefs, the result is a multiplication of sects, and not any univocal or useful definition.

2. If there are belief commitments which are relatively widespread among sects, they usually turn out to be either so vacuous or so unimportant as to be of little concern to any religious group. This has been the case with beliefs in immortality, moral verities, or the facts of order and design. Similarity in vague formulation has usually obscured the most basic differences of interpretation of these generalities.

3. Definitions based upon beliefs err in including those who do not wish to be included, and excluding those who wish to be included. It is not simply that there is a basic fallacy involved in separating believers from unbelievers, but that when an issue as important as religion is decided by stipulative definitions, the impression is given of determining ultimate, let alone true, matters by much too nominal a procedure. It will, therefore, be more fruitful to let the men and movements that we study specify the beliefs which are held to be essential. We shall still be in a position to determine what is philosophically relevant with regard to whether these beliefs are indeed true or of ultimate value concern.

IS RELIGION A MATTER OF FEELING?

The acceptance of feeling in preference to belief as the distinguishing element of religion has had serious and widespread support. Probably more nineteenth- and twentieth-century Protestant theologians and philosophers of religion have taken this option than any other. Friedrich Schleiermacher [2] believed that feeling was by far a more adequate criterion of a "real definition" of religion than was belief. It was not that religion had no contemplative element in it, but that religious contemplation was not a matter of objective facts, so much as of basic feelings and immediate awareness of properties in the world. The nature of these data of feeling was such that religious knowledge must be assigned a radically different meaning from scientific knowledge. Men have an immediate consciousness of deity, and associated with this consciousness are feelings of a kind and magnitude which distinguish religion from all other human interests.

Josiah Royce, the distinguished Harvard Idealist, supported Schleiermacher's analysis of the essential meaning of religion. He saw religion as that which added enthusiasm to obedience to the moral code. There were, he admitted, beliefs which were a part of religion, and there were mandates which admonished appropriate behavior, but, more than any of these, religion properly entailed feelings.

> A religion must teach some moral code, must in some way inspire a strong feeling of devotion to that code, and in so doing must show something in the nature of things that answers to that code or that serves to reinforce the feeling. A religion is therefore practical, emotional, and theoretical; it teaches us to do, to feel, and to believe, and it teaches the belief as a means to its teaching of the action and the feeling.[3]

Rudolf Otto expressed even more directly the idea of feeling as a basis for religion. It was his judgment that orthodox Christianity had committed a serious blunder when it had slighted, throughout its history, the noncognitive element, and had substituted a narrow, one-sided rational theologizing. The expression *mysterium tremendum* identified for Otto a "wholly (holy) other," about which we do not so much speculate as feel. He concluded, on the basis of wide experience with Eastern and Western religions, that certain feelings characterized the religious manifestations. In the presence of this *mysterium tremendum* men reacted with feelings of awe, overpoweringness, and urgency.[4] Associated with the mystical experience by which man became aware of the "wholly other" were feelings, in addition, of fascination. While Otto admitted that there were cognitions which man could have concerning these "numinous experiences," their basic qualities transcended expression, and hence feeling terms were more appropriate when attempting to elucidate the meanings associated with religion. Such an explanation as this has distinct advantages over all definitions in terms of belief. For one thing, feelings are more vague, and perhaps more ubiquitous, and thus do not produce the sectarian divisiveness which precise beliefs do. In addition, because of these very properties, definitions based on feelings can include persons of widely different beliefs. This has led many definers of religion to feel that definitions based upon feelings more closely approximate "real definitions."

A comparable stress upon the feeling element may be seen in the remarks of H. Richard Niebuhr to the effect that religion means "confidence in certain realities as sources of value." [5] Here the emphasis is upon the feelings associated with the realities and not the cognitive proofs of them. The explication of Durant Drake, although it contains cognitive elements, puts primary stress upon feeling, for religion meets the emotional needs for consolation and inspiration, as well as comprehension. [6]

William E. Hocking's investigation of the nature of religion led him to ask to what degree intelligence, or the rational component, was essential. Does religion require metaphysical speculations and theoretical conjectures, or is there some human attribute more basic to the fundamental religious spirit? The rhetorical question, "how far, on the other hand, religion appeals to something in us deeper than the intellect, —to faith, to feeling, to the subconscious, to the instinctive, to the essential will," [7] is answered with a clear affirmation that here in the affective nature of man lies the essential religious element. Man's awareness of an "Other than himself" [8] produces feelings of alienation between man and his world, although at the same time the wounds of alienation created by religion are also given the appropriate balm by religion. With religion so inextricably connected with feeling, there may be doubt as to the role of reason at all. How, for example, are religious truths to be established? Are these determined by logical inferences? Hocking assumed that religious faith rested upon immediate, empirical, real experiences in which man saw reality for what it was directly. This much can be done without logical speculation. The role of reason is to determine where in the total system of things the religious events fit, but reason is not needed to determine that the data to which religious persons refer do exist.

There have been contenders for the feeling-essence of religion whose views have implied that religion has been judged and found wanting. Let us note two such formulations, even though the inferences the authors draw from them are premature. Sigmund Freud based his analysis of religion upon a highly speculative thesis about the psychological genesis and evolution of man. He found religion to be rooted in fear, ignorance, insecurity, and the unwillingness of men to assume their mature responsibilities. On the strength of these theses, Freud concluded that religion was the expression of neuroses rooted in the infancy of the race, and hence that as men matured the need for religion would evaporate. Indeed, he conjectured that children reared without exposure to religion would mature both more quickly and more easily. It is pertinent to note that even if his theory is correct, his assertion of the need for an irreligious experiment is hasty. It is not, however, within the province of this section to determine the truth or falsity of Freud's psychological history. Our concern, after all, is with the significance and truth of religion, and for these ends the origin and history of religion are scarcely premises. If what religion talks about exists as described, then religious statements will be true no matter what their origin. If contemporary religious meanings have normative worth, then these will remain, even if religious sentiments did in fact have a neurotic genesis.

Ludwig Feuerbach saw religion as man's reification of himself. As men became conscious of their potentialities, they translated these human sentiments into metaphysical universals. This process has separated man from the authentic roots of his religion—namely, himself, for the essence of Christianity is a message of man's inalienable worth. Real religion asserts Man, not God, for God is, after all, Man reified to cosmic worth.[9]

The attempt to define religion in terms of the appropriate feelings of awe, mystery, dependence, worth, or worship has encountered the same essential problems as confronted belief definitions. Where the feeling is asserted with any precision, it fails to be universally present among those who call themselves religious. Where the feeling is kept vague, and hence may appear to be ubiquitous, it fails to challenge any religious persons as being of worth. Many religious philosophers object to the apparent lack of interest in cognitive matters which definitions based upon feelings demonstrate. And again, feeling definitions appear too undiscriminating, for the same human feelings have been applied to every human experience. The feelings of awe and reverence, for example, have been attached to referents of quite different values. The injunction in the Decalogue, "Thou shalt have no other gods before me," suggests that men have commonly associated these feelings with experiences of doubtful worth. If there are ways of determining that this has occurred, then obviously feeling alone is not the meaning of religion. The so-called "finer sentiments" are usually linked with familial love and political patriotism, not to mention self-esteem. To define religion solely in terms of feelings would result in a functionless lumping of man's values. In addition, if religion really means feeling, then the centuries of theological speculation to the contrary would certainly exhibit a cosmic misunderstanding.

IS RELIGION A KIND OF ETHICS?

In this approach to the definition of religion the important element is action. It is what the religious person does, far more than what he thinks or feels, that distinguishes him as being religious. In spite of the emphasis upon deeds which this approach to religion stresses, it would be misleading to imagine that any definition of religion excludes all other approaches. Defining religion as the performance of certain rites or moral deeds is a case in point. Probably most persons who insisted that religion meant the performance of appropriate actions also recognized both feelings and beliefs as relevant. The ancient prophet who asked, "What doth Jehovah require of thee, but to do justly, and to love kindness, and to walk humbly with thy God?" [10] obviously believed that there was a God, and that there were proper feelings associated with this God, but the emphasis seems to be upon the resulting deeds which ought to follow. Let the question remain open as to whether Micah would be disturbed by a man who performed the righteous deeds but did not believe in a God.

The essential emphasis of the Israelite prophets of the eighth, seventh, and sixth centuries B.C. was upon action, rather than belief. Indeed, most of the subsequent social concern which has characterized the Judeo-Christian traditions is traced to these prophetic and utilitarian seers. What confuses part of the issue is that most of the opponents of these same prophets, in their own day were also men who stressed deeds. The chief difference lay in the nature and intent of the deeds themselves. The priestly cult endorsed ritual ceremony, which consisted essentially of overt deeds. In part, the prophets objected to priestly liturgies simply because they did not possess survival value for the race. It is equally true that the prophets objected to the beliefs and feelings which such mechanical genuflexions seemed to presuppose. The prophet Amos denounced those who robbed poor widows of their homes or who persecuted the impoverished; he did not seem excited about the unbelievers. In spite of the priestly implications involved, the emphasis of ritual Judaism has traditionally been upon what a person does, rather than upon what a person either feels or believes. In spite of the feeling of non-Jews that dietary laws are somewhat unrealistic and indefensible, the fact remains that faithfulness to Judaism results in practical action. The remarks attributed to Jesus when he announced his intended mission has linked him also to this commitment to act. "The Spirit of the Lord is upon me, because he anointed me to preach good tidings to the poor: He hath sent me to proclaim release to the captives, and recovering of sight to the blind, to set at liberty them that are bruised." [11]

It was in the spirit of these great religious social prophets that Saint Francis of Assisi (1182–1226 A.D.) raised his voice in protest against the lack of "holy living" in the Italy of his day. Francis saw the spiritual leaders of the church enmeshed in petty intrigue and in internecine warfare which set one city against another. Protests against corruption had already been made by the Albigenses in southern France and the Patarenes in Milan. Both groups found the church so worldly and the clergy so dissolute that they rejected the church and denounced the Pope. The Amalricians, followers of Amalric of Bena, declared that the Pope was Antichrist and the church was Babylon. The Waldensians, under Peter Waldo, denounced the papal armies and condemned war of any kind. The spiritually sensitive believed that they confronted two alternatives, equally distasteful. On the one hand, there were the theological speculations of the church; and on the other hand, there were the world-rejecting monasteries. The arguments of the former seemed sterile, and the escape of the latter seemed nihilistic. Into such a context Saint Francis introduced an essential revival of the moral requisites of the Sermon on the Mount and of the great Hebrew prophets. While Francis rejected the example of the conventional clergy and denounced the schools, he did propose a functional poverty of material goods and a missionary healing program which led him first to his work with the leper colony near Rome. The commission to a life of practical service Francis found in the Scriptures, read one morning while he attended Mass at the Chapel of the Little Portion on February 24, 1209. The minister read from the New Testament, "As ye go, preach, saying, The kingdom of Heaven is at hand. Heal the sick, cleanse the lepers, raise the dead, cast out devils: freely ye have received, freely give. Provide neither gold, nor silver, nor brass in your purses, nor scrip for your journey, neither two coats, neither shoes, nor yet staves. . . ." [12] Here in the life of Saint Francis we find a clear distinction between the practical deeds of religion and the theological speculations about religion. Francis engaged in no theoretical dispute, and when some of his followers wished to speculate about the semantic niceties of the Rule of the Order, he insisted that the message was perfectly clear as to the righteous deeds which were required. In a comment on the futility of philosophic disputation of religion he stated: "Suppose that you had subtlety and learning enough to know all things, that you were acquainted with all languages, the courses of the stars and all the rest, what is there in that to be proud of? A single demon knows more on these subjects than all the men in this world put together. But there is one thing that the demon is incapable of, and which is the glory of man: to be faithful to God through love to man." [13]

All through the Middle Ages there were Roman Catholic spokesmen for a religion defined in terms of social action, and for a minimization of the element of belief. The Protestant Reformation inherited this tradition and directed it toward attacks against alcohol, prostitution, gambling, card playing, and a host of lesser peccadilloes. This emphasis upon deeds which religion was believed to entail produced the lack of interest in theology which the Quaker movement typified.

During the nineteenth century and the beginning of the twentieth there emerged in Protestant Christianity, in particular, a trend called the Social Gospel movement. This represented another attempt to strip away from religion the dominance of the element of belief. It was a renewed effort to shift from theologizing to action. Among the more active spokesmen were included the Baptist, Walter Rauschenbusch; the Methodist, Harry Ward; the Presbyterian, Norman Thomas; and the Congregationalist, Jerome Davis. Protestant clergymen in large numbers joined actively in social, economic, and political pressure movements. Religion was a matter of doing things, not essentially of believing. Obviously these actionists had some beliefs, but their major emphasis was upon practical programs. It was during this period that clergymen wrote such earthy treatises as *Would Jesus Join a Labor Union?* or *Was Jesus the First Socialist?* In both instances the answers were resoundingly in the affirmative.

While the members of these groups did not deny traditional religious beliefs, in their enthusiasm for action they did by-pass such speculative issues as the Trinity, immortality, the divinity of Jesus, and the arguments for the existence of God.

This attempt to define religion in terms of ethical deeds posed, however, some of the same practical problems which other definitions of religion had faced. Persons who called themselves religious, even within the same sect, could not or at least did not agree on which deeds were the essential ones. This impasse was well illustrated at the World Council of Churches which met at Amsterdam in 1948. Christian delegates advocated a wide range of possible social reforms and economic systems. H. Richard Niebuhr, from the United States, asserted that it has been the shame of the Christian church that it has been so middle-class. "That it should carry out its mission to the men in the middle classes of capitalistic society is doubtless a part of the Church's order, but that the mission should result in the formation of a middle-class church which defends the secular outlook and interests of that class is an evident corruption." [14] Edmund Schlink (Germany) deplored the fact that the German churches during the Nazi regime had frequently denied communion to those who were anti-Nazi.[15] Capitalism was up for more than passing criticism. Wilhelm Pauck (United States) was convinced that "the good life cannot be attained until society is rebuilt, and until the principle of capitalistic free enterprise in particular has been recognized as irreconcilable with the democratic faith in the freedom of all men." [16] John Bennett (United States) pointed out that the working class had rejected the church because "the majority of lay people are Republicans, conservative in economic and social thinking, accepting the capitalistic order." [17] John Foster Dulles (United States) recognized that a free society may be capitalist, socialist, or communist. Concerning the ends of Soviet Communism, Dulles said, "There is nothing in these long-term ends irreconcilable with what Christians seek." [18] J. L. Hromadka, a professor from Prague, saw that "the phenomenon of communism is in its essential structure different

from that of nazism." [19] Communism is part of the age-old
struggle of man for liberty and for freedom from exploitation.

In spite of these specific recommendations with regard
to the social emphases which Christianity was asserted to
entail, the Council meetings were not productive of any
general agreement. Many delegates from the West still felt
that capitalistic democracy was "Christian," while others
sounded the clarion call for a form of socialism. Communism
had its supporters also, and the net result was an exhibition
of the inability of putative Christians to define their religion
in terms of the deeds to be performed.

The debates which have characterized social programs
in the United States reflect not merely a difference of opinion
over what is to be done in the name of religion, but how these
deeds are to be done. This is to say that it has been not
merely the ends which posed the difficulty, but the means to
these ends. For every religious proposal that the federal government is best fitted to effect the necessary reforms in
society, there have been others who insisted that unless the
changes are brought about by free enterprise on the part of
individuals the ends are not worth the means. It has not been
so much a matter whether hungry persons are to be fed or
the sick healed, but rather how these matters are to be
resolved, that has divided serious religious men.

In spite of the inherent difficulties in defining religion in
terms of action, there has usually been a general sympathy
among those claiming religious sentiments for programs
which minister to basic human needs. At least as far back
as the Hebrew prophets (eighth century B.C.) or the compassionate Buddha (sixth century B.C.) there have been nuclei of
reformers who insisted on utilitarian ends as inherent in religion. Virtually every movement laying claim to being religious has had its Saint Francis.

RELIGION NOMINALLY DEFINED

Our survey of the classes of definitions of religion has revealed certain persistent difficulties. What ap-

pears as generally present in all groups associated in the name of religion turns out to be of no serious moment for any group. What is of great importance turns out not to be universally present. Each group specifies the locus of value and the meaning of its mission, and the consequence is that religious persons are in houses divided against themselves. When earnest religious leaders make the meaning of their religion precise, then they exclude a majority of the rest of mankind as being, by definition, irreligious. If, instead of precision, a more vague and inclusive definition is proposed, then many are included in the class of religious persons who would much rather be excluded. Finally, the most serious implication which has followed from the attempt at definition has been the temptation, to which men normally succumb, to use the definition of religion as a premise in an argument, the conclusion of which is held to be true. It is hard, in an area so highly charged with emotion, to look upon the definition dispassionately. Even though it is recognized that definitions are, after all, stipulative, and hence neither true nor false, it still seems to many religious persons as if the fate of religion depended upon proper definitions, rather than upon true descriptions. In religion, perhaps more than in any other area, definitions have appeared to be much more than linguistic conventions to aid in communication. They have functioned as criteria of truth and falsity, and as ways of separating the pious from the impious. Many religious persons, armed with a definition, will still reason from the following type of syllogism:

"To be religious means to believe in God."

"Mr. Smith does not believe in God."

"Therefore Mr. Smith is not religious."

Or again:

"If true religion leads a man to minister to the sick and needy,"

"And if Mr. Jones' sect does not so minister,"

"Then the sect of Mr. Jones is obviously not a true religion."

It is perfectly clear from the first syllogism that Mr. Smith does not believe in God, although the second premise alone would have conveyed this information. On the other hand, it is equally clear, *by definition,* that Mr. Smith is not religious, but this is not a very astounding bit of factual information in view of the plethora of definitions of religion. Much the same conclusion follows from the second syllogism. As a matter of fact some sect may not have a social service program; indeed, many sects which do have such programs would still maintain that these are not what characterize the essence of their faith. The labels of "true religion" or "false religion," however, are merely epithets, by which one religion defends itself against all others. Were we to get involved in the definition of religion (true or false, right or wrong, useful or useless, noble or repugnant) we would dissipate our energies on a matter which could never be resolved.

In view of these observations, let us decide to allow each person and group to define religion. This will enable us to know what "religion" means sufficiently to follow the discussion. When we study Saint Augustine, we will deal with his definition of religion. By the same token, when we analyze the cosmological arguments for God given by Saint Thomas, we shall use his definitions for God and for religion. After all, the problems of both religion and philosophy of religion are not definitional. We wish to know whether what religion talks about (however defined) is true or false. We want to determine whether the aims of religion (however defined) are morally worthy, psychologically compelling, or candidates for ultimate concern. Definitions are prerequisites to understanding, but they are not sufficient to determine either truth or value.

It clearly does not follow from this decision that we shall never know what religion is. We shall always know what it is, for the person who defines it. Philosophically this is all we need to know.

III

Why Do We Have Religion?

YOU MAY HAVE asked yourself why man's concern with religion has been so constant and so widespread. Few movements rival religion for endurance, for emotional attachment, and for influence in so wide an area of human experience and concern. The data of religion are so much more ancient and so much more plentiful than those of virtually any other subject that it seems pertinent to inquire as to the sources of its vitality. The question, "Why do we have religion?" is capable of a variety of interpretations. One may be asking for the origins of religion, or for the reasons for its persistence, or for the consequences which give it warrant pragmatically, or for the psychological elements in it which have made it so compelling and of such concern; or this may be a disguised epistemological question asking for the evidences of its truth or falsity. We shall consider several hypotheses as answers to the original question. On the legitimate assumption that the answers to a question shed light on what the question was interpreted to mean, we shall then have a variety of theories from which to choose to account for the phenomenon of religious activity and interest.

4 1

IS RELIGION INHERITED?

According to one theory the religious interests and institutions that exist at the moment will be functionally related to what has already existed in the society. This would account, for example, for the fact that most of the students in a course in philosophy of religion in an American college will be from the Judeo-Christian tradition. According to this theory, most students come with this religious concern simply because they come from communities where this was already the accepted religion. It is assumed that most of us do not choose our religion, but inherit it. Children hold the religious views of their parents not because these children have evaluated them and found them adequate, but because religion is absorbed by these children without conscious effort. Religion is not alone in being accepted in this unintentional fashion. Politics and ethics are also assumed to be inherited and thus continued by one generation simply because the last generation provided the atmosphere. This is as simple as pointing out that most Roman Catholics had Roman Catholic parents, or that the average citizen of Ceylon is likely to be a Buddhist. It should be no surprise if the average citizen of Moscow is sympathetic to communism, while the average citizen of New York is sympathetic to capitalism. In all of this, it is not a matter of deliberate choosing that accounts for these interests; it is, rather, the mere fact that our culture supplies us with the emotionally active options which we absorb without much critical thinking. If one were to consider a typical small American town, where the churches were all Christian, it would seem quite incredible if from this town there emerged any Buddhists, Hindus, or Moslems. This is not just a matter of not knowing what other religions have to offer, for even where such general information is available, we do not find people choosing religions that are alien to what already exists in the society.

There are certain difficulties with the universal application of this theory. If, for example, one were to assume that it adequately accounted for the existence of religious concerns, it would be difficult to explain how Buddhists do come from non-Buddhist backgrounds, or how a Protestant could come from Roman Catholic parents. It would be even more difficult to explain how religious revolutions take place, where the members of the revolution certainly appear to be choosing against their own cultural heritage. How, for example, would this theory explain the origin of religion in the first place? Would it have to predicate that religion always existed and that there never was a time when it did not? Even assuming that this was actually the case, and that religion has always been, the theory would still not explain why the religion of today resembles so little the religion of yesterday. In spite of these difficulties, however, the role of cultural heritage in maintaining religion is not to be dismissed.

WAS RELIGION INVENTED BECAUSE THE WORLD WAS SO GRIM?

The grimness of the world has been most clearly seen in those natural catastrophes which constantly threaten man's survival. These natural events which men face, but do not appear to cause, have been traditionally called "natural evils." They include such sources of human misery as disease, hurricanes, tidal waves, killing frost, floods, and the like. Suppose we were to predicate that primitive, genetic man, confronted with all these hazards and without any knowledge of medical science or meteorology, concluded that life in such a world would be intolerable unless there were some explanation of these events. Is it too fantastic to suppose that he predicated the existence of supernatural beings whose actions caused these evils? Having asserted that there were such beings, is it not conceivable that he then tried to find the means of pacifying these beings so that the evils either would not occur or at least might be avoided? To put the questions in this way might lead one to suspect that genetic man was being credited with both an imagination and an intelligence which far surpass any he could be expected to have. Whether or not this does predicate a rather ideal primitive man, it is true that primitive religions did have an-

43

swers to precisely such problems. Natural catastrophes were interpreted as being caused by unseen powers, and the possible motives which prompted these powers to act in such fashion were of particular concern to early religious thinkers. It gave comfort to a Vedic Hindu to know at least that Rudra, one of the pantheon of Hindu gods, was in some measure the cause of natural evils. The predecessors of Job did take comfort in the claim that natural evils were punishment for moral evils. When it was no longer possible for Job to be comforted with this explanation, he invented another to take its place. Few subjects have involved more time and concern among religious persons than these questions of natural evil. Even if it is doubtful that religions were invented to answer the problems raised by disease and disaster, it is clear that religions do spend a preponderance of their energies speaking to this point. While it is true that Mary Baker Eddy made her claims because she believed that they were true, it is also true that her religious movement has prospered precisely because of the answers that it gives to the gruesomeness of the world of natural evils.

This theory intends, however, to say more than this. It is not merely that religions do explain why men suffer, but that these religions were invented for the purposes of explaining why men suffer. It could be inferred, therefore, that if the world could be tidied up so that all natural evils were eliminated, then there would be no excuse left for the existence of religion. That this might occur was at one time a very real fear on the part of certain religious leaders who blocked the attempts at slum clearance, at raising standards of health, or at providing adequate wages. They suspected that if we did make the world a Garden of Eden, religion would disappear on the ground that it served no function. There is a simple sense in which this fear would appear to have some basis. It has been a fact of introspective experience that one might turn to religion for comfort in a time of natural crisis, though normally one would not be motivated to think of religious matters. At any rate, religious dogmas are commonly intended to take the sting out of the heartlessness of the world. It may still be doubtful that religion was originally invented for this purpose or that religion serves no other aim than this.

This theory does not appear, for example, to explain all the theological ideas which do not intend to account for natural evil. What would prompt a theologian to propose the dogma of the seven sacraments of the Roman Catholic Church? Is there any sense in which the doctrine of the Trinity is meant to answer the problem of natural evil? If the theory were the only one used to account for religion, how would we explain the emergence of so many different sects, whose differences are not based on their solutions to the problem of natural evil?

WAS RELIGION DESIGNED BY POLITICAL SCHEMERS?

A third view accounts for religion on the grounds that it is and was a weapon in the struggle of princes against their serfs, or of tribal chieftains against their subjects. To put the matter quite simply and boldly, we imagine a chief, troubled by the fact that he is losing his grip over his followers, inventing, by a stroke of imaginative genius, the whole religious panoply. He could then say to his people, "If you revolt against me, you revolt against the omnipotent power or powers which guide the world. I am a mere man, but I govern by the authority of a power greater than us all." While it may seem incredible to assert such a theory seriously to account for the origin of religion, it has been asserted seriously to account for the maintenance of religion. Machiavelli noted concerning ecclesiastical kingdoms, "They are acquired either by ability or by fortune; but are maintained without either, for they are sustained by ancient religious customs, which are so powerful and of such quality that they keep their princes in power in whatever manner they proceed and live. These princes alone have states without defending them, have subjects without governing them. . . ." [1] Machiavelli considered the vitally useful role which religion had played and could play as a plain fact with which any aspirant to leadership ought to be cognizant. There were times, to be sure, when he looked at some religions as dangerous. The Church of Rome, for example, he judged as deficient on two relevant counts. In the first place, it had "destroyed all piety and religion in Italy." [2] And in the second place, "the Church has kept and still keeps our country divided." [3] In spite of these debits which religions have accumulated from the point of view of a monarch, he still believed that religion could be used by the shrewd leader for his own ends.

> It is therefore the duty of princes and heads of republics to uphold the foundations of the religion of their countries, for then it is easy to keep their people religious, and consequently well conducted and united. And therefore everything that tends to favor religion (even though it were believed to be false) should be received and availed of to strengthen it; and this should be done the more, the wiser the rulers are, and the better they understand the natural course of things. [4]

Thomas Hobbes wrote in the same essential spirit as did Machiavelli. In neither case did religion seem to be of concern other than as it might be used for purposes of control by a designing monarch. In his analysis of the origins of religions he singled out four "Naturall seeds of Religion."

> And in these foure things, Opinion of Ghosts, Ignorance of second causes, Devotion towards what men fear, and Taking of things Casuall for Prognostiques, consisteth the Naturall seed of Religion; which by reason of the different Fancies, Judgements, and Passions of severall men, hath grown up into ceremonies so different, that those which are used by one man, are for the most part ridiculous to another. [5]

In the long process by which religions emerged, virtually everything in nature was at one time called a god. This reification of the natural course of things gave primitive man an explanation of the fortuitous and unpredictable quality of things. The shrewd monarch will take note of the seriousness with which men of all ages have taken these verbalizations of their fears, and will, as a consequence, take special care to fulfill three ends. In the first place, the ruler will take care to impress upon his people that all laws and decrees of the monarch proceed, not from the whim of the monarch, but from the decrees of the gods in whom the people already believe. In the second place, the wise monarch will take care to impress his subjects with the thesis that what is prohibited by law is also prohibited by the gods. Third, he will urge the citizens to practice ceremonies, sacrifices, and festivals of a religious nature. These aid in keeping the citizen convinced that failures in war, famines, and any other social catastrophes all occur through the displeasure of the gods rather than the incompetence of the monarch. Thus the cure for such ills, from the point of view of the subjects, will always be more religion. This serves to keep any onus of failure away from the king, and at the same time gives the people the impression that they have a share in their destinies. Hobbes observed that the Romans had had great success by these strategies, and that given religion and a little bread most subjects are kept in a pacific state. If a prince is truly wise, he will see to it that the faith of his subjects does not rest upon miracles, on the fulfillment of all petitions, or upon virtuous pastors; for when these fail, then the faith will fail. By inventive skill the prince will foresee every contingency so that both he, as the spokesman for religion, and the faith in the religion will always survive no matter what happens.

One doctrine common to most religions in the past must be particularly attacked by the monarch. This is the thesis that what a man does against conscience is a religious sin. Such a view places the church and the state as antagonists of each other, and suggests that the insights of religious men might not correspond to those of prelates in the state. The monarch cannot afford to have this subversive doctrine in circulation, since, sooner or later, it will lead to the dissolution of the state.[6] In order to gain the absolute obedience of his subjects, the monarch must go on the assumption, which in turn he impresses upon his subjects, that "it is with the mysteries of our Religion, as with wholesome pills for the sick, which swallowed whole, have the vertue to cure; but chewed, are for the most part cast up again without effect."[7]

In the implementation of this program there are several doctrines which the monarch must explain to his people. First, he must assert that a true prophet works miracles and does not teach anything contrary to what is already established in the state. The unlikelihood that miracles will be performed, in the first place, puts an effective check on any would-be prophets; and the latter idea prevents a prophet, who is yet supposed to have done the impossible, from working any harm to the monarch. Second, he must declare that the Kingdom of God, which both Jews and Christians teach, really means a state in which the people vote to have God as their sovereign. Since the monarch is the symbol of this type of kingdom, his position will not be jeopardized. Third, the monarch must define the church as "a company of men professing Christian Religion, united in the person of one Sovereign; at whose command they ought to assemble, and without whose authority they ought not to assemble." [8] Fourth, he must assert that the real aims of all Christians are not of this world. This effectively cuts the power of priests and bishops to command obedience, and when coupled with the previous ideas, gives the secular monarch all power. In support of the apostolic succession of secular monarchs, Hobbes asserted the thesis that the apostolic succession really began with Constantine (324–337 A.D.) as the first pope, and that thus all civil leaders are his successors.[9] The whole message is then summed up in two requirements for salvation: faith in Christ (which has no social implications) and obedience to the laws.

In the thought of both of these men religion is a convenient and effective tool of social and political control. It was, in part, for this reason that Karl Marx called the Judeo-Christian religion the "opium of the people."

If the above is considered as a positive function of control exercised by religion in political affairs, it may also be noted that religion has served a function in supporting or attacking a wide variety of economic viewpoints. At the conclusion of his book on *Religion and the Rise of Capitalism*, R. H. Tawney observed that the Church of England had been a weapon in support of the capitalist economic theory by encouraging the idea that "the very heart of religion was a spirit which made indifference to the gross world of external circumstances appear, not a defect, but an ornament of the soul." [10] Here the religious institution aided an economic theory by claiming that religion and the economic processes had nothing in common, and hence left the impression that a religious criticism of economic practices was improper. It was claimed, therefore, that religion had been a weapon in the struggle for power both by its intervention and by its withdrawal.

This constituted, in part, Tawney's answer to the question which first prompted him to write his book. In the early pages we find him asking:

> Has religious opinion in the past regarded questions of social organization and economic conduct as irrelevant to the life of the spirit, or has it endeavored not only to christianize the individual but to make a Christian civilization? Can religion admit the existence of a sharp antithesis between personal morality and the practices which are permissible in business? Does the idea of a Church involve the acceptance of any particular standard of social ethics, and, if so, ought a Church to endeavor to enforce it as among the obligations incumbent on its members? [11]

As far as the church of the third century was concerned, Tawney saw it as having been absorbed and diluted by the secular culture to the point where it was a mere tool of scheming monarchs. The Protestant churches of the seventeenth and eighteenth centuries became, in effect, religions of trade or capitalism. Religiosity and economic thrift and shrewdness were identified. Here, again, the church had no word to speak which was other than a sanction of the *status quo*. While Puritanism was not guilty of this capitalizing of religion, it erred in "training its pupils to the mastery of others through the mastery of self, it prized as a crown of glory the qualities which arm the spiritual athlete for his solitary contest with a hostile world, and dismissed concern with the social order as the prop of weaklings and the Capua of the soul." [12] Here religion makes no judgments of the world at all, and leaving the arena to political and economic aspirants, it retires to its dreams of a future world. The modern church is castigated by Tawney for its assumption that "the attainment of material riches is the supreme object of human endeavor, and the final criterion of human success." [13] Thus the church and its religious message are subverted to being tools of economic and political barons.

No explication of the thesis that religion is a weapon in the power struggle would be complete without at least some reference to Karl Marx. He saw institutional Christianity as "parsonpower," [14] as a force to "demoralize immature masses." [15] The abolition of the church as an effective social or economic agency was essential to the redemption of man.

> The so-called Christian State needs the Christian religion in order to complete itself as a state. The Democratic State, the real State, does not need religion for its political completion. [16]

The theory is probably right in its claim that religion has been used as a convenient weapon in the economic and political struggles. The theory has limitations, however, if one assumes that this is the only purpose religion has served, or that this explains the creation and maintenance of religious interests. The historical origins of religions do not support the thesis that power was the motivation for their creation. The theologies of religions, in addition, do not commonly make the sorts of claims which could be of use in furthering the pursuit of power, or any other worldly aim.

In support of his theses Marx showed some incisiveness and ingenuity. As a confirmed member of the Lutheran church he attended its services and heard sermons. He noted that the clergy were prone to read passages from the Sermon on the Mount which urged men not to fill their barns with this world's goods, to give their cloaks when asked for their coats, and in general to be obedient citizens. Now, Marx asked himself, to whom are these recommendations given? Clearly they are not for the priests, since the churches of Europe possess the largest and best-filled barns and they do not evidence any tendency to empty them in honor of their Lord. Nor are the financiers the intended recipients of these words of advice, for they continue in their positions of economic power. Ultimately, there is only one group for whom these actions are intended, namely, those who possess no barns to begin with. To make empty-barnness a mark of religiosity effectively removes the masses of the proletariat from competition in the economic struggle. Thus the church serves as the "barking dog of capitalism" and the witting servant of the power struggle.

And yet here, as in Machiavelli and Hobbes, it seems as if the authors are explaining not so much why men have religion, as a use to which religion may be and has been put. While this may be what some have had in mind when they asked for the *raison d'être* of religion, it is clearly not the whole story—nor even, probably, what most persons have in mind when they ask about the existence of religion.

IS RELIGION PSYCHOLOGICALLY DEMANDED?

If some of the theories so far considered appear to be destructive of the basic value which religions claim to possess, there is another explanation which has no such tendency. Here it is claimed that a variety of basic human wants prompted the emergence of the phenomena of religion as means to the fulfillment of these needs. The kinds of wants appeared to vary widely from the commonly approved to the seldom approved. Among these basic human urges have been mentioned the need for personal security in a world of hazard, the need for cosmic support for otherwise essentially human values, the spontaneous response of awe and wonder, the need for a father figure to play on a world scale the functions which a biological father plays on a local scale, the need for solace in the presence of inexplicable fears, and the need simply to know what life's dramas are all about. Let us consider a few of the representative explanations which account for religion as the fundamental human response to unmet wants and desires.

In an essentially psychological account Gerald Heard deprecates the notion that intellect has ever played a basic role in religious creation, and lays the primary causal force in the seat of human emotions. It is not that man has not, in fact, spent considerable energy reasoning about his survival problems, but, rather, that the mere presence of such rational efforts indicates a more basic emotional lack. He conjectures that "far below sympathetic magic lies sympathetic mimicry. The emotional behaviour pattern would reach a very considerable elaboration, real ritual would be present before it became so complex, so varied and separated by so many steps from the emotion-provoking object, that it would, as it were, break the surface of consciousness, by its elaborateness awake speculation, make the constituent wonder what he was doing, and thus compel him to project a compensatory intellectualising explanation." [17] The emotions thus aroused were rooted in matters of common purpose, such as food getting, social order, or health. The archetype of this hypothesis he found in the behavior of apes, which, if true, would lend an age to religion which would have it antedate the emergence of man. He conjectured as follows:

> But, prior to the rationalisations which were to culminate in sympathetic magic, religion must have gone through a long period when it was still completely "nonprecipitant," i.e. when it is still so flexible, so spontaneous that it can be completely unsummoned and unordered. It is still altogether a dromena—a dance—and has as yet no hint in it of a drama—a representation. It has no more of ritual about it than has a round of applause, or, perhaps it were more apt to say, than the choric bellowings of the roaring monkeys. . . . At the stage when man first became human we must presume that the common yearning must have coalesced with the common play, which, to meet it, has risen to the common rhythm. [18]

The idea of immortality, which is a product of much later rationalizing, fundamentally expresses the urge to return to that state of belonging to the primitive herd, and to feel at one with the group effort for survival. By reason man has distorted this basic urge for communion with the group into a belief in personal immortality, which he conceives as the zenith of religious expectation. Clearly, at this point, man's reason has done his emotions a disservice, by putting forth an essentially private objective which dooms the social end to failure. Heard remarks:

> So at the level of the religion of magic, the first reflective men could not grasp—and to-day religious people are little advanced in this essential knowledge—that it was working magic *with the group* that was their real salvation.[19]

And thus religion originated in primal emotional needs. Although the modern trappings, the contribution of philosophers, with which religion is gilded obfuscate its genetic purpose, there is yet in the subconscious of the race a yearning for this same social solidarity.

In Freud we find an account which closely resembles that of Heard in that it finds the genetic cause lost in a rubble of intellectualization. The real motive for religion, according to his theory, lay in man's emotional need for solace and relief from the natural evils which plagued him. Man was threatened with personal extinction, and he rose to the occasion by humanizing nature. When nature was considered to be impersonal, there was nothing man could do to rectify the situation, but if the events of life were the work of personalized deities, then man could take steps and assume a responsibility. For if there are gods, endowed with properties identical with those of the ancestral fathers, then "we can try to exorcise them, to appease them, to bribe them, and so rob them of part of their power by thus influencing them." [20] The survival of the religious belief in miracles is merely an indication that although the gods can be influenced, they have not completely resigned themselves to being the pawns of designing men. Freud summarized this position:

> I have tried to show that religious ideas have sprung from the same need as all the other achievements of culture: from the necessity for defending itself against the crushing supremacy of nature. And there was a second motive: the eager desire to correct the so painfully felt imperfections of culture.[21]

With Freud also, the vast structures of systematic theology and philosophy of religion serve merely to cover the real essence of religion. Men did not reflect cognitively about nature, and then create religion. Dogmas "are not the residue of experience, or the final result of reflection; they are illusions, fulfilments of the oldest, strongest and most insistent wishes of mankind." [22] These religious illusions, whose future Freud is discussing, gain their meaning simply from the fact that they arise in emotions and are sanctioned by them. Since Freud was convinced that mature persons could resolve these same emotions more effectively by personal responsibility than by religion, he was quite willing that an experiment of irreligion be carried out, which would replace this obsessional neurosis (called religion) by healthy activity. Religion may have had a proper place in the infancy of the race (though Freud doubted even this), but, clearly, mature persons have no need for religion.

A similar justification for the source of the religious urge is found in the reflections of C. J. Jung, the psychotherapist. According to him, man will never rest with the certitudes of mathematics or the high probabilities of scientific explanation. Man has spiritual needs which no factual reports can assuage. The "fictional and imaginative processes" [23] to which religions appeal are what give meaning to life. The alternatives confronting man are quite clear: if science is posed as being sufficient, then men will have no *raison d'être;* if religion is admitted, then the impersonal becomes warm and the otherwise pointless natural events become endowed with significant meaning. Unlike Freud, who suspected that the need for religion would vanish with emotional maturity, Jung intimated that the emotional needs which religion meets will always be a part of the human situation. With Jung there is a recognition that life will always be larger than logic, and that intellect may not, at the point of religion, be man's best guide.

While the many problems which religions have constructed for man may not all be functional, they are not, at any rate, simply a sign of man's neuroses. They are far more an indication of the ambiguity of human existence and the dilemma of being human. Jung spoke of this problem as follows:

> Healing may be called a religious problem. In the sphere of social or national relations, the state of suffering may be civil war, and this state is to be cured by the Christian virtue of forgiveness for those who hate us. That which we try with the conviction of good Christians to apply to external situations, we must also apply to the inner state in the treatment of neuroses. This is why modern man has heard enough about guilt and sin. He is sorely enough beset by his own bad conscience, and wants rather to learn how he is to reconcile himself with his own nature—how he is to love the enemy in his own heart and call the wolf his brother.[24]

Feuerbach found the essence of religion to be something within man—not a set of events to be reported, like objects of science, and to be treated with a proper emotional awe or reverence. He cites Saint Augustine with favor as recognizing that God is closer and more understandable to man than corporeal objects. Unlike Saint Augustine, however, he asserts that God is not anything apart from man. Indeed, God is simply man's highest aspirations objectified. "Religion is the solemn unveiling of man's hidden treasures, the revelation of his most intimate thoughts, the open confession of what he secretly loves."[25]

The religious man, however, may not usually be aware that this is what his religion really is. In fact, for Feuerbach, unawareness of this is considered to be basic to the peculiar

55

nature of religion. Religion is basically self-knowledge reified and objectified.

> Hence, the historical progress of religion consists in this: that that which during an earlier stage of religion was regarded as something objective is now regarded as something subjective, so that that which was formerly viewed and worshipped as God is now recognized as something human. The later stage of religion recognizes the earlier stage as a stage of idolatry, a stage at which man prayed to his own nature, and at which man objectified himself without recognizing the religious object for what it was: his own nature.[26]

Santayana's explanation of the role of religion, although essentially autobiographical, stresses the emotional solace, the aesthetic stimulus, and the challenge to the imagination which have been the concomitants or the consequences of religious emphases. Life without religion would lack luster and verve, even though, with religion, life gains no insights into truth. He observed: "Their chief anxiety has been to offer imaginary remedies for mortal ills, some of which are incurable essentially, while others might have been really cured by well-directed effort." [27] But even in spite of this, religion for Santayana meets emotional wants of such magnitude that its continued presence is both warranted and assured.

Henri Bergson has traced a thesis as to the twofold sources from which religion has sprung. On the one hand there is a vast accrual from the heritage of man's past during which instinct and intelligence accumulated data for the resolution of life-and-death issues. "Looked at from this point of view, religion is then a defensive reaction of nature against the dissolvent power of intelligence." [28] Instinct alone would have counseled man adequately for his own protection, but man, being a creature of intelligence, is able to destroy himself. Nature rises to the occasion by supplying in man this myth-making function, of which religion is an expression, to curb the evil consequences which reason might have produced. Among the disasters of which reason has been the parent are egoism, depression in the face of failure, and the dissolution of society through revolt. Nature reacts to these potential calamities by creating in man both custom and the myth-making function, which serve as deterrents. The myths which this form of "static religion" produces are, however, quite unsatisfactory to intelligence. May there not be another source for a religion called "dynamic" which may speak even to the needs of sophisticated men? Bergson finds such an additional element in the *élan vital* of a mystical intuition.

> But we know that all around intelligence there lingers still a fringe of intuition, vague and evanescent. Can we not fasten upon it, intensify it, and above all, consummate it in action, for it has become pure contemplation only through a weakening in its principle, and, if we may put it so, by an abstraction practised on itself? [29]

This mystical spirit, though not the possession of all men—indeed, few men ever experience it—yet speaks to the innermost being of men, and is prompted by a source which is nature itself. Both of these "sources" of religion have their roots, not in the inventiveness of man's imagination, but in the inexorable life processes of "nature."

There has been a long tradition for the belief that religion serves the function of giving to human ethical and moral standards a cosmic support and significance. Perhaps, even, religion was consciously invented for this pragmatic end. Without the aura which religion provides, ethical maxims would be mere culture-bound mores. The common assumption of so many religious laymen and professional evangelists that if there were no belief in God, there would be no reason to do right rather than wrong, is an expression of this conviction. Religion gives to moral commands a dignity and a sanction which they would not otherwise possess. Part of the suspicion of the ancient leaders of Athens of the teaching of Socrates was that it was impious, and that, hence, it undermined the moral fabric of the citizens. The sentiments of Crito in Berkeley's dialogue are in this tradition.

> It puts me in mind of my friend Lamprocles, who needed but one argument against infidels. I observed, said he, that as infidelity grew, there grew corruption of

every kind, and new vices. This simple observation on matter of fact was sufficient to make him, notwithstanding the remonstrance of several ingenious men, imbue and season the minds of his children betimes with the principles of religion.[30]

This universal need for metaphysical support for ethics and morals appears to have been operative in most religions. This may be apparent from no other fact than that every religion has produced moral commandments, and that these same commandments were rooted in the deity to which that religion was committed.

William E. Hocking expressed this sentiment when he averred that religion originated as "the spirit of the sacred past which organizes and sanctifies these relics, providing a place where the Zeitgeist may worship at the shrine of its own emancipation." [31] He saw the chief marks of the religious spirit as a "fearless and original valuation of things." [32] As such, religion is the parent and precursor of the arts. It foresees and commands that that which only the long evolution of man will actually fulfill ought to be the present accomplishment of men. "Religion is anticipated attainment." [33] It requires that men be perfect right now, even though such perfection will never be a fact in the near future. Religion thus provides the vision of the good and the assurance that victory is within the powers of men.

Attempts to make a case for the morality-producing properties of religion commonly founder on the ambiguity of the empirical data which are supposed to support it. There is no compelling evidence to support the supposition that religious commitments produce any particular kind of moral behavior. This does not mean that religious persons are morally insensitive, but simply that religion has not spoken with a univocal word on moral matters. Serious Christians have endorsed capitalism, communism, socialism, and the Robinson Crusoe view in economics. They have both supported and attacked child labor, anti-Semitism, democracy, war, pacifism, capital punishment, integration, and the general strike. It is one thing to say that religion serves the function of lending sanction to moral behavior, and quite another thing to show that religion has any unique insights into what would be proper action. While there has been a common allegiance among Jews and Christians on the matter of the Ten Commandments, the interpretations as to what kinds of behavior these commandments entail have been so contradictory as to cast serious doubt on the efficacy or adequacy of the religious sanction.

In addition, this explanation suffers from the same incompleteness as did that which asserted that religion was invented to aid in the power struggle. Would it seem likely that genetic man would have been so shrewdly calculating as to invent religion in order that his local virtues should be given a cosmic endorsement? Even if our original man had been so pragmatic in his surmise, would there be any reason to laud his decision? That religion has functioned as a powerful support for moral actions may be conceded, but this concession is a far cry from evidence that this explains the genesis of religion. Here again we have, perhaps, a clear indication that religion may be used, once it has emerged, to lend support for a variety of ends. It seems highly doubtful, however, that if this were the only motive, religion would ever have persisted with the vitality that it has demonstrated. And on the other hand, the drive exhibited by loyal Marxists raises a question as to whether religion is either sufficient or necessary for moral enthusiasm and commitment. Perhaps, as C. J. Jung suggests,[34] both Communism and Freudian psychology function as if they were religions, and consequently they stimulate the drives which their adherents do express for moral commitment.

Indeed, our problem may now be asked anew in the face of these putative answers. Why do we have religion? Are the social and theological interests associated with religion to be explained by the utilitarian ends which it serves? Suppose that all of the above theories were true and that religions have been invented for these various purposes, have we answered any philosophical question? Would such theories imply that religion is, therefore, either significant or true? Let us turn our attention to such matters and see whether the reasons for having religion, or the accounts of its origin, are actually matters of great philosophic moment.

IS THE ORIGIN OF RELIGION IMPORTANT TO PHILOSOPHY?

Suppose we were to premise that all of these theories together, or any one of these theories by itself, accounted for the motivation for having some religion. Suppose it were true that we have religion precisely for these reasons. The philosophical question would still remain unanswered. In philosophy of religion we wish to know whether any of the statements of religion are true, and whether some of them may be false. No amount of theorizing about the motivational causes for religious expression can determine whether anything which religion asserts is true. This may be expressed in a maxim: "The origin of an idea has no epistemological bearing on the truth of an idea." Even if religion were the result of neurosis, the statements of the religion might still be true. If, as some have suggested, Jesus was paranoid, that he had delusions of grandeur, it is still an open question whether any of Jesus' claims are true.[35] Neurotic persons can make true statements, just as normal persons can make false statements. The truth of a statement will not be a function of the psychic health of the person who makes the statement. It will be a function of whether what the person talks about exists as described. If, for example, there were data to prove that the statement "God exists" is true, it would be quite irrelevant if the motive for making the assertion about God were grounded in infantile traumata.

Even if Marx were correct in saying that religion was prompted by power-hungry chiefs and kings, this fact would not affect the truth or falsity of what these same chiefs or kings asserted. To be sure, if it were conceded that either Freud or Marx was correct, this fact might well affect the emotional enthusiasm with which we approach religion; but here again, the motivation or lack of it does not determine truth or falsity. It may be doubted whether it is always true that the origin of an idea does not affect the truth of an idea. What if a religion asserted a religious claim concerning its own origin? What if a Christian theologian, for example, made the religious claim that Christianity originated in the act by which God incarnated himself in Jesus? Thus it would be claimed that an act of God, prompted by a desire of God, got the whole religion started. Would this, even if it were a fact, affect the truth of Jesus' statements? No. It would still be necessary to show that what Jesus talked about existed as he described it. If, however, some religious person wished to argue that since it was God's idea in the first place, the idea must therefore be true, it would then have to be demonstrated that a God-prompted idea is always a true idea. This is not an easy venture. The conventional approach to this type of claim is to postulate that since God is omnipropertied, his ideas must consistently be correct. But this merely shifts the question. We would then have to ask concerning God's omni-propertiedness. Even after this had been satisfactorily demonstrated, it would still have to be shown that no omnipropertied being had ever erred. If one wished to claim now that an omnipropertied being could not err by definition, then the nature of a definition would lead us to conclude that while such a definition is consistent and that the inference from omni-propertiedness to the making of true statements is valid, there would still remain the question as to whether either the definition or the inference meets the requirements which true statements must meet.

The fear that the origin of an idea does have a bearing on the truth of an idea has prompted some religious persons to fear the social sciences. Data such as those presented in Max Weber's *The Protestant Ethic and the Spirit of Capitalism*, R. H. Tawney's *Religion and the Rise of Capitalism,* or Karl Marx's *The Civil War in France* have suggested that religion is affected by the social milieu in which it finds itself. This has appeared to give to religion a "kiss of death." Religion appears to be as susceptible to influence as any other essentially human institution. Even if one doubted Freud's thesis that religion was invented through the promptings of neurosis, the invincibility of religion still seemed to be shaken. It seemed to have its feet in the same clay which clung to all human strivings. Biological hypotheses such as that of Charles Darwin also contributed to the apparent fallibility of religious insights. Can religious people accept the findings of the social sciences without giving up religion altogether? It has seemed to many that they can. But this would be to confuse our emotions with our epistemology. Even if the data of the social sciences were to affect our feelings toward the worth of religion, they would not affect the philosophical problem of which religious statements, if any, are true. It may not be possible in fact for individuals to make this distinction. Feelings cannot be ignored, particularly when it has been observed that these same feelings may prompt one to lose interest in the question of the truth or falsity of religious statements. It is not that the origins of religion prove the falsity of religion, but that the origins of religion may prove the irrelevance or worthlessness of religion. If one ever drew this inference from the data of the social sciences, he might never exert himself to prove or to disprove the statements of religion. This is a real psychological possibility, but in this regard religion is not the only field in which this could occur. It is a common fact that some persons find some areas unimportant and, hence, not worth the effort. This attitude plagues most of the disciplines on the average college campus. To pursue this problem leads us, however, to the psychology of motivation and away from the epistemological question of the truth or falsity of the statements of the subject in question.

IV

The Idea *of* God: *to* What Does *the* Term Refer?

T HE WIDESPREAD NATURE of the belief in some god has led many to suppose that this, more than any other commitment, expresses the essential nature of religion. Probably no idea associated with religion has a greater antiquity. Indeed, it has been noted that "the earliest known representation of a deity is in the Caverne des Trois Frères in Ariège, and dates to the late Paleolithic period"[1] (c. 25,000 B.C.). Consistent with the recommendations in the first chapter, it is appropriate to ask what the term "God" means before we become involved in the secondary issue of the existence of such a being. In most discussions of the "bull session" variety it is commonly assumed that the word "God" means the same to every person. If this were indeed the case, then the problem of the existence of a god would be a much simpler task than it has in fact proved to be. The fact of the matter is that the term "God" has been attached to a variety of meanings so disparate that when it is discovered that two persons believe in a god, we are not particularly informed as to whether the two persons are even referring to the same world of discourse.

It will not be our purpose to entertain the fruitless question, "What does the term 'God' really mean?" since, as we have seen, this is a matter of definition and will be subject to all the vicissitudes and vagaries to which definitions are subject. Our problem, rather, concerns the gamut of actual meanings assigned to "God" and an analysis of what these meanings entail. Once we decide what we wish "God" to mean, we shall be in a position to determine whether a being with such attributes actually exists. But we shall not assume that there either is or should be one single and univocal meaning for "God." The sheer variety of meanings which have been assigned would preclude our deriving any such conclusion from the facts of putatively religious beliefs. In addition, we shall not preclude the possibility that ideas of God change. One Christian theologian maintained that both univocality and persistence were inimical to religion.

> How to escape sin, suffering, sorrow, and death, how to win compensations for the frustrations of endeavor, how to discover the values which are possible to experience, how to find courage and strength for the common social tasks,—this is the aim of every religion, and these are the conditions which determine the content of the idea of God. Accordingly, different peoples in different ages and countries, and the same people in different times and conditions, develop different ideas of God.[2]

From this situation the author drew two conclusions. In the first place, an idea of God which is adequate for one age and its problems may not suffice for another age. Indeed, the same people may alter their beliefs about a God as they confront new and urgent problems. In the second place, since every idea of God is a functional thing, there must be, at any given moment in time, a wide variety of notions of God to take care of the variety of human needs. Ideas of God will vary, and they should change. It will become clear that while these two ideas appear correct as reports of what actually occurs, few believers in a God ever share these opinions about their own meanings. Ideas about God are generally asserted in a positive tone and do not concede any possibility of alteration or difference of opinion as being possible, let alone desirable. In this chapter we shall merely accept these two matters as the facts of the case: on the one hand, there is a plethora of defined meanings for God, and on the other hand, each is asserted with absolute assurance of its being proper. If we face these matters objectively, we may conclude that many kinds of gods are believed in. It will be the subject of the next chapter to inquire whether some of these gods, so defined, actually exist. We shall divide some of the various meanings of "God" into two general classifications based on the number of referents claimed to be involved.

A MULTIVERSE REQUIRES MANY GODS

Polytheism is the belief in two or more gods. David Hume conjectured that genetically primitive religions began with polytheism. He attributed this to a preoccupation of primitive men with the contingencies of everyday experience. The imminent possibility of disease, hurricanes, floods, killing cold, burning heat, and the casualties caused by falling trees and earthquakes all impressed early man with the multiplicity and lack of unity of the world in which he lived. He had no evidence which would indicate that he lived in an orderly universe amenable to the direction of a single deity. Indeed, the soundest inference from the confusion with which he was confronted was to conclude that many gods were operating the affairs of this world, and that frequently they carried on at cross-purposes with each other. While polytheism seemed, thus, to be the obvious state of affairs, the fact remained that within a particular locale one god received all the attention. For this particular community it was as if there were but one god whose concern was directed to their own private problems. Early religious leaders were perfectly aware that neighboring communities had their gods also, but there was neither sufficient cosmic awareness nor practical need for fraternization to lead any particular community to be concerned with what other gods were doing. It seemed as natural for each area to have its private male or female deity as to have its own tribal chieftain. However, the monotheism which this state of thinking entailed was of a purely practical nature. If anyone were asked, he would admit the existence and efficacy of other gods for other persons and places. This mood seems to have been apparent among the Jews who occupied Canaan shortly after the Egyptian exodus. They conceded that there were Baal gods. For Jews, however, Jehovah was adequate, and it was their claim that even in this new land he would prove to be quite capable of holding his own in any exigency.

As soon as tribes intermingled, however, there emerged a practical and theoretical polytheism. Symbolic of the tribal marriage, the gods of each tribe married also. If the merger came as a consequence of war, the conquered people's gods assumed a lesser role. If the merger was effected peacefully, then the gods all shared coequal powers.[3] In the case of the Canaanitic Jews, we see the problem which even a conquering tribe faced in keeping the gods of the conquered in their proper place. The prophetic leaders of the Jews insisted on the superiority of Jehovah over the Baalim. The rank and file of the Jews, however, were not so concerned with retaining the purity of their religion. This situation was prompted essentially by the fact that the gods of the Canaanites were agricultural fertility gods. The Jews were, by and large, farmers, and they were quite ready to take advantage of almost any source which promised abundant crops and fertile herds. The simple fact that biblical prophets denounced so frequently the Canaanization of Judaism would suggest that the rank-and-file Jews accepted Baal deities. A further reason for this Jewish concern with Baal religion derived from the lack of any clear idea of immortality in Judaism. The Baal religion, on the other hand, asserted immortality with the Baal gods in charge. Since intimations of immortality were emerging in Judaism, it seemed the better part of discretion for many to pacify Jehovah for earthly affairs, and yet to take cognizance of the Baal gods for the possible future life.

With an abundance of gods, a wide range of earthly phenomena could each be given supernatural control. This was clearly expressed in the polytheism of the early Greek religions. Gods were assigned as the efficient causes of rain, healthy crops, fertile herds, and, indeed, anything deemed important for human affairs. The Greek gods were divided into categories of greater and lesser deities primarily in terms of their effectiveness for granting human petitions.[4] As the gods failed to fulfill their pragmatic functions they were replaced with more potent ones. Indeed, the spirit of Greece contributed to an ease in accepting gods from alien lands and of multiplying them as necessity demanded. This same open-mindedness and receptiveness to new gods characterized early Roman religion as well.[5] In the ancient Roman pantheon there were at one time 30,000 gods, each with his or her assigned tasks. Surely with such a wealth of divinities no Roman need ever be without a god for his wish fulfillments. For both the Greeks and the Romans these gods possessed essentially anthropomorphic attributes and were commonly subject to the same weaknesses of character which plagued men. The Zoroastrian religion [6] flourished during this same period under the benediction of both Greeks and Romans and under the aegis of two gods. In orthodox Vedic Hinduism 330 million gods were asserted.

Within the class of polytheism two emphases may be distinguished. On the one hand, there was henotheism, which asserted that there were many gods, but that one of these gods was more potent (for a particular group) than any of the others. According to biblical criticism there was a stage in early Judaism when henotheism was the accepted interpretation. This view was assigned as being the meaning of the story of Elijah and the priests of Baal.[7] It is perhaps not crucial whether the story is true or not. What is crucial is that it reflected a phase when Jews admitted the existence of other gods but denied their ultimate power. The historical reading of the Hindu literature appears to illustrate the same henotheistic theme. Although there were 330 million gods, one of them normally functioned as the supreme power. The concept of Brahma, for example, functions as a synthesizing and unifying force in what is otherwise a simple polytheism. For many Hindus the god Indra functioned as the henotheistically strongest god.

The other way in which polytheism has been expressed has been called kathenotheism. This is the thesis that there are many gods and that they take turns being the most powerful. A view of Vedic Hinduism seems to suggest this notion. Here it was indicated that the natural phenomena which dominate at the moment point to which of all the many gods happen to be ruling at the time. A storm god obviously governs during storms, a sun god during the day, a night god during the night, and a pretty sadistic deity during pestilence and famine. Some biblical references have been interpreted as expressing this same idea. Biblical critics have held that there was a time when the Jews believed in an immortality which was governed by the Baal gods and in which Jehovah took no part. While the god of the Jews was supreme in this mortal life, the Baal gods ruled in the next life. This kathenotheism was amply demonstrated in both the Greek and the Roman religions, where gods perennially battled for dominance, and where these Olympian struggles were expressed on earth as changing phenomena.

The appeal of some form of polytheism has been both widespread and enduring. Margaret Murray noted that as late as the seventeenth century the worship of a plurality of deities still prevailed in essentially Christian circles.[8] The avowed assumption was that everyone was a professing Christian, but covertly and often even quite openly, both laymen and clergy alike participated in the pagan and polytheistic festivals. On occasion, even bishops acted as spokesmen for the horned gods and led the people in rites to propitiate these deities. In 1282 the priest, Christian of course, still found no incongruity in leading his Inverkeithing parishioners in a fertility dance in the churchyard. In 1453, during the trial of Joan of Arc, the Prior of Saint-Germain led his people in a ceremony to pay homage to a horned pagan god in the form of an animal. This kind of practice gave rise to the accusation, well into the seventeenth century, that a major portion of the Christian clergy practiced witchcraft on the side. While the accusation of Moslem thinkers that the Christian Trinity is an expression of polytheism is debatable, there are many other Christian notions which could well be carried over from periods when belief in many deities was accepted even by polite company.

A UNIVERSE MEANS ONE GOD

The greatest fertility of imagination has been demonstrated in developing views of a single, universal, and essentially non-anthropomorphic deity. David Hume conjectured that the idea of monotheism could not have developed until there had first emerged a sense of law-abiding universality for the world in which man lived. The data which supported such a position he called "facts of nature," to distinguish them from the disparate natural evils and contingencies which he called "events of life." [9] Some proposed that the idea of monotheism first arose when different cultures, each with its own deity and its own creation-myth, came into contact with each other. Certainly the creation problem did pose a contradiction for polytheism, unless it was presumed that one of the many gods had done the job of bringing the world into being. This seemed unlikely. The similarity of the accounts of creation, in the face of the plurality of putative creators, led to the general feeling that there must be but one deity. Whatever may have been the motives prompting the belief, the fact is that monotheism has been found universally, even in those religions whose predecessors were strictly polytheistic.

Pantheism: everything is God

While the term "pantheism" means literally that God is all that there is, or that all is God, probably no religious thinker ever meant this in any literal sense that one could walk on God, breathe pieces of God, or drive a chunk of God called a nail into another chunk of God called a board.

This view intended, rather, to assert the doctrine of the universal immanence of God in whatever fashion the characteristics of the God would entail. In Spinoza's pantheism "God" refers to the systematic and mechanical order which the physical universe possesses. It is not that God is to be built up lump by lump from the matter of the world, but that the understanding of the whole interlocking and necessary system of causes and effects, and the meaning of this system, are to be understood in the context of the idea of God. In *The Ethics* Spinoza defined "God" as follows:

> VI. By God, I mean a being absolutely infinite—
> that is, a substance consisting in infinite attributes, of
> which each expresses eternal and infinite essentiality.
> . . . I say absolutely infinite, not infinite after its kind:
> for, of a thing infinite only after its kind, infinite attri-
> butes may be denied; but that which is absolutely infinite,
> contains in its essence whatever expresses reality, and
> involves no negation.[10]

In his analysis of the implications of such an idea of God, Spinoza insisted that apart from God, no substance can be granted to exist. After all, if God is a universal and necessary substance, it would be contradictory to have anything outside of God. Everything that is, must be in God, and as a consequence the substance of God must be infinitely extended. He summarized this thesis by predicating: "All things, I repeat, are in God, and all things which come to pass, come to pass solely through the laws of the infinite nature of God, and follow . . . from the necessity of his essence." [11] Whatever individual things there are, such as persons, trees, or planets, are nothing but "modifications of the attributes of God." It follows, therefore, as many medieval mystics have asserted, that everything which is, is in God. It would follow from such a view of God that the conventional idea that one can pray that God may alter the course of events for him is clearly absurd.

A similar pantheism can be found in the theorizing of Hegel. In the Hegelian pantheism, the term "God" stands for the *élan vital* which accounts for the dialectic of human and nonhuman processes. Any attempt to understand any aspect of the universe of things necessarily involves God, for apart from God there is nothing. If in Spinoza's account God appears to be material, while in Hegel's account God appears to be ideational or mental, the fact remains that for both of them God was immanent in what there is. One cannot get away from God. In both of these theories the God thus portrayed is more nearly a process than a person. This is not the sort of God to whom one prays with any hope of reciprocal relations.

Of all the views of monotheism, pantheism is the most unified and systematic. No element of the universe is apart from God. So strictly is this unity pressed that pantheists have traditionally had difficulty in explaining how either natural or moral evil could be possible. Some idealistic pantheists like Hegel and Mary Baker Eddy, in effect, denied that there were any natural evils, for to admit these events seemed to raise a doubt that God was everything and that everything was God. Both Spinoza and Hegel had difficulty in accounting for human freedom in a world in which there were no other efficient causes than the one God. In spite of these difficulties, however, pantheism has attracted religious persons because of the immanent and absolute role which was assigned to God.

In spite of this relatively happy reception enjoyed by pantheism, there have been stern opponents from the camp of Christians. John Calvin, for example, in a remark which betrayed an abysmal misunderstanding of the meaning of pantheism, averred that "its true tendency is to set up a shadowy deity and to banish all ideas of the true God, the proper object of fear and worship. I confess, indeed, that the expression, that nature is God, may be used in a pious sense by a pious mind: but, as it is harsh and inconsistent with strict propriety of speech, nature being rather an order prescribed by God, it is dangerous in matters so momentous and demanding peculiar caution to confound the deity with the inferior course of his works." [12]

71

Deistic supernaturalism: the far-off God

There was a time when deism referred to the view that God was to be identified with natural processes, which made of it a kind of naturalism. The term "deistic supernaturalism," however, asserted a far-off God, whose sole contact with the universe had been to create it. From creation on, the God remained aloof and indifferent to the result of his creation. The arguments for the deistic supernatural view appear to have stemmed from the awareness of the preponderance of natural evils in the world and from the assumed innate sinfulness of man. If these evils do abound, then it ill behooves religion to allow God to be associated too closely with this tawdry realm. Some have inferred platonically that the world of matter was too deceptive and unreal to have any God in it. Others inferred, in the spirit of John Calvin, that man's evil nature so permeates the whole process of life that God could not be imagined to be having any part in what was happening. Soren Kierkegaard, the nineteenth-century Danish theologian, put forth this doctrine of the wholly-other God. The whole dialectic of human experience in values seemed to support deistic supernaturalism. When man at his best affirmed values, then God always said "No." When God affirmed values, then man said "No." Emotionally and intellectually man and God were separated by an unbridgeable gulf. In the words of Emil Brunner, a contemporary exponent of this deistic reasoning, "Revelation issues from a region which, as such, is not accessible to man. The absolutely Mysterious is not only partially hidden from the natural knowledge of man; it is wholly inaccessible to man's natural faculties for research and discovery." [13] The abyss between human reason and divine nature cannot be crossed. Human reason and divine reason do not touch at any point. Human will and the divine notion of the good have nothing in common. "The object of faith is something which is absurd to reason." [14] With God so unknowable, so alien to human emotions, it seemed obvious that God and the world could not be closely related. Man's alienation from God thus finds its re-

72

flection in God's alienation from man. This situation was recognized to produce in man an essentially anxious quality. The
sense of uneasiness, dread, fear and trembling, or nausea held
man in a grip of stark indecisiveness. This very thesis of an
indifferent, remote God seemed to find its correlate in the
alienations of the world of human experience. Man is, as a
matter of fact, separated from his fellows, from his ideals,
from his needs, and from knowledge of the ultimates. The
ultimate alienation is expressed in this idea of a remote and
unapproachable God. All of this gives to deistic supernaturalism an apparent realism. Experience seems to indicate that
the ultimate source of value and the realm of existential fact
have no common ground on which to meet. While some deists
have intimated that a divine-human encounter could occur,[15]
the nature of the elements in the encounter, and the fact that
such encounters are rare, still leave man with the feeling
that for all practical purposes God is dead.[16]

Naturalism: the process God

A contemporary class of meanings for the term
"God" which has had particular appeal to those of a scientific
temper may be called naturalistic. In this view the history
of biological, geological, moral, and social evolution play a
dominant role. Just as the ancient pre-Socratics had been
convinced that matter had within it tendencies which led to
order and plan, so the modern scientists could have been and
have been equally impressed with these phenomena within
the range of the modern interpretation of matter. Patterns of
order can be ascribed to geological history. Systems or order
can be read into man's biological development. It seemed
natural, therefore, to pay some attention to this apparent
tendency of the universe of man and the world to produce
the kind of plan which led the nineteenth-century biologists
to coin the phrase, "Ontogeny recapitulates phylogeny." Some
religious thinkers referred the term "God" to this tendency to
order. It may have been a tendency to conserve moral value,
in the tradition of Fichte's conception of God as "the moral
order of the universe." Henry Nelson Wieman related God to

73

"the growth of meaning and value in the world." [17] Samuel
Alexander distinguished between "God" and "deity." Deity was
identified as the inevitable movement toward evolutionary
perfection. Each emergent in the biological scheme points to
a next stage yet to come. This evolving tendency was deity.

> As actual, God does not possess the quality of deity
> but is the universe as tending to that quality. This nisus
> in the universe, though not present to sense, is yet pres-
> ent to reflection upon experience. Only in this sense of
> straining towards deity can there be an infinite actual
> God.[18]

This view differs from deistic supernaturalism in that it places
God in the world. It shares with pantheism some of the im-
personalism which that theory possesses. The chief deterrent
to any widespread use of this meaning for God has been the
difficulty of relating it significantly to the common religious
expectation that relations with God are possible. It seems unlikely that the experiences of prayer or worship, as commonly
understood, would have any meaning within the context of
an impersonal process.

Neo-orthodoxy: the ground of being

Neo-orthodoxy has been the particular contribution of metaphysical theologians, and because of the eso-
teric nature of its meaning, it probably has little appeal to
the average religious citizen. A primary function of defining
God in terms of the ground of being was to combine the virtues of philosophy with the aims of religion in such a way
that they supported each other. Saint Bonaventura (1221–
1274 A.D.), a Franciscan monk, noted in his reflection on the
Divine Unity:

> If you wish then to contemplate the invisible traits
> of God in so far as they belong to the unity of His essence,
> fix your gaze upon Being itself, and see that Being is most
> certain in itself; for it cannot be thought not to be, since
> the purest Being occurs only in full flight from Non-
> Being. . . . For everything which is thought of is either

thought of as Non-Being, or as Being-in-potency or as Being-in-actuality. If, therefore, Non-Being is intelligible only through Being, and if Being-in-potency can be understood only through Being-in-actuality, and if Being is the name of that pure actuality of Being, Being then is what first enters the intellect, and that Being is pure actuality. . . . It remains, therefore, that that Being is divine Being.[19]

Such a Being is grasped both as an experiential intuition or encounter, and as a philosophical insight into the nature of things.

This position is in direct opposition to views which present God either as a far-off creature, or as a creator who is metaphysically unconnected with the realm of human experience. If God is the ground of all that there is, then it ill behooves man to speak too slightingly of the world of created things. This analysis is also antithetical to those tendencies to assign to the God predicable properties which commonly border on the anthropomorphic. In discussing this tendency Etienne Gilson, a distinguished contemporary Roman Catholic philosopher, speaks of

a Christian metaphysics of being, where the supreme principle is a God whose true name is "He who is." A pure act of existing, taken as such and without any limitation, necessarily is all that which it is possible to be. We cannot even say that such a God has knowledge, love, or anything else; he is it in his own right, for the very reason that, were he not everything and anything that it is possible to be, he could be called "He who is" but with some added qualification. . . . If, on the other hand, such a God actually is or exists, his self-sufficiency is so perfect that there can be no necessity for anything else to exist.[20]

This is the point of view expressed in the writings of Paul Tillich, the contemporary Harvard theologian. He is particularly insistent that the former personal properties which Christians and Jews had assigned to God must be abandoned in favor of the view that God is the "ground of being." While he recognizes that "that which is the ultimate concern of a person cannot be less than a person," [21] he maintains that it must be much more than a person. The traditional arguments for the existence of God erred in assigning to God attributes which he does not possess. Tillich concluded:

> But they perverted their insight when in spite of this assertion they spoke of the existence of God and tried to argue in favor of it. Actually they did not mean "existence." They meant the reality, the validity, the truth of the idea of God, an idea which did not carry the connotation of something or someone who might or might not exist. . . . God does not exist. He is being-itself beyond essence and existence.[22]

Our very language about God, however, gives the impression that he is more than this ontological ground. In an attempt to satisfy this general desire for a language about God that will give us an idea of what the term refers to, Tillich stated:

> "God" is the answer to the question implied in man's finitude; he is the name for that which concerns man ultimately. This does not mean that first there is a being called God and then the demand that man should be ultimately concerned about him. It means that whatever concerns a man ultimately becomes god for him . . .[23]

It is not inappropriate to mention under this category the view developed by Leibniz in his *Monadology*. A monad was an ideational entity, windowless and alone. Each person was such a monad; indeed, everything in the universe of things was a monad. All monads, as mental entities, operated in a pre-established harmonious fashion due to an original initiation by the great Monad (God). Concerning this divine Monad Leibniz stated:

> 47. God alone is the ultimate unity or the original simple substance, of which all created or derivative Monads are the products, and arise, so to speak, through the continual outflashings of the divinity from moment to moment, limited by the receptivity of the creature to whom limitation is an essential.[24]

Such a Monad of all monads operated essentially as a ground of being.

The traditional problems of religious Christians and Jews, however, would all be obviated by such a meaning for God. The problems with which we shall be concerned require that the term "God," at least, be assigned some other meaning.

Personalism: the sensitive God

The last meaning attached to the term "God" which we shall consider contains characteristics essentially like those possessed by man. Such views of God express his meaning in terms of personality, and hence they have been called "personalistic." This was the view maintained by E. S. Brightman, a distinguished philosopher in the personalistic tradition.[25] According to him the term "God" refers to a being possessing intelligence, emotions, and will. Like man, God thinks, feels, and makes decisions. Unlike man, God possesses these attributes in an absolute form. Existing coeternal with God, however, is a brute datum which Brightman calls the Given. This Given is not the product of God's will, and it functions as a deterrent to the beneficent divine plan. It is the Given which accounts for the presence of natural evils. Consequently, although God is omniscient and omnigood, he is limited in his power by the ineradicable Given. What God lacks in power he more than makes up for in his sensitivity to the plight of man in a world of natural evil and by the assurance that God and man are co-sufferers. This view presents a God of understandably human qualities and with the traditional biblical properties of sensitive concern, but the God so designated is finite in point of power. This predication of a finitely powerful God, as we shall see later, rests upon the need to solve the problem of natural evil.

William James's God also had personalistic attributes, and, like Brightman's God, was finite. James observed: "The line of least resistance, then, it seems to me, both in theology and in philosophy, is to accept, along with the superhuman consciousness, the notion that it is not all-embracing, the notion, in other words, that there is a God, but that he is finite, either in power or in knowledge, or in both at once." [26]

H. G. Wells shared this finite view of a God with limitations. His God weighed alternatives, increased in stature and in wisdom, and, in general, exhibited the virtues of an imaginative and intelligent person. While non-monarchists may have difficulty in appreciating "the Invisible King" as an appellation for God, there will be no doubt that Wells aimed to portray a God of exceptionally human properties. With regard to the finite aspect of God, Wells observed: "It comes as no great shock to those who have grasped the full implications of the statement that God is Finite, to hear it asserted that the first purpose of God is the attainment of clear knowledge, of knowledge as a means to more knowledge, and of knowledge as a means to power." [27]

Jacob Boehme, the medieval mystic, furthered the view of God which portrayed him as a kind of personalized ground of being. In an essay on the divine intuition he wrote:

> God is the eternal One, or the greatest gentleness (stillness), so far as he exists in himself independently of his motion and manifestation. But in his motion he is called a God in trinity; that is, a triune Being, where we speak of three and yet but of one, and in accordance with which he is called the eternal Power and Word. This is the precious and supreme ground, and thus to be considered: The divine will shuts itself in a place to selfhood, as to power, and becomes active in itself; but also by its activity goes forth, and makes for itself an object, viz. wisdom, through which the ground and origin of all beings has arisen. [28]

The personalistic position was urged by Borden P. Bowne, a nineteenth-century personalist, who referred to God as "ever-acting Intelligence and Will." [29] Henri Bergson portrayed a God of love "who effectively reveals Himself, Who illumines and warms privileged souls with His presence." [30] This same interpretation of a God who is a person was expressed by William E. Hocking in his remark that God is "an Other Mind, an individual Subject, wholly active." [31]

The Idea *of* God: *to* What Does *the* Term Refer?

In all of these versions of a personal deity there appears to be a rough correspondence with the views of God found expressed in the Old and New Testaments. Scriptural references in significant number seem to imply this view. God is talked to by Moses and Elijah. Jacob wrestles with God. Adam walks with God in the cool of the evening. Amos credits God with feelings of anger. Hosea endows God with feelings of forgiveness and love. Jesus speaks of God as like a father, a shepherd, or a friend. These great characters out of the Judeo-Christian past refer to God as if he could understand and see the wisdom of their varied proposals. The famous "seven last words" of Jesus stand, for many Christians, as an archetype of communication with a deity believed to be personally responsive.

In some instances the idea of a personal God has been pressed in order to conclude that there really is no objective being of the sort described. Ludwig Feuerbach (1804–1872) felt that traditional Christians had paid too little attention to the attributes of God, and that they had demonstrated this omission through their preoccupation with the question of the existence of God. As this was developed in traditional thought, the moral greatness of the God was purchased at the price of a demeaning of the moral worth of man. Speaking of the God of Catholicism Feuerbach insisted:

> He has a profound, heartfelt, truly religious significance, and is, therefore, a religious need only when real life is emptied of its meaning. The more empty life becomes, the richer and fuller becomes God. The impoverishing of the real world and the enriching of the Deity is one and the same act. Only an impoverished humanity has a rich God.[32]

As an alternative to this Feuerbach proposed: "But God as a morally perfect being is nothing else than the realized idea and the fulfilled law of morality. God is the moral nature of man posited as the absolute being."[33]

A much more derogatory conclusion based on the assumption that God means a personalized being was drawn by Sigmund Freud, for whom the predication of God is a sign of a fundamental neurosis. Freud developed this theory simply:

> Now when the child grows up and finds that he is destined to remain a child forever, and that he can never do without protection against unknown and mighty powers, he invests these with the traits of the father-figure; he creates for himself the gods, of whom he is afraid, whom he seeks to propitiate, and to whom he nevertheless entrusts the task of protecting him. Thus the longing-for-the-father explanation is identical with the other, the need for protection against the consequences of human weakness. . . .[34]

The pictures drawn by both Feuerbach and Freud are not, however, so much meanings of the term "God" as they are arguments that the term really has no reified meaning at all.

In all of the above interpretations of what the term "God" means we find the believers endowing the referent of "God" with the attributes deemed by them most important. Kant considered this tendency of man to anthropomorphize his God from two evaluative perspectives. On the one hand, he deplored the situation where "we create Him in the form in which we believe we shall be able most easily to win Him over to our advantage and ourselves escape from the wearisome uninterrupted effort of working upon the innermost part of our moral disposition." [35] Kant found this tendency which commonly resulted in penance, prayer, and self-castigation, with no moral improvement of the participant, as inimical to true religion. He concluded from this the following proposition: "Whatever, over and above good life-conduct, man fancies that he can do to become well-pleasing to God is mere religious illusion and pseudo-service of God." [36] This danger relates to man's practical relations with God. On the other hand, anthropomorphization may be quite harmless from the perspective of the theoretical representation of God. If one can assume that for all of the various believers God serves some function, we could infer from the properties with which they endow him what it is about the world of experience that needs explanation.

Pantheism stresses the order of the universe. On the one hand the materialistic pantheists point to the mechanical cause-and-effect structure. On the other hand, the idealistic pantheists concentrate on the values implicit in the essentially human aspect of world history. Neither comes out with a God to whom prayer would be directed, but this merely indicates that they feel most in need of a unified account.

Deism puts its stress upon the natural evils, upon the disorder created by man, upon the apparent dichotomy between man and the physical world. To make God too close to such events would seem to detract from his intelligence and goodness. While the remote God which they posit appears completely indifferent to affairs in this world, the alternative of putting him in the world seems to them the greater evil.

Naturalists find significance where the pantheists do. Unlike the pantheists, however, the naturalists doubt that God is so universally distributed. God is the symbol of order, but that is not all that there is. While natural evil appears to have no consistent place in a pantheistic world, these evils do have some account in a naturalistic explanation. Pantheism leaves the human role unexplained. Naturalism takes the human role seriously.

The personalistic account aims to include both the fact of material order and the human desire for participation in that order. In this view, while God is the cause of this systematic universe, he is not so close to it as to be inseparable from it. God and the world are distinguishable. On the other hand, the personalist God is immanent enough so that the despair which has been a concomitant of deism is absent. The relation between God and the world is for the personalist a fairly complicated one. Both natural evil and natural good, both order and chaos, are expressed in this world. God cannot be identified too closely with the world or he becomes responsible for matters which would raise a doubt as to his morals and his intelligence.

With such imaginatively different ideas of the term

"God," it is clear that when we are confronted with the question, "Does God exist?" it is not obvious what is being asked. In the traditional arguments for the existence of God it is not self-evident what kind of God the defense establishes, nor is it clear whether more than one god could be established by the same argument. We will turn now to the problems entailed in proving the existence of a God of some specified characteristics.

V

---◆◆◆---

Arguments *for*
the Existence *of* God

THERE ARE two questions which philosophers have asked
concerning the term "God." The first is, "What does the
term mean?" After meaning has been assigned, a second question is raised, "Does there exist some being which corresponds
to this meaning?" We discussed the first of these questions in
the preceding chapter and we noted then that the assignment of meaning determines both the nature of the God and
the human evaluation of the worthiness or significance of the
God. Each attempt to predicate content for the idea of God
establishes, at the same time, an evaluation of the importance
of the concept. Each of the views mentioned in the preceding
chapter delineates the area of influence of God and, hence,
the domain of the significance of the term "God." The problem
of the present chapter is to consider some of the traditional
approaches to the proof that a god of some sort exists.

Occasionally an argument leaves open the question of
the kind of god that is demonstrated to exist, and in some
arguments of the number of gods is left unspecified. With each
argument we shall identify some of the major supporters,

analyze what the argument claims, and point out some of the
criticisms that the argument has had to face.

THE ONTOLOGICAL ARGUMENT

The spirit of this approach to proving the existence of God has its genesis in the metaphysics of Plato, for
whom the necessity of absolute forms seemed demanded by
the nature of ethical experience as well as by the intellectual
intuition which true philosophers had. In the tradition of the
Western world laymen and experts alike have testified to
the ineluctable belief in the existence of the very things we
find it possible to talk about. This is not to ignore the obvious
fact that man's imagination has frequently exceeded what
in fact does exist. It does point, however, to the tendency to
suppose that the mere ability to imagine a thing lends some
weight to the supposition that the thing exists.

Some awareness of what the term "being" or "existence"
meant to the ancient Greeks is a precondition to appreciating
what the ontologists meant when they saw intuitively that
a being, than which a greater cannot be conceived, must
exist. "Being" was thought by Aristotle to be the most universal
concept. While other terms can be applied to a limited range
of objects, "being" can be applied to everything.[1] Aristotle opposed the notion that "being" could be a highest genus. It
was assumed that every genus had its differentiae, and that
these very differentiae are what make the genus explicable.
If, however, being were a genus, then the differentiae would
not possess being, and, thus, they would not exist. If the differentiae were imagined to possess being, then each of the
differentiae would contain all of the genus, which would reverse the signification of the classification of genera. A genus
has its own differentiating characteristics. The differentiating characteristics cannot be said to have the genus of which
they are properties. For every genus and for all differentiae,
existence or being must be presumed. On the other hand,
"being" cannot be thought of as what is left over after all the
properties of objects, such as color, taste, etc., are removed.

If this were the way one arrived at "being," then "being" would be the same as nothing. Some modern thinkers [2] assert that "being" can be comprehended only by an intuition. Even after the intuition of "being" has been achieved, all one can say about it is that *it is*. Through the ages this question of "being" has entailed a simple distinction—between existence and essence. While the former is concerned with the observation *that* a thing is, the latter is concerned with observing *what* a thing is.

What does "existence" mean? What do we add to a concept or a thing when we say of it that it exists? Immanuel Kant drew together the threads of centuries of discussion on this question when he showed that the idea of existence does not add anything to a concept. The term "to exist" is not, therefore, a predicative one. This idea has been expressed in the present century among logicians by the stipulation that the verb "to be" is a mere logical connective which has no content function. In common conversation there is a tendency to identify "existence" with sense data. When a man says that the lights are on, the verb "are" conveys the fact that he sees them. When one says that the telephone is ringing, the verb "is" conveys the fact that we hear something. The difficulty with illustrations of this sort is that the verb "to be" is compounded with other verbs which are predicative. We understand the sense data implied by the statement, "John runs," but we do not understand any new sense data when we reformulate the sentence to read, "John is running." All of this discussion contributes to the complexity of the problem of appreciating the ontological insight into the existence of God.

While the ontological approach has been advocated by Saint Bonaventura (1221–1274), Gottfried Wilhelm von Leibniz (1646–1716), and Georg Wilhelm Friedrich Hegel (1770–1831) the chief proponents have been Saint Anselm (1033–1109) and René Descartes (1596–1650). The classical formulation of Anselm's thesis is to be found in the body of a prayer which occurs in his *Proslogium*. After noting that he has the idea of a being than which none greater could be conceived, he concludes, "Therefore, if that, than which noth-

ing greater can be conceived, exists in the understanding
alone, the very being, than which nothing greater can be conceived, is one, than which a greater can be conceived." [3] From
this statement Anselm sees intuitively that God must exist. If
God did not exist, then it would be false that Anselm had an
idea of a being than which none greater could be conceived.
This could be deduced from the fact that a being who did
exist in fact would be greater than a being who merely existed
in the understanding. There is an obvious, though trivial,
sense in which we can see that what Anselm says is correct.
There appear to be two options before us. Either the being so
conceived is imaginary alone, or else the being exists. A being which lacked existence would, indeed, be less than one
who possessed it. Since an intuition is incomprehensible unless one has it, there may be some advantage in considering
the claim of Anselm as if it were a deduction with premises.
In effect what he is saying would, then, appear as follows:
I have an idea of a being who has all properties. That is, he
is perfect. Now everyone knows that perfection entails existence as one of its properties. It follows, therefore, that God
exists. If God did not exist, then the original premise, that I
have an idea of an omnipropertied being, would be false.

While the explication of Descartes, like that of Anselm,
is essentially an intuition, Descartes did structure the argument so that it appeared to be a deduction from premises
whose truth was obvious. To imagine, however, that either
Anselm or Descartes intended the ontological defense to have
the force of a syllogism would be a gross distortion. In his
Reply to the Second Objections [4] Descartes structures the
argument in several ways, a synthesized form of which we
will consider. The following premises would be asserted.

1. I have an idea of an omnipropertied being. This being not
   only has all significant properties, but he has them in a
   universal degree.
2. Every effect must have a cause which contains at least as
   many properties as the effect.
3. If, then, we consider the idea I have expressed in premise

1 as an effect, it must have had a cause. The cause, of course, must be omnipropertied, or else the second premise would be denied.

4. I am not the cause of this idea, for then I would be omnipropertied. If I were omnipropertied, I would know that I possessed all properties and that I possessed them in an absolute degree. Since I do not know this, it follows that I am not omnipropertied, and hence I am not the cause of the idea.

5. But the effect, expressed by the first premise, must have a cause. Therefore we may say that an omnipropertied cause of the idea exists. This is the same as saying that God exists.

Gaunilon, a monk of Marmountier, and a contemporary of Anselm, raised several objections to this manner of argument. While the criticisms are pointed and incisive, they attack the deductive formulation rather than the more basic intuition which Anselm intended. Gaunilon observes, in the first place, that Anselm claims that this idea of the omnipropertied being is in his understanding and that hence the being must exist. But could it not be said with equal correctness that all manner of ideas are in my understanding, and that some of them are mere fictions—that is, that they do not exist in fact? Why would not an Anselmian admit that all these other ideas must demand existence equally with the idea of God? Is it not true that to assert that understanding that I have an idea is the same as understanding that the referent of the idea exists, blurs the necessary epistemological distinction between having an idea and knowing that the idea is true? Once this distinction is obliterated, one would have to admit all entertained ideas as being true ideas.

Now Anselm would have a clear reply to make to such an objection. He would point out that he is not claiming that existence can be inferred from any existential statement. On the contrary, we can and do entertain numerous fictions which we formulate as existential statements. The idea of a God, however, is not an ordinary assertion, for it involves a being with the qualities of absolute wisdom, power, and good-ness. It just so happens, Anselm would insist, that the sen-tence about God is the only one where an analysis of the es-sence of the idea entails the existence of the referent of the idea. If Gaunilon were to say that he has an idea of a unicorn which possesses wisdom, power, and goodness in the same cos-mic fashion as Anselm's God, then Anselm would point out that the unicorn of Gaunilon and the God of Anselm are one and the same being. If Gaunilon were to press this identifica-tion as incorrect on the ground that the unicorn had a long horn in the middle of his forehead while God had no horn, Anselm might be prompted to make two observations. First he might remind Gaunilon that the possession of a horn is not a divine quality. Second, he might remind Gaunilon that the Anselmian idea was intuited. He could well ask Gaunilon, "Do you really mean what you seem to be saying, or are you just playing games with me? I, Anselm, really have intuited my idea, while you have merely created your idea as a clever fic-tion." I suspect that Gaunilon would have to admit that he really didn't intuit the idea of a perfect unicorn, and hence would have to admit that there was at least this difference between his idea and that of Anselm. It remains to be seen, however, whether this concession saves the ontological argu-ment.

A second question raised by Gaunilon refers to the ability to conceive such an idea as one of an omnipropertied being. How can we say that we know what an idea means when we have no data, even conjectural, as to what would be the case if the idea were true? I could conceive of a man whom I have never known, because after all I do know some men. How could I conceive of a God whom I have never known, unless I already knew some gods? While it is true that we could give defined meanings to the words in the sentence, "I have an idea of an omnipropertied being," this is a far cry from the kind of ostensive or denotative meanings which must occur before we can say that an idea is more than a definition, or that its meaning is more than one of words alone.

A third objection raised by Gaunilon concerns the

claimed impossibility that this being might not exist. Anselm said that if the being did not exist, then it would have to be the case that I did not have an idea of an omnipropertied creature in the first place. Might not this be the very case? Why is it so obvious that I really had the idea of an omnipropertied being? On the other hand, why would it be so impossible for me to have an idea which indeed is omnipropertied, even though the referent of the idea did not in fact exist? To prove that such an omni-creature really exists, we must go to the creature, not to the idea of the creature. Once we have proved the existence of a thing, we can entertain the idea of that thing with some assurance that the idea is true. On the other hand, if I consider my own existence, and contemplate the assurance with which I accept my existence as a fact, do I not also recognize that my possible nonexistence is not a self-contradiction?

Gaunilon summarizes his final objection by asserting: "Moreover, it is said that the non-existence of this being is inconceivable. It might better be said, perhaps, that its non-existence, or the possibility of its non-existence, is unintelligible. For according to the true meaning of the word, unreal objects are unintelligible. Yet their existence is conceivable. . . ." [5]

Benedict Spinoza (1632–1677) certainly deserves mention as one of the philosophers who found the ontological argument plausible. Like Anselm, he believed that this argument had the ring of certitude, and that it was logically impossible that it be invalid. In his *Ethics* he formulated this in a proposition: "God, or substance, consisting of infinite attributes, of which each expresses eternal and infinite essentiality, necessarily exists." The proof of this he defended by a *reductio ad absurdum* argument. "If this be denied, conceive, if possible, that God does not exist; then his essence does not involve existence. But this (by Prop. vii.) is absurd. Therefore God necessarily exists." [6] Clearly this defense rests on an implicit idea of the nature of essence and existence, and it has been at these two points that objectors have usually directed their attack. His argument is much weaker when he proposes later that "it follows therefrom that a thing necessarily exists, if no cause or reason be granted which prevents its existence." [7] This latter requires only the weak requirement of logical consistency, which, if pressed, permits an incredible number of fictions to be asserted as real.

In reflecting on the long history of objection to and support of the ontological argument for God, Paul Tillich concluded that those who attack arguments for the existence of God are really criticizing their logical form, while those who support the arguments are really defending their meaning. The ontological argument, says Tillich, points to the infinite and unconditioned which he felt that thinking implies. It is this meaning which is significant. As a proof of the existence of God, it fails utterly.[8] Tillich's objection is not so much that the logic of the argument is unsound as that the type of meaning thus assigned to God is unauthentic. The kind of God the argument proves is not the "ground of being" which is Tillich's concern.

The objection of Etienne Gilson stems essentially from this same dissatisfaction. Descartes' God is a mere philosophical first principle of a first cause whose sole property is to create. As Gilson notes, "Now it is quite true that a Creator is an eminently Christian God, but a God whose very essence is to be a creator is not a Christian God at all. The essence of the true Christian God is not to create but to be." [9] This remark, by itself, is not quite fair to Descartes, nor does it account for Gilson's distaste for what Descartes did. What is more to the point of Gilson's criticism is that Descartes claimed to establish this God by reason alone and without the aid of the supernatural revelation which the Roman Catholic church can uniquely provide. What Gilson finds so objectionable is that philosophy and theology are separated in Descartes. It is Descartes' claim that philosophy alone can arrive at the same conclusions that theology does, that disturbs Gilson. This feeling that the ontological argument is too skeletal, too bare, too remote from theology proper has fairly well reflected the general distaste of religious persons for this manner of proof for

the existence of God. It is not so much that it is illogical as
that it is sterile and emotionally uncompelling.

THE TELEOLOGICAL ARGUMENT

This argument gets its name from the Greek
word *telos,* which means purpose, order, design, plan, or system. The simplicity and directness of the analogy on which
this defense rests have made it one of the most psychologically compelling defenses for the existence of God that have
ever been proposed. The skeletal plan of the argument rests
on the claim that we live in a world where order is found. It
is further predicated that order cannot reasonably be derived
from chance or contingency, and that, hence, an ordering
mind is required to account for the world as we find it. Theologians have been impressed with Eddington's illustration [10]
that an army of monkeys banging on an army of typewriters
for a finitely long period of time could produce all the books in
the British Museum with greater probability than the chance
that all the molecules in a vessel would at any moment all be in
one half of the vessel. Some have used this illustration to indicate that even a monkey mind, as a cause of order, is more
likely than chance as a cause of order. Parenthetically, this
overlooks Eddington's point, which was that chance may imi-
tate order when the numbers are large.

To say that there is order in the world and hence that
the teleological argument is plausible has usually meant one
or more of the following facts: It could mean that there are
events in nature or in human inventiveness which are geometric in form. They have a shape which is of such and
such a type, called an orderly shape. The greater the variety
of geometries and the greater their complexity, the larger
will be the list of possible geometric or ordered patterns. Secondly, the term "order" has meant that the event in question
could be fitted into a cause-and-effect scheme. If it is noted
that there is a resembling contiguity between flipping
switches and lights going on, it may then be asserted that the

event in question is an orderly event. This is to say that a cause and an effect can be distinguished. A third meaning with which the term "order" has been associated is essentially pragmatic. When events serve human needs, meet human desires or wants, or fulfill human aspirations, it is claimed that these events are orderly or purposive. Using these three criteria, individually or collectively, we can isolate a vast list of events which are orderly in one or more of the above senses.

The traditional teleological argument has assumed, further, that this list of orderly events can be divided into two categories. In the former category will be found events like chairs, houses, electric lights, and books. In the second category will be found events like planets, trees, oceans, and human bodies. It is maintained that from events of the first sort a human designer can be inferred. If we see a chair, it is assumed that we can reasonably infer a chairmaker. Indeed, to deny that we can do this seems to be too incredible to believe, for then chairs would just have occurred by chance. On the strength of the plausibility of this inference it is then asserted that a like conclusion must be drawn from the facts of order in the second category. If it is inconceivable that a reasonable man would deny chairmakers when he is confronted by chairs, would it not be equally inconceivable that a reasonable man would deny a maker for planets and human bodies? If we called the events like books and chairs O_1 and the events like planets and human bodies O_2, then the analogical inference would appear as follows: If from O_1 we reasonably infer D_1 (human designers), then may we not equally reason that from O_2 a D_2 (nonhuman designer) may be inferred?

The teleological arguments of both Joseph Butler in *Analogy of Religion* (1736), and William Paley in *Natural Theology* (1802), run in this fashion. Each of these men reasoned that if the world began with the order specified in the book of Genesis and if animals all appeared with a remarkable adaptation to their environment it is clear that so much order could not have been the consequence of mere accident. A designer is required to make sense of it all. The theories of evolution undermined this argument by showing that creation did not begin full-blown but that a long process of selection occurred in which tremendous waste was a concomitant. One could not assert a creator who made all creatures adjusted to their environment from the start. This led to a revision of the teleological approach in a form called the "wider argument" by Peter Bertocci.[11] This argument stresses the "arrival" of the fittest instead of the "survival" of the fittest. It calls attention to the remarkable fact that orderly events did occur even though vast numbers of creatures did not survive in the process. He presents what he calls a sevenfold larger argument. This argument rests on the following "orderly" events: the purposive relation between matter and life, the relevance of thought to reality, the interrelation of moral effort and the order of nature, the interrelation between value and nature, the sense in which the world is good for man, and the significance of aesthetic and religious experience. The implication he draws is, "If the above are to be humanly meaningful and explicable, then we must infer a God." In spite of the critical approach with which Immanuel Kant analyzed this argument for the existence of God he did recognize that "this argument always deserves to be mentioned with respect. It is the oldest, the clearest, and that most in conformity with the common reason of humanity."[12]

The degree to which the common man remains impressed with this type of inference is so great that any who reject the obvious facts are deemed to be invincibly ignorant. After indicating that "the creatures of this sensible world signify the invisible things of God," Saint Bonaventura concluded that "from all this it follows that the invisible things of God are clearly seen, from the creation of the world, being understood by the things that are made; so that those who are unwilling to give heed to them and to know God in them all, to bless Him and to love Him, are inexcusable."[13]

Berkeley, speaking through the lips of Euphranor, expressed the obvious sense in which orderly events seemed to entail an orderer of these events. He observed that there is a remarkable order in the relations of both plants and animals to their environment, and in the movements of the planets in the solar system. Everywhere we turn there are evidences of the "unity of counsel and design." [14] The fact that laws of nature are operative equally in all parts of our earth is not to be taken lightly. What more reasonable conclusion, therefore, than that there is a divine "Agent, Spirit, or Mind"?

The teleological argument has not been without its opponents. Some objectors have opposed all arguments for the existence of God and, consequently, have opposed the teleological argument. Kant maintained that this argument went beyond the powers of the mind because it transcended the empirical data which were its premises. "This proof can at most, therefore, demonstrate the existence of an architect of the world, whose efforts are limited by the capabilities of the material with which he works, but not of a creator of the world, to whom all things are subject. Thus this argument is utterly insufficient for the task before us—a demonstration of the existence of an all-sufficient being." [15] We simply do not possess the kind of information that would enable us to infer a transfinite being, nor do we have the kind of facts which indicate that there even ought to be such a being. We would have to show the insufficiency of matter to explain its own order before we could move on to demonstrate the existence of a being who accounts for the order.

Friedrich Schleiermacher, like Kant, doubts the efficacy of all arguments to prove the existence of God. His objection, however, stems from his conviction that all such approaches to God miss the essence of religion. He referred to all arguments for God as "analyses of the nature of an incomprehensible Being, wherein everything runs to cold argufying, and the highest can be treated in the tone of a common controversy," and he concluded that "this is certainly—let me appeal to your own feeling—not the character of religion." [16] The essence of religion is a feeling of God. Once one has this feeling, he could, if he wished, reason to the characteristics which the God possesses. There is, however, no religious reason why the God needs to be endowed with personal, impersonal, creative, omniscient, or any other qualities. "But to which

94

idea he will attach himself depends purely on what he requires it for, and whether his imagination chiefly inclines towards existence and nature or consciousness and thought. [17]

In his *Dialogues* David Hume singled out a number of the objections to the teleological approach which are worth noting. In the first place, the analogy is not clear. It is assumed by the teleologist that the order of the O_1 variety is like the order of the O_2 variety, but this is not clearly the case. In the former instance the orderly events are considered to be like paintings which require a painter. This assumption is reasonably confirmed by the facts. It is further assumed, however, that the whole of the order of nature is patterned after this little area of human creations. This is not warranted by the data. "What peculiar privilege has this little agitation of the brain which we call thought, that we must thus make it the model of the whole universe?" [18] The world of nature is more like an organism than a work of art, more like a vegetable than a painting. Organisms are explained in the sciences as containing their own principle of order. No appeal to an outside designer is warranted.[19] A second objection, crucial only if one is convinced that one God is all that one should have, is that if any inference to a designer is warranted, it would be more commensurate with the human analogy to conclude many designers rather than merely one. Most human constructs are the product of joint efforts. Why might this not be the case in the world of nature? Teleologists have argued, in reply, that the unity of the world of nature presupposes a single designer; but this could easily have been the result of cooperative deities.[20] A third objection raised is the assumption implicit that the whole world of order demands a cause. What this assumption overlooks is that the order of the world was humanly predicated. The uniformity of nature is a judgment of an organizing human mind. Where does the need for a divine mind arise? While the events of the world are what they are, the claim that these events are orderly is a human decision, and hence, a human designer is all that is required.

The essence of the Humean objection is well summarized

in a footnote in the *Dialogues*. The whole issue between those who assert and those who deny the arguments for a God is purely verbal "or, at least, regards only the degrees of doubt and assurance which we ought to indulge with regard to all reasoning." [21] While the dogmatists stress the necessity of having some belief, the skeptics stress the difficulties of having any belief. Skeptics admit that we must frequently draw conclusions even in the face of difficulties. Dogmatists admit that we do face difficulties even when we feel that we must draw conclusions. A final objection which Hume raised relates to the supposed abundance of orderly, in the sense of utilitarian to man, events. Hume asks whether the world is not different in fact from what we would expect from a transfinite being, and he answers his question in the affirmative. We would expect an all-good being to have done much better by man than to fill the world with so much disease, and to have such a multitude of potential hazards as hurricanes, tidal waves, earthquakes, killing cold, and burning heat. The world being what it is, a deathtrap for man, no empirical argument for a God on teleological data can ever be justified. Hume was willing to concede that the idea of a deity might still be consistent with the world of experience, although the existence of such a deity could not be inferred. And even here, Hume felt that consistency required that the deity be predicated as finite so that natural evil and a God could at least be imagined together without contradiction. This concession of Hume's may be all that religious persons require, although it may seem unlikely that the mere intellectual possibility of a God would suffice for faith. Indeed, could it not also be said that the idea of spirits of a wide variety of attributes is also consistent with the world, since logical consistency is not a very discriminating criterion?

For all the objections which have been raised against the teleological argument for the existence of a God, it still remains the approach most compatible with the sentiments of most persons who believe in any argument at all. It has an appeal to common sense and common wishes which is hard to match. Order presupposes an orderer. This is a simple inference of everyday magnitude.

Arguments *for the* Existence *of* God

In the words of Saint Thomas Aquinas, the most distinguished proponent of the cosmological argument, this is a defense of a First Cause. The bases of the argument are classes of data considered as effects. In the context of Aristotle's maxim that every effect must have a cause, the cosmologist argues that these classes of data must have a cause. In general, what is intended is not merely the establishment of a cause, but of a First, Necessary, and Sufficient Cause. At the time that Saint Thomas entered upon the task of analyzing the so-called arguments for the existence of God, the prevailing approach had been that of Saint Anselm and Saint Bonaventura. For both of these men the existence of God was self-evident. Their problem was, rather, one of showing the essential knowableness of God. For them, God was being, by definition, and hence to speak of God was to speak of being. In the traditional dichotomy between being and essence, Anselm and Bonaventura both sought to prove the essence of God rather than the existence of God. Saint Thomas replaced this approach by the quest for proof of the existence of God. While Anselm and Bonaventura both believed that the existence of God was self-evident, Saint Thomas devoted an article to showing that this was not the case. His thesis rested on the epistemological premise that the only beings directly accessible to our knowledge are sensible things. God is not a sensible thing, or at any rate we have no sensible knowledge to this effect. In opposing Anselm, Aquinas notes that there is no contradiction in imagining that there does not exist a being than which a greater cannot be conceived. The Anselmian God is not self-evident. Only demonstration from evidence can establish God's existence. While the assumption of Anselm and Bonaventura, that we could have such perfect knowledge of essences in this life that we could see that a being than which a greater could not be conceived must exist, does not harm them personally, it is dangerous to others in the sense that it may lead an unbeliever to suppose that proofs for God are really intuitive and hence undemonstrable.

Although Saint Thomas is generally considered to be the most famous exponent of the cosmological argument, he was by no means its inventor. The distinguished Jewish philosopher, Moses Maimonides (1135–1204), had already formulated the essential premises of this type of argument. Maimonides, in a series of "Propositions," predicated the premises from which he inferred that a First Cause must exist. He noted that "when an object moves, there must be some agent that moves it, from without." [22] Again he asserted that "everything that passes over from a state of potentiality to that of actuality, is caused to do so by some external agent." [23] And again, "A thing which owes its existence to certain causes has in itself merely the possibility of existence." [24] A final proposition may be noted: "Everything that exists potentially, and whose essence includes a certain state of possibility, may at some time be without actual existence." [25]

From these postulates several possibilities may be inferred. In the first place, an explanation for motion which never rose above the plain facts of experience would move backward in time infinitely. Since an infinitely regressive explanation was considered, in this Aristotelian structure, to be inadmissible, some element in the essential argument must be missing. In the second place, if every potentially existing thing may at some time not exist, there may have been a time when nothing existed, and hence it would be impossible to explain how anything came to exist after this. The only state of affairs consistent with what we know to be the case, and with what we insist must logically be avoided, is to predicate a Prime Mover. Since the whole argument by Maimonides centers on the cause of motion, he concluded that "it may thus be considered as proved that the efficient cause of the motion of the sphere, if that motion be eternal, is neither itself corporeal nor does it reside in a corporeal object. . . . This Prime Motor of the sphere is God, praised be His name!" [26]

Saint Thomas asserted that we can demonstrate the existence of God from either of two approaches: from cause to effect, or from effect to cause. It is the latter way that he chooses, primarily because the effects are what we know best.[27] If any reader of Saint Thomas found it impossible to accept his arguments for God, there was nothing to prevent him from accepting God on faith. Thomas presents five arguments for the existence of God. Each of them reasons from effect to cause. His most important argument is that which reasons from motion, as an effect, to a First Cause of this motion. He calls this argument "the first and more manifest way." [28] It is perhaps the most easily understood of all the arguments. The premises are somewhat as follows:

1. It is a fact of experience that some things move. (By experience he means at the sense level.)
2. It is a logical derivation that no thing can move itself. This is defended on several bases.
   a. Motion is a change of something from potentiality to actuality.
   b. No thing can have both potential motion and actual motion. To say that a thing possesses potential motion is to say that it is not moving, but that it could move.
   c. It is clear from this that if a potentially moving thing comes to move, it could not have done this itself. To be the cause of its own motion it would have to possess motion already, since the cause of any effect must contain the properties of the effect.
3. It is clear that to explain any event of motion will take us in a regression. A is moved by B, which is moved by C, and so on infinitely.
4. But an infinite regression cannot account for motion because we would never get to a first cause in this way.
Therefore: There must be a First Cause which is the efficient Mover of all motion. Everyone understands that this First Cause is God.

The second argument which Saint Thomas proposes rests on an analysis of what it means to have an efficient cause or to be an efficient cause. It is clear from the above argument that no thing in the space-time world could be the first efficient cause because it would then have to be prior to itself, which is impossible. Hence, there must be a First Efficient Cause.

The third argument rests on the distinction between what it means to exist possibly or contingently, on the one hand, and necessarily, on the other hand. In the world of nature all things are found to exist only possibly. This means that it would not be a contradiction for them not to exist. If there are things which might not exist, it follows that if we go back in time we will come to the time before they existed. If we go sufficiently far back in time, we should come to a time when none of the contingently existing things, of which the world of nature is composed, existed. Now, if there was a time when no contingent things existed, how could there ever have occurred the first contingent thing? The only way to explain this is to posit that there must be something which exists necessarily. It cannot be true that everything is contingent. This necessarily existing being we call God.

The fourth argument is based on the fact that we make moral judgments. In these judgments we assert that some things are better or worse than others. No such judgment would be possible unless there were a maximum good which we used as the measure of all actual moral distinctions. An appeal is made, at this point, to Aristotle's *Metaphysics*, Book Delta, 2, to the effect that only the maximum of any genus can be the cause of everything in that genus, and whatever is greatest in truth is also greatest in being. To avoid any infinite regression we move directly to God as the First Cause.

The fifth and final argument is essentially like the teleological one previously discussed. We see that natural objects which do not possess intelligence act intelligently. To explain such orderly effects requires an ordering cause. This being we call God.

Saint Thomas did not invent these arguments, as he makes perfectly clear. The Old Testament [29] and the New Testament [30] both contain implicit cosmological arguments. Plato had discussed such arguments in the *Laws*, Book X, together with some prevailing theories that the order of the world can be explained by chance. Many of the Stoics had also formulated general cosmological appeals for the existence of a God.[31] The Neoplatonism of Plotinus had put fetters on this type of argument for the existence of God, for Plotinus had minimized the importance of the world of human experience, and demeaned empirical observation. Yet Saint Thomas was not the first Christian theologian after Plotinus to return to the world of experience for evidences for God. His first argument he borrowed essentially from Aristotle with some of the variations which already existed in the writing of Albertus Magnus, Moses Maimonides, and Peter Lombard. His second argument he takes also from Aristotle and from the versions of Avicenna and Albertus Magnus. The third argument had previously been expounded by Avicenna and Maimonides. The fourth argument comes more or less directly from Aristotle, and perhaps derivatively from Saint Augustine. The fifth argument has its roots in Christian scripture, in particular the book of Genesis, and the form of the argument had already been given by Saint John of Damascus. While these arguments agree in structure, they differ in the data, considered as effects, from which the First Cause is inferred. In this whole enterprise of proving God's existence, Saint Thomas functions as a philosopher, not as a theologian. The existence of God is not, after all, a theological problem. It is philosophical. Religiously God is known by faith. Only a philosopher would require, let alone be persuaded by, evidential proofs.

The cosmological argument has not been without its opponents. These include men like David Hume, who objected to all proofs for God's existence on logical grounds, and men like Paul Tillich, who objected equally to all proofs for God on religious grounds. It may be questioned whether Thomas was correct in his stipulation that motion or existence need to be accounted for; and more specifically, whether it is tenable to say that whatever moves must have been moved by something outside itself. This thesis has been declared incompatible with modern dynamic science.[32] Even William of Occam made this attack and anticipated modern notions of inertia. The thesis was also challenged by Nicholas Autrecourt

and Jean Buridan. In modern science both motion and existence are assumed; they are not explained. This assumption
has been expressed under the maxim "Energy (or matter) is
neither created nor destroyed." This is where we begin our
inquiry. We may also question whether an infinite sequence of
explanations is so incomplete and unreasonable as Saint
Thomas assumed. Contemporary physical science rejects any
need for ultimate first causes. It assumes that an unending
series of causal relations constitutes a legitimate explanation.
This does not undermine Saint Thomas' metaphysical principle with regard to cause and effect. What this objection does
is to make the problem one of the psychology of belief. It becomes a question of what an adequate explanation really is,
and in addition, it is still problematic whether Saint Thomas'
metaphysical principle with regard to cause and effect is
true. It can be noted that while science does rest its case with
regressive explanations, and while in science these are considered adeqate, the Thomists still deny that this gives a complete picture. In his argument from the nature of contingent
being Thomas predicated that if we go back far enough in
time we shall come to a time when no contingent thing existed. This assumption may be questioned. There is no logical
necessity for concluding that because a contingent thing may
not exist in the future, therefore there must have been a time
in the past when no contingent things existed. There could
be an infinite sequence running into the past. Thomists would
still maintain, however, that even if there were an infinite
regressive sequence of contingent beings, this sequence would
not be self-explanatory.

While Immanuel Kant remarked of the cosmological argument that it "is at least natural, and not only goes far to
persuade the common understanding, but shows itself deserv-
ing of respect from the speculative intellect," [33] he nonetheless attacked it on the grounds that it too transcended the
bounds of human reason. While the cosmological argument
begins with experience and hence gives the illusion of being
empirical, it is really a disguised form of the old ontological
argument. What Thomas does is to reason from the possibility

of a necessarily existing cause to the existence of such a cause. This repeats the ontological confusion between having a conception and knowing that there exists a referent of the conception. Kant attacks the Thomist thesis that everything contingent must have a cause on the grounds that this has meaning only in the sensuous world, while Saint Thomas uses this to go to a nonsensuous world. In addition, Kant observes that contingency and necessity are mere categories set up by the human mind. They need have no correspondence with anything in fact. Actually, necessity has no place in nature or in any content area. He notes, further, that even if an infinite series of causes were impossible, it does not follow that there must be a First Cause, just because this is the only way we can conceive of having a start to a series. Thomas' fourth way leads to the absurdity that any range of any attribute then points to a God as the maximum of that attribute. It is true that Saint Thomas' theory is logically consistent and thus possible, but this is not sufficient warrant for moving to the assertion that this theorized pattern is true. It is because the cosmological argument reduces to the ontological argument, which Thomas had already rejected, that Kant is led on the same grounds to dismiss the cosmological defense.

THE MORAL ARGUMENT

While the moral argument for belief in God has had many formulations, the defense of Plato is quite typical. Belief in the gods is justified essentially on the grounds that we would not be able to account for moral action if there were no gods. While Plato gives no neatly structured inference, the implicit premises may at least be identified.[34]

1. Let us assume that a society of good persons is the end of endeavor. Accepting this will provide the motivation for pressing through the remainder of the inference.
2. Let us assume that "to know is to do." This means that if persons know what is good they will inevitably do what is right. This proposition is convertible; hence, if persons do

what is right, it follows that they must have known what is good.

3. Let it be admitted that no man who believe in the gods ever committed an unholy act or uttered an unlawful word. If this is an instance of premise No. 2, then it too should be convertible.

4. It follows from the above that if persons who do the right know the gods, and if only knowledge of what is really the case can produce right action, then it must be the case that the gods exist.

It is clear that for Plato this argument proved the existence of an unspecified number of gods. There did not appear to be any logical reason for concluding that there was only one being. It could well be that the polytheism in the conclusion reflects more the precommitments of Plato than it does any inherent data in the premises. If this were so it would be a further illustration of the thesis held by Saint Thomas that arguments for the existence of God are not intended to stand alone, but that they presuppose faith commitments. Plato was, perhaps, the first thinker to advocate that the holding of false theological beliefs should be treated as a crime against the state. He recommended that the first offense be punishable by five years in prison and that the second be punished by death.

While Kant denies the possibility of any transcendental proofs of the existence of God, he does recommend a practical justification for God on moral grounds.[35] Kant supposed that there are certain practical moral laws which are absolutely necessary. For these moral laws to possess obligatory power, a being must be postulated. The necessity alluded to is, however, practical. It is not transcendental. It is still true that no unconditioned practical law, such as the categorical imperative, can be proved by speculative reason. If, however, we predicate that the laws of actions of rational beings entail autonomy, freedom, etc., and that these must necessarily involve an obligation, then it can at least be postulated that there is a practical necessity for a God. This is not to be confused with the claims that have been made for the other arguments for the existence of God. Kant is not saying that the practical necessity proves that there is a God. It is only that a God lends the element of obligation which a categorical command requires.

IS ANY ARGUMENT FOR GOD POSSIBLE?

The feelings of many religious devotees were well expressed by Alciphron in Berkeley's *Dialogue:*

> First then let me tell you I am not to be persuaded by metaphysical arguments; such, for instance, as are drawn from the idea of an all-perfect being, or the absurdity of an infinite progression of causes. This sort of arguments I have always found dry and jejune; and, as they are not suited to my way of thinking, they may perhaps puzzle, but will never convince me. Secondly, I am not to be persuaded by the authority either of past or present ages, of mankind in general, or of particular wise men, all which passeth for little or nothing with a man of sound argument and free thought. Thirdly, all proofs drawn from utility or convenience are foreign to the purpose. They may prove indeed the usefulness of the notion, but not the existence of the thing.[36]

Alciphron further found it unwarranted that he should be put in the position of having to prove that a God did not exist, when the affirmative position has already been demonstrated to have no proof.

When all is said and done, where do all these arguments for the existence of God leave the religious person? Are these arguments sufficient or necessary to establish that there is a cosmic being? If all arguments for the existence of God prove to be illogical, does this mean that there are no grounds for asserting God? A number of the men whom we have studied so far have responded to these questions with a firm negative. We have already noted, for example, that Saint Augustine, Saint Anselm, Saint Thomas, and Schleiermacher never believed that the commitment for God depended upon logical argument. None of these men would claim that, apart from faith in God, arguments could provide the religious basis for belief. The essential inference to be drawn from the arguments which some of them did offer was that it illustrated that reason was at least compatible with faith. It was never asserted that reason was a substitute for faith; nor was it claimed that faith without reason was incredible.

John Calvin (1509–1564), the Protestant reformer, shared the Augustinian suspicion of arguments that claim to prove the existence of God. He did not intend in his *Institutes* to defend on philosophic grounds what is really a matter of faith. Nonetheless, he did indicate his conviction that belief in God was innate and universal. "We lay it down as a position not to be controverted, that the human mind, even by natural instinct, possesses some sense of a Deity." [37] He implemented this by the claim that all nations and tribes, no matter how primitive or ignorant, were in fact firmly persuaded of the existence of a God. While there is serious doubt as to the truth of this claim, particularly with regard to a Christian view of God, the nature of his assumption is at least clear. As an aside, he noted that it is precisely this instinct which raises man above the animals. While this is not intended as a proof in any logical sense, it is intended as a warrant of the ubiquitousness of the belief in God. His ground for objection to all arguments for the existence of God is that they miss the essential warmth of religious experience. "Cold and frivolous, then, are the speculations of those who employ themselves in disquisitions on the essence of God when it would be more interesting to us to become acquainted with his character and to know what is agreeable to his nature. . . . What benefit arises from the knowledge of a God with whom we have no concern?" [38]

In spite of his obvious distaste for rational defenses for God's existence, it must be noted that he did believe that the amazing orderliness of both man and the universe entailed a Maker of great skill. The proof of this planning was seen in medicine, astronomy, and the whole of physics. While skilled scientists were in the best position, because of their knowledge, to be aware of the remarkable order, Calvin yet assumed that scientific ignorance was no real deterrent to seeing the obvious divine architecture.

Blaise Pascal (1623–1662), a Roman Catholic won over to Jansenism,[39] denied all metaphysical proof for God. If we know God at all it is because of the reasons of the heart—that is, faith. Man is such a nothing compared with God, so far removed from God in comprehension, that he is incapable of giving any proofs for God's existence. Notwithstanding all this, Pascal formulated what has come to be called his "Wager." While it is not a proof for God, it is intended to supply motivation to believe in God. In accordance with Aristotle's Law of the Excluded Middle he posed the following options: Either God exists or God does not exist. If God exists, we can either believe it or disbelieve it. If God does not exist, we can either believe it or disbelieve it. These exhaust the options before us. Although we cannot prove God's existence or nonexistence, we can show what odds attach to each of the options. If God does not in fact exist, it makes no difference whether we believe or disbelieve; hence these options may be disregarded. If God does exist and we disbelieve it, possible disastrous consequences may result. If God does exist and we believe it, possible beneficial consequences may ensue. The odds, therefore, are all against disbelief in a God, and in favor of belief in a God. It is doubtful whether Pascal ever thought that this neat formula would, by itself, ever lead anyone to believe in a God. By the same mode of reasoning one could equally be led to gamble on the existence of unicorns, witches, and gremlins. There is some evidence from the psychology of motivation that would indicate that if the emotional stakes are high, men will gamble even without a formula of odds; and on the other hand, that if the emotional stakes are low, men will not act even if the argument is invincible. There is, after all, a great gulf between this conniving gambler's attitude and the actions of Abraham, Isaac, and Jacob, who risked their destinies in a choice between the all and the nothing, with no cognitive odds to give assurance.

In addition to the psychological limitations of the "Wager," certain logical objections can be made. If Pascal does not, indeed, know God on rational grounds, how does he know that the odds are in favor of belief and against disbelief? Suppose God wished to remain hidden. Suppose, therefore, that he punished all believers and rewarded all disbelievers. The "Wager" implicitly assumes information which, by virtue of his premises, Pascal could not have.

Ludwig Feuerbach (1804–1872), disclaimed the relevance of all arguments for the existence of God. The assurance of God, is after all, internal. We know God intuitively if we know God at all. Since all arguments are external, they miss the emotional heart of religion. A further problem involves the use of the term "existence" [40] in arguments for the existence of God. Normally the term "existence" means "availability to sense observation." Since God is not available to sense observation, what could the "existence" of God possibly mean to religious persons? All arguments for God make a common error similar to that to which Kant pointed. They attempt to infer a factual, empirical conclusion from premises which are analytic or definitional. Since belief in God is belief in a special type of datum, a special mode of proof is required. Logic will not do. And, yet, although Feuerbach finds that arguments for the existence of God are "contradictory to the essential nature of religion," he insists that the difficulty lies in the form of the arguments. Since religion is a matter of internal feeling, and since arguments presuppose religion to be concerned with objective facts, there is an element of discord. He concludes:

> The proof, therefore, is discordant with religious feeling only to the extent that it presents the implicit assumption of religion as a formal deduction, exhibits it in logical form, and therefore distinguishes what religion unites without analysis. [41]

The internally felt God of real religion becomes, in all arguments, an external God who appears to have reality apart from man's feelings and thoughts. This leads men to suppose that "out there" there is a God who can be apprehended by the senses. Since this latter is obviously not the case, the result is indifference as far as a God is concerned. On the psychological side it is asserted that religious inspiration is inversely proportional to the degree to which arguments are empirical or logical. Arguments for the existence of God are, therefore, subversive of religious faith.

Thomas Huxley (1825–1895) opposed all religious proofs on essentially Kantian grounds. In his essay on agnosticism he concluded, "But let him not delude himself with the notion that his faith is evidence of the objective reality of that in which he trusts. Such evidence is to be obtained only by the use of the methods of science, as applied to history and to literature, and it amounts at present to very little." [42]

No discussion of the arguments for the existence of a God would be complete without some consideration of the position called atheism. The term has, unfortunately, functioned more as an epithet than as a description of a univocal position, and this confounds attempts to approach the whole subject with the proper degree of dispassionate inquiry. For centuries it was common to call anyone who believed in a God other than the acceptable one an atheist. Thus in a society of persons who believed in a miracle-working God, those who contended for a law-abiding God were atheists; in a community of believers in a personal, retributive deity, those who endorsed deism or naturalism were clearly atheists. To use the term in these ways is, however, to make of it a mere expletive with no essential or clear meaning. It has been much more fruitful to consider that the term "atheism" designates a class of persons who do not believe in the existence of any deity of any sort. Such persons would also reject all arguments for the existence of a deity. A typical atheistic reaction to conventional theology was expressed by Chapman Cohen. "If they already believed, the arguments were enough to provide them with sufficient justification to go on believing. If they did not already believe, the arguments were powerless." [43] It was, at least, the atheist contention that the case for God was both invalid and irrelevant. Since it appeared to be clearly established that belief in God cannot be based on either science or philosophy, there was nothing left of the God issue save the history of the belief.

Charles F. Potter, an avowed humanist, classified at least four different senses in which the term "atheism" may be said to have functioned. There is "agnostic atheism," which is the position of a man who feels that the evidence for a God is too weak to warrant an affirmative answer, and, at the same time, that there is no adequate argument to warrant belief in the nonexistence of a deity. He simply says, "I do not know." Secondly, there is "negative atheism," which is the position of the person who states that although there is no evidence either for or against the god thesis, he would not be interested in a god even if there were one. For all practical purposes his dismissal of the issue is equivalent to the denial of a god. Third, there is the position which Potter calls "dogmatic atheism." This position asserts that there is evidence to warrant the conclusion, "I know that there is no God." Finally, Potter distinguishes "moral atheism." This position denies not only the existence of a deity, but also of the predicates normally associated with such a deity.[44] Let us consider each of these categories from the point of view of the cognitive presuppositions entailed.

With regard to the first position, that of agnostic atheism, Potter indicates that this is where most humanists would place themselves, on the grounds that the other positions presuppose information which it would be presumptuous to claim to possess. Two humanists who support this evaluation are cited. Alfred W. Hobart asserted: "Atheism really denotes a dogmatic position, i.e., the denial of God without reservation. I have yet to meet a humanist who is an atheist in this sense of the word."[45] E. Stanton Hodgin, also a humanist, supported the same view. "The Humanist is not anti-theistic; to call him an atheist is most unjust and betrays the limitations of the accuser."[46] Since, for all practical purposes, the humanist says, "We do not believe that there is a God," it may not be clear what the distinction is between the first and the second categories. This is particularly evident when it is noted that a man could belong in the class of agnostic atheists and not really be asserting that he doesn't believe that there is a God. He merely observes that there is not enough evidence either way. Now to hold this position presupposes the question of a God to be theoretically provable, and only practically unproved. If a humanist shared the views of A. J. Ayer that the whole question of a nonsensible deity is "meaningless," in the sense that no data could ever be gathered, in principle, for either belief or unbelief, he would not fit under any of the four categories which Potter lists. It would seem that the only distinction between the first and the second types of atheists is one of psychology. Do we wish to withhold judgment (hence the first position) or do we feel that we might just as well say, in the absence of any adequate affirmative information, that we do not believe in a deity? It may be convenient for our purposes to place A. J. Ayer under the second category with the understanding that this position entails the belief that the whole question of God makes no empirical sense at all. It is not that "no God" has been established, but simply that deities, being like gremlins and witches, are groundless fictions.

The third position, that of dogmatic atheism, is clearly distinguishable from all the other views. Here it is claimed that there are counterarguments of a positive sort which prove, in the same way in which any other scientific matter would be proved, that there is no God. The famous book by Jean Meslier takes the stand that atheism is a cognitively justified position in view of the following facts.

1. All definitions of "gods" are negative. They merely indicate what a god is not, and thus the term never has any positive meaning.
2. By definition supersensible gods are unknowable, and hence, any positive argument for a god is impossible.
3. What arguments there are for a god rest upon primitive fear. The facts seem to indicate that man invented gods because he was afraid. As another committed atheist then concluded: "And to bury his gods is, after all, the

only real apology that man can offer for having created them." [47] Cohen pressed this further when he concluded that if belief in gods originated in ignorance, we are then justified in dismissing the whole idea of such beings. But this would be to commit the fallacy of origins, and to suppose that the origin of an idea has a bearing on the truth of an idea, which it clearly does not. Plato, for example, believed that the earth was round for the naïve reason that the gods would have made the world in the shape of the most perfect figure, which is a circle. Since, as a matter of fact, the world is more or less round, it should be obvious that we cannot dismiss any idea simply on the grounds that it was initiated in ignorance.

4. The God described by Christians and Jews, in particular, is so immoral that no thinking man of decent impulses could possibly subscribe to such a creature.

5. Belief in such a God makes for immorality. Atheists, on the other hand, have adequate motives for virtuous living.[48]

6. All children are atheists and are indoctrined with theism at an age when they are incapable of reasoning otherwise. [Parenthetically, what would Meslier infer from the fact that all children are unscientific?]

7. There is too much natural evil in the world to warrant the inference that there is a Providence or an Architect who has human interests at heart. The facts would seem to warrant, on the other hand, that man is not the end of creation, and that like the woolly mammoth he too will sink into some tar pits and be remembered only as an archaeological show piece.

8. Nature is, after all, self-explanatory, and thus the chief teleological arguments for a God are vitiated.

9. To speak of a pure spirit who is at the same time endowed with properties of will and intellect is to utter a self-contradiction.

10. The facts of evolution mean atheism, i.e., no God.[49]

From all such facts as these man's reason leads him to irreligion and to atheism. In all honesty, therefore, man ought to stand up and be counted as a full-fledged atheist in the third sense of the term. Teller notes, for example, that Christians are cowards, since they keep the God fiction, while atheists are courageous in their disbelief.[50] Even Potter, who does not wish to be called an atheist, admitted that "when man gets to the point where he realizes that God was man's own creation for a temporary purpose, he needs God no longer." [51] In the light of the overwhelming facts, Meslier believed that the position of skepticism or agnosticism was simply the combined result of a superficial examination of the facts and cowardice.

In view of these varied options it would seem as if at least three positions could be denoted. Which one we wish to designate as atheist will be a matter of personal taste. In the first place, there is the stand that, while the issue of God is theoretically provable, it is not proved in fact. It would seem egregious to call this position atheism. In the second place, there is the position that the issue of God is not theoretically or practically provable, and hence to say, "I do not believe in any God," does not entail positive evidence that such and such a God does not exist. It simply makes an assertion in the same spirit in which we would say that Santa Claus, elves, and phlogiston are unacceptable as candidates for existence. There seems to be no reason why such a position could not be called atheist consistently with past usage and philological meanings, as long as it was made clear that we were not claiming to know that God did not exist, but merely that we knew that it could not be proved either way. The third position, and the one it would seem is most entitled to the name "atheism," asserts that there is evidence which shows that no God exists, or at least no God of the properties assumed in the major arguments for the existence of a God. Such an atheist claims to have cognitive information on a matter which is not, as A. J. Ayer said, meaningless. Such a contender could assert, "I know on evidential grounds that the probabilities are against the existence of a God." The second position, it would seem, merely denies the legitimacy of arguments for God. Although its supporters may say that they do not believe in any God, this is not a statement of knowledge. The third position, however, represents what might succinctly be called "authentic atheism."

We have considered the question, "Are any arguments for God possible?" All arguments have met with objections on two essential points. First, men like Feuerbach, Schleiermacher, Kant, James, and the contemporary Quaker mystic, Rufus Jones, object on the grounds that all arguments miss the essential spirit of religious commitment. The assurance of God is internal, immediate, personal. All arguments are external, mediated, and objective. To attempt to prove the existence of God to an unbeliever presupposes that God is an object of knowledge like other data, and that by objective, neutral analysis one may be led to believe in God. Like the experience of love, the experience of God is a report of an inner awareness. All arguments are, therefore, psychologically unsound if we suppose that they will lead persons not otherwise persuaded to believe in God. The second class of objections rests on logical grounds. Men like Kant, Hume, and Feuerbach maintained that all arguments for a necessary, absolute, or transfinite being transcend the limits of human experience, human understanding, or human reason. The data of human cognition do not warrant the claim of the existence of God. The attitude of Saint Anselm, Saint Thomas, and Descartes toward their own arguments for God is in support of the thesis that arguments alone do not confirm that there is a God. These men were convinced that no one would be persuaded to believe by the arguments unless he first had faith in God. If one had faith in God, one would not actually need the arguments. This led to the inference that the function of all arguments was not actually to prove that God existed, but to show that reason was compatible with the commitments of faith; and, more, to show that the attributes of the God, assumed by faith, did have some rationale.

VI

The Problems *of* Religious Knowledge

WHEN A PERSON SAYS, "I know that such-and-such is the case," what does he mean to assert in religion? What is the essential nature of the claim to religious knowledge? Is religious knowledge like scientific knowledge, at least in the sense that certain epistemological requirements have been met? Does the term "knowledge" mean the same in the statements: "I know that God exists," and "I know that Mount Everest exists"? It is necessary for the purpose of understanding religious claims to indicate some of the various meanings in philosophies of religion of the assertion: "I know that certain dogmas are true."

Plato's remarks, particularly in Book X of the *Laws*, still stand as a paradigm of what religious persons most commonly mean by the claim of religious knowledge. Plato's thesis needs to be understood in the context of his whole theory of knowledge. This entails the doctrine of reminiscence and presupposes that every person in this world has already had a prior existence in a realm of absolute, universal ideas. In this former life men lived without the distracting influence of physical bodies, limited as they are to sense experiences, and enjoyed an association with pure and unchangeable universals. All of their knowledge was apodictic, or certain, and they never suffered the doubts and anxieties which mere statements of probability arouse. In this ideal life men did not have the problem, which we face in this realm of space and time, of having to relate statements with the states of affairs which they designated. Unlike us, they did not have to ask themselves: "Now, is this statement which I have just expressed a true statement?" They intuited, as self-evident and immediate, the truth of the ideas which they confronted. These ideas were not particular or concrete. They moved in an aura of perfect knowledge. They did not meet particular cows, states, or moral practices; but, instead, they faced only the perfect cow, the perfect state, and the absolute good. The question, "How do you know that your knowledge is correct?" never had occasion to be asked. All knowledge was immediate and inerrant.

In this world of space and time, however, we confront particulars and our information is gained by fallible experiences. The goal of education is to draw out of persons their formerly learned knowledge of absolutes. This never proves to be an easy task, because the students are constantly caught in the relativity of their finite sense experiences. Nonetheless, Plato assumed that through a shrewd dialectic of question and answer, men could be led to recall the pure and unchangeable truths which they possessed as innate ideas from birth. Obviously, if Plato's theory is accepted, then religious knowledge is gained from within rather than from without. Introspection, rather than observation, was the proper procedure. As this was applied to religion, it meant that it was not necessary for the devout seeker to study this temporal world so much as to introspect into his own understanding. By virtue of this assumption of inborn knowledge, the primary Platonic procedure is best expressed by the term "intuition." We would then assume that every human being who engaged in the proper kind of dialectic discussion could suddenly come upon the ultimate insights, and that the truth of these insights would dawn with immediate certitude. There is not, as a consequence, in the Platonic dialogues any attempt at mustering the empirical data which would corroborate religious truth. Nor is there any effort, such as we find in Aristotle, to specify the fundamental intuitive postulates from which religious knowledge, like any other knowledge, might be inferred. On the contrary, the basic insights appear immediately, self-evidently, and with no need for further justification. It would be a misunderstanding of the procedure of Plato to ask, "But what are the premises which warrant these religious statements?" For in fact, the claim of knowledge of the absolute is a claim which is premiseless. If this seems to be an odd state of affairs, it can be appreciated at least that it is implicit in the definition of an intuition that it have no premises as grounds for an inference.

Probably the preponderance of religious thinkers, both in the Orient and in the Occident, fit most nearly into this Platonic pattern. The basic information called religion, and the certitude which this information carries within itself, are not the result of either deductive inference or empirical observation. If we assume that this is really the case for religion, there are certain practical problems of communication which become insurmountable. Intuition, either as a test of truth or as a criterion of truth, suffers from two fundamental limitations. In the first place, intuitions are by their nature incommunicable. If we were to ask a person who claimed to have intuitive insights what the intuitions meant, or more basically how he got the intuitions, no communicable answer could be given. For to explain the meaning of any statement normally consists in showing the premises from which it came. Since this is impossible in the case of intuition, no explanation could be given in the normal fashion. This means, in effect, that a person who has an intuition can never explain to a person who does not have it what the intuition means. Nor can the person who has the intuition explain how any other person might have the same experience.

A second difficulty with intuition arises out of the problem of attempting to show why an intuition is true. Here also, the acceptable procedure for justifying statements is to construct an argument, either deductive or inductive, in which the premises are of such a nature that the listener can see clearly that the conclusion follows. But intuition, by definition, prevents us from doing precisely this. The dilemma involved in operating from an intuitive frame of reference has been well expressed in the theological writings of Paul Tillich. For Tillich the ultimate commitment to which Christians are bound is fundamentally a self-evident, immediate, and intuitive insight. If a person has no insight of the Christian sort, there is no known way in which he can be enlightened. Where communication is carried out among persons who purportedly have had a common Christian revelation, the language is always symbolic and never literal. While these symbols may be informative for persons who already know the basic Christian meanings, they are empty for the unbeliever. This would appear to mean, in effect, that if a person had the basic intuition he would not need enlightenment; while if, on the other hand, he did not have the intuition, then there would be no possible way for him to be enlightened.

This search for self-evident and informative statements in religion reached a high point in the philosophical speculations of Descartes. His procedure, commonly called "Cartesian doubt," was to begin by disclaiming any certain information whatsoever. "I doubt," Descartes appeared to say, "that any of the information which I received in my Jesuit training is self-evidently true. It will be my task, therefore, to see whether I can discover some statements which contain inerrant information of the world in which man lives in some real sense." These statements will not need to have any empirical evidence to support them. They will be statements of such a nature that analysis of the statements alone will reveal their truth. The first such proposition which Descartes believed that he had discovered was his famous "I think, therefore I exist." He believed that this was an informative sentence, and that its contrary entailed self-contradiction. This is to say that if a man asserted, "I think, therefore I exist," it would be impossible for him without self-contradiction to imagine that the contrary of this statement was true. To suppose this latter to be possible would be the same as claiming that while it is true that "I think," it is not true that "I exist." Or, it may mean that while it is true that I am aware that I exist, it is not true that I am thinking. It may also mean that I know that I am not thinking and not existing. Descartes believed that a serious analysis of these three options would reveal that it would be self-contradictory to assert any one of them. He concluded, therefore, that the original remark, "I think, therefore I exist," was a statement whose truth was self-evident and incontrovertible. Now the value of such a statement, assuming that it could be found, is that it would then be possible to use it as a premise in a deductive argument, such that the conclusion would be absolutely true. As we shall see in our later discussion, one of the fundamental problems of both induction and deduction is to find premises which are absolutely true, for unless premises of this degree of certitude are possible, all religion would rest upon statements of probability. On the assumption that probabilities are inimical to religion, religiously acceptable knowledge would be out of the question.

Specifically in the area of religion, Descartes believed that he had found a similar statement whose evidence for truth could be determined by an analysis of the statement alone. This religious sentence read somewhat as follows: "If I have an idea of an absolutely perfect being, whose perfection entails all properties worth having, then it follows necessarily that this being must exist. For if it were true that this being did not exist, then it could not have been true that I had an idea of a perfect and omnipropertied being." This conclusion was obvious since a nonexisting being would lack the property of existence. While it is not our concern at this moment to determine whether this particular claim is really true, it is interesting to note that intuitively self-evident propositions have seemed to be absolutely essential in the history of Christian theologizing. It will follow, therefore, that if some of the religious discussions which we attempt to analyze presuppose intuitive premises, we shall be in a difficult position to determine either what is meant or whether what is meant is really true.

The intent of the medieval mystics supported the perennial search for indubitable intuitions. It was the hope, for example, of Jacob Boehme and Meister Eckhart to show that religious persons under the proper situations could have immediate awareness of religious certainty. The awareness involved in a mystical experience is somewhat comparable to that which is experienced in being in love. Just as it would be improper to ask a person who is undergoing the experience of love to give the premises which justify his claim that he is in love, so it would be equally improper to require the Christian mystic to give any further evidence of his religious insights beyond his own immediate mystical experience. While it is still quite proper to investigate the knowledge claims of intuitively religious persons, it will again be obvious that there will be severe epistemological limitations in all attempts at communication of meaning and certification of truth. It may be, therefore, that we shall have to conclude, if religion consists only of intuitions, that philosophy of religion can never involve epistemology. If to philosophize about religion means to supply the proper premises for valid inferences, then intuitive religion would be philosophically out of bounds.

In view of the serious limitations which the intuitive method entails, the assumptions with which we shall operate are that the claims of religious knowledge rest on available data and require for their defense a logical inference. If it turns out that the data on which religion is claimed to depend are not available for general inspection, then we shall have to turn in a negative epistemological report, and direct our attention to the normative significance of religion.

If our investigation of the normative essence of religion reveals that the norms are subjective, then our problem will be further complicated. Perhaps we shall find that the philosophical problem of religion is much like that of ethics—namely, one of attempting to prove that a certain class of moral obligations and ethical goods are indeed worth while. The problems involved in this kind of analysis have been well developed by Immanuel Kant. Since Kant's case for religion rested upon ethics, and provided a kind of emotional sanction for the obligatoriness of moral requirements, all that Kant really had to show was that religion logically functioned in this way. While in his later writings he was led to reject this point of view, he does give us some insight into what is involved in attempting to justify the normative meaning claims of religion as opposed to any supposed descriptive claims of religion.

Let it be understood, at the outset, that the question of whether there is any religious knowledge is itself disputable. Although the title of this chapter suggests not only that there may be religious knowledge but that there are some problems in defending it, it ought not to be concluded prematurely that it has been demonstrated that religious knowledge is a fact. We might still wish to choose the available alternative supplied by some contemporary religious existentialists— namely, that there is no religious knowledge, and that no serious religious-minded person would ever make the claim that there was.

On the assumption, however, that religious knowledge has been claimed to be a problem, the issues involved would seem to fall into three general areas. First, what does the term "truth" mean? Second, what are the criteria or tests by which it may be determined that any religious statement is in fact true? And third, what are the logical methods by which inferences may be validated? If we have some true statements, we may then wish to know what further truth can be inferred.

THE DEFINITION OF "TRUTH"

The most ancient meaning of the word "truth" comes to us from Aristotle. It has been called the "correspondence definition of 'truth.'" The stipulated meaning of this definition as it interprets truth is as follows: A sentence is true if, and only if, what the sentence talks about exists as described. In Aristotle's system he predicated that to say of anything, when it exists, that it exists, is true; while to say of anything, when it does not exist, that it really does exist, is false. If, for example, we were to assert the sentence, "The door in this room is open," when in fact the door was closed, we would be asserting a falsehood. The state of affairs of the "closed door" is what leads us to assign falsity to the claim that the door is open. All of this means, very simply, that any sentence will be false if what it refers to either does not in fact exist, or exists in some fashion opposed to what our sentence claimed. This is what the term "truth" appears to mean in normal discourse. The sentence "There is immortality" is true if, and only if, there is in fact something which corresponds to the meaning of our assertion. Truth is a property of sentences which are descriptive of the world and intend, therefore, to give information about states of affairs outside of the sentence which indicates these states of affairs. Now, when a religious person says that the sentence "God exists" is true, he normally means this in the correspondence sense. He means to assert that the statement "God exists" tells us something about the world, and that "out there" there is a state of affairs which the sentence "God exists" correctly describes. It is clear that this correspondence meaning of "truth" presupposes that we can check the referent of any sentence which is claimed to be true to see whether it does or does not exist as described. If we were asked what a true sentence was good for, we would obviously reply that it tells us something reliable about the world.

The difficulty, however, of ascertaining that the referent of some descriptions does in fact exist has prompted alternative definitions of "truth." The second definition which we shall consider came into being and continues to enjoy popularity primarily because it does not require us to check the referent before we assert truth. This definition has been called the "coherence definition of 'truth,'" and it found its most explicit expression in the writings of G. W. F. Hegel, a nineteenth-century German philosopher. What we need to establish in order to show that a sentence satisfies the coherence definition is that the sentence in question is coherent with a long list of already coherent sentences. Ideally, the latter sentences should themselves be provable in the correspondence sense of truth, although if this is not the case, the mere occurrence of a long coherent list should be able to prove every one of the sentences true. When such an interlocking consistency exists, then it is considered warranted to infer the existence of the referent of the original statement. A coherently true sentence, therefore, must be capable of being fitted into a system.

This is the common idea of truth appealed to in courts of law. The attorney for the defense cannot recreate the past events which would absolve his client. What he does instead is to get a list of testimonies as to where his client was at the time the crime was committed, which will be coherent with the claim of his innocence. It is commonly true that the statements of testimony are themselves unprovable save in the coherence meaning of "truth," but if the evidence constitutes a large enough body of consistent assertions, then innocence is usually inferred to be true. This will mean that there did exist a state of affairs in the past consistent with the plea of innocence.

It is essentially to this meaning of "truth" that the teleologist appeals when he asserts that the existence of God is coherent with the existence of orderly events in the world. When he has collected a large enough mass of orderly events, he concludes that the hypothesis of a designing God is coherent with these events, and hence the hypothesis is descriptively true. No teleologist ever intended to suggest that when he asserted the existence of God, this meant that he had found God and confirmed his existence. Coherence was all that he claimed as evidence for his conclusion that God existed in fact.

While this coherence definition appears to be strikingly different from the correspondence definition, it may just as easily be considered to be a special case of correspondence, in which the determination of the existence of the referent is by means of the existence of the coherent list. Coherence could, therefore, be considered not so much a new definition of "truth" as a specification of what must exist in order to assume that the referent exists. This interlocking dependence of correspondence and coherence has been reflected for centuries in the development and confirmation of scientific hypotheses. In any case, both of these definitions make the same final claim: a true sentence has a referent which exists.

Contemporary pragmatic thinkers have coined what appears to be a third definition. In the language of William James, "Ideas become true just in so far as they help us to get into satisfactory relation with other parts of our experience." [1] This instrumental view defines the truth property of a sentence without appealing to any referent in the sense in which the two previous definitions did. In his essay on "What Pragmatism Means" James concluded: "If theological ideas prove to have a value for concrete life, they will be true, for pragmatism, in the sense of being good for so much. For how much more they are true, will depend entirely on their relations to the other truths that also have to be acknowledged." [2] This means quite simply that a theological idea is true if it has value for human living in establishing satisfactory relations with other acknowledged truths. We would not have to find the referent of God or immortality, for it would be sufficient to show the usefulness of the ideas of God and immortality for human ends. Among these ends would be listed the desire for feeling at home in the world and the desire for cosmic support for values, as well as the more direct human wish for mental and physical health.

This pragmatic definition, like the coherence definition, is not so much a new definition as it is a specification of what would be considered an adequate test of truth. In the case of all three of these purported definitions it is assumed that true sentences will serve the same function—namely, that they will be useful for predicting future events. They will enable us to explain our world in such a way that experience can be ordered and systematized. While there are these common elements in all the definitions of "truth," the pragmatic conception does entail a shift in emphasis which it is important to note. In this case no assertion is made concerning the existence of the referent of a true sentence. The correspondence definition requires the knowledge that the referent exists before truth can be properly assigned; the coherence definition infers the existence of the referent from the existence of the coherent list. Unlike either of these, the pragmatic definition neither asserts nor infers any referent at all. If the sentence in question is useful for predictive purposes, or if it fulfills human emotions, then it is considered to be true, and any question about existing referents is considered to be irrelevant. It would, of course, be theoretically possible for a sentence to be both predictably useful and emotionally satisfying even though what it talked about did not in fact exist. This interesting possibility is not, however, of live and compelling concern to a pragmatist.

All of this discussion of definitions of "truth" leads us to the question, "What shall 'truth' mean in the study of philosophies of religion?" We have two options which we shall alternately choose. At the outset of any investigation we shall assume that it is the correspondence definition of "truth" that is involved. If the particular person or argument we are studying states a preference for any other defined meaning, we shall operate with this new definition. In any case, we wish to know what implications follow for any utilized meaning for the claim to truth. If the assumption is that true sentences are those which are useful for some prescribed end, then we need to determine whether in fact these sentences have such usefulness. If coherence is the claim, then coherence is what we shall look for. If, finally, true sentences correctly describe the states of affairs claimed to exist in the world of experience, then it will be appropriate to ask: "By what tests is existence certified?" In a very real sense, the tests of truth reveal the meaning of the claim for truth.

THE TESTS OF TRUTH

It is the function of a test of truth to determine whether a given sentence satisfies the requirements of the definition of "truth." For the sake of simplicity and compliance with common usage, we shall assume that "truth" has a meaning in accordance with the correspondence definition. A sentence will be called true, unless otherwise specified, if, and only if, what the sentence talks about exists as described. The question which the test of truth must answer is "What is the sentence talking about?" or "What must exist in order for a sentence to be called true?"

Let us illustrate this in a few commonplace situations where all of us are familiar with both the test and its application. If a friend should tell us, "Your porch lights are lit," we assume that a look at the proper spot on the porch ceiling will determine whether he has made a true statement. What must exist, in this instance, is a look of such-and-such a sort which we interpret as being "a look at lights which are on." The test, therefore, is sense experience, and the minimum interpretation of what must exist is an appropriate sensation. In this simple instance, what we have done is to let the choice of the test determine what is supposed to be the referent of the problematic sentence whose truth concerns us. To say, "The porch lights are lit," is to assert that if you go out on the porch a certain sensation will occur. This is the very least that would be intended, although it may not be the most intended. We might also intend to assert the fact that whether you look at the porch ceiling or not there is a state of affairs which means "the lights are on." Your look merely acquainted you with the fact; it did not create the fact. We can, for our purposes, waive the niceties of this distinction and concentrate upon the sensation.

A second illustration may be drawn from archaeology, where what we assert cannot be seen directly, as could the lights on the porch. If an archaeologist should assert, "There was a time in human history when men had no metal implements," he would probably mean that if we look at the artifacts in certain geological strata we will find only stone implements—or, at least, we will find no metal implements. The scientist in question does not expect that sense experience will be able to recreate primitive men using nonmetal implements. The test involved, however, is sense experience. Looking in the proper places will prove or disprove the original assertion. What will exist are artifacts as far as the direct test is concerned. In the context, however, of a complex of other theories it will also be the intention of the archaeologist to claim that if we could go back in time we would be able to have direct sense confirmation of the statement.

In religion proper the tests are rarely simple sensations. Nonetheless, the classical teleological arguments for the existence of a designing God come very close to being confirmed by sense experiences. The teleologist may formulate the following conditional statement: "If we live in an orderly world, we may infer that an orderer brought this about." A host of sensations which we fit into a matrix of unity may constitute the test which confirms the antecedent: "We live in an orderly world." Sense experience does not confirm, however, that the inference to a designing God is valid. What normally confirms this for the teleologist is a coherence test. If the original conditional statement would be "incoherent" when we accept the order but deny the designing God, then the logical test of coherence would urge the acceptance of the designing God thesis. In this argument two kinds of "facts" are up for question. In the first place there are claimed events of order, which sense experience confirms after a fashion. In the second place there is a claimed coherence, which logic confirms in its fashion. Relating these two kinds of facts is an avowed inference. In the case of this last item, logic is said to be the test which applies a degree of probability to what the facts of order are claimed to imply.

Unlike the simple situation of the porch lights, however, this latter situation faces some complication if we expect that true sentences are supposed to be useful for future predictions. It is quite clear what would be involved if we predicted, "If you go out on the porch, and if the lights are on, then there should be shadows cast upon the floor." It is not so clear what would be the prediction for the future if we assumed that a designing God did exist, other than the circular claim that we should then expect to find orderly objects.

Where sense experience is used for religious confirmation, it is seldom, if ever, intended that the sensation confronts or means the religious referent. There is usually a coherent sequence of events, and the sensation touches only one end of this sequence. We are familiar with this sequential procedure in the establishment of complex theories of science. Certain claims with regard to atoms are given a probability, not by seeing atoms, but by visual sensations of occurrences, such as those in the Wilson cloud chamber, which are in turn connected sequentially with intermediate hypotheses; and only after this do we get to the final inference: "There are atoms." While assertions of a God are like assertions of atoms in the sense that the confirmation is indirect, it is not obvious that the two types of claims have equal use in predictive situations in the future. None but a religious mystic has ever claimed that there are any elementary sense proofs for a God. Yet even for the mystic it has not been claimed that we sense God in the ordinary meaning of the term.

It has generally been understood by religiously interested persons that the vast number of conventional tests of truth are inapplicable to religious matters. No one would ever suppose that there are, or ever will be, religious thermometers, spectroscopes, rulers, or scales. No one has ever seriously supposed that the five senses could directly apprehend the referents of religious assertions, such as God or immortality. The awareness of this fact was well expressed by Ludwig Feuerbach when he asserted that religious matters represented a peculiar kind of data, and that the verification of these data required a peculiarly different kind of procedure. Perhaps the data of religion are not so peculiar as Feuerbach contended, but one thing is clear: these data are not available to simple sense confirmation or denial.

More than this, religious arguments possess a claim to value. To assert the existence of God is not merely to contend that there is a being "out there," but to insist that the universe of man has moral values structured within it. This state of affairs has led many contemporary religious seekers to minimize the descriptive element in religion in favor of the element of moral significance. It is not that religious arguments intend to establish the mere existence of a God, so much as to establish the implicit moral meaning of life. This was probably part of the message of Paul Tillich when he insisted that the existence of God was not of religious concern, while the meaning of God was of religious concern. The religious problem, therefore, may be seen as one of showing that the religious claims are not only coherent with the assignment of meaning to facts, but that they are the only claims coherent with the predication of value.

After we have decided on a definition of truth and on tests of truth, there is still a further epistemological matter to be considered. This is the problem of logical inference. If we have in our possession some true sentences, we may wish to know whether further truth can be inferred using these true statements as premises.

THE METHODS: INDUCTION AND DEDUCTION

In the long history of philosophic speculation two primary and distinctive methods of inference have been developed: induction and deduction. Their function is to show how it is possible to infer conclusions from truths already known. If we have certain premises, we can infer certain conclusions. If a religious person wishes to be logical, or wishes to prove some religious matter, he has at his disposal these two fundamental approaches.

Induction and deduction are logics or systems of rules of valid inference. While there are many specific deductive systems, each with its own rules, all deductive approaches share certain general characteristics. The same is the case for inductive systems. We shall itemize these characteristics and show how they affect religious arguments.

Induction
1. If the premises are true, and a valid inference is drawn, the conclusion may still be false.

Deduction
1. If the premises are true, and a valid inference is drawn, the conclusion must be true.

It is a property of all inductions that a false conclusion may be asserted even though no error in inference has been made. If, for example, we were studying the number of legs on the cows in our community, and we discovered that all of the n cows we examined had four legs, we might reasonably predict that the next cow, or even that all the rest of the cows, had four legs also. If the next animal which was a cow were to have three legs, our prediction would have been false, even though it had been reasonably made. In any induction, no matter how consistent the premises have been, it is always possible that disconfirming evidence may falsify the conclusion.

On the other hand, it is a property of all deductions that the conclusion will always be true, if the premises were true. It is assumed, of course, that no error in inference was made.

> If all cows eat grass;
> If this is a cow;
> Then: this cow eats grass.

If the premises are true, then the conclusion must be true. No disconfirming evidence could ever occur. It must be noted, however, that the argument entails a conditional "if." There will be a real problem for all deductions to show that the premises are actually true. Quite aside from this question, it will still be the case that, if the premises are true, the conclusion must be true.

Induction
    2. The conclusion is not contained in the premises.
Deduction
    2. The conclusion is contained in the premises.

To say that the conclusion of an induction is not contained in the premises is another way of saying that the conclusion is a prediction of what will be the case, and not an assertion of what is now known to be the case. In the illustration of studying the legs on cows, it will be noted that while I studied n cows, my conclusion concerned the $(n + 1)$th cow. This was a cow not studied in the premises. It follows from this that the conclusion of an induction gives logically new information. It tells me something that I did not previously know. It asserts something that I did not previously observe.

The conclusion of a deduction, however, is contained in the premises from which it is drawn. This means that the conclusion does not contain any logically new information. It reasserts information already found in the premises. If we were to analyze the deductive argument with regard to the cows, we would see that this is the case. To say that all cows eat grass is to say that all of the class of cows is included in the class of grass eaters. To say that this is a cow is to say that it is included in the class of cows. It is clear from this that the conclusion that this cow eats grass was already contained in the information given in the premises. Obviously, therefore, if the premises of a deduction are true, the conclusion must be true. The fact that the conclusion is contained in the premises explains why the first rule is clearly the case.

Induction

3. Contradictory premises are permitted, and hence contradictory conclusions are possible.

Deduction

3. Contradictory premises are not permitted, and hence contradictory conclusions are not possible.

To say that contradictory premises are permitted is not to say that self-contradictions are allowed. A self-contradiction would be a sentence that asserts and denies the same fact at the same time. For example, to say that the lights in this room are on and they are not on would be a self-contradiction. Self-contradictions are not permitted in any logic, inductive or deductive. The following illustrations show what this means for the respective logics. If I were attempting an induction where the problem was, "What color are crows?" my premises, based upon observations, might appear as follows:

Crow$_1$ is black.
Crow$_2$ is black.
Crow$_3$ is black.
Crow$_4$ is not black.

Now, given these premises, I wish to make a prediction as to the color of the next crow which I will see. I might predict that crow, will be black. If this crow is not black, this situation would illustrate the first rule with regard to induction: if the premises are true, and the inference is valid, the conclusion may still be false. In any case, it is possible to draw an inductive conclusion where the data are not univocal.

In deduction, on the contrary, I cannot have premises which are contradictory or ambiguous in the sense that they do not indicate clearly and univocally which ideas I have in mind. This may be understood in view of the fact that while the premises of induction are reports about the world, the premises of deduction are ideas. We expect that the facts will be disparate and conflicting, but that predictions can still be made. In deduction, on the other hand, where our aim is to see what is entailed in a given set of ideas, conflict among these ideas would make it quite impossible to draw any conclusion other than that we are confused. Since the conclusion of a deduction is always implicit in the premises, and is expressed, therefore, as a certainty, it is clear that contradictory premises would make this impossible. No univocal certainty would ever be possible from multivocal or conflicting premises.

Suppose, for example, that we were to make a deduction from the following ideas about crows:

All crows are black.
X is a crow.
Therefore, X is black.

We can see that the conclusion is necessarily entailed in the ideas expressed in the premises. Suppose, on the other hand, that we were to list as our premises the following ideas:

All crows are black.
Some crows are not black.
X is a crow.

It would be clear that we could not draw any conclusion about the color of X as being necessarily contained in the premises. While some probability estimate might be hazarded, such an estimate would not be valid in a deduction. Nor would it be possible to deduce anything from the following premises:

Some crows are black.
Some crows are not black.
X is a crow.

All of this means essentially that the premises of a deduction must be univocal or noncontradictory if any conclusion is to be validly drawn. The premises of an induction, however, may express multivocal or contradictory possibilities without making it impossible to draw conclusions. To be sure, when the data are conflicting, it will be possible, in induction, to draw conflicting conclusions. Suppose, for example, that we were trying to make a teleological argument for the existence of a God. Our premises would consist of the facts of order in the world, but we could not ignore the facts of dysteleology or disorder. No serious teleologist has, in fact, been able to ignore the natural tychisms discussed by John Stuart Mill in his essay on "Nature." As a consequence of this abundance of order and disorder at the level of existence, many inductive conclusions have been possible about theodicy.

When we contrast this ambivalent and equivocal situation in induction with the clear and single-minded certainty which deductions about God possess, we can see the role which the permission or prohibition of conflicting premises entails. Once again, however, we must remember that induction starts with the facts, while deduction starts with postulated ideas. Induction was designed as a method of inference from conflicting facts, while deduction was designed as a method of inference from consistent ideas.

Induction

4. Additional information may alter the truth or falsity of the conclusion.

Deduction

4. Additional information cannot alter the truth or falsity of the conclusion.

In induction, where the conclusion is not contained in the premises, and where contradictory information is permitted in the premises, it will always be possible that new data may lead to a reassessment of the truth status of the conclusion. If I predict that the next cow I see will have four legs, but the next cow has only three legs, then my prediction is falsified. The possibility of disconfirming evidence will always be present. When we are dealing with the inductive arguments for the existence of God, this fact will mean that the possibility will arise that the conclusion is false, and that there really is no God. One of the risks which any philosopher of religion must face, if he believes that an inductive proof of God can be given, is that an inductive argument for the non-existence of God may also be asserted. For any empirical statement there will always be some probability that it will be disconfirmed. This fact has suggested to most theologians that inductive proofs for God are both psychologically and logically inadequate for religious purposes.

Because the conclusion of deduction is contained in the premises, and because contradictory premises are not permitted, no additional information can ever alter the truth status of the conclusion. The only kinds of premises which could do this are prohibited—namely, the contradictory ones. This fact has led to far greater enthusiasm on the part of religious philosophers for deductive arguments. If the conclusion is true, it will always be so. Even Immanuel Kant, who doubted that any argument for God could be justified, still admitted that if reason alone could suffice to prove the existence of God, the deductive ontological argument would be the one to prefer.[3] The real problem remaining for the deductive proofs for God is that of finding premises which are true in any absolute sense. The conclusion of a deduction is true only if the premises are true. The search for true premises engaged Descartes when he constructed his ontological argument. It seemed evident to him that only intuited premises could supply the required certitude in such a way that no doubt could be raised and that no additional data could disconfirm this certitude.

Saint Bonaventura, the Franciscan Roman Catholic, believed that religious knowledge was possible both in the inductive and in the deductive sense. On the side of induction, he insisted that empirical observation of the events in the world revealed the nature of the cause of the world, on the grounds that the cause of any effect contains the essential properties which the effect possesses. On the assumption that we can understand the worldly effects, it should follow that we can understand the divine cause to the same degree. The simple fact that we do not generally have this knowledge of God is due, simply, to the concupiscence and fleshly interests which we permit to dominate us. These prevent what would otherwise be a clear inference from the world to God.[4] The real certitude, however, comes through deduction from absolute premises. In his analysis of the nature of the defining process, he asserts that every definition is understood in terms of more universal ideas, and so on until we get to the most universal idea, which is God. Man's problem, now, is to get an incorrigibly clear and correct notion of God, so that by a series of deductions we may arrive at a true knowledge of man and his world. No sum of inductions can provide us with certitude about the meaning of God. Such knowledge must come intuitively or immediately in such a fashion that doubt cannot be raised. Once we have this clear meaning of God, man's intellect is able to grasp the necessary connections entailed in a strict deduction.[5] That such immediate knowledge of God is possible is the thesis of his book, *The Mind's Road to God.*

The analysis of these two logical methods reveals a dilemma for all who would use logic to prove statements to be true. This dilemma has special psychological significance for religious thinkers. If we use deduction, our conclusions will be true with certainty, but we will never learn anything logically new. In addition to this we face the thorny problem of getting true premises in the first place. If we use induction, our conclusions will be logically new, but we will never be able to prove them with any certainty. It will always be possible that new information may prove our original conclusions to be false. (Logically speaking, there is no way in which we can learn both something new and something true at the same time. If we attempt to prove the existence of God by deduction, then, it is clear, we must already know in our premises that God exists. (Only on this condition can we be certain of the truth of our conclusion./ If we attempt to prove the existence of God by induction, then, although our premises do not have to beg the conclusion as in deduction, we can never have the assurance of certitude about our conclusion. It appears that this certitude is an essential property of any religious commitment, but at the same time the religious person wants his claims to have the assurance of content. On the horns of this dilemma religious knowledge claims have traditionally been caught. On the face of it, the choice for the certitude of deduction carries with it the suspicion that only the inference is valid, while the content of the conclusion remains in doubt. If, on the other hand, we choose the informative procedures of induction, we then sacrifice the certitude without which religious claims seem to be in vain. How shall this problem be solved? In the chapters which follow we will note two basic resolutions. On the one hand, some will claim that religious arguments can avoid the dilemma, and on the other, some will concede that the assurance of certitude must be purchased at the price of relinquishing the hope for religious knowledge in the common meaning of the term "knowledge."

Whatever implications seem to follow from this analysis of the nature of truth and the methods of proving it, as applied to the problems of religious knowledge, it must still be kept in mind that for a good many philosophers of religion this is not the essential problem. If we emphasize, as W. E. Hocking does, the role of the will in the establishment of religious information and religious certitude, then these epistemological considerations turn out to be essentially peripheral. An introspective and psychological analysis of the nature of human emotions would be far more to the point. If, on the other hand, we stress, as does Paul Tillich, the basically intuitive element in religion and were to describe the essence of religion in terms of an encounter with ultimate reality, then once again, such empirical or logical issues of truth or falsity, and the proof thereof, turn out to be beside the point. It would be difficult, however, in a course in which communication is both expected and desired, to operate at the Tillichian level. Unless we assume that what religion talks about is available for public inspection, very little can be done. Only Christians who had had the intuitive insights would be able to understand each other in terms of their religious symbolism, and fundamentally, for them, this procedure would be irrelevant. While it will still remain an open option whether one wishes to decide, after all is said and done, for the fundamental ineffability and incommunicability of religion, it is hardly an adequate starting point. We shall investigate, therefore, some of the classical arguments for immortality, and for the solving of the problem of natural evil. We shall presuppose that these arguments must be amenable to the elementary rules of logical discourse. Our analysis and criticism of these arguments presupposes the possibility of religious knowledge.

VII

The Problem *of* Natural Evil

THE PROBLEM of evil was formulated by Philo as the unanswered questions of Epicurus. "Is he [God] willing to prevent evil, but not able? then is he impotent. Is he able, but not willing? then is he malevolent. Is he both able and willing? whence then is evil?" [1]

The solution to the problem of natural evil has historically been called the province of theodicy. This was the discipline which disclosed the ways of God in dealing with human beings, with special reference to natural evil. If God is wise, good, and powerful, why do human beings suffer? This was the crucial question which drove the Gautama Buddha to leave his home and wander for seven years as a mendicant. This was the question which Descartes evaded because he had no intuitions on this score. Concern with this problem led some of the early Christian church fathers to develop patripassianism, the view that God the Father suffered in Christ. According to Praxeus, the second-century founder of this view, God descended into the Virgin and was born as Christ, and hence it was proper to speak of "the suffering God." While this view was declared heretical because it seemed to make God a changing creature, it has always held some fascination among religious laymen, for God and men are pictured as co-workers and co-sufferers.

Some would hold, with Tillich, that the initial question rests on a misconception. The question of natural evil can be asked only existentially—that is, by the person about himself. It cannot be asked as a generalization for others. Since, in his theory, God is the ground of being, ultimate unity must prevail, and no good-evil distinctions are possible metaphysically. Any answer to the question of natural evil would have to arise out of the existential encounter of individual questioners. Any attempt at a general theory would be a perversion. A long tradition of religious speculation has, however, assumed that general theories were possible. This is due essentially to the tendency to attribute characteristics to God, and hence to assume that he faces moral problems just as man does. It is with this latter supposition that we are concerned in this chapter.

Once men have established the existence of God to their satisfaction, their religious problems begin anew. Questions must now be raised concerning the purported character of this God. It could well be that some omni-being does exist, but what if this being were basically evil, stupid, or impotent? The possibility that this might be the case arose whenever men were depressed by the natural catastrophes which are all too common in this world. Diseases unnumbered lay waste the physical and mental powers of man. Hurricanes and floods destroy the material advances which he may make, removing either life itself or the means by which life could tolerably be maintained. When to these we add tidal waves, killing frost, burning heat, earthquakes, volcanoes, rattlesnakes, Gila monsters, natural poisons in vast numbers, any serious man begins to wonder whether the God that he has just established may not be a cosmic tyrant, an omnipotent Borgia, or a universal sadist. The problem of how to save the character of the God in the presence of the ubiquitous natural evils is what has been known as the "problem of natural evil." Two premises need to be assumed to be true before this problem is urgently clear:

1. There are events harmful to man and not caused by man. These events are not rare and exceptional, but widespread and common.
2. There is a transfinite God. The minimum properties which this God possesses are omnipotence, omniscience, and omnigoodness.

It seemed clear to religious persons that if man is not the cause of these evils, then God must be. This becomes more obvious in the traditional Judeo-Christian assumption that God made the world *ex nihilo* (out of nothing). If there had been something here in the first place, perhaps one could excuse the God on the grounds that he had to use the available stuff, and that, consequently, he had to make the best job he could with fallible material in much the same sense that a human artist must. This option raises a further question as to whether God is really the Creator, if there was some material which he did not create. The problem has seemed clear. There are evils in the world, and they are due to a transfinite God. How can these two facts be reconciled? The study of this and comparable problems has been called theodicy. It is the investigation of the problem of how and why God operates the way he appears to operate.

Of all the religious problems this has seemed to be the most pressing. More ingenuity and energy have been expended in attempting to resolve this issue than any other. In the ancient Vedic scriptures, illustrative of thinking about 3000 B.C., the fact of evil posed real questions about the operation of the gods. The hymns addressed to the god Rudra raise these urgent questions. Why do the righteous perish? Why do catastrophes happen to people for no apparent reason? The god Rudra becomes symbolic of this irrational, incomprehensible force. While no clear answer to this problem of theodicy is asserted, the awareness that it is a problem is obvious.

> Kill not our great or our small, our growing one or
> our full-grown man, our father or our mother. Injure
> not, O Rudra, our dear selves. Injure us not in our cattle
> or horses. In thy wrath, O Rudra, slay not our heroes. We
> invoke thee ever with sacrifices.[2]

While there is a clear awareness of the occurrence of natural
evils, there is not the same issue which would harass a
monotheist. Rudra was not claimed to be a helper of the
Aryans. He was admitted to be malevolent. This will at least
save the character of other gods. The monotheist, however,
must account for all this in the context of the same god. The
same god who creates good must also be the author of evil.
In monotheism there are no other gods to whom the blame
can be passed. In the subsequent developments in Hinduism,
however, the easy appeal to a Rudra was found to be inadequate. Hindus, like monotheists, felt compelled to discover
reasons for this gruesome state of affairs in which beings of
great insight still created events that caused great misery.
The wise sayings attributed to the Gautama Buddha are
essentially concerned with this problem of human suffering.
The book of Job begins with this issue. The Gospels evidence
concern with the problem, notably in the discussion of why
the Tower of Siloam fell. Roman Catholic and Protestant
theologians alike have felt impelled to discuss the question
of natural evil.

We shall discuss a number of the solutions which have
been proposed, analyzing what they mean, what the appeal
has been, and what problems still seem to remain after all
the defenses have been mustered. The solutions may, on
occasion, redefine the premises or even deny them. In the
variations which these solutions exhibit we shall also see the
wide differences in the analyses of what the initial problem
really is.

MAN'S FREEDOM REQUIRES NATURAL EVIL

The theory of free will admits the truth of the
two premises which we posed as constituting the problem of

natural evil. There are natural evils, and there is a transfinite being. The rationale by which this God deigned to create natural evils predicates the following premises as being admittedly true.

1. Free will is the basic postulate of human morality. If men did not have freedom to choose, then moral culpability or praise would have no meaning.
2. The cosmic being credited freedom with this essential function as being the precondition of moral responsibility.
3. Moral responsibility is presupposed to be of intrinsic merit, and hence it needs no justification.
4. If there were a world in which all choices led to the same morally qualitative results, then human freedom would have no meaning. If human freedom had no meaning, moral responsibility would be a null class. There are two conditions under which all choices could be said to lead to the same qualitative results:
    a. If all consequences were good.
    b. If all consequences were bad.

Conclusion: It seems obvious, therefore, that a transfinite being who admitted the intrinsic value of moral responsibility would have to create a world in which some actions exposed man to natural good and some exposed him to natural evil. Without such radically different consequences to actions, there would be no point in being free, and hence no practical meaning to moral responsibility.

This solution has had considerable support from Judaism, Protestantism, and Roman Catholicism. While Immanuel Kant is no theologian, his defense of human freedom as the ground of human dignity and responsibility has lent a luster to this position. The chief merit claimed for this solution is that it emphasizes what appears to be a fact of human experience; namely, that if natural evils are to be avoided, human choices must be made. If we are to eliminate the scourge of certain diseases, men must choose to conduct medical research and find the cures, if such exist. Since we do assume that many of the great evils that plague man can be eliminated by intelligent insight, the force of the solution is obvious. Only responsible choices can free mankind from the fetters of natural evil. Modern Existentialism, particularly the irreligious variety, has predicated this "dreadful freedom" which men face, in which cosmic responsibility to avoid or eliminate natural evils is theirs. The alternative to this position appears to be resignation to fate or a doubtful refuge in predestination.

This answer to the question of natural evil raises new problems which seem to cast a doubt as to whether it really "saves the character of God." In the first place, this solution seems to miss the essential problem. The disturbing matter is, "Why do natural evils exist?" This solution answers, rather, the question, "What shall we do in a world where natural evils exist?" To say that the natural evils had to exist because human responsibility requires them is essentially a psychological reason, not a logical one. This solution aims to show that the motivation to choose presupposes good and evil consequences to the alternative choices. Without such radically different consequences, there would be no incentive to choose at all. It is doubtful whether any psychological data exist to support this contention. Most daily choice situations are not between natural good and natural evil, even though the existence of the evils does prompt many choices.

A second problem with this solution concerns the number and seriousness of the natural evils which do exist. John Stuart Mill was particularly bothered by what appeared to him to be a superabundance of evils. "Everything in short, which the worst men commit either against life or property is perpetrated on a larger scale by natural agents." [3] It is not merely the sheer number of natural evils, which appears out of all proportion to their function, but the seriousness of these evils. As Mill noted, hurricanes lay waste on an incredible scale, a single frost can destroy all the efforts of a season, "nature impales men, breaks them as if on the wheel, casts them to be devoured by wild beasts, burns them to death, crushes them with stones like the first Christian martyr, starves them with hunger, freezes them with cold, poisons them by the quick or slow venom of her exhalations, and has hundreds of other hideous deaths in reserve."[4] If a cosmic mind wished to impress on men the importance of choice, it scarcely seems required that there be such a plethora of evils or that they be so utterly destructive. If, for example, there is a motivating power to disease in impressing on men the significance of their choices, would not the point be made effectively with just one disease of the magnitude of the common cold? Why do there need to be cancer, tuberculosis, leprosy, or heart disease? If we were to construct an analogy at the human level, it would appear obvious that a human parent who confronted his children with consequences of the scope supplied in nature would be considered immoral. How much more, therefore, would a cosmic being stand judged by such wanton multiplication of evil!

A third problem with this solution relates to the distribution of the natural evils, if their function is to impress on man the importance of moral choice. It would seem just that the consequences of the alternatives should be real options to the person who confronts them and not to the innocent or ignorant bystanders. How is the moral choice improved or made more significant to the person born blind? Where is the choice for the infant stricken by disease? If one were to reply that these events make choice more important for the parents, friends, or members of the society in which they occur, then we would be tempted to raise a question of justice. The children thus afflicted are being used as means for the moral growth of others, and this is not in accord with human standards of justice. Not only should the punishment fit the crime, but it should fit the criminal as well. If my moral sensitivity to choice needs to be sharpened, the failure to become aware of this should result in consequences to me, not to my neighbors. If, on the other hand, it were to be observed that we live in an interlocking world where the errors of the fathers are visited on the children, this would fail to absolve the character of a God whose imagination is supposed to be boundless and whose will for man is supposed to be beyond reproach. That we live in a world where such visitations occur, we will admit. What is not so admissible is that the world had to be this way in order for moral responsibility to be important.

If it is objected that all such criticisms as these are finite judgments of fallible man, and that while man would be indicted for such behavior, God ought to be commended for it, such objection becomes flippant and evasive. The only bases on which we are able to conjecture approval or disapproval, rightness or wrongness, truth or falsity, are human bases. To doubt that human beings are even in a position to analyze the solutions will mean that they are equally incapable of comprehending that there was a problem in the first place.

NATURAL EVILS ARE PUNISHMENT FOR MORAL EVIL

According to the analysis of Leibniz in his theodicy, a world of finite creatures must be a world of sinful creatures. A world of sinful creatures requires the punishment of natural evil in order that justice may prevail. Since God is transfinite, he has provided the minimum number of evils commensurate with this end; hence the maxim may be asserted that "this is the best possible world." While this theory raises questions as to the reasons for moral evil, they are not considered germane to the problem of natural evil. This is also the view with which the book of Job begins, and which constitutes the problem in the book. It was assumed by Job and his tormentors that natural evils were punishment for moral evil. In the context of this assumption, the moral goodness of Job introduces a contradiction. If Job was as good as he appeared to be, how is it possible that he received all these natural evils?

Moses Maimonides presents punishment for moral evil as one of three explanations to account for natural evil. There is a class of evils of this type which man brings upon himself. "This class of evils originates in man's vices, such as excessive desire for eating, drinking, and love; indulgence in these things in undue measure, or in improper manner, or partaking of bad food. This course brings diseases and afflictions upon body and soul alike." [5] The Epic of Gilgamesh, out of the Akkadian literature of 3000 B.C., maintained this theory also. The gods ordained that disease, death, and old age should be man's lot because man sins. Moral transgressions cause the sufferings of natural evil. The New Testament has many references to sowing sin and reaping natural evil. All of them aim to indicate that there is a justice in this plan. Great moral sins require great natural evils. In implementing this solution some Hindus and some theosophists have believed that the incidence of natural evils in the world corresponds in a one-one correlation to the number of moral evils committed in previous incarnations.

This solution has appeared to satisfy some theologians on a number of points. It is in the spirit of the Aristotelian desire for causal explanation. In this fashion each natural evil has its final cause in moral evil. The theory fits in well with the sixteenth-century commitment to excessive original sin. With the weight of sin so great, the justice of God demands retribution. In addition to this, it has some support in fact. We do, on occasion, bring the natural evils on ourselves. There is an obvious correlation between some human action and the experiencing of natural catastrophes. The moralist may point to the relation between the act of swimming in December and catching a cold, playing with matches and getting burned, or overindulgence in alcohol and experiencing a hangover. It is from simple facts such as these that the punishment thesis generalizes to a similar explanation for cancer, the Dust Bowl of the 1930's, and the latest epidemic of poliomyelitis.

The objections to such an explanation for natural evil have ranged from moral to logical. In the first place, it is objected that this solution misses the basic question. While the answer does indicate obvious and empirically founded causal connections between some human action and some natural evils, it does not really explain why there were any natural evils in the beginning. The problem is not one of figuring out what to do with natural evils, but to give plausible reasons why there should be any. To say that they exist in order to punish moral evils raises serious questions about the character of God. If this is, indeed, the mode of operation of the cosmic being, then we should criticize him for being outmoded in his penal theory. The modern versions of penology, for which the late Warden Lawes was a spokesman, reject the punitive aspect in favor of a rehabilitation program. We do not advocate the pit, the rack, the cat-o'-nine-tails, or the thumbscrew. In theory, at least, men are imprisoned in order to rehabilitate them, if possible. We are not slapping their wrists, we are taking their pulse. If God continues to operate in the medieval fashion, and if he is still claimed to be moral, then there is no way of understanding his moral aims or his character. If the punitive thesis is the one held by the cosmic being, then it would appear likely that he is immoral, ignorant, or at least callous to the finer human sentiments.

A second difficulty with this view is the one which troubled Job and the ancient Hebrews. There is something skewed in the distribution of natural evils. If these evils are to serve as punishment, then those committing the greatest number of moral evils ought to suffer the greatest number of natural evils. We would expect that the greatest scoundrels are in hospitals, that the floods destroy the farms of evil men, that frosts kill the crops of sinners, or that boatloads of rascals are the ones which sink into the sea. That this does not appear to be a defensible thesis is what bothered Job. He was a moral man, and yet he had natural evils come to him in a proportion not experienced by known evil persons. The hypothesis discussed in the book of Job that God was playing games with the Devil, using Job as the pawn, scarcely saves God's cosmic character. It was in part this objection which prompted Voltaire to write *Candide* in opposition to the Leibnizian thesis that the distribution of natural evils for moral evils was in proper balance. The Lisbon earthquake of 1755 provided the departure point for Voltaire's question. Were all the men, women, and children who perished in that holocaust evil? Were they so much more evil than those who were spared that their destruction was morally required? With all the recognized scoundrels in any given society, it would appear most likely that God is asleep on the job, or that he has turned this administrative matter over to a heartless monster. In either case his character stands judged as wanting in normal human decency and normal human intelligence. When we consider the children born deformed or dead, the ignorant savages penalized by disease, it seems incredible to claim that God has a retributive plan in operation. The punishment should fit the criminal. If God operates by punishing the nth generations for the sins of past generations, this is scarcely just by human standards. While it is clear that the kind of a world in which we live is precisely this way, that the bystanders are punished for the errors of others, the initial problem was not to describe what kind of world we have, but, rather, to explain why we do have the kind of world we have.

Among the many views held by Jews at the time of Jesus' ministry was the one that natural evils were punishment for moral evils. On one occasion (Luke 13:4–5) Jesus asked whether his hearers thought that the tower in Siloam had fallen on the greatest sinners. While Jesus clearly doubted that this had happened, he did warn his listeners that unless they repented they too would perish. Such an answer does not destroy the punishment thesis, although it does indicate that there were sinners who did not die when the tower fell. However, when Jesus was asked whose sins had caused the man to be born blind (John 9:1–3) he expressed doubt that sin had been the cause.

Both of the above objections raise such questions concerning the character of God that he must be either evil or incomprehensible. If he is perfect love, then punishment is incredible. If he is intelligent, then he should have been able to figure out a way of handling human sin without committing such errors in application. No parent could operate in the fashion attributed to God without being indicted by society as cruel, neurotic, or sadistic. Some religious thinkers have rested in the view expressed by John Laird. "There is a great deal of pain in the world, and much of it is peculiarly revolting, but I do not see how we are able to conjecture whether there is more of it, or less, than a divine regime would permit." [6] But this is to take refuge in ignorance, and to admit that the whole problem is beyond the ken of mortal man. In addition to this, it is difficult to maintain this bland confidence in a world which has so much of obvious human destruction in it.

NATURAL EVIL BUILDS CHARACTER

When Machiavelli wrote that "soft climate produces soft men," [7] he was reflecting a commonly held thesis that great personality grows out of harsh, challenging, and perhaps even cruel situations. Hegel developed this conjecture in his *Philosophy of History*.[8] Perhaps the great civilizations of the past have emerged because of the challenges of nature which they faced. In the warm climates there were too few spurs to imaginative thinking. Life was too easy to maintain, and, hence a weak, undisciplined, and unorganized citizenry was produced. An aspect of this solution is suggested in the book of Job. The dialogue between God and the Devil discusses the possibility that Job's faithfulness was not fundamentally great on the grounds that it was never tested by the vicissitudes of natural evil. The visitation of the catastrophes on Job and his family was to test this hypothesis. The spirit of the story would seem to indicate that the original doubt was groundless. Nonetheless, it is indicated that the purification and discipline of the natural evils was salutary in Job's case. It is commonly believed that the production of great art, music, and poetry requires personal suffering. The inference from this theory is that the kind of character required to produce something great will not be produced by an environment of milk and honey. Analogies are made to sports in this regard. The bodily discipline required for feats of athletic prowess is likened to the natural evils required for feats of moral character. Natural evils toughen the spirit. At the everyday level of human experience we can recall persons who faced trials and rose triumphant above them. It seems an easy inference from these facts to the thesis that natural evils were put into the world by a cosmic being precisely for this purpose. While we may laud those who are able to rise above their environmental evils, there is serious doubt as to whether this fact justifies the evils in the first place.

A first difficulty with this theory concerns its claim to produce high character, and its assertion that without such evils the great character would not have been produced. How would a Christian be able to press this thesis with regard to the character of Christ? If the tales are correct, he did not face any of the vicious personal limitations which plague so many born on the wrong side of the tracks. He appeared to be healthy, free from neuroses, untroubled by hurricanes, earthquakes, tidal waves, or any other of the events which were the lot of Job. Yet his character was pure, refined, and disciplined. Was he an exception to the theory? If he was, then he is no example of any use to the vast number of human beings who do not have it anywhere near so easy. The psychological data seem to indicate that more spirits are debased by suffering than are ever refined. When penology was punitive, great character was not the result. When natural catastrophes, such as floods, occur, the first step required is usually to call out the national guard to curb the animality, theft, and general destructiveness which seem to be the consequences of the natural evil of flood. That heroic deeds are performed in these crises is undeniable, but this is not the point. The original claim was that natural evils somehow raised the moral level of mankind, and that without these evils men would be swine, or mere vegetables. Even if it could be defended that without natural evils men are a rather diffident and debased lot, it still could not be established that natural evils make any improvement on this situation. Excessive suffering crushes most people; it does not lift them. If these things are psychologically and sociologically the case, then it cannot be maintained that a cosmic mind operates by flying in the face of them. If God knows what we know about the results of natural evils to human personality, he would have to be stupid, immoral, or impotent to act as it is claimed that he acts. In summarizing the claim that natural evils have an affirmative value, John Laird remarked, "Such arguments, then, must be accorded a certain weight, but although they are empirical they are also rather highhanded in what they say of empirical fact. We find empirically that some (perhaps much) suffering has a beneficial function, and we are entitled to surmise that frequently, when this beneficial function is not apparent, it may nevertheless occur. On the other hand, it would also be legitimate to surmise that some of the apparent benefits of suffering are illusory; and in any case we should be flying a very speculative kite if we maintained that all suffering must be beneficial because we know that some of it is." [9]

A second problem implicit in most solutions to the problem of natural evil is that the distribution appears unrelated to the need for disciplined character. Does deformity at birth help the character of the infant? Even assuming that it might at some later date, the *modus operandi* is so gruesome that it would be hard to get enthusiastic about the fact. If the theory is sound, we would expect that disease strikes more often on callous souls than on any other, and that hospitals are really institutions where characters of high integrity are built. Graduates from hospital beds should certainly be at least a notch above the common run of healthy animals. What evidence we have does not support either thesis: neither the notion that brutish spirits experience most natural evils, nor the notion that ex-sufferers are morally elect. Job was concerned with the former part. Why do the righteous suffer and the virtuous perish, while the evil men prosper? If this solution reflects God's judgment on natural evil, there has clearly been a break in the administration somewhere. Our deep-seated suspicion of the whole idea of spiritual purification is reflected in our attitude toward those called saints. What is so astounding about them is that they were as noble as they were, in spite of, not because of, the natural evils which surrounded them. If, when all is said, God really does operate in this way, there would seem to be no happy reason why men should follow his example.

NATURAL GOODS NECESSITATE NATURAL EVILS

This solution has enjoyed a certain popularity because of its common-sense plausibility. When Moses Maimonides reflected on the causes of natural evil, this was his first answer. We must have evil if we are to have the kind of good we endorse. "Genesis can only take place through destruction, and without the destruction of the individual members of the species the species themselves would not exist permanently. Thus the true kindness, and beneficence, and goodness of God is clear. He who thinks that he can have flesh and bones without being subject to any external influence, or any of the accidents of matter, unconsciously wishes to reconcile two opposites, viz., to be at the same time subject and not subject to change." [10] God was under a logical requirement when he put natural evil in the world, for the possibility of natural good requires the possibility of natural evil. Although Josiah Royce rejected most of the conventional explanations of the reason why natural evil is logically required, he did maintain the thesis on somewhat original grounds. "Yet now, in the moral experience, we have found a wholly different relation of evil part to good whole. My good act is good just because of the evil that exists in it as conquered element. Without the evil moment actual in it, the total act could be at best innocent, not good." [11] F. R. Tennant was equally suspicious of most explanations of the supposed usefulness of natural evil, but it still appeared to him to be a matter of inexorable logic that evil should be in the world. There simply must be physical evil. "It must be shewn that pain is either a necessary by-product of an order of things requisite for the emergence of the higher goods, or an essential instrument of organic evolution, or both. Short of this we cannot refute the charge that the world is a clumsy arrangement or an imperfectly adjusted mechanism." [12] The former he sees as accounting for human suffering. The latter accounts for animal suffering. In the kind of world in which we live, where human development is desired, we must logically have natural evil. When William James asserted that a world without gross evils would be insipid, lackadaisical, and wishy-washy, he was stressing the psychological necessity of natural evil for the production of moral progress. This psychological warrant resembles the theory that we need natural evils for the purification of great spirits.[13]

John Calvin defended a form of this explanation for natural evil. According to him, natural evils nurtured a proper contempt for this world, and a consequent expectation of a much better life to come. The host of natural evils teach us the vanity of the present life. Men, being naturally hedonistic, would wallow in the pleasures of this present world if it were sufficiently pleasant. Under these circumstances men would never aspire to immortality if the world of mortal life were too alluring. He conjectured, therefore, that God in his wisdom planted the vicissitudes of the flesh and the spirit to turn man's thoughts toward immortality. This makes of natural evils a necessary psychological contrast to the ultimate goods.[14]

Jacob Boehme entertained the question why God did not eliminate all the natural evils so that only good would prevail. His answer fits the pattern of psychological and logical contrast. He remarked:

> Nothing without contrariety can become manifest to itself; for if it has nothing to resist it, it goes continually of itself outwards, and returns not again into itself. But if it return not again into itself, as into that out of which it originally went, it knows nothing of its primal being.[15]

Like Calvin, Boehme saw natural evils as the psychic spurs which compel men to think about God and prevent them from resting content in the mere world of space and time.

A first difficulty raised by this solution revolves around the claim of logical necessity. It was said that a world of natural good logically requires natural evil. This assumption stems from a double misunderstanding. In the first place, there are no necessities in nature. There is no empirical state of affairs which is ever other than contingent. Physical events are the way they are. None of them have to be what they are necessarily. This position derives essentially from the nature of induction, the conclusions of which are probable at best. They are never necessarily true. A second misunderstanding may grow out of a reading into Aristotle's law of excluded middle. Aristotle's law asserts that the negation of any class is always possible. Given some class A, we can predicate the class non-A. The conceivability of the negated class does not, however, carry with it the assurance that the class has any members. The negation of the class of natural good, for example, may be an empty, null class. Assuming God to be an Aristotelian, we can assume that God predicated the class of non-goods, but we do not need to feel that he was under any necessity of giving members to the class. Logically, therefore, natural evil is under no necessity to exist.

A second problem is posed by the claim of psychological necessity. It is assumed that no one would appreciate the good or would labor for the good if there were no natural evil. There is a double issue involved. As far as the former claim is concerned, there appears to be evidence that we do appreciate health, good food, friends, etc., even though we have no experience of their opposites. Must the child drink sour milk before it can appreciate sweet milk? Must a man be unhappily married to appreciate an adequate marriage? There is a popular convention to the effect that the presence of prostitutes in a society raises the value of virgins. While contrasts may well supply motivation, does this mean that disease is justified on the grounds that it makes us appreciate health? Under such circumstances one would be tempted to recommend that we waive concern with whether the good is appreciated, if the price we have to pay is widespread disease. What this solution calls attention to is that in a world of good and evil we make distinctions. We may love the good and hate the evil. But all of this is after the fact, *post hoc*. Our problem was, "Why is there natural evil?" This solution merely tells us what our reactions are in a world in which there is natural evil. Even granting that natural evil is a psychological contrast to natural good of some consequence, there would still be the objection that there is far more natural evil than is needed to make this point. If sickness is needed to appreciate health, it is unlikely that leprosy, cancer, tuberculosis, and a thousand other diseases are needed before we can understand that health is good. There is more sand in the Sahara Desert than is required to lead us to appreciate our fertile acre. The question that we are raising is not whether we do in fact make contrasts between events experienced as good or bad, but whether there is any psychological necessity for doing so. Let us suppose that there is a psychological necessity for evil in order to appreciate good or to recognize it. Let us imagine that we are at a livestock-judging show and that our problem is to choose the best cow. Assuming we have criteria for identifying this cow, we should be able to say, "There she stands. She is the best cow." Suppose, now, that all of the other cows were removed and we were to bring a new judge, who uses the same criteria. We ask him, "Is this a good cow?" Does he need the poorer cows around for contrast to make his decision? Why would he need them? If he has criteria in the first place, he would not need any poor cows in fact in order to make his assignment of value. If, on the other hand, he had no criteria, then no number of cows would ever enable him to discover anything other than difference. He needs the preestablished criteria to tell which cow is good; he does not need poor cows. This is not to deny that since all judges of cows have already seen bad and good cows (by their criteria), they will in fact make comparisons, but this is beside the point. Our objection was not that people do not compare, but that there is no "psychological necessity" for doing so. Even if a "bad cow" were still claimed to be required, it is not required that she be an existent cow. A fictitious cow should do just as well.

THERE IS NO EVIL

This alternative is not, strictly speaking, a solution to the problem of natural evil. It is a restatement of the premises in such a way that the problem no longer exists. The original problem presupposed that we admitted the existence of natural evils. If there are no natural evils, then there is no problem to begin with. The popularity of this position, however, warrants that it be given a place in the list of historic solutions.

There are two senses in which the denial of natural evil has been meant, although in both instances it is the ultimate reality rather than the apparent reality which is being denied. To say that an event is not ultimately real has meant in some Christian Science circles that the event is due to an "error of mortal mind." Such believers stress the psychic roots of ailments such as headaches, neuritis, hay fever, and sinusitis. If man gains the proper mental attitude, the apparent reality of these sicknesses disappears. The first interpretation of the denial of the ultimacy of natural evil emphasizes the event. This view, while not denying the apparent reality of the experience, denies the ultimate reality. This position has particular application to psychosomatic ills. No one has meant to hold this view for such overwhelming facts as earthquakes, cyclones, and bodily dismemberment. There is, on the other hand, some plausibility in the Christian Science rejection of the ultimacy of headaches and muscle cramps, particularly in view of their contention that an event which is psychically rooted is not ultimately real. The second interpretation emphasizes the judgment that an event is evil. This position was held by St. Augustine, Moses Maimonides, G. W. F. Hegel, and Josiah Royce. These men do not deny earthquakes or headaches, but they deny that these are evil. In a world where everything is created by God there cannot really be any genuine evils.

Saint Augustine makes a very complete analysis of various theories concerning evil.[16] Each of them is dismissed as incompatible with the character of a transfinite God. His final word is that since God is good, and since he is the author of all there is, everything must really be good. "I perceived therefore, and it was manifested to me, that Thou madest all things good, nor is there any substance at all, which Thou madest . . . because each is good, and altogether very good,

because our God 'made all things very good.' . . ." [17] Moses
Maimonides held the position that evils are merely negations.
They are not the positive presence of anything. "It cannot
be said of God that He directly creates evil, or He has the
direct intention to produce evil; this is impossible. His works
are all perfectly good. He only produces existence, and all
existence is good; whilst evils are of a negative character, and
cannot be acted upon." [18] In the full sweep of the dialectic of
Hegel we see that evil is only apparent, a chimera, the result
of truncated vision. The whole is good. While the part may
appear to be evil, this error of mortal mind disappears when
the whole grand plan is unfolded. Christian Science, as
explicated by its founder, Mary Baker Eddy, shares this
Hegelian insight. Only good is positive, and hence real. Evil
is an illusion, a negation, and hence not real.

Leibniz held essentially that evil could not be real if God
were transfinite. Since God is perfect, it must follow that
what appears to be evil to man is actually an unknown, but
not unknowable, good. The admission that there may be real
evils in the world is an indictment of the character of the
perfect God. If God is indeed perfect, then it must follow
that whatever he does is done with the best intent and in the
best possible way. Leibniz' thesis of a "best possible world" lent
itself to caricature, as in the case of Voltaire's *Candide,* but
he was well aware that man can at any moment imagine
things better than they are. His "best possible world" was not
intended to be the best humanly thinkable world, but simply
that the nature of God required that this be as good a world
at every moment as it could divinely be made to be. [19] In the
conclusion to his *Monadology* he defended this belief in harmony and reasserted that, in God's good time, everything will
work out for the best.

The denial of evil is a natural consequence of the
pantheist position. If everything that there is is God, if God is
the only real reality, if the ultimate account of reality reveals
only God, then, it follows that there cannot be any metaphysical reality to evil. The original problem of natural evil is,
therefore, the result of an incomplete analysis based on a

finite picture of the infinite plan. Evil is an incorrect idea in the mind of man.

The chief difficulties with this view as a solution to the problem of natural evil are psychological. The position which denies the reality of the judgment of the evil of natural events defies human experience and human emotions. Even if the quality of evil is really unreal, the fact still remains that we experience this unreality with a vividness which defies all denial. J. M. E. McTaggart attacks the solution on two scores relative to this psychological difficulty. "There is no judgment about the good of whose truth we are more certain than the judgment that what is painful or sinful cannot be perfectly good. If we distrust this judgment, we have no reason to put any trust in any judgment of good or evil." [20] On the other hand, he avers that while we may err in thinking natural diseases evil, for we may be deluded or mistaken, "a delusion or a mistake is as real as anything else . . . it seems certain that a delusion or an error which hid from us the goodness of the universe would itself be an evil. And so there would be real evil after all." [21] To assert that all of this is merely the error of mortal mind strains both emotions and credulity. This is not to prove that evil is really real, but only that the denial that it is real is psychologically fantastic.

When William James pointed out the traditional difficulties with what he called the "theoretic way," one of his major contentions was that an emotionally intolerable position led to no practical consequences, and hence it would be pragmatically absurd to call it true.[22] This raises no logical objection to the original solution that evils are not real. It is logically possible that evils are illusions. The point of the objection is that it would be psychologically incomprehensible to believe in the nonexistence of something which is so widely and deeply felt to be a fact. If pain is not real, what could be real?

THE ANSWER OF BLIND FAITH

Many devout persons of religious faith feel that all intelligible explanations appear absurd. None seem to save the character of the transfinite God to whom they are committed. The classic response of this type appears in the words of Job, "Though He slay me, yet will I trust in Him." [23] We finite creatures cannot explain natural evils, but they must be for some good end, if God is good at all. Josiah Royce said that "however inexplicable they must now be to us, they are in themselves nothing that God vainly wishes to have otherwise." [24] Saint Augustine felt this to be the only adequate answer of religious faith. "For if it were not a good that evil should exist, its existence would not be permitted by the omnipotent Good God, who without doubt can as easily refuse to permit what He does not wish, as bring about what He does wish." [25] The Indian mystic, Tagore, saw no logical resolution to the problem of natural evil. He concluded, therefore, that "we must take it for granted that it could not be otherwise; that creation must be imperfect, must be gradual, and it is futile to ask the question why we are." [26]

Such stoic resignation and religious confidence have held positions of high esteem in religious circles. After all, if the essence of religion is faith, there is no other conclusion possible once reason has proved incompetent. While this is an attitude which can be taken with regard to the problem of natural evil, it is clear that it is not a solution. It is, rather, the claim and admission that no solution can be given. Once this point has been reached, faith steps in to provide at least grounds for assurance that all things work together for good, human experience to the contrary. In the wisdom literature of ancient Akkad the same last word is spoken with regard to natural evil. Throughout the Epic of Gilgamesh the existence of natural evils poses the question: "Why do these catastrophes occur to men?" The answers are always shrouded in mystery, and hence the message is that man cannot know what the gods have in mind when they send natural evils to afflict him.[27]

The objection of Spinoza to all attempts to reconcile natural evil and the character of God stems not from religious faith, but from a conviction that there is a basic error in premises. This error resulted from an analogy with human experience. It was noted by ancient man that human beings had purposes, that they projected plans not yet fulfilled, that they considered alternatives—that they were, in short, self-conscious creators. From the events in the natural world men made a similar inference to the supposition that there must be a first cause of all these occurrences. It was a natural leap to the position that this first cause likewise had purposes, projected plans not yet fulfilled, and considered alternatives. What more natural, therefore, than that the question should arise, "What did God have in mind when he created natural evil?" Such a question errs on several points. It overlooks the obvious fact that nature can be self-explained in the natural sciences without any appeal to a first cause. The whys and wherefores of all natural phenomena are explicable by analysis of the essential properties which these phenomena possess. In blaming God for every event for which we have not yet found the natural cause, we cast aspersions on his character, and make of him "the sanctuary of ignorance." [28] Finally, all formulations of the initial problem overlook the fact that classifications of good and evil are human-oriented artificial classifications. We act "as though there were any order in nature, except in relation to our imagination—and say that God has created all things in order." [29] Are good and bad to be defined by their relation to human desire, or to the degree to which they offend the human senses? He concludes: "There is no need to show at length, that nature has no particular goal in view, and that final causes are mere human figments." [30]

GOD IS FINITE

There is a long tradition for the position that there are some things which God cannot do, and that hence, in power at least, he is not absolute. Plato preferred the gods not to be omnipotent, this preference being based, in part, on the thesis that infinity is not an admirable quality. The gods cannot be the author of evil. They must be thought of only as being the authors of good. The gods are limited not only by the rational principles of order and control, but also by the

disorderliness of matter. There is a "drag" which obstructs
the gods. This "drag" is illustrated by matter with its recalci-
trancy and deception. The gods did not create matter. It
was coeternal with the gods, and hence outside their plan.
This is not to say that the gods are impotent, but that there
was at least one thing which they could not avoid. Even Saint
Thomas Aquinas, who held to an absolute God, admitted that
there was one limitation of God. He could not do the impossible. This logical limitation was interpreted in the tradition
of the logic of Aristotle. God could not evade the laws of
identity, noncontradiction, or excluded middle. This may
prompt the quip that it was odd that God should be thus
circumscribed by Aristotle. However, if God is to be logical,
there must be some things which he could not be permitted
to be able to do; namely, the illogical things. In addition to
this Saint Thomas admitted a second limitation. This is the
limitation which even absolute gods are under when they
choose. Every existential choice precludes all the other things
that might have been chosen. To choose is to self-limit oneself. God, being a creator, imposed upon himself this obvious
restraint. Once God chose the kind of world he was going to
make, and made it, then he was prevented from making any
of the other kinds of world that could have been made. While
he could have wiped the cosmic slate clean and started over,
any new start would have subjected him to the same limitation.

Moses Maimonides anticipated this analysis of Saint
Thomas. While Maimonides was not willing to call the inability of God to do the illogical a limitation, the fact remained that "we do not ascribe to God the power of doing
what is impossible." [31] Maimonides had no patience with the
old self-contradictory question, "Can God build a stone so big
that he cannot lift it?" It must be presupposed that a God who
is transfinite must be subject to the minimal requirements of
logical consistency. After all, if an act is impossible, no one
would call a creature weak who could not perform it. Strictly
speaking, however, the recognition of logical limits does not
support the kind of limited-God theory that we have in mind.

The classic formulation and defense of the limited-God thesis was made by John Stuart Mill in his essay on *Nature*. After one has analyzed all the proposed solutions to the problem of natural evil, the problem still remains, "Is the moral character of the God saved?" Every solution which we have considered, save the one which denies natural evil, predicates a god whose character is lower than that of a good man and whose intelligence is less than profound. There appears to be an impossibility in maintaining that God is at the same time all-good, all-wise, and all-powerful. All the former affirmative solutions save God's power at the expense of his goodness and intelligence. Here is a solution that saves God's goodness and intelligence at the expense of his power. Mill maintained, as did E. S. Brightman, that we must choose between goodness and intelligence, on the one hand, and power on the other. We cannot have a god with all three attributes when we have the kind of world we have. Mill averred: "The only admissible moral theory of Creation is that the Principle of Good cannot at once and altogether subdue the powers of evil, either physical or moral; could not place mankind in a world free from the necessity of an incessant struggle with the maleficent powers, or make them always victorious in the struggle, but could and did make them capable of carrying on the fight with vigour and with progressively increasing success." [32] The assumption that God struggles against the natural evils will give more psychological support to men in this world than any alternative theory. This makes men co-workers with God, a God who suffers with men in their struggles. Mill felt sure that even persons subscribing to alternative theories really did not believe that God was omnipotent in any strict sense. The goodness and wisdom of God would be jeopardized if we maintained omnipotence with any rigor.

This theory gains its support from its assertion that, after all, goodness and intelligence are more important than power. This is true at the level of human character judgments. A saint is a person who is good, and usually intelligent, but the power element is not pertinent. A weak saint is not a contradiction in terms. An immoral saint would be a contradiction. A stupid saint, while not a contradiction, would be unpalatable under most circumstances. Notwithstanding this, even the invincible ignorance of Friar Juniper, the friend of Saint Francis of Assisi, could not overshadow the beneficence of his character.[33] When it comes to a choice as to the attribute we could not afford to deny to a god, goodness wins first place. Intelligence would be desirable, while power seems expendable. We could reason as follows. If a person could identify the point at which a god was less than good, then, theoretically, a person could be more good than this god. The same would hold true for intelligence. Power, however, is not of the same order. If man can show where a god is less than omnipotent, it does not follow that the man is more potent than the god. It would seem obvious that religious persons would want their god to have higher attributes than they themselves possess. It follows, therefore, that power is the only attribute in which a god could be limited while remaining a god in the popular sense.

This solution assumes the same relation between the original premises in the problem of natural evil that is predicated by those who deny that natural evil exists. It is assumed that the two premises cannot be reconciled, that they are basically contradictory. We must choose, therefore, between denying natural evils and denying the transfinite nature of God. This solution prefers to deny the second premise, essentially on the grounds that to deny the first premise has insuperable psychological obstacles, and that, in addition, there would still remain germane moral objections to the apparent reality of evils, such as pain, even if in reality these evils do not exist.

The chief difficulties with such a solution are psychological. Logically the solution is consistent, although there may be serious doubt as to whether it is true. The psychological problem is essentially this: "Would a less than omnipotent god be worth the effort? Would such a being supply the religious and moral fervor which a God normally supplies?" While there are clearly many persons who find this limitation no obstacle, this will scarcely pacify the objectors. If a god must be transfinite, then the creature designated by this solution is not a god. While it may be germane to note that Hindu gods are not claimed to be omnipotent, it would also have to be added that they do not play the function which the Judeo-Christian God does. While McTaggart admits that the limited-God solution is probably the one best in accord with the moral character of God, he insists that there are consequences of potential damage to the whole god hypothesis. If God is limited at all in his struggle with natural evil, might it not be the case that he will in the end "be doomed to almost total defeat"? [34] Some may feel that to admit the least little impotency to God leads ultimately to the reluctant conclusion that God is powerless. The question of whether there is any logical reason for this inference becomes irrelevant in face of the widespread unwillingness of religious laymen to accept a God who is anything but absolute.

We have considered seven "solutions" to the problem of natural evil. Two of these, the fifth and the seventh, are restatements of the problem rather than solutions to the original issue. The five essential solutions all have the same Achilles heel—namely, the apparent impossibility of reconciling the fact of natural evil with the character of a transfinite God. The fifth and seventh reformulations aim to avoid this contradiction. While they do resolve the problem of irreconcilable premises, they raise new psychological issues of their own. The choice among these seven alternatives is, probably, a function of the personality of the chooser. To which kinds of difficulties can one reconcile himself? The simple fact that there are seven solutions, at least, suggests that we differ on what is acceptable. Suppose we are still to ask, "But which one of these solutions is true?" If we could prove the truth of the second premise, which asserts a transfinite, or unlimited, God, we could at least prove that some solutions are consistent. Few religious persons would claim to be able to do more than this. Theodicy, as a systematic account of the plans of God, is admittedly presumptive on the part of man. In spite of this, no problem rivals that of natural evil for psychological urgency. Every would-be theologian cuts his religious teeth on the attempt to resolve the character of God in the face of cosmic tragedy.

VIII

The Problem *of* Immortality

THE RELIGIOUS ATTITUDES toward immortality have reflected two opposing positions. There are those who, like Unamuno, maintain that the question of immortality is the only problem that "strikes at the very root of our being."[1] It is a problem which every man would wish to have answered in the affirmative. Everyone would, if he could, live forever. The desire for immortality, says Unamuno, is inseparable from the desire for God. The two beliefs go hand in hand. It is not that the universality and seriousness of the desire for immortality prove that there must be immortality, but, rather, that these make for the urgent and tragic quality which all discussions of immortality have. Plutarch wrote in the same spirit that "the hope of eternity and the yearning for life, is the oldest, as it is the greatest, of human desires."[2] Immanuel Kant held that belief in immortality was a necessary characteristic of any group which would wish to be called religious. He predicated that "since no religion can be conceived which involves no belief in a future life, Judaism, which, when taken in its purity, is seen to lack this belief, is not a religious faith at all." [3] On the other hand, there are those who, like Spinoza, assert that "a free man thinks of nothing less than of death, and his wisdom is a meditation not of death but of life." [4]

WHAT DOES IMMORTALITY MEAN?

The initial question which must be answered is, "What do you mean by immortality?" The answer to this definitional problem will determine what may be considered to be the evidence supporting or refuting immortality.

In Hinduism the religious devotees long for a metaphysical oneness with the principle of unity, Brahma, which does not entail or require self-awareness. While there is self-awareness in reincarnation, this is not what they consider to be the ultimate immortality. The goal is to become a "drop in the ocean of Brahma," in which experience one is no longer self-aware or self-identifying. An endless self-conscious life holds no appeal for many Oriental religious persons. Self-consciousness with all its attendant desires and pains is the thing to be avoided, not prolonged. The essential doctrine of the Upanishads refers to the belief that the soul of man and the soul of the universe are ideally one. The former is called Atman, the latter Brahma. While both polytheism and monotheism are in the Upanishads, the dominant theme is an attempt to answer the metaphysical religious question in some unitary fashion. The subjective soul (Atman) whose nature had been outlined in the Vedic period and the objective many gods (now unified under Brahma) found a synthesis in Brahma-Atman. This symbolized the union of objective and subjective. The famous formula, *"Tat tvam asi"* ("that art thou"), of the Chandogya Upanishad, specified this union of man and the universe. It has at least the spirit in common with Martin Buber's "I—Thou" and with Emil Brunner's "Divine-Human Encounter." Ultimate reality lies in the understanding of Atman as well as Brahma. The role of the self is the heart of the Upanishadic emphasis. Brahma alone will not suffice. To grasp the unity of self and world is the goal of the Upanishads. This unity is not a clear, cognitive whole, nor is it unambiguously a simple monism. The apparent negativism in references to Brahma-Atman is due to the nature of the issue. It entails an inner encounter of faith which cannot be intellectually expressed for those who have not had the encounter. To say that the view of Brahma is pantheistic would presume that the Upanishads are more specific than they are. While Brahma contains the universe, the universe does not exhaust Brahma. Brahma is immanent, but whether Brahma is pantheistic could not be clearly explicated. The Upanishads are not theological treatises. The stress is on spiritual experience, and not on theological reasoning. This explains the Upanishadic idea that while Brahma can be experienced, Brahma cannot be known.

It follows from this that the objective of these writings is not so much to explicate the truth as to provide a basis for inner peace. All solutions put forth in the Upanishads are tentative, not fixed or final. These many-sided writings have been the bases for the most divergent of Hindu views. As one Hindu has put it, "When disputes arise all schools turn to the Upanishads." [5] There are generally said to be 108 Upanishads. Only ten of these are said to be of primary importance. Some are pre-Buddhist and some are post-Buddhist. Both Tagore and Radhakrishnan maintain that Buddha is really in the spirit of the Upanishads, and that his movement is not really so heretical from Hinduism as is usually supposed. The motivation for writing these new scriptures grew out of dissatisfaction with the naïveté of the Vedas, on the one hand, and a feeling that the forms of Brahmanic worship were incomprehensible, ambiguous, or perhaps even empty. Serious doubts were raised as to the efficacy of Brahmanic ceremony or sacrificial acts that depended upon knowledge of Brahma, which it was impossible to obtain. All in all these writings possess the caution, latitude, and tolerance which have characterized subsequent Hindu dogma.

Speculation about the relation of the individual to the universe led naturally to reflection about how the union of the subjective soul with Brahma was to be achieved. Recognition that the event of union had occurred was called "entering

Nirvana." It was gained essentially by a mystical experience. To attain this mystic state one needed to achieve a condition neither conscious nor unconscious. Consciousness, because it maintains the subject-object distinction in knowledge, is defective. In unconsciousness everything is obliterated; hence it too is defective. The only Western term appropriate to what is experienced is, perhaps, intuition. What appears as negativism to many Westerners when they attempt to understand the Nirvana experience, is really the limitation of language which cannot explain in any cognitive fashion what is fundamentally an inner subjective awareness. About all one can do rationally is to indicate what the experience is not.

This limitation imposed by the natural language, which was set up for empirical discourse, ought not to be unknown to Western religious men. Saint Augustine, the medieval mystics, the modern neo-orthodox religious existentialists, such as Jaspers and Tillich, have all recognized that there are experiences which cannot be rationally accounted for. Tillich maintains, for example, that faith is not a matter of intellectual or volitional effort. We cannot think our way to faith any more than we can will our way to faith. To suppose that we could do these things errs in its analysis of what faith is. Faith is not an object of knowledge, hence neither reason nor will can lead us to it. If we have faith, we can think or will about it, but if we do not have the primitive encounter of faith, no amount of thinking or willing can lead us to it. Anyone who can appreciate the communication dilemma of Tillich can appreciate the problem that Hindus face when they attempt to explain to nonbelievers what the Nirvana experience is like. In this Hindu doctrine, as in Tillich's doctrine of the encounter, religion is an inward affair, necessarily involving a human participant. Language fails to express what has been essentially experienced, even as it fails in the love experience to make clear to one who has never been in love exactly what is going on.

If one must be a Brahman to be in a position to have the Nirvana experience, it was natural that the Upanishadic writers were concerned with whatever steps could be set forth to show how one could at least achieve the Brahman caste. The doctrine of Karma was intended to give this account. The term "Karma" meant deeds or works, and the general theory of Karma asserted that the deeds in a given incarnation affected the next incarnation. If one lived well, he might move up the caste scale in the next life. If one lived poorly, he might move down the caste scale in the next life. One of the clearest statements of this belief is found in the Chandogya Upanishad. "Those who are of pleasant conduct here—the prospect is, indeed, that they will enter a pleasant womb, either the womb of a Brahman, or the womb of a Kshatriya, or the womb of a Vaishya. But those who are of stinking conduct here—the prospect is, indeed, that they will enter either the womb of a dog, or the womb of a swine, or the womb of an outcaste." [6]

There were two views of the working out of Karma. The more moderate view expressed Karma as the law that what a man sows, that shall he also reap. A man's conscious good deeds in this present life so shape his soul that in the next incarnation this soul can fit into a more glorious body. This is a moral law of nature from which there is no escape. You must do good if you are to advance. If you do evil, you will retrogress. The Christian idea of praying to a God for forgiveness for sins is alien to Karma. Immoral action has certain fruits by virtue of a law, and no petitions can change the law. There was a more extreme view of Karma which asserted that even involuntary actions determined one's destiny. It was not simply a matter of consciously deciding to do good. Every sneeze, every chance occurrence, affected one's future. This appeared to mean that the individual person had no control over his next incarnation. He was in the hands of a fate which had taken the future out of the jurisdiction of human plan.

When the moderate view of Karma became linked with the caste system, a religious defense of caste could be made. The political, social, and economic lot of a man was his own fault. There was no point in complaining about the breaks or of raising the question of natural evil—"Why does God permit this to happen to me?" These things happen to me because of the way I lived in previous incarnations. What Judeo-Christians hold to be the rule within a given mortal life is held by the Hindus to hold across incarnations. As greater detail was worked out in the Karma steps, it was natural to increase the number of caste stages through which a soul might pass. Castes became subdivided until there were several thousand possible caste steps. In the early formulation of four castes, it might have been hoped that four incarnations would suffice to lead the most miserable soul to the status of a Brahman. With thousands of castes, and with the introduction of animal and insect forms as possible future incarnation shapes, a sense of overwhelming length and effort emerged. The cycle of incarnation development was depressing. The hope for the Brahman state on the part of a Shudra was so remote as to be inconceivable.

The early optimism of the Vedas became overshadowed by the cosmically long period of possible rebirths. It was against this, in part, that the later splinter groups, Buddhism and Jainism, protested. If men are to avoid utter despair, salvation must be achievable in a reasonably short span of rebirths. Samsara, or the cycle of rebirth, became for the Upanishadic thinker a desperate and gruesome thing to contemplate. Where the notion of rebirth had once been a source of hope, it was now the basis for despair. And yet within it all there was the sense of order and plan. No event was haphazard, no incarnation was an accident. "The law of karma," said a contemporary Hindu, "is the counter-part in the moral world of the physical law of uniformity. It is the law of the conservation of moral energy." [7] All suffering from natural evils had explanations. It was either punishment for moral evil, or it served the function of purifying the spirit in its upward march.

Coupled with the theory of the reincarnation of souls into many human forms was the thesis of the transmigration of souls, in which the soul may inhabit animals or plants. There were two views of the soul. There was the temporal soul, or temporal aspect of the soul, which was the soul of which we are aware in a given incarnation. There was also the eternal soul, or the eternal aspect of the soul, of which we are not aware in a given incarnation, but which is the soul that trans-migrates across incarnations. It was this latter soul that the early Buddhists rejected along with the transmigration theory, although they kept the temporal soul and the reincarnation theory. The general premises for this rejection seem to rest on the lack of empirical or experiential evidence for an eternal soul. A strong argument in support of this view was the lack of any memory links between incarnations.

The belief in both reincarnation and transmigration was not peculiar to Hinduism. Indeed, these views were rather widely held. Burial practices in certain sections of Africa, Australia, and North America suggest this conviction. The body is buried near the birthplace on the theory that it will be reinhabited. There seems to be no evidence that there was any indigenous Roman belief in metempsychosis, but both Horace and Vergil allude to Romans influenced by the Pythagoreans to accept the theory. Pherecydes, a Greek thinker of about 600 B.C., is said to have been the first of his countrymen to introduce the idea of transmigration of souls, reincarnation, or metempsychosis. The view was held by Pythagoras as well as by both the Orphic and Dionysian cults. The most distinguished Greek supporter was Plato, who developed the position in the *Phaedo, Phaedrus, Timaeus,* and the *Republic*.

The general spirit of Hinduism favors a view of im-mortality which does not entail self-conscious awareness. In the earnest search for oneness with Brahma, ego concerns vanish, and in the ultimate Nirvana we are no longer self-aware or self-identifying. The common belief among the Westerners, on the other hand, is that there will be more time during which self-aware persons will be consciously participat-ing. Even within the Judeo-Christian tradition, however, this common Western idea of self-conscious immortality is not universal. Some have held to an immortality of influence in the tradition of John Donne. "No man is an island, entire of itself; every man is a piece of the continent, a part of the main; if a clod be washed away by the sea, Europe is the less, as well as if a promontory were; as well as if a manor of thy friends or of thine own; any man's death diminishes me, because I am involved in mankind; and therefore never send to know for whom the bell tolls; it tolls for thee." [8] Here we find immortality not merely because we are remembered, but because in a pantheistic sense we are part of the Whole, and the Whole is never lost. The comfort which such a thesis holds has been little appreciated by most self-conscious persons. They want more than this. Being remembered is no substitute for remembering for oneself.

Yet Leo Tolstoy found such a conception not only psycho- logically adequate, but the only view consistent with the Christian position. He found the origin of this view in the Old Testament. The Jews did not talk about a life beyond the grave, in the conventional "Heaven" sense. The life we now live is good, and if we follow the laws of God we will experience immortality right now. Immortality is a quality of life experienced now, and not another life to be experienced in some other world. While later Christians viewed this present life as basically evil and hence postulated a new world for the new life of immortality, Jesus based his views upon the Old Testament and asserted immortality to be a quality of this present life. Note, says Tolstoy, that when Christ was asked by the young man how one could gain eternal life, he did not reply with any promise of life beyond the grave. "He says 'live' simply, and does not add 'forever' . . . the accomplishment of the will of God is the eternal life." [9] So live that your life is united with humanity and this shall be your immortality. The perpetuity to which Tolstoy refers is not one of bodily perpetuation in one's children. The line may die out and a people may perish. It is the life with Christ which is the immortality of Christians, for Christ never dies. When one lives the present life in the spirit of Christ, he gains his immortality in this present life.

Jesus, according to Tolstoy, opposed the doctrine of the resurrection at every occasion when the issue was discussed. The later Christian idea of personal survival after the death of the body played no part in the convictions of Jesus. For Jesus immortality was a quality of living in the present life, and therefore the way each person lived determined whether he would find his own immortality. Instead of immortality being a divine prize for shrewd living, it was an existentially won state of mind in which the individual was the key instrument. Another life beyond the grave is not, according to Tolstoy, part of the Christian promise.

Another view which shares some of the essential consequences of Tolstoy's position was expressed by John M. E. McTaggart. The whole idea of life beyond the grave is presumptuous, egregious, and impious. This is one of the dogmas of religion which deserve to be stricken from the records. The view developed by A. Seth Pringle-Pattison is an almost identical counterpart of that of Tolstoy. Mere endless duration of time does not contribute to the worthiness of human existence. After all, such duration could be shared by the commonest matter. What is more important about the concept of immortality is that it lends a tone of stability and a note of assurance that the present life is in the hands of a power which will not pass away. Immortality reveals a God in control of life, and the basic quality of enduring is his, not man's.[10] Further in the same vein he remarks, "He who has tasted eternal life is not wont to be troubled in heart about the question of his personal survival. . . . His immortality lies for him in his union with the eternal object on which his affections are set, and he seeks no other assurance." [11]

The metaphysical idealist, Josiah Royce, was equally unconvinced of the assurance of personal immortality. Royce did not wish to go beyond the reasonable data of science in making claims about immortality. Indeed, no man should really claim to have knowledge which transcends science. Faith may go beyond experience, but knowledge should contain itself within experience or within that which can be deduced from experience. The fact is that science gives no data about personal immortality. In spite of this plea of ignorance for personal eternalness he still felt qualified to assert that the Hegelian Whole of things was indestructible.

"Whatever happens to our poor selves, we know that the Whole is perfect." [12] This knowledge seemed, to Royce, adequate to give to man all the assurance which he needed, without the further private guarantee of endless personal survival. Since Royce, like Hegel, found ultimate reality to be the Whole, rather than individual personality, it is understandable that he was not particularly concerned about private immortality.

The above is reflected in the thought of Santayana, a most unorthodox Roman Catholic thinker. Immortality belongs to man solely by virtue of his reason. As man thinks, he finds an "immortality" in real satisfactions of the moment, in logical insights into timeless relations, and in ethical ideas of excellence.[13] Beyond these there is no "pie in the sky." "By becoming the spectator and confessor of his own death and of universal mutation, he will have identified himself with what is spiritual in all spirits and masterful in all apprehension; and so conceiving himself, he may truly feel and know that he is eternal." [14]

While the conclusion that there is no other world with another life is held by humanists, such as Corliss Lamont, it has none of the metaphysical element found in Tolstoy, Pringle-Pattison, or Santayana. For humanists, since the distinction between mind and body is chimerical, the expectation of immortality is an illusion. Whatever richness man may hope to achieve, he will gain it now or not at all.

A view of immortality which combines a putative description and an adverse evaluation has had vogue both within and without the circle of religious devotees. Sigmund Freud, who would scarcely be classed with the promoters of religion, saw the idea of immortality as a sign of man's basic uneasiness, frailty, and despair. The human longing for immortal bliss is reflected in the making of a myth to banish an otherwise intolerable and neurosis-producing situation. Immortality is a fiction which depressed and infantile men invented, on the theory that the misery of our present existence must have its compensation in an immortality of delight. From the father-figure which man invented, called God, each of his children will someday receive the gift of immortality as proof of his love. It was quite obvious to Freud that mature, self-respecting, and self-asserting men would have no psychological need for the solacing prospect of a future life. The expectation of immortality is like the child's expectation that Santa Claus will fill his empty stocking. This belief combines retreat from reality, the abnegation of personal responsibility, and the longing for a world of myth and fantasy to replace this cold and heartless life.[15]

Ludwig Feuerbach developed an analysis similar to that of Freud, in that the expectation of immortality was rooted in human inadequacy and in childlike delusions of importance. He predicated that man found the present world alien to his wishes and desires. Man assumed that there must be something better in store for him, so he invented God as the reified picture of himself, and had this God promise immortality. This type of reasoning Feuerbach saw as an interesting inversion of traditionally avowed belief. Man's assurance of God rested upon man's assurance of immortality. If there were no immortality, then there could not be a God. The requirement that there be immortality rested, in turn, upon man's assurance that he deserved something better than the present life had to offer.

A strictly materialistic idea of immortality was explicated by August Weismann. Immortality in his thesis was more than genetic, it was cellular and atomic. The term "immortality" does not mean life without a beginning or end, but "life, which, when it has once originated, continues without limit, accompanied or unaccompanied by modification (viz. specific changes in unicellular organisms, or in the germ-plasm of multicellular forms). This immortality is a movement of organic material, which always recurs in a cycle . . . and must at some future time, by the operation of external causes, come to an end." [16] His argument on behalf of this meaning for immortality is that it gives a scientific conception to an otherwise mythological term. While such an explication does lend a scientific note to immortality, one wonders what motivation might prompt any person, religious or irreligious, to adopt it as the meaning for immortality. The divergence from common meanings associated with immortality implicit in this idea is reminiscent of Protagoras' reconstruction of the laws of grammar, which paid little attention to how the Greeks actually spoke. One thing is clear, however: the question as to whether there is immortality is certainly a different one from that usually asked.

In order to approach the question "Is there immortality?" it will be necessary to specify which meaning of the term we have in mind. It will make more sense in the traditional religious contexts to suppose that immortality means, at least, more time during which there will be some self-conscious awareness. We shall assume that the question of immortality does not refer to biological matters, but to mental or "spiritual" continuation. If this is scientifically unpalatable, it is at least what Moslems, Jews, and Christians normally mean.

The arguments for an immortality of this general sort may be divided into two classes: those which derive from human desires and those which derive from purported factual data which reveal another life.

THE PRAGMATIC ARGUMENT

Fundamentally the great appeal of immortality is due to its promise that we will keep on living. Since most people find life tolerably endurable, at least most of the time, the idea of immortality has been emotionally satisfying and, according to William James, psychologically constructive. If a theory for which empirical data are lacking promotes emotional satisfaction of a constructive sort, and if it frees men from debilitating fears that prevent effective living, then, pragmatically, such a theory ought to be endorsed. While it may be objected that this approach is self-deceptive or delusory,[17] it is doubtful that most pragmatic believers in immortality are deceiving themselves. They are, rather, making their lives more endurable and reducing their anxieties by a conscious decision of faith. Plato's arguments in the *Phaedo* appear to be motivated by this simple and understandable desire to reduce anxiety. Charles S. Peirce once remarked that most, if not all, reasoning on emotionally important matters consists in finding "reasons for what the heart desires." This desire to live longer is almost universal. While the universality of a desire is not a datum which could prove immortality, it is a datum which accounts for the widespread approval which the idea of immortality enjoys. It may be objected that a mature man ought to be able to accept the prospect of his annihilation without so much fuss. The facts seem quite clear that we do not live forever. Why should our mere desire blind us to the brute fact that we are going to die, and that will be the end? In reflecting upon this stoic advice, C. D. Broad observed, "It is easy enough to think of anyone else as having really ceased to exist; but it is almost impossible to give more than a cold intellectual assent to the same proposition about oneself." [18] This is a psychological datum which, of course, provides only the motivation for the belief in immortality, and not the proof that there is immortality. Nonetheless, the recognition of this attitude will at least shed light on the reasons why so many cling to the expectation of immortality, even when no empirical facts seem to support it.

Ashley Montagu, for example,[19] sees no reason why immortality of influence ought not to be enough. Let us live on in the remembrance of others who were influenced by us! If one could be impressed by recognizing that he is a cog in psycho-biological, social evolution, and from this awareness gain solace from an otherwise pointless death, no pragmatic objection could be raised. It does not follow, however, that the desire for something more is the sign of an emotional glutton. The desire to live on is not very surprising, even though proof that we actually do live on seems quite incredibly impossible. It has been asserted that even if believing in immortality because it is so emotionally satisfying is to make the wish father to the thought, since there is really no evidence either pro or con, it would still be absurd to deny our wishes, when the alternative is equally indefensible.

It is precisely at this point, however, that the Buddhist finds his objection to an immortality of a self-aware type. The endless cycle of reincarnations with all the pain caused by desires and their frustration is something to be escaped, not something to be prolonged. The Judeo-Christian immortality continues on an endless scale a type of experience which the Eastern religious man wants to abolish. Even the psychic annihilation which oneness with Brahma entails seems preferable to endless personal struggle. Many Christians apparently share this Eastern distaste for endless life. These Christians speak of immortality as rest, peace, inactivity. These are words which might be used to describe the psychic mood which Nirvana entails. Feelings of this type do not attack the immortality theory, however, any more than those of the opposing type support it. What these feelings do suggest is that the emotional urges which lead many to predicate an endless life are not universally experienced. As a minimum inference from this we might observe that there does not appear to be any universal intuition or instinct for immortality.

While we shall discuss Plato's metaphysical argument for immortality in the next section, it is well to note at this point that in his discussions of the subject in the *Phaedo* and the *Gorgias* he is aware that a metaphysical argument alone is not sufficient to establish either logical or psychological grounds for the commitment for immortality. What is of far greater motivational force is that moral justice requires immortality. The very manner in which Socrates met his death demonstrated an assurance that it was not merely his metaphysical nature, but his moral character, which made further life necessary. The whole way in which the righteous perish and the wicked seem to prosper calls for immortality on the simple and inexorable grounds of elemental justice. Even when we admit that this is not an argument which proves immortality, we still sense that the idea gives meaning to all the metaphysical premises of Plato. If there is no immortality, then his discussions of justice and of the absolute good become empty in the face of the empirical misery which "good" men experience.

A more directly pragmatic argument for immortality was noted by Euphranor in Berkeley's *Alciphron*.[20] Here it appears that immortality serves the function of a sanction to moral living. The simple wish for immortal blessedness and the fear of immortal torment lead men to virtuous living. By inference we might draw the conclusion that moral living requires immortality, on the assumption that if this present life were all that man had, men would behave like "eat, drink, and be merry" hedonists. This hardly constitutes a proof of immortality, so much as it makes a case for the use of belief in immortality. If we were to be attracted to this type of pleading, a host of fictions would then be "demonstrated" on the simple grounds that they are psychic spurs to some kind of already approved end. The remarks of William James to the effect that morality makes more sense under a theistic hypothesis are in the same vein. They do not prove that there is an immortal state, but they do show that belief in immortality is pragmatically functional.[21]

It has been a common practice of evangelists to exhort belief in immortality on the grounds that it is an aid to moral living. It has been assumed by them that loss of faith in God's divine judgment will result in moral decline. If there were no promise of eternal blessedness or fear of eternal punishment, most people would lack any motive for abiding by any moral rules. One of the logical consequences of the view of "double predestination" was to remove this pragmatic function from immortality. If, as Calvin claimed, immortality was a gift of God, and not a reward for good deeds done, then it would have been reasonable for Calvinists to wonder why they should exert moral effort at all. If men were so afflicted by original sin, as Calvin seemed to believe, that they were incapable of doing deeds sufficiently worthy to warrant salvation, then belief in immortality could serve no utilitarian function.

The defense of Immanuel Kant is likewise essentially pragmatic. After he showed the impossibility of rational or empirical proof of immortality, he went on to show the necessity for believing in further life. He granted that immortality cannot be established by speculative reason, but he insisted that it is a postulate of morality. The moral law requires that men bring their wills in accord with the categorical imperative. The facts of human life show that this will not be accomplished in any time less than infinite. If what ought to be done really can be done, as Kant assured us, then immortality is required in order that the endless progress of men may become actual. Here, as in the preceding argument of Plato, we have not so much a proof of immortality as an assurance that the moral enterprise of man requires immortality. It may still be the case that there is no immortality, but if so, the idea of man's moral progress becomes incredible if not indefensible.

This same aspect of the moral defense for immortality was reflected in the comment of F. H. Bradley that "reflection on morality leads beyond it." [22] No culture-bound ethical analysis has ever sufficed, or will ever suffice. All moral discussions which are caught within a finite time will fail to be persuasive.

The explication by William E. Hocking proffers a pragmatic defense which purports to rest upon facts of human experience. The facts are that the ascription of meaning to human life is best approached by indirection. That is, we see the meaning of the present only in relation to the past and the future. To understand this present world requires, therefore, an "other world," [23] not just in imagination, but in reality. It is equally a fact that men live as if there were more time, or at least as if there were no temporal end to their existence. Living in this context of an eternal expectation elicits the best from men. It is not, however, the mere extension of the quality of currently felt experiences. Mere continuation of the duration of time is "a sign of a certain lack of inner dignity." [24] If one merely had more time, then he could either perpetuate the mediocrity which he has already demonstrated, or live further at a level far below the high achievements which have marked his past.

There is always the possibility, however, that people will merely spin their heaven out of their fertile imaginations, and that it will have no more reality than a conventional fairy tale. Hocking considers this as a possibility, but insists that if men "responsibly imagine," [25] the results of their imaginings will at least be "structurally possible in the given universe." [26] It is at this point that the role of the concrete experiences of freedom in a world of other people, and of live options, may show men the meaning of immortality, even if these experiences and options do not demonstrate the reality of immortality.

Fundamentally, pragmatic arguments for immortality have always been more enlightening for the question, "What does immortality mean?" than they have for the question, "Does immortality exist?" These pragmatic defenses rest for their greatest appeal upon the desires and hopes of man, not merely for additional time, but for additional meaningful time. The wealth of personal testimony regarding the importance of the belief indicates, if nothing else, that the expectation of immortality has shed a long and hope-producing ray of influence over the lives of those who have shared this dream. Even though William James in the preface to his Ingersoll Lectures on immortality admitted that the idea of immortality had never occupied a significant place in his feelings, the fact remains that there have been many for whom the opposite has been the case.[27]

THE METAPHYSICAL ARGUMENT

In the *Phaedo* Plato proposes an analysis of the soul in which eternal life is inherent. The analysis presupposes, however, prior agreement on the doctrine of a previous existence during which souls lived without bodies. It follows that if souls are immortal, then they are imperishable. If souls were able once before to exist without bodies, there is no reason why they should not be able to do this again. Plato mentions three entities which appear already to possess immortality and hence to possess imperishability. They are gods, the essential form of life, and the immortal in general. There is an empty circularity in all of this unless one can have the vision or the intuition of the soul as immortal to begin with. If one can have the vision, then it follows that the soul is indestructible.

One of the arguments for immortality given by Saint Augustine approximates an ontological defense based upon an analysis of the supposed metaphysical nature of statements in mathematics and the mind of man which discovers these statements. The premises of this ontological argument appear as follows.

    a. Science is eternal: it exists and is unchangeable.
    b. Whatever is eternal cannot reside in anything which is not eternal. (The term "reside" is used to express the relation of effect to cause: i.e., the effect resides in its cause.)
    c. Whatever is eternal, such as science, makes equally eternal that which is its vehicle.
    d. Science is in the mind of man, since it is a product of human thinking.
    e. Since that which the mind thinks is eternal, then the mind that does the thinking must also be eternal. Hence there is an immortality enjoyed by the mind.

A further argument is given by Saint Augustine in which he begins with certain specific mathematical truths, such as that two plus two equals four. On the assumption that this is an eternal truth, and that the mind is the seat of this truth, and that death can never occur to things which never change, then it follows that the mind which thinks eternal ideas must itself be an eternal mind; thus immortality exists for human minds at least.[28]

    The modern temper is too remote from this type of speculation to be much impressed. We look for the empirical data in vain in Saint Augustine's explication. Furthermore, the contemporary analyses of the nature of mathematical truth leave us unconvinced by any derivation from this field to immortality. We recognize that "two plus two is four" is certain precisely because it is defined so, and that it is incontestable because no claim is being made for the descriptive truth of mathematical statements. Man gives to mathematics what eternality it possesses. The modern mood is further unmoved by the medieval insistence that the cause of an eternal idea must itself be eternal, for this smacks either of drawing a definition from a definition or of deducing a matter of fact from a definition. In the former case, the result is empty and uninformative. In the latter case, the inference is invalid. As we recall our investigation of the nature of deduction and induction, the inference of Saint Augustine gives the impression of being made up out of whole cloth.

A more detailed analysis of the metaphysical nature of the incorrigible, or incorruptible (immortal) soul is found in Saint Thomas, who follows in the footsteps of Aristotle. As we have already seen in our analysis of the role of arguments for the existence of God, Saint Thomas does not intend to prove to an unbeliever that the soul is immortal, but rather to demonstrate to one who is already committed to the immortality thesis that it is according to reason to believe it. The argument begins with the assumption, therefore, that the soul is and must be immortal. The hypothetical thread which holds the argument together is the axiom that whatever follows from something by reason of its nature cannot be taken away from it. Saint Thomas notes that animality cannot be taken away from the nature of man, just as the property of evenness or oddness cannot be taken away from the nature of a number. Since everything that is has a form, it follows that existence cannot be separated from form. If the form of a thing ceased to be, the thing would cease to be. Some forms depend upon matter for their survival. The problem is, however, "Does there exist a form which can exist by itself without matter?" He asserts that the intellect is such a form. Since the intellect grasps universals, it could not be the result of a bodily organ. Each bodily organ is limited by its nature. The intellect appears to have no limitation; hence it has no bodily basis. This intellectual principle by which men understand is a form which has existence apart from the limitations of matter, and hence it is not subject to the decay of matter. It follows that the intellectual principle is incorruptible (immortal). This principle is either a man's soul or a function of his soul. It follows, therefore, that the soul is immortal. Thomas notes two additional arguments for the soul's immortality. On the one hand, it is the mind which grasps the concepts of corruptibility and incorruptibility. If the mind were corruptible it could not grasp incorruptibility. The second argument calls attention to the universality of the desire for immortality. Men do wish to be immortal. Since existence is desirable in its own right, it is reasonable that men should want to live forever. Since it is reasonable, and since God is on the side of reasonableness, it is clear that the desire for immortality cannot be in vain, but must have foundation in fact. It would be absurd that a reasonable idea, in this sense, should be false.

This is the type of inference which Immanuel Kant assailed so vigorously. Apart from the assumption in the argument that there is a soul in the first place, there is the more important element of ontologizing from the term "existence." Kant remarked that all arguments for the existence of God really reduce to the ontological intuition of necessary existence. From whence comes this insight that some entity must necessarily exist? After all, there are no factual data for which anything more than probability can be established. The method of induction, which is the proper procedure for discovering facts about the world, cannot prove that there are any events which exist by necessity. This means simply that inductions which aim to establish the existence either of God or of immortality can show that if certain causes exist, both God and immortality might well follow as effects. But at no point can induction show that there are necessarily existing causes or that there are some uncaused necessarily existing effects. While deduction is designed to establish its conclusions with necessity, one of two prices must be paid by the person using this method. Either he must accept his premises as true without proof, or he must have premises which are like definitions. If he takes the former alternative, then he will be accused of begging the whole problem, which is, "Are there necessarily true facts?" If he takes the second alternative, then his premises will be empty of information about the world, and his conclusion will share the same emptiness. The statement, for example, that evenness or oddness is a necessary property of numbers is based on the definitions of numbers bestowed upon them by mathematicians. We can classify our numbers in a great variety of ways: divisible by 9 and not divisible by 9; even and not even; positive and not positive; cardinal and not cardinal. All of these classifications follow from the way in which numbers are initially predicated.

Kant also raised a question concerning the predicative nature of existence. He maintained that this is not a term like "green," "run," "jump," or "salty." Indeed, even the deductive necessity of "green" as a property of grass does not warrant that grass will be found to be green. Likewise, even if existence were a predicate, there is no way of deductively showing that it would have to be. The certitude of deduction is always a function of the certitude of the premises. Where the premises are analytic, we can waive problems of existence, but then we can never show existence. Where the premises are synthetic, we can never show necessity for existence.

Historically, Judeo-Christians have had a preference for an argument which, in effect, reasons from the purported nature of God to the necessity of an immortal life. We may structure the inference by specifying the following premises.

1. If there is a God who is all-good, all-powerful, and all-wise, it may be assumed that he would do, and would want to do, whatever coherence required.
2. If we agree that human persons have an intrinsic value, that they are of supreme worth, and that they are, thus, made in the image of God, and
3. If we agree that there is not enough time in this mortal life for the development of the potential which human persons have, if we agree that all persons die with vast untapped resources,

   THEN:

   It would follow that absurdity, chaos, disorder, incompatibility with the facts could all be avoided if, and only if, there is really more time. Hence, man must be immortal, or else God is not transfinite.

All who are impressed by the idea of coherence feel an affinity for this reasoning. To be sure, the argument would not be able to get off the ground if we did not already believe in a God who possessed certain qualities. For those who believe, however, the inference is compelling. The alternative which we would face if we accepted the premises but denied the conclusion would be that we live in a world which makes no human sense. While it may well be that this is precisely the kind of world we do live in, most religious persons would not consider this possibility until after all other alternatives had been conclusively disproved. The unlikelihood of this ever happening is so apparent that the conclusion that immortality exists has great psychological weight. It is a conclusion which is consistent with the premises, and it is assumed that this implies both consistency and order in our world.

Objections to this mode of reasoning have usually raised questions about the demonstrability of the premises. This argument presupposes a God of such and such properties, and this in itself is a grand unverified assumption. The doubters raise all the traditional objections to arguments for the existence of a God in the first place. If there are serious doubts as to the truth of this particular premise, then there must be serious doubts as to the necessity of immortality. It will be impossible to assert that immortality is necessary if the existence of God is, at best, probable.

If one holds to the existentialist position that man creates for himself whatever value he possesses, and that, hence, there is no intrinsic significance which man may be said to have, then a doubt may be cast upon the second premise. If value is humanly invented and humanly bestowed, it would not follow that the universe had any obligations in the matter of immortality. Further, if biological evolution is more than a fiction, the human species may ultimately be extinct. Man will then appear to have been of no more cosmic significance than the woolly mammoth or the saber-toothed tiger.

While Immanuel Kant held no brief for those who thought that the existence of God or of immortality could be proved by reasoning from empirical data, he did believe that the mind demanded both to save the categorical nature of the moral law. When one has predicated, as Kant did, the role of freedom in moral responsibility, it follows consistently that one would also predicate immortality to give a cosmic setting to the supreme attribute of human freedom. God, the starry heavens above, and the moral law within were all assumptions which, for Kant, were required by the mind. Between a mental requirement and an existential fact, there is, however, a great unfilled gap. That this gap cannot be filled by reason at any empirical level did not detract from Kant's avowal that the mind did require these ideas for the sake of logical consistency.

do require of the mind nec., exist?

THE APPEAL TO THE PSYCHIC

To a Thomas, a Meister Eckhart, or a Jacob Boehme the assurance both of God and of immortality is immediate. Encounters of the type they assert give immediate evidence for the religiously devout. Psychological observations concerning the nature of such experiences to the effect that they are signs of neurosis or psychosis all miss the mystics' point. These men had experiences which, no matter how we psychoanalyze them, were exceedingly real. If these are psychotic, then, *vive* psychosis!

The modern counterpart of these experiences is to be found in claims of extrasensory perception, ectoplasmic visions, and audible discussions with disembodied spirits. A fascinating collection of reports is available for discussion. They include reports from séances of a semi-public sort, and a wide variety of private "supernatural" phenomena. People have claimed to have talked with departed relatives, written in the handwriting of former friends, seen shadow forms which looked like persons, and had a host of similar experiences. The inference which they draw is that these must be immortal spirits and that there is, therefore, immortality. "If that wasn't my departed Uncle John, then who was it?" This is the tenor of the argument. Its appeal has been undeniable. It supports a widespread human penchant for the fantastic, the weird, the inexplicable.

The major problems which have been encountered in making inferences from psychic phenomena to immortality have centered on two issues: first, the quality of the experiences which have been reported; and second, the propriety of the inference of immortality even assuming the psychic reports to be correct. On the former matter we have the reports of a large number of conversations. What is appalling is the triviality of the comments made. One might imagine that if these are departed spirits, then their minds must have degenerated. One could hope for comments of the stature of Plato's dialogues instead of the childish dialogue, "How are you?" "Fine." "Are you happy?" "Yes." "Will I see you again?" "Someday." The least that a departed spirit could be expected to do is to make significant comments. A person who has no more important things to say than to comment on his health and emotional life hardly seems to be worthy of being given an infinite amount of time. A. E. Taylor, commenting upon the vacuity of psychic messages, observed, "I do not think it too much to say of the most harmless of these 'messages from beyond the tomb' that, if they are what they claim to be, we can only hope that the unseen world, like the seen, has its homes for the feeble-minded, and that it is with their inmates that our occultists are in communication." [29]

Criticisms of the legitimacy of the inference have been more incisive. On the one hand, even the firm believers commonly admit that 99 percent of the events may be self-deception. The psychological contention that almost all such events can be explained in accordance with contemporary psychically accountable occurrences supports this admission. The small remainder of ESP occurrences are under the surveillance of trained researchers. The fact that psychology cannot yet explain these phenomena is no warrant for the inference that they must, therefore, have a supernatural origin. Even if we were to admit the correctness of the reports of psychic events, there is still a methodological problem. If events occur which cannot be synthesized into any available scientific hypothesis, what criteria must we establish if we are to pose a new hypothesis, such as that immortal spirits exist? C. D. Broad has suggested a number of equally "plausible" alternatives to the immortality hypothesis. He suggests, for example, that these data may support the conclusion that there is a very extended and complicated telepathy among living persons. This theory could account for all the psychic events. Secondly, he suggests that these psychic mysteries may imply the action of nonhuman spirits who impersonate dead human beings.[30] In neither of these hypothetical possibilities is the idea of immortality required. They are as consistent as the belief in immortality, even though the motivation to accept them does not come anywhere near that prompting the religious commitment to a life beyond the grave. The inference of immortality would appear, therefore, to be unparsimonious, a multiplication of entities beyond necessity. Perhaps, as F. H. Bradley commented, curiosity about spirits is not "in the proper sense religious at all." [31]

IS ANY ARGUMENT POSSIBLE?

From the point of view of contemporary physiological psychology, the whole immortality hypothesis is unconfirmable. If we are to study man scientifically, then we must define him operationally in terms of observable elements such as gross behavior and neuromuscular or cerebral activity. When man is so defined—and he must be so defined to be studied scientifically—then there does not appear to be any part of man which could survive the body, for indeed, man is defined in terms of this same body. In effect this means that there will be no evidence for a supersensible soul. Bodily death, and hence total human obliteration, seems to be a stark fact. It is no substitute to claim that we may be remembered by those still alive, or to assert the emotionally vacuous correlate of the principle of conservation of energy, that nothing is really lost.

This psychological position is a function of an epistemological one. In the tradition of logical empiricism it is predicated that no statement has any empirical meaning unless it is at least possible to make the kinds of observations required for assigning a probability weight. The physical laws which both prescribe and permit observation will clearly fail to allow the possibility that a disembodied soul might be found. It follows from this that the assertion that there is a disembodied immortal spirit is unverifiable, neither true nor false. Given this epistemological rule, no facts can be asserted to exist unless some sense data, directly or indirectly observed, occur. It would appear that we could make no prediction on the immortal-soul thesis which could ever be tested. It is interesting to note, however, that Moritz Schlick, a positivist in the Vienna Circle tradition, insisted in a debate with A. J. Ayer, an English positivist, that the immortality thesis was not meaningless. These men were not discussing the question of a disembodied spirit, but rather whether it would be possible to be aware of another life after this one. Schlick maintained that it could be verified by a person who attended his own funeral and knew that he was doing so. The mere fact that no one had reported doing so was hardly evidence that it could not be done. The absence of any evidence for survival after bodily death cannot be considered logically as very significant evidence against immortality.

The substance of James's Ingersoll Lectures on immortality is an attack upon the thesis that if physiological psychology is accepted, immortality must be rejected. It has not been established by the physiological psychologists that there is more than a contingent relation between mental processes and physical processes. Indeed, as both James and Kant aver, the death of the body may actually permit the proper functioning of the mind, on the somewhat Platonic thesis that the body functions essentially as a distorter of rational processes, and at best neutrally as a vehicle of or context for the mental operations. All that James intended to show was that immortality is a thesis consistent with science. He did not claim to show that immortality was empirically demonstrable, nor did he even intend to prove that the hope for immortality was universally of great pragmatic importance. This is obvious from the fact that he admitted that the immortality thesis had never occupied much of his own attention or concern.

The materialistic or physiological thesis, which asserts that personal continuation would be inconsistent with bodily death, may itself be subjected to some criticisms. Neither this thesis nor the preceding one is a validated metaphysic, and even if either were true, it does not follow logically that immortality could not be. It merely shows that from these premises we could never know that it existed. If materialism really were inconsistent with immortality, it would seem odd, to say the least, that idealists in metaphysics, such as F. H. Bradley and Hermann Lotze, should claim that their systems do not entail immortality either. While Lotze suggested, as a thesis consistent with his metaphysics, that souls will be immortal as long as their existence is necessary to the Absolute,[32] his basic stand on the epistemological question was that there was not, metaphysically speaking, any evidence for immortality. C. D. Broad concluded his analysis of the probability of immortality and the weight of the scientific data against it with the note: "Whenever we are told that 'Science proves so-and-so to be impossible' we must remember that this is merely a rhetorical form of 'Professor X and most of his colleagues assert so-and-so to be impossible.'" [33] The only empirical impossibilities would be self-contradictions, and it is not clear that immortality is such, even though it is clear that bodiless minds are inconsistent with the materialistic definition of man. Abraham Edel, a naturalist with as consistent a systematic basis for rejecting immortality as that of materialism, still contended that "questions about immortality are not well answered merely by showing that all perceptible consequences that could be deduced from the hypothesis that Mr. A now is a disembodied spirit are not verified or are unverifiable. They are better answered by examining the content of the idea until it appears as the demand for a richer quality of life in the context of collective insecurity engendered by the lack of control over nature and the conflicts of man against man." [34]

Purely rational arguments either for or against immortality have not been, historically, of much significance. The desire for immortality, where it is strong, has never required empirical verification for support. The lack of data to support immortality despite all efforts to establish them prompts very few to doubt immortality with much conviction. The belief in a future life has been one of those commitments which the eager assert without evidence, yet with great emotional comfort. The doubter, on the other hand, although he may lack the emotional drive to believe, also lacks the emotional concern to disbelieve affirmatively.

Frederick Barnard, president of Columbia University from 1864 to 1889, expressed the pragmatic potency of the affirmative belief. "Much as I love truth in the abstract I love my sense of immortality still more; and if the final outcome of all the boasted discoveries of modern science is to disclose to men that they are more evanescent than the shadow of the swallow's wing upon the lake . . . if this, after all, is the best that science can give one, give me then, I pray, no more of science. I will live on in my simple ignorance, as my father did before me; and when I shall at length be sent to my final repose, let me . . . lie down to pleasant, even though they may be deceitful, dreams." [35] Here is the emotional urge to believe in the absence of all evidence. Admittedly it is not an argument for immortality. It suggests, however, that the choices to believe or to disbelieve are functions of one's personality. Neither the affirmation nor the denial of immortality has any empirical evidence to support it.

There appear to be no empirical reasons for believing in immortality, but, then, there are no empirical reasons for disbelieving either. In such a situation a scientist would make no commitment. He would withhold judgment until either confirming or disconfirming data could be found. It seems to be a property of the religious temper, however, to follow the heart's desires in these matters. This is what faith commonly means. We commit ourselves before there are any scientific data to support us. This is similar to the commitment to belief in a God. The religious person is certain of his conclusion before there are any known premises. Arguments for immortality, like arguments for a God, are usually after the fact and beside the point.

IX

Is Religion *a* Matter *of* Knowledge?

I N MOST of the discussions concerning arguments for the existence of God, for solutions to the problem of natural evil, and for proofs of immortality, it was presumed that the subject before us—namely, religion—admitted of some logical defense. It was assumed that religious knowledge is possible. Since the available logical methods are induction and deduction, it was claimed by various defenders that inductive or deductive proofs for religious statements were possible. We shall now consider two types of views to the effect that religious knowledge is not possible. While the conclusion of both of these positions is the same, the premises which warrant the conclusion and the implications that follow from the conclusion differ.

The claim that some religious arguments transcend human experience, and are thus indefensible, has already been noted in our discussion of Immanuel Kant with regard to the existence of God and the proofs of immortality. We have further had occasion to consider objections to all reasoned defenses of religion from the point of view of a man such as Ludwig Feuerbach. His objection was that religion was an affair of the heart and that it rested on an internal assurance. The purpose of the inductive method is to establish the reality of some objects which have at least the property of being "out there." Since religion involves nothing external to the believer, no logic is really relevant to the issue of truth in religion. Religion being what it is, logic misses its essential core. In addition to this, Feuerbach noted that the expectation that there could be absolutely true premises gained by revelation was human self-deception. After all, Feuerbach insisted, man had created his gods in his own image, so that there really were no religious facts in existence. This fact, coupled with the semantic meaning of "existence," which entailed the claim that what was being discussed could be the object of a sensation, made all rational arguments hitherto put forth either contradictory or irrelevant. The following analyses rest on two divergent sources: on the one hand, the nature of logic; and on the other, the nature of religion and the nature of man, and hence of metaphysics.

REASON AND FAITH DO NOT CONFLICT: THE MEDIEVAL VIEW

The relation between reason and faith underwent a series of changes during the Middle Ages in the thinking of Roman Catholic theologians. For Saint Augustine epistemology was never the requisite introduction to religious metaphysics. In spite of his writings relating to the role of reason in faith, he never intended to develop a systematic theology. Reason, for Saint Augustine, as for Spinoza, was a means of helping men to achieve the beatific vision. At no time did Saint Augustine claim that man could reason his way to God. If he had been primarily interested in epistemology he would normally have been expected to be concerned with the question: "How is certainty possible?" He assumed, on the contrary, that of course we have certainty, and he directed his attention rather to the question: "How and why is it that we do, as a matter of fact, have knowledge of some certitudes?"

In his explication of the answer to this question he began with those areas where certainty is clearly in our possession —namely, in logic and in mathematics. We know for certain that $7 - 5 = 2$. We know also that either there is one world, or there is more than one world (he denies the possibility that there may be no world at all). We know that either there is a finite number of worlds, or there is an infinite number of worlds. Such propositions as these assert that we know for certain the principle of contradiction as well as the principle of the excluded middle. In addition to sentences such as the above, there are immediate experiences of man which indicate that certitude is an accomplished human fact. For example, the fact that we have doubts shows that we are certain of something—that is, that we do doubt. In his development of this position we find a version of the later Cartesian dictum, "I think, therefore I am," which now reads, "I doubt, therefore, I am certain that I do not possess an absolute insight." There is also a kind of certitude known by inner experience. We are certain, Augustine assumed, of our own existence, that we are alive, and that we understand. The fact that finite human minds can have such certainty becomes the basis for arguments both for the existence of God and for the immutability of the human soul.[1] Like Plato, Saint Augustine was more concerned with knowledge of the immutable than with knowledge that leads to God.

When we assess the Augustinian confidence in human reason, we find that it does not impinge significantly upon the area of religion. He was willing to admit that our sense experience has added immeasurably to our store of earthly knowledge. This he was quite willing to concede even though sensations are private. The important areas of human knowledge, however, are those which involve knowledge of eternal truths (mathematics and logic), common to all men. One of the difficulties which Augustine considered was this question: If the human mind can grasp eternal truths, and if eternal ideas are in the mind of God, does it not follow that the human mind grasps something of the essence of God? While Augustine's answers appear equivocal, one simple fact argues for a negative answer in his writing: he asserted that man's ability to grasp eternal truths was one of the proofs for the existence of God. This indicates that one could grasp eternal truths, but still not know God.

In spite of all that Saint Augustine had to say about human reason, there was never any question but that faith had logical and psychological priority. The function of reason was to make sense of faith. Under no conditions could reason jeopardize faith. In general this was the position of Catholic thinkers up through Saint Thomas. What disagreements there were centered on the degree to which the role of reason was significant. For Saint Augustine, at least, reason did not play a great enough part to result in systematic theology.

It was John Scotus Erigena (815?–877?) who produced the first great system of the Middle Ages. He maintained that reason was prior to authority, because true authority rested on truths found by reason. The authorities in question were the church councils, the Fathers, the theologians, or, indeed, anyone who interpreted church dogma. Prior to Erigena all questions of the proper interpretations of dogma were resolved by appeal to these authorities. In view of the many different interpretations put forth by conflicting authorities, this suggestion of Erigena was a step in the direction of bringing a univocal church view. He proposed that the authoritative claims of all theologians be grounded in some rationale. When Erigena asserted that reason was the final authority, he did not mean that a revealed dogma, such as the Trinity, rested upon reason. The priority of reason was in the domain of the explications of the Church Fathers as to what the dogmas meant or what they entailed. Reason was not required to establish that there was such a state of affairs as the Trinity. It followed, therefore, that while the dogma of the Trinity was final and absolute, the interpretations of the Trinity were tentative and probable. While he defended his own right, and that of others, to interpret dogma, he did not in any sense advocate a right to reject dogma.

In his arguments for God he insisted that we could not know what God is, but only that God is. As a consequence, all statements referring to God must be made in the negative —for example, "God is not wisdom, substance, or love." God is, according to Erigena, much more than these, but since we cannot know what the "more than" means, we cannot know affirmatively what God is. Like Saint Augustine, Erigena held that God had created the world *ex nihilo* (from nothing). Since the expression "from nothing" had posed considerable difficulty in the past, he explained it in such a way that an idea of cause and effect could still be maintained. To say that God had created the world "from nothing" meant that there was no thing in the space-time world from which the present world was made. God used no "thing." From the point of view of customary usage, the expression "from nothing" meant "from no physical or comprehensible thing." Whatever it was that God had used, it was ineffable to man, and what is ineffable to man may properly be called "nothing." As an interesting aside, we may note that Erigena claimed that persons before the Fall were not sexually differentiated. One consequence of the Fall was that sex was brought into the world. This would contradict the common Protestant Fundamentalist thesis that the cause of the Fall was sexual sin. After the resurrection, it was assumed, everyone would return to the sexless bliss of Eden. Erigena supported this position by appeals to Saint Paul, Saint Gregory, and Maximus.

In general we may say that Erigena insisted that revelation should be reasonable. He did not go so far as to recommend that a dogma should be abandoned if it could not be made reasonable. The dialectical subtlety which he used to fulfill this end, however, roused the particular objections of Saint Peter Damien (1007–1072). Since dialectics were not necessary for salvation, and since they did not really touch dogma, Damien had no sympathy with dialecticians. They put their faith in the principle of contradiction and presumed to judge theology by it. On the contrary, the Saint insisted, theology may refute the principle of contradiction, for God, after all, is not bound by a mere postulate of Aristotle. Objections of this type were not, however, sufficient to stem the flow of dialectical effort.

Saint Anselm (1033–1109) reasserted the basic Augustinian position with regard to reason and faith. "I do not seek to understand that I may believe, but I believe, in order to understand." [2] Faith and reason do not conflict, but faith has priority. It is the task of reason to show that faith is reasonable. If reason cannot do this, it should hold its peace. There was in Anselm's works no clear distinction between theology and philosophy. He gave reasons for the belief in God in the same spirit in which he gave reasons for the belief in the Trinity. In the Thomistic tradition, discourses to prove the existence of God would be called philosophy, while explications of the Trinity would be called theology. As a consequence, Saint Thomas would deny that there could be reasons for the Trinity, although he did allow that explications of what the Trinity means could be given. It must be remembered that Saint Anselm at no time doubted the revealed dogma. His belief that a rationale, even for dogma, could be given indicated the esteemed position which reason now occupied. We have noted in a previous section that Saint Anselm is famed for his ontological argument for the existence of God. It should also be remembered that he gave a posteriori arguments as well. His argument for God based on the facts of degrees of wisdom, and judgments about degrees of perfection, was an anticipation of the careful cosmological arguments of Saint Thomas.

Abelard (1079–1142) pressed the role of reason to a more extreme position than any other major Roman Catholic theologian. He held that if we do not understand rationally what faith is all about, then we should not assert that faith. He was a gifted dialectician. In the face of the obvious disagreements of the Church Fathers on matters of Christian belief (he noted 158 propositions on which the Fathers contradicted themselves), and since the time of supernatural revelation was assumed to have ended, it was clear that only reason could solve the situation. If Christians were to convince nonbelievers, they would have to develop a consistent and reasonable mode of persuasion. The success of Moslem missionaries in making converts among European intellectuals added to this urgency. In part because of the attack on him by William of Champeaux and by Saint Bernard, he was accused of heresy by Pope Innocent II and forbidden to teach any more. In spite of the fact that he contributed to the general fear of dialectic on the part of theologians, he did prepare for the great theological dialectic of the Scholastics.

The school of St. Victor in Paris, which had an Augustinian orientation, produced two chief scholars who added to the medieval resolution of the relation between reason and faith. Hugh of St. Victor (1096?–1141), a man of broad humanitarian sympathies, advocated learning in all the arts and sciences. In religion he urged the development of empirical arguments for the existence of God. These were based upon varied data, but all of them could be considered as proofs that rest upon experience. From the internal experience of the soul, which must have had a cause, he inferred cosmologically that there must be a God. From the external change of events in the space-time world, which must have had a beginning, he reasoned to a God as the cause. From the harmony of animal needs with a world which supplies those needs, he reasoned teleologically to a designing God. Like Saint Albert and Saint Thomas after him, he defended the position that an infinitely regressive argument is logically inadequate. In spite of all his enthusiasm for reason as the distinguishing attribute of man, he nonetheless insisted that it was no substitute for faith. Richard of St. Victor (d. 1173) also stressed the role of reason in religion and maintained that all arguments for God rested upon experience.

One of the truly great synthesizers in the Roman Catholic church in this matter of faith and reason was Saint Albert (Albertus Magnus, 1206–1280). His work was so important in preparing for the structure of Thomism that he has been called "Thomas' Socrates." [3] As a member of the Dominican order he spent the latter years of his life in scholarly activity. As a young professor in Paris he had Saint Thomas as one of his students. While he was sensitive to the differences between Aristotelian and Christian thought, this did not prevent him from embracing large sections of Aristotle's philosophy. In his enthusiasm for empirical observation in the field of the sciences he represented one of the early spokesmen for the a posteriori procedure.

Saint Albert, unlike Saint Anselm, distinguished between theology and philosophy. Theology dealt with dogma and operated by means of the supernatural light of faith. Philosophy was concerned with first principles and utilized the light of reason. He urged the use of philosophic reason in theology, even though he was aware that reason does not confirm dogma, on the grounds that reason could clarify meaning and interpretation. Philosophy, he insisted, was particularly helpful to the theologian in answering the attacks of opponents. Saint Albert borrowed from Aristotle the idea of a first necessary cause, which is the primary axiom in all cosmological arguments for the existence of God. Consonant with the Neoplatonists, however, he still held that God transcends all our thinking, and that, consequently, we know better what God is not than what he is. He held, also, that the immortality of the soul can be proved by reason. It was his genius to have seen the value to the Christian church of both Aristotle and the Arab Aristotelians. He saw that a rationale could be given to Christianity by adapting Aristotle to Christian dogma. It was this side of his thought which Saint Thomas developed, and which produced, as a consequence, the grand philosophic scheme of Thomism.

In the work of Saint Thomas (c. 1224–1274) the Roman Catholic Christian position on the relation of reason and faith reached a plateau from which there has been comparatively little retrogression.[4] In Saint Thomas the distinction between philosophy and theology was drawn in such a way that both the uniqueness and the relatedness of the two approaches were preserved. In the area of revealed theology some issues, such as the existence of God, were held to be demonstrable by reason, while others, such as the Eucharist, were not demonstrable. In either case, however, the light of faith took precedence over the light of philosophy. In the former area the term "mundane theology" indicated that reason and faith can corroborate each other. In the latter area, the term "revealed theology" indicated that while reason can explain, it cannot prove dogmas. Saint Thomas is not to be considered as either a philosopher or a theologian, nor as both a philosopher and a theologian, but, rather, as a theologian-philosopher. The two fields were inextricably related, and each would suffer by separation from the other.

His Aristotelianism was clearly distinguished by the fact that he began his mundane speculation, not with the inner life (as did Saint Bonaventura), but with the sense experiences of man in the world of space and time. While Saint Thomas believed that it was theoretically possible to discover a true metaphysics by the use of reason alone, he still insisted that such a metaphysics would be incomplete.[5] Reason alone, for example, could not discover man's divine destiny, nor could it arrive at the revealed dogmas which only faith could discover. But the metaphysics of Aristotle, which was both pagan and limited to reason, was a clear case of the incredible accomplishments which philosophy without theology could achieve. While the philosophic approach of Saint Thomas was in the spirit and pattern of Aristotle, his theology was still in the spirit and method of Saint Augustine. This latter was simply a reflection of his assumption that the ultimates of faith could not be established by reason alone.

The major achievement of Thomas was his defense of reason in religion. A man did not have to sacrifice his intelligence in order to be a man of faith. Indeed, this very thesis made it possible for pious men to pursue scientific studies with the secure conviction that they would not undermine religion. While a little study in this area was seen to be a dangerous thing, Thomas insisted that a wise philosopher would discover from his study of God and man that human beings seek a good beyond reason. Thus some faculty was needed to supplement reason, though not to contradict it. He assumed that the goodness and wisdom of God had provided supernatural guidance (faith) to fill this need. When such a position as this is pressed, it becomes clear that there never could be any real conflict between religion and science. Since both mundane theology and science have the support of reason, they must agree. In matters of revealed theology which are beyond reason, science has nothing to say either pro or con. A serious Thomist, therefore, need never face the problems of the Fundamentalist Protestant over whether geology and Genesis conflict or whether biological evolution threatens the Garden of Eden tale. It became apparent, however, that reason may make faith unnecessary in those areas where reason alone is competent. Would this not mean that any increase in knowledge would be followed by a concomitant decrease in faith? While an affirmative answer was given by Thomas, his additional remarks took away any sting which might have been inferred. "The reasons which are brought forward in support of the authority of faith are not demonstrations which can bring intellectual vision to the human intellect; and so the unseen is not removed . . . and hence such reasons do not diminish the merit or measure of faith. On the other hand, though demonstrative reasons in support of the preambles of faith, but not of the articles of faith (which depend on revelation), diminish the measure of faith, since they make the thing believed to be seen; yet they do not diminish the measure of charity, which makes the will ready to believe them, even if they are unseen." [6]

If we are to ask the question, "Is religion a matter of knowledge?" in the context of this Roman Catholic tradition, a qualified negative answer would seem to be required. While there was no question but that reason could put forth shrewd arguments for the existence of God, Thomas never assumed that reason alone would ever be sufficient to persuade an unbeliever to believe in a God. It was assumed that his readers already accepted by faith that there was a God. The most that reason could hope to accomplish was a demonstration that at this point reason and faith were consistent. It followed, therefore, that even in the area of mundane theology man could have knowledge of religion even though religion was not actually a matter of knowledge. In revealed theology the case was even stronger. In this area, the most that reason could hope to accomplish was to explicate the meaning of the revealed dogmas. Reason clearly could not offer a single cognitive argument to show the rationale of the dogmas. This is not to say that a Thomist would doubt that there can be a history of religion, a psychology of religion, or a philosophy of religion. What it does mean is that these are not to be confused with religion itself. Philosophy of religion is a matter of knowledge, but religion is basically a matter of faith.

Let us turn now to three further positions consistent with this conclusion. While all of the men we shall consider agree that religion is not a matter of knowledge, they disagree sharply on what follows from this decision.

FAITH IS NONSENSE: THE POSITIVIST VIEW

Alfred Jules Ayer, a British positivist, attacked the possibility of religious knowledge on the grounds that the nature of truth and verification, and the nature of religious statements, preclude the possibility that there could ever be genuine religious knowledge. Professor Ayer was chiefly concerned to indicate the requirements which any indicative sentence must meet if we are to say that it is possible to verify it. After several false starts at a stipulated rule, he finally concluded that "a statement is directly verifiable if it is either itself an observation-statement, or is such that in conjunction with one or more observation-statements it entails at least one observation-statement which is not deducible from these other premises alone; and I propose to say that a statement is indirectly verifiable if it satisfies the following conditions: first, that in conjunction with certain other premises it entails one or more directly verifiable statements which are not deducible from these other premises alone; and secondly, that these other premises do not include any statement that is not either analytic, or directly verifiable, or capable of being independently established as indirectly verifiable." [7]

What this rule essentially means is that no statement can be considered empirically significant unless some observable facts can be predicted from the statement. If it is assumed that religious statements do not refer to observables or entail any observables, then it would follow that no probability of truth or falsity can be assigned to religious statements. This would mean that religious statements are "meaningless" in the positivist or empiricist sense of the term. If no religious statements can be verified as probably true or probably false, then religious knowledge is clearly impossible.

In order to assess what this would mean, we need to explicate the nature of the positivist rule which declares religious knowledge to be impossible. The positivists and empiricists are aware that the epistemological rule with regard to meaningfulness is not itself meaningful. The rule is neither true nor false. While at first hearing this may appear to undercut the strength of the claim that knowledge of religious statements is impossible, it does not follow obviously that this is so. Every attempt to prove truth or falsity presupposes some epistemological stipulations with regard to meanings of the terms. "Truth" needs to be defined, and the "methods of inference" and the "tests of truth" need also to be given some agreed-upon meanings. Whenever we deal with the defining of terms, we are removed from questions of truth or falsity, because until we have taken care of the semantic question there is no way of determining what we could possibly mean by such a question as "Is this statement true?" At this point the problem is, rather, one of analyzing whether such defined meanings are fruitful, whether they enable us to make useful distinctions, and above all, whether they are of such a sort that it would be possible to show that any given sentence "X" could satisfy the requirements. If it is objected that this initial rule of the positivists implies that religious statements are meaningless, it must also be noted that no matter what rule we put in its place, some sentences would still be classified as meaningless. A rule which was so broad that it permitted any statement whatsoever to be considered empirically significant would be functionally useless. We would then have to share the area of knowledge with phrenologists, palmists, crystal gazers, and readers of horoscopes. Whatever the rule, some statements will be true, some false, and some neither.

The actual question is, rather, which statements would you be willing to have within and which without the knowledge category? The strong claim which Ayer's position has rests on the fact that it is implicitly accepted by scientists. Meaningful sentences must have operationally defined equivalents which are, in theory at least, capable of being observed. The remarkable contributions of experimental physiological psychology are due directly to their requirement that man be studied as a neuromuscular–cerebral–gross-behavioral creature. Clinical psychology, as well, operates on this observation data level. The whole experimental structure would be radically altered if we were to redefine verifiability so that immortality could become a matter of knowledge.

Ayer discusses this same issue in the context of the God problem. We have only two methods for inferring a God, deduction and induction. No matter which logic we use, the premises must be empirical descriptions. If they were analytic tautologies they would not be informative, and hence the conclusion would be uninformative. All empirical propositions, however, are probable at best. This would mean that any conclusion that there is a God would be a statement of probable truth or falsity. If "God exists" were an empirical statement, it should be possible to deduce other empirical or experimental propositions from it. Since this cannot be done, it follows that the original term "God" was not an empirical term. What is more, the term "God" is of such a nature that no conceivable factual premises could significantly entail it.

While all of this may seem abhorrent to religious persons, the result is not so gruesome as it would appear. If theism is not a tenable position, neither is atheism nor agosticism. It would follow, further, that there is no conflict between science and religion. While this means that there can be no religious knowledge, it also means that there can be no scientific refutation of religious faith. While there appears to be an inference on Ayer's part that religion must be rejected if religious knowledge is not possible, this inference is emotive rather than logical. Men like Immanuel Kant and George Santayana denied the possibility of religious knowledge, but emotionally they reacted favorably to religion nonetheless. The point is that even if religious knowledge is denied, the pragmatic value of religion and the emotional approval of religion are still consistent positions.

FAITH IS BEYOND KNOWLEDGE: THE EXISTENTIAL VIEW

The religious existentialist is in a long tradition of Judeo-Christian theologians who maintain that religion is a matter of internal assurance. Religion asserts faith commitments. It cannot claim knowledge. Soren Kierkegaard, who was certainly a prophet of this position, was proud to assert that religion was not a matter of rationality. Indeed, it was a source of great concern to him that so many religious persons thought that religious knowledge was possible. "The misfortune is not that Christian truth is never uttered . . . but that it is uttered in such a way that at least the generality of men attach to it no significance whatever." [8] He referred to the penchant for religious knowledge which had given rise to theologizing reasons for the existence of God, immortality, or the value of prayer. The absurdity of all such knowledgeable attempts was clear when we understood that the religious person was like the lover, not like the scientist. "But dost thou believe it could occur to him [the lover], dost thou believe it would be possible for him, dost thou not believe that it would be an abomination to him, to talk in such a way as to try to prove by three reasons that there is after all something in this thing of being in love?—pretty much as when the parson proves by three reasons that it is profitable to pray, so that this thing of prayer has sunk so low in price that there must be three reasons alleged to bring it a little bit into repute." [9]

In explicating what he called the determinants of faith or religion he showed that they entailed a relationship with God in which the individual was absolutely alone from church, home, friends, or state. The religious relationship was absolutely particular. In addition it involved a resignation with respect to the finite goods of this world. There was a double movement of the spirit in which the person, after infinite resignation to God, lived again in the finite, but in a God relationship which had no dependence on the understanding. The final teleological suspension of the ethical represented the awareness that divine ethics and human ethics are incommensurate. "For me the love of God is, both in a direct and in an inverse sense, incommensurable with the whole of reality." [10] Indeed, God and man cannot even talk together, for they have no language in common.

What does being Christianly religious mean? Kierkegaard considered several popular misconceptions. To say that a Christian was one who accepted the doctrines of Christianity did not answer the question, for it was still necessary to ask, "What are the Christian doctrines?" If the Christian was not the one who merely accepted a doctrine but clung to it in a certain way, and bet his life on it, then "How is a Christian different from a lover or from any committed person?" If a Christian was one who had undergone certain sacraments, such as baptism, then it still needed to be shown that baptism was either an orthodox doctrine, or that it made an emotional difference. Even those who emphasized baptism complained at how few Christians there were among the baptized. No, Christianity was none of these things. "Christianity does not lend itself to objective observation, precisely because it proposes to intensify subjectivity to the utmost." [11] What this means essentially is that Christianity is not a matter of probability statements. If Christianity were a matter of knowledge, then by virtue of the nature of induction and of deduction with informative premises, Christianity would be a set of approximate or probable statements. Nor is Christianity a matter of objective knowledge. Awareness of the Christian commitment is not like awareness of the color of grass. The grass is objective to me and my wishes, emotions, and thoughts. The grass remains what it is independently of what I think or feel. Religion, however, has no outside objective referent. It is a matter of inward experience or possession. It is precisely because scientific knowledge is approximate and because it is indifferent to the inner experience of the knower that science or reason cannot reach religion.

Is Religion *a* Matter *of* Knowledge?

In the nineteenth century, during which Kierkegaard lived, there was a movement of Christian biblical critics who thought that the truth of Christianity could be ascertained by a historical analysis of the Bible. But all biblical study results in mere approximations in historical time, while faith needs an eternal referent. Such approximations are "incommensurable with an infinite personal interest in an eternal happiness." [12] All such biblical scholarship is objective, while the problem of the Christian is subjective. Christians posit inspiration and, consequently, must object vigorously to critical investigations both by those in favor of Christianity and by those against it. Indeed, "if all the angels in heaven were to put their heads together, they could still bring to pass only an approximation, because an approximation is the only certainty attainable for historical knowledge—but also an inadequate basis for an eternal happiness." [13] What holds for the inadequacy of biblical analysis holds also for analysis of church history. While the Christian church has lasted an impressively long time, Hinduism has lasted much longer. No one will ever become a Christian through historical or biblical study. If one is already a Christian, it will be a matter of indifference what either history or biblical criticism reveals.

Here is a point at which all objective philosophers err. Christianity is not an objective given. The subject matter is not objective data but human subjectivity itself. In fact, if any trace of objectivity remains in Christianity, "it is at once a sign that the subject seeks to shirk something of the pain and crises of the decision." [14] Since the predominant mood of the Established Church of Denmark was that of historians and biblical critics, it followed that Christianity really did not exist in organized Danish religious movements. The inner assurance of religion was lost in the theological speculation of pretenders to religion. Religious knowledge is not merely irrelevant or impious, it is impossible.

A contemporary defender of a similar view is Paul Tillich. While the language in which his views are set forth gives the impression of rational theologizing, his position clearly is that religious knowledge, in the ordinary meaning of the term, does not exist. While he does refer to a "reason" beyond reason, as does Karl Jaspers,[15] the new use of "reason" bears no cognitive relation to either induction or deduction. "The object of theology," he asserts, "is what concerns us ultimately. Only those propositions are theological which deal with their object insofar as it can be a matter of ultimate concern for us."[16] This concern is infinite, unconditional, independent of situations, personal, participatory; it involves passion and interest, and entails personal choice or commitment. This concern must be of such a nature as to threaten or aid our very being. It must touch us at the point of our ultimate destiny. This rules out political, economic, or social concerns, as well as many so-called "religious" matters which are not actually of ultimate concern. This faith commitment involves the total person and indicates by its noncognitive nature that man is not essentially a creature of reason.

The grasping of this faith arises in a personal, immediate encounter. No one can even talk about this faith unless he has it, because this faith is not an object of knowledge, but a subjective experience. In his little book, *The Dynamics of Faith,* which is probably the simplest and clearest account of his position, he defends this view of faith against alternative theories. Faith is not an act of knowledge with a low degree of evidence.[17] There are, therefore, no objects to which we can attach probabilities by any demonstrative approach. If you can know the contents of "faith" it is not faith. Hence it is improper to speak of faith in the Bible, in Moses' Ten Commandments, or in God. These are matters on which traditional theologians claim there is not sufficient empirical evidence, so that faith is required to fill the evidential gap. But this makes faith a matter of weak reason, and, according to Tillich, this would subvert the absoluteness of the religious commitment. In the second place, faith is not an act of the will to atone for a lack of scientific evidence.[18] In a traditional Roman Catholic position this will to believe is given by the grace of God. This reverses the proper order, according to Tillich. If we have faith, we can be expected to will to believe. If we do not have the faith, no will to believe could ever create it. "Our oscillating will cannot produce the certainty which belongs to faith." [19] Nor, in the third place, is faith to be identified with a mere subjective emotion grounded in no content and without a demand to be obeyed. This would be to make faith whimsical and essentially an invention of human feelings. No, faith is none of these things. It is rather the name for a direct personal encounter with the "ground of being." The assertion of this faith is not the conclusion of a premised argument. It is the report of an immediate divine-human encounter.

The language of faith is symbolic, not literal. This is to say that the statements of faith are not descriptions which could be confirmed or refuted by evidence. Religious symbols, according to Tillich, have the following properties which set them apart from conventional linguistic symbols: [20]

1. They participate in the reality of that which they symbolize. The meaning of this is hard to grasp directly. Hence it may help if we note the meaning of the claim that conventional linguistic symbols do not share in the reality of that to which they point. If we were to take a symbol such as "Chevrolet," which points to a literal automobile, we could note that the Chevrolet car itself was made of metal, plastics, wire, and rubber, while the symbol was not. We could ride in the Chevrolet but not in "Chevrolet." Linguistic symbols claim none of the essential properties of the things which they symbolize. Indeed, these linguistic symbols have a remoteness from their referents which indicates that they differ radically from the thing to which they point. Religious symbols, such as "God," are the negation of this. While it would seem odd to express ourselves in this fashion, we might say that whatever we can do with God can be done also with "God." Religious symbols have ontological roots in the things to which they point. The symbol "God" originates in God. Even this may be unclear unless we recognize that for Tillich the meaning of the symbol is what concerns us and not any literal sign token.

2. Religious symbols cannot be intentionally created or destroyed. Linguistic symbols, on the contrary, can be either created or destroyed by acts of human will. "Chevrolet" can

be replaced by "Chevvy" or "Corvair." The only limits to the changing or creation of linguistic symbols are human imagination and clear communicability. Religious symbols are quite otherwise. No man deliberated and then invented "God" or "The Incarnation." These symbols cannot be intentionally created, because they arise out of an initial encounter with the referents which they symbolize. The first person to encounter the Incarnation saw immediately the symbolic meaning "Incarnation." The meaning of the "Incarnation" could never change unless someone had a new encounter with Incarnation which carried this new symbolic meaning. Tillich discusses what this means in the context of "water" as the symbolic meaning of "baptism." [21] It was not that some primitive man considered the possible elements which might be used for baptism, and concluded that water would be best because it was so precious. No, what really happened was that the first religious person to have an encounter with "baptism" (not to be confused with the actual events of baptizing) saw immediately that "water" was, of course, the symbol. By the same token, "bread" as symbolic of Jesus' body and "wine" as symbolic of Jesus' blood in the Eucharist encounter came from the original encounter itself. The first Christian to encounter the meaning of the Eucharist saw with his mind's eye (as if there were a tag affixed to the encounter) that "bread" and "wine" were the appropriate and authentic symbols. While no one is surprised when Chevrolets are called by new names or when the "long, low look" replaces the short, high look, or when ownership of such a car now symbolizes a degree of business success which the old Chevrolet never suggested, the religious person would be flabbergasted to have this occur for religious symbols. We are aware that modern businessmen do intentionally consider changing symbols of their products, and commonly do change them. We do not expect that theologians will confer on the desirability of replacing the "Atonement" with "Un-Atonement." The Atonement encounter precludes any deliberate changing of symbols.

3. Religious symbols open up levels of awareness not otherwise available to man. On the other hand, men may

utilize and value Chevrolets without even knowing about the symbols of them. Indeed, it would be peculiar to say that a knowledge of the symbol "Chevrolet" opens up for man levels of reality otherwise closed to him. In part, this may mean that religious symbols have this emancipating property simply because the encounters which they symbolize are so unavailable. The meanings are all that most persons will ever have of religion. It is more than this that is entailed, however, for religious symbols tell us something about ourselves which no other symbols could reveal. These religious symbols give us roots and meaning which we would otherwise not possess.

4. Religious symbols are not easily replaceable. Linguistic symbols, on the other hand, may be altered to suit the fancy of their creators. Since religious symbols cannot be intentionally created or destroyed, it may seem improbable that the occasion would ever arise when replacement of religious symbols would occur. At least two events could conceivably bring this about. In the first place, a new encounter with ultimate reality may reveal new symbols and, hence, give rise to the need for a replacement of the old symbols with the new. This contingency, however, is considered highly improbable—indeed, impossible—if the present Christian message is authentic. Another situation, which is more probable, might arise when a person reared in Judaism with its symbols is "converted" to Christianity with its new symbols. In such an event replacement of symbols would be required, and, as a minimum, it could be reported that this would not be easily effected.

Since the referents of religious symbols have the properties of privacy, incommunicability, and inaccessibility to objective examination, it would be inappropriate to speak of the truth or falsity of religious symbols. Tillich considers it proper to speak of the adequacy or inadequacy of symbols to portray faith; but since the referent of faith symbols is not publicly ascertainable, it would be meaningless to make truth claims for these symbols. It follows, equally, that it would be inappropriate to assert the existence of the referents of religious faith. It is true that theologians have for centuries been proposing arguments to prove the existence of God, and have,

hence, asserted the truth of religious statements. Tillich insisted that all these endeavors were really meant only as assertions of ultimate concern. No theologian ever intended the
logical form of his "arguments" to carry the significance. If
Tillich is right in this assumption, he is equally right in his
dismissal of all critics of cosmological, ontological, or teleological defenses for God.

Karl Jaspers and Rudolf Bultmann discussed a related
matter in the role of myth in the Christian religion.[22] Jaspers
maintained that the myths are symbols of faith. As such they
are neither true nor false. While he advocates demythologiza-
tion, he does not mean by this term the destruction of the
myths, nor the replacement of them by facts. He merely advocates recognizing them as myths to avoid meaningless arguments over their descriptive correctness. He calls this "break-
ing the myth." Bultmann, on the other hand, requires religious
statements to be factually correct, and advocates, therefore,
throwing out the myths. Tillich would concur with Jaspers and
oppose Bultmann.

While the conclusion that religious knowledge is impossible is shared by A. J. Ayer, Kierkegaard, and Tillich, they
differ both in the premises from which this conclusion follows
and in the inferences which are drawn for religion from this
fact. To be sure, they all agree that the nature of human
logic precludes the kind of absolute certainty which religion
demands. All three agree that religious statements are not
empirically informative. Ayer, however, stresses the requirement of epistemology for empirical verification in order that a
statement be significant. Since religious statements cannot
meet this requirement, he effectively advocates the dismissal
of religion on the grounds that it contains no cognitive assertions. Kierkegaard and Tillich, on the other hand, stress the
requirements of religious faith for ultimate meaning. Since no
statement of science can fulfill this requirement, they advocate the dismissal of science from religion. This situation,
where opposed inferences are drawn from similar statements,
indicates that the position that there is no religious knowledge
is not intrinsically inimical to religion. One point should be

noted—namely, that the inferences of both Ayer and Tillich are decisional matters. Whether religion is to be damned or praised for its lack of cognitive content will not be determined by a cognitive argument.

This situation has given rise to a lively contemporary issue concerning the usefulness of religion in the university teaching program. Is it necessary, for example, to include the concept of a "personal God" in such fields as chemistry, physics, or sociology in order that these fields be adequately integrated? Is a scientific education without the idea of God somehow incomplete in the sense that the science is not quite correct? The question is not whether the idea of God should be mentioned, for this would be required in any course which dealt with the religious ideas of the past or present. The question is whether a commitment to God is required, and whether this same commitment should be advocated or promoted by the university. Are God concepts functionless in the sense that they make no demonstrable difference to the academic enterprise? Suppose, for example, we were to discuss this question in the light of the view that God is like a father, that he punishes sin and rewards virtue, that he created the galaxy of all galaxies in time or out of time, from something or from nothing, that he is the necessary cause of all that is, that he has a Book in which he explains what he has in mind for the human race, that he receives requests and, on occasion, makes replies, and that he is that which provides value for the universe. Would such a concept have a necessary place in a university? It would be understood, of course, that such a concept might have a very different function in a church or for the personal peace of mind of a believer. Now, the notion of the uselessness of an idea is open to many interpretations. We might decide that any concept is useless if it fulfills one or more of the following conditions:

1. The statement in question cannot be assigned any significant probability weight by any department on the campus. No area has data which could make such an assignment possible.

2. The statement, when assumed to be true without

proof, leads to no specifiable consequences. Indeed, whether the idea is true or false, the scientific results remain the same.

3. No predictions of a testable sort can be made on the basis of the statement. Now, it would seem clear that Hume, Feuerbach, Kant, Kierkegaard, and Tillich would all agree that the concept of God is useless for a scientific education.

Does such a conclusion not make presuppositions about the nature and aims of the academic institution? Yes, it would appear that the university was assumed to be essentially concerned with the communication of demonstrable facts in the physical, biological, and social areas. But, surely, the university is also concerned with man's humanistic heritage, and is it not true that the concept of such a personal God is also part of our milieu? If this is assumed, then the concept of such a God would be part of the matter studied, along with information about Osiris and Isis, Ahriman and Ahura-Mazda, and the 330,000,000 gods of Hinduism. We might assume, however, that the discussion of the concept is not what is meant by the question of the uselessness or irrelevance of the idea of God. What is at stake here is, rather whether any concept of God is necessary for the adequate explication of the subject matter. If some concept is necessary, then it would be assumed that it is possible to assign a weight of academic respectability to this belief. The fact is that the sciences operate in blithe indifference to all God theories. Mathematics, physics, biology, and logic are all taught independently of theology. Further, it is generally assumed that belief or lack of belief in any God concept is intellectually irrelevant to good teaching or to adequate research. Suppose a psychology professor had convictions on the thesis that God punished sin and rewarded virtue. Would the facts of psychology with regard to disease and catastrophe in human experience come out any differently from what they would if the professor doubted this thesis? Clearly not. Suppose a physical scientist believed that a God created the heaven and the earth. Would his report of the age, constituency, and origin of the earth come out any differently from what he would report if he doubted this? Obviously not. Suppose a biologist believed that in some sense the Bible account of Genesis was correct. Would we expect his data on biological evolution to come out differently? We would hope that they would not if he aims to be a scientist. In the aforementioned sense, it would be clear, therefore, that concepts of God are useless for a university.

Even where two theologians might agree on the above analysis, at least two emotional responses might be forthcoming. A theologian might assert the uselessness of a God concept with a sigh of relief on the grounds that such a distinction saved religion. Feuerbach, Keirkegaard, and Tillich would seem to fit into this category. On the other hand, a theologian might admit the uselessness of God concepts with a moan of pain, for this would mean that such ideas could never be assigned a truth status and their referents could never be asserted to exist. Many medieval Catholic theologians would fit into this category, and not a small number of "liberal" Protestant thinkers who aspire to scientific respectability for their religion. There are traditions to support both the desirability and undesirability of useless religious concepts in the sense defined. There are, equally, traditions to support the scientific tenability of religious statements. The decision remains open for religious aspirants. One matter, however, is clear. Both Kierkegaard and Tillich deny the possibility of religious knowledge, and at the same time they hold that this is in the interests of the salvation of religion.

FAITH IS AN ILLUSION: FREUD

Freud not only denied religious knowledge, but insisted that even when the illusion of such knowledge is presented to religious persons, it is insufficient to motivate them by itself. The desires of man are so overwhelmingly potent that all argument pales into insignificance beside them.

When the question is asked, "What are the warrants for believing religious dogma?" three answers are usually given: [23]

1. Since our forefathers believed them, and since so many persons have found this adequate, we too should believe the dogma.

2. Religious literature abounds in religious arguments,

and these arguments have stood the test of time. If they were not valid arguments, would they not have been dismissed long ago?

3. It is irreligious to question the dogma, for such questions inevitably undermine the faith.

This last sentiment Freud saw as peculiar. Indeed, the natural inference from the prohibition against thinking is that the religious leaders know that their dogma cannot be defended, and this is why they make a religious dogma out of unquestioning obedience. As far as the first two "warrants" for religious belief are concerned, they would fail to be accepted in any field of science. The beliefs of primitive men are notoriously incorrect in every other area, since our ancestors were obviously less informed than we. Why should we imagine that religion poses any different situation? Is it not odd that the arguments for God and immortality, which are most persuasive, are the very ones which have been put forth in the far past? Why are there no new arguments in religion, considering that we have so much more information than our ancestors had? It is not just because religious arguments are so old that Freud raises his doubts, but because there have not been any new arguments. It does seem odd that persons who were in every other way less informed than we should have been able to exhaust the religious questions.

Freud takes particular issue with two alternatives which propose to avoid the problems of religious knowledge by admitting that religious knowledge is impossible, but maintaining that religious commitments are still defensible. The one option is that taken by Kierkegaard and may be traced all the way back to Saint Paul in the New Testament. This is to hold that the logical absurdity of religious claims is simply due to the fact that religion is beyond reason, and, hence, does not have to possess a rationale. The very multiplicity of religious claims still requires, however, that we ask, "Why should we accept this particular set of 'absurd' dogmas rather than some others?" How will the religious evangelist be able to make a case for his preferences when he is speaking to persons with another set of equally noncognitive preferences?

Is Religion *a* Matter *of* Knowledge?

The second alternative is that expressed by Immanuel Kant and William James, both of whom admitted that religious knowledge was not possible. This option consists of predicating religion as an "as if," which is justified on the grounds that it is so useful for human emotions and for already agreed-upon human ends. But why should we accept mere feeling as a better guide than reason in those precise areas where the stakes are the greatest? James saw the answer to such a question as obvious. It was precisely because the issues were great that reliance on emotions was warranted. Even if we admit that religious dogma are fictions, we still recognize that the alternative to accepting them will be emotional despair and death. The problem was that James believed that the emotional consequences of religious commitment were beneficial to man, while Freud insisted that the consequences of religion were disastrous. This is an empirical matter on which we have a wide accumulation of data. The facts do not, however, permit a univocal answer. Psychologists such as Carl Jung and Rollo May reported some religious commitments as favorable to healthy personality, while Freud reported the opposite. This very disparity of consequence may indicate that religion is not every man's tonic, since some appear to be sickened by imbibing it. The initial question, however, is still before us: "Is religious knowledge possible or desirable?"

THE LIMITATION OF RELIGION BY REASON: KANT

In *Religion within the Limits of Reason Alone* (1793) Kant analyzed the implications for religion of his earlier-established theses with regard to the limits of human reason. In the *Critique of Pure Reason* he had developed two basic convictions which influenced his religious conclusions. In the first place, reason alone gives us the phenomenal world, which, for all its law and order, is still not all that there is. Reason unaided cannot rise one iota above the everyday world of sense experience. In the second place, intuition, or firsthand contact with reality, reveals the possibility of a noumenal world. While these intuitive data furnish the mind with the raw materials for knowledge, and are, hence, essential to knowledge, they do not themselves constitute knowledge. This noumenal world is so structured that it cannot be grasped by man through reason alone. The relation between these two worlds was made clear through his discussion of the "Antinomies." These consisted of pairs of exclusive and purportedly exhaustive disjuncts, each of which led to absurdity when assumed to be true.

The Third Antinomy may be referred to as illustrating the essential problem. The thesis declares that every event has a natural cause in an *ad infinitum* sequence. But if this is so, then there is no room for freedom. The antithesis asserts that there is freedom, but if this is so, then scientific explanation becomes impossible. The dilemma here is one between science and religion. The two fields appear to be mortal enemies in the Third Antinomy. If the thesis is asserted, then freedom (and to this degree, faith) is lost. If the antithesis is asserted, then scientific respectability is sacrificed. Kant resolved the Antinomies in two general ways. On the one hand, he asserted that the whole problem arises only in the context of the phenomenal world. When applied to the noumenal world of things-in-themselves, these two options are meaningless. As applied specifically to the Third and Fourth Antinomies, Kant proposed a second solution. In this he asserted that while the theses apply to the phenomenal world, the antitheses apply to the noumenal world. Both may thus be true for their respective worlds. By this solution Kant put science and religion in two distinct and unrelated fields. This fact led one scholar of Kant to remark: "By banishing religion from the field of science, and science from the sphere of religion, he afforded freedom and independence to both." [24] At that stage (the *Critique of Pure Reason*) this solution was offered as a hypothesis only, since speculative reason cannot prove anything with regard to either immortality or God.

In 1763 Kant wrote an essay, "The Only Possible Argument for the Demonstration of the Existence of God." Here he affirmed that while it is necessary to be convinced of the existence of God, it is not necessary to be able to demonstrate it. In this essay his solution is a priori and speculative. While he rejected the Anselm-Descartes formulation of the ontological argument, he did claim that since it was impossible that nothing should exist, something must necessarily exist. In addition he held that this something was the ground of all else and must be simple, unchangeable, and eternal. Moreover, we can, he asserted, think of a being who does not reason discursively as man does, but is one who grasps intuitively the whole as such. For such a being, to conceive a plan is identical with having effected it. Any assurance, however, which man may have about such a being, as also about freedom and immortality, is of a moral nature only. There is nothing scientific or cognitive about such moral certitude. Even though the notion of God lacks any requisite rationale, he still claimed that theism was superior to all other types of explanation.

A dichotomy persists throughout the analysis of religion in *Religion within the Limits of Reason Alone*. Two accounts are contrasted—namely, what may be said for religion theoretically and what may be asserted practically. From the theoretical point of view Kant stated that "so far as morality is based upon the conception of man as a free agent who, just because he is free, binds himself through his reason to unconditioned laws, it stands in need neither of the idea of another Being over him, for him to apprehend his duty, nor of an incentive other than the law itself, for him to do his duty. At least it is man's own fault if he is subject to such a need." [25] On the practical side, however, morality "leads ineluctably to religion," [26] specifically through the idea of a moral lawgiver. Practically, such a God gives objective reality to otherwise subjectively necessary duties. Kant's later thinking, however, rejected this moral argument in order to purify his ethics of both heteronomy and hedonism, which the God thesis had introduced. Yet at this point in his development he maintained that "the idea of a moral Governor of the world is a task presented to our practical reason. It concerns us not so much to know what God is in Himself (His nature) as what He is for us as moral beings." [27]

In this essay religion is virtually reduced to morals, and the idea of a moral governor as he introduced it seems out of place. At one point he stated: "Religion is (subjectively regarded) the recognition of all duties as divine commands." [28] Somewhat later he restated this: "The one true religion comprises nothing but laws, that is, those practical principles of whose unconditioned necessity we can become aware, and which we therefore recognize as revealed through pure reason (not empirically)." [29] The moral improvement of man is "the real end of all religion of reason." [30] The inner moral certitudes which Kant was sure that all men could experience constituted the religious assurance. While from the theoretical position this moral confidence is a "mystery" (that is, it cannot be cognized or given an empirically grounded defense), from the practical position it can be known by each single individual. This practical assurance he called "a pure rational faith." Essentially in his development, such a faith has its ground in the person, and needs no external sanction; and yet he did feel at this stage in his thinking that there was some merit in adding to the inner experience an element of divine command. Though he saw this divine element later as an extraneous addition, it seemed desirable (and perhaps prudential in view of his difficulties with the pietist leaders in Germany) to introduce it.

So far, it would seem that a religion which was indeed within the limits of reason alone could, at best, predicate God and immortality as practically valuable and as theoretically possible, but in no sense could reason establish any logical defense for the truth of the statements concerning these two states of affairs. Reason lays down two requirements which any respectable religion ought to satisfy. First, the religious person ought to maintain a due modesty in his revelatory pronouncements. Second, he ought to use the scriptural narratives (if he uses them at all) in the interests of morality. With regard to the first of these requisites, Kant was aware that the average person requires more than mere reason in his religion. He demands revelation. Kant was not insisting that revelation be abandoned, but only that it be used with due awareness of its limitations. After all, revelations are beyond human rational powers to authenticate. Consequently, to assert these revelations as if they were cognitively certain would be hypocrisy. What is even more important, from Kant's view, is that a religion which bases itself upon revelation gives up "any rightful claim to universality." [31] Only a religion which is rooted in the universal claims of duty can ever become a truly universal religion.

With regard to the second requisite of respectable religion, Kant found that common ecclesiastical practice was considerably in default. Several specific ills deserve mention. There is, in the first place, the matter of original sin which seems to be so important to pietistic Christianity. In part, Kant's position rested on his view of man as a compartmentalized creature. Man has three predispositions, each arising by virtue of his being a certain type of creature. He has a predisposition to animality, by virtue of being a living thing. He has a predisposition to humanity, by virtue of being a rational being. He has a predisposition to personality, by virtue of being an accountable individual. While such a segmented view of man is alien to the prevailing psychological analyses of human nature, the conclusions of Kant would not be essentially changed even if he were to accept a more integrated picture of what man is like.

Essentially, the origin of evil in human nature may be considered from two points of view. There is, on the one hand, the question of the origin of evil in reason, which is concerned with the existence of evil. There is, on the other hand, the question of the origin of evil in time, which is concerned with the occurrence of evil in fact. Only the former question is of Kantian concern, since it alone involves the proper role of will in morality. It is a man's universal duty to rise to the ideal of moral perfection. To accomplish this requires a sense of personal responsibility, and an awareness that moral growth "begins not in the improvement of his practices but rather in the transforming of his cast of mind." [32] The latter view, which concentrates upon the origin of evil in time, has led the churches to hold that man is morally incompetent, and this, clearly, undermines practical morality in fact. Kant made the simple observation that "we may note that since we take for granted that man is by nature sound of body (as at birth he usually is), no reason appears why, by nature, his soul should not be deemed similarly healthy and free from evil." [33] The very notion of a moral culpability which was inherited, and which involved no act of will on the part of the inheritor, was inconceivable. Such a view undermined the basis of moral responsibility, and Kant therefore considered it "the most inept" explanation of the nature of evil which religion had invented.[34]

A second area in which ecclesiastical religion fostered practices inimical to the moral life was in "atonement" theories. In general, prevailing practice and belief in atonement were such as to lead to an evasion of human moral responsibility. Church practice gave the clear impression that virtue consisted in acts of penance designed to improve man's status with God, as if virtue could be bought by the performance of essentially mechanical genuflections. In this regard Kant asserted firmly that "the illusion of being able to accomplish anything in the way of justifying ourselves before God through acts of religious worship is religious *superstition*. . . ." [35] A man can do these things, he points out, without ever really being moral. By the same token, attempts to justify oneself by communion with God are religious *fanaticism*. This whole practice he called "fetish-worship," and the religious organization which promoted it he called "clericalism." [36] What was anathema in this procedure was that it undermined moral responsibility, and, in fact, it seldom resulted in any moral greatness. Indeed, religions which preach election or grace turn out rather shoddy characters.

Our original question, "Is religion a matter of knowledge?" has been answered in a variety of ways by Judeo-Christian theologians and philosophers. In part the answer depends upon what we mean by knowledge. On the simple assumption that knowledge consists of statements provable as true, the problem has been to find a method and the tests which could accomplish this end. If, on the other hand, knowledge is more intuitively defined, then perhaps the claims of certain religious persons to have immediate religious insights constitute sufficient grounds for the possibility of religious knowledge. The problem with this latter assumption, however, is that we then have to give up the requirement that claims of religious knowledge be provable. There is, at this point, an interesting historical question. How many religious thinkers ever in fact thought that religious knowledge was possible? Or, how many religious writers really imagined that religious knowledge, if possible, was significantly important to religion?

There has appeared to be a decisional element involved in this whole question. Perhaps religious persons will simply have to decide, first of all, whether they wish religion to be a matter of knowledge. On the assumption, rejected by some, that we should be logically consistent in religion, men might be able to decide whether religious knowledge would be advantageous in terms of the use to which they propose to put religious statements. Where religious persons have decided against the possibility of religious knowledge, no necessary disadvantages seem to have followed for religion. Where religious knowledge has been claimed to be possible, then the real problems have emerged. Are there really valid religious arguments, and are there actually empirical or experiential data to prove religious claims true?

X

The Problem *of* Inerrant Scripture

WHILE MOST of the major religions of the world have written scriptures, those in the Judeo-Christian tradition face a type of problem which is somewhat unique to them. In part, these problems which are peculiar to Jews, Christians, and Moslems stem from the early Jewish premise that their God not only spoke to men but that he wrote books as well. While all religions which possess a divine being have maintained that he communicated with mankind, only the above-mentioned groups fostered the thesis that the god put his inerrant words down on the pages of books. While devout Hindus may discover eternal insights, these insights always share an inescapable human property. They are always humanly discovered and humanly spoken or written. The Jews, however, put forth the claim that God himself announced insights, and that these were either spoken or written by persons who did not taint the revelations with any human fallibility. There was no chance of human error, no possibility of superfluous words, and no risk that the human factor had individualized the message or made it culture-bound. So precise was this purportedly divine writing that each diacritic mark was held to possess eternal significance. The New Testament remark became a mandate, that not one jot or tittle should be changed in the "authentic" text. The person who happened to be the amanuensis functioned as a mere tape recorder, and none of his personality touched the original message.

When this initial thesis of the absolutely nonhuman authorship of the scripture became coupled with the Greek belief in rational explanations for every phenomenon, then it posed very naturally the subsequent religious issues over the meaning of the scripture. For centuries the scholars of Judaism, Christianity, and Islam have pored over the sacred texts in the attempt to find the univocal and absolute rationale which they present. If the scriptures are inerrant, then the problem was to find a way to indicate inerrantly what the inerrant message was.

The belief in inerrant scriptures remains as a dogma of the faith in spite of the inability of man to substantiate this by any outside data. It is not that men have not tried to show scientifically that the creation of the world did occur as the book of Genesis records, or that the Flood took place; for scores of books are still in print which aim to show the empirical foundation for scriptural "history." Attempts of this sort must, however, come to terms with the phenomenon of parallels between the Bible and the writings of other, more ancient peoples. For example, the creation story is part of many cultures. Both Persian and Chinese similitudes of the Genesis tale are available. The idea of a six-day creation has its equivalent in the Zend-Avesta of the Persians, in Chaldean cosmogony, in Chinese myths, and in Etruscan legends. Would it not be a remarkable fact that the inerrant insights of the Old Testament should have been anticipated by so many other writings which are not considered to be inerrant? The same parallel situations occur in the case of the Flood story. Companion accounts are present in the writings of the Chaldeans, Parsees, Hindus, Persians, Greeks, Celts, and ancient Scandinavians. The same universality has been noted for the theme of the man swallowed by the big fish (Jonah story), and for the varied experiences of the erstwhile strong man (the Samson and Delilah story). The most striking parallels, however, occur in the case of the notion of miraculous birth for the messiah of the movement. Scores of half-man, half-god personalities were announced to be of virgin birth, spiritual conception, or in some fashion not tainted by the normal processes associated with being born. Such accounts were given for all of the following persons before Jesus: Krishna, Buddha, Codom, Lao-tsze, Confucius, Horus, Ra, Zoroaster, Hercules, Prometheus, Mercury, Apollo, Alexander the Great, Cyrus the Persian, Pythagoras, and even Plato. In each instance there are accounts which contain claims to authenticity. Where does this leave the person committed to the view of biblical inerrancy? Why should one account be considered more authentic than any other, since each is vouched for by a written testimony? To be sure, the orthodox Christian has tended to answer this question by raising another question: "How could an inerrant God have written an errant book?" [1] But this question begs the question with which we are concerned, and assumes that, of course, the Bible is authentic, inspired, infallible, and inerrant, and that the only real question relates to what we propose to infer from this dogma.

A recent Roman Catholic writer on this subject [2] asserted the authenticity of the Gospels on the grounds of the following suppositions. If we doubt the miracles reported in the Gospels, then how can we explain the impact which Christ made on his contemporaries? If we deny the inerrancy of the Gospels, then we cannot substantiate the place and authority of the Roman Catholic Church. If we suppose that the Gospels are the fabrication of mere human minds, then we must endow the writers with more ingenuity than mortal men are capable of expressing. If the Gospels are contrived, then we would expect the stories to be more embellished than they actually are; since the Gospels show remarkable restraint, they must be authentic. Finally, a religion as "wonderful" as Christianity must be authentic, and, hence, must have an inerrant scripture. It should be sufficient in investigating these double claims to see that they are far from making a convincing case. The same holds for the traditional attempts to let the Bible authenticate the Bible, by quoting passages within the scripture which indicate that what has been written is unquestionable. This is a procedure which would be quite unacceptable in any other field, and one which Christians would scarcely accept when presented by a Moslem for the inerrancy of the Koran.

No such problems have ever plagued the Hindu seer. The Upanishads, for example, were anonymous as to authorship. No one either knew or cared who wrote them, for if these Hindu insights made sense it was clearly not a function of authorship, human or divine. This was a far cry from the intense Jewish concern, for example, with the authorship of the canonical Old Testament books. The early Jew was concerned not only with who the author was but when he lived as well. Indeed, the prevailing view of the pre-Christian era Jews was that no book written after the death of the prophet Ezra could possibly be considered as authentic. The Christian scholars of the first three centuries had a similar concern with the problem of authorship. It was not that in either case the author was held responsible or given credit for what was written, but that God would have spoken officially only to men of stature in the community of the faithful. In addition, the Hindu philosopher never imagined that one could speak logically, factually, or informatively about ultimate matters. The Hindu scriptures were, therefore, admittedly poetry and myth. The authors "were not builders of systems but recorders of experience." [3] This is not to say that the Hindu ignored his holy books. The scriptures were diligently read in the company of a teacher. There was, however, no slavish study of the letter of the Word. Indeed, if a Hindu found some scriptural remarks to be incompatible with experience, he would reject the scripture. The Bhagavad-Gita records a discussion over the question of how one reaches true religion. The reply was: "Not by argument. Not by scriptures and doctrines; they cannot help. The path to religion is trodden by saints." [4] The same general opinion prevailed in Buddhism, for which "there is no canon comparable to the Bible for Christianity or the Koran for Islam." [5] Zen, in particular, because of its noncognitive, nondualistic approach, lay no stress upon scripture. The problems of biblical analysis or interpretation were always remote from the Zen spirit.[6] Zen, like the Hinayana tradition in Buddhism, held that Buddha wrote not a word. Clearly we do not find here the crying Christian concern with the proper and authentic interpretation of the word of God. Neither Hinduism nor Buddhism was ever a religion of a book. Nor were the seers of either group troubled by any need to make literal or metaphysical sense out of what had been written. Let us consider some of the elements which made up the Judeo-Christian commitment to biblical interpretation as necessary to salvation.

THE OLD TESTAMENT CLAIMS

At a moment in the history of the Hebrew people which is usually dated around 621 B.C., the importance of a book containing the sacred revelations of God to the Hebrew people became explicitly clear. For millennia these people had found their religious rallying point in their leaders, like Abraham and Moses; in symbolic artifacts, like the Ark of the Covenant; in the Temple in Jerusalem; and in the priestly classes who carried out the sacred rites within this Temple. In successive exiles the Hebrew people were carried far from their sacred land of Canaan and from the efficacious ritual of Temple priests. During these periods they had to conjure with the thorny question, "If our God is in the Temple at Jerusalem, is he not too far away from us in exile to be of any real help?" It was during the Babylonian and Assyrian exiles that the leaders of the Jews (laymen) invented the synagogue. This was a lay study house and a symbolic substitute for the distant Temple. Here the loyal Jews gathered to study their sacred heritage and to meditate on the disastrous sequence of events which had led to their displacement from the promised land. It was during this period that their prophetic leaders probably began the writing of the books which ultimately became the Old Testament. This substitution of a book for the Temple came as a direct consequence of the need for a new focal point which would symbolize the unity of the tribes and the perpetuity of the divine presence in their affairs. Judaism reveals, perhaps more than any other religion, a preoccupation with scripture, detailed analyses of passages, and commentaries which surpass in complexity the writings which they intended to clarify.

In the light of recent Christian biblical criticism, assisted by archaeological findings and linguistic tools, a wealth of varied notions has emerged with regard to the meaning and significance of this ancient document. In particular we shall have occasion to note the overwhelming sense of historical development which is revealed with regard to the religion of the Jews. No religion in the history of man shows so clearly the pattern which all ancient religions probably followed in emerging from primitive witchcraft to profound moral insights. In this picture Judaism is somewhat unique. One of the great archaeologists of our time has observed that "Buddhism and Zoroastrianism do possess conscious historical traditions, but these traditions are almost entirely attached to the persons of their founders, and modern historians find the greatest difficulty in offering any systematic reconstruction of their subsequent early history." [7] From the point of view of understanding the premises for the position that religions evolve, a grasp of the development of Judaism forms an intellectual spearhead which has pierced the dim veil hanging over the early history of all religious movements. The Old Testament is the document which gives us this ancient panoramic picture.

In addition to this historical contribution which the Old Testament provides, it stands also as the divine scripture for at least three of the major religious movements of the world. Judaism, Christianity, and Islam all study this book with pious reverence, and look to it for insights into both man and the ultimate. This was the book to which Jesus referred, although in the truncated form which was then canonized, as the source of final truth. It is easy to forget that when Saint Paul commended the reading of scriptures for "teaching, for reproof, for correction, for instruction in righteousness" he was talking about the Pentateuch and the Prophets of the Old Testament. This was the sacred book of the Christians for the first several centuries of their institutional life. So seriously did these early Christians regard the Old Testament that it was the norm for deciding which of the many available writings would be accepted as the New Testament. Eusebius, a fourth-century Christian historian, observed that among the criteria applied to determine New Testament canonicity a major one was the Old Testament.[8] Respect for Old Testament ideas was the basic requirement which all subsequent scripture had to satisfy. Any new book which spoke slightingly of the Old Testament God or the Old Testament prophets was rejected out of hand. These early Christians were not replacing the Old with the New Testament. They intended to shed new light on the ancient and honorable book which had been their heritage from the centuries of Judaism. It has been contended that Jesus never intended that a new book should even be written, and if this is the case, it may follow that he did not intend to create a new religion either. Both Friedrich Nietzsche and Soren Kierkegaard developed the thesis that Saint Paul institutionalized the differences between Judaism and Christianity. It was Paul who first enlisted Gentile Christians who had no roots in Judaism. It was also Paul whose ambiguous and conflicting views on Judaism made the clear separation of Christianity from its obvious religious roots. On the one hand Paul had said that the Law (Pentateuch) was holy (cf. Romans 7:12), permanent (cf. Romans 3:31), and that yet, on the other hand, this same Law was of interim use only (cf. Galatians 3:16–19). Paul had asserted the un-Jewish motto, "The just shall live by faith" (cf. Romans 1:17), and had assumed therefrom that the purpose of the Law was to show man that he could not achieve salvation by works. The Jews had held the reverse position.

Notwithstanding the conflicting attitudes of Paul toward the Old Testament, it was the book which Christians read in their Sabbath services. After all, this was the book which foretold the coming of the Messiah. Early in the second century A.D., as noted by Clement of Alexandria, Christians read the Old Testament to find evidence that the coming of Christ was in the orthodox Jewish tradition. In Acts 2:22–36 Peter attempted to prove that the resurrection of Christ was foretold in Psalms 16:8–11. Similar prophecy was believed to exist in Jonah 2:1; Psalms 89:4–5; 132:11; and 110:1. Peter also aimed to show in Acts 3:12–26 that Jesus was a prophet sent by God and predicted in the Old Testament (cf. Deuteronomy 18:15, 19; and Genesis 12:3), and that his crucifixion (Acts 4:8–12) was known and planned by God in the Old Testament (cf. Psalms 2, 22, 69, 118; and Isaiah 53). Paul, in spite of some anti-Jewish views, did lead the way for the expropriation of the Old Testament by the Christians. It is not our concern at this point to raise the obvious questions about the purported predictions of Christianity claimed to exist in the Old Testament. Suffice it to say that the Jews have found themselves amazingly unable to find such predictive information in their book. Indeed, the general tenor of modern biblical criticism is to look with suspicion on all such attempts to read Pauline Christianity back into the Old Testament. But aside from the empirical problems entailed in making a crystal ball out of the Old Testament, the fact remains that the Old Testament was the first Christian book. Its importance was reasserted in the fourth and fifth centuries by Saint Augustine when he used it as a model both for his moral concern and for the City of God.

WHO CANONIZED THE SCRIPTURE? THE OLD TESTAMENT

The idea of an inspired scripture appears to have emerged with the discovery in 621 B.C. of a Book, assumed later to be Deuteronomy, by Hilkiah, the high priest of the Jerusalem Temple. It is little short of incredible that the scriptural account of its "discovery" should be correct.

It would be hard to imagine a document of this length and importance lying unnoticed for long, and what would be even more astounding would be that no one was even aware of the existence of the book or that it had ever been written. Nonetheless, the scriptural tale probably indicates that there came a time in the history of the Hebrew people when the importance of a book superseded that of the Temple, and the leadership of laymen replaced that of priests. The conviction that this book which was discovered was Deuteronomy was held as early as the fourth century A.D. by Saint Jerome, a priest of the Latin church. The idea had come to him while he was engaged in his monumental translation of the scriptures into the Latin Vulgate version. The significance of this theory was not realized by biblical scholars, however, until 1806, when the German scholar DeWette reached the same conclusion. He saw the tale as symbolic of the ripeness of the time for a written word to replace priestly authority. Since the priestly authority which was to be replaced had an absolute appeal, it may not have been surprising that the earliest Hebrew proponents of scripture insisted that the books came directly from God, and that, hence, they had an authenticity which no merely human artistry could have produced. While tradition assigned the authorship of this first book to Moses, the unlikelihood that it could have lain for six centuries forgotten led nineteenth-century biblical critics to hold that the book was probably written about the time it was "found."

The remainder of the Pentateuch (the first five books in the Old Testament) [9] was probably compiled during the sixth and fifth centuries and canonized about 400 B.C. These five books remained for centuries the zenith of divine insight for the Jews. When the Samaritan schism occurred (335 B.C.) and this group of Jews withdrew from the main body of Judaism to build their own temple at Gerezim, they took with them the Pentateuch as their sole and authentic scripture. Like the Sadducees, the Samaritans never accepted the later canonized books. These five books are the Law referred to in the New Testament phrase "the Law and the Prophets."

The body of Old Testament books called the Prophets was probably canonized around 200 B.C. These books were normally divided for convenience and for chronological identification into the Former Prophets and the Latter Prophets. The Former include Joshua, Judges, Samuel, and Kings. The Latter include Isaiah, Jeremiah, Ezekiel, and the twelve minor prophets. Each of these books had to receive canonical status independently. There appear to have been at least two criteria which each book had to meet before acceptance as canonical. First, there had to be a popular demand and interest which would have caused the books in question to be retained and recopied. The second, and more essential, requirement was that it be demonstrated that the book was written before the end of the period of Ezra. The belief that the period of divine communication was completed by Ezra's time was widely held. Ben Sira, a Jewish leader about 180 B.C., wrote in Ecclesiasticus 44–49 that pre-Ezra authorship of sacred scripture was required. Since it was known that Ben Sira wrote Ecclesiasticus after this time, it never became canonical. The same requirement was asserted in the equally uncanonical work, II Esdras 14:45–46. The thesis was set forth again by Josephus, the first-century Jewish historian, in *Against Apion* 1:8. It was the opinion of many early Christian theologians, notably Tertullian, Irenaeus, and Clement of Alexandria. In 1536 the Jewish scholar, Elias Levita, stated this position once more. Since contemporary biblical scholarship supports the post-Ezra authorship of many of the Old Testament books, it is unlikely that the pre-Ezra requisite ever functioned as more than a fiction.

The remainder of the Old Testament, as we possess it, was not canonized until 90 A.D. at a council held at Jamnia. These documents, called the Writings (Hagiographa) had great difficulty being accepted because they appeared clearly to have been composed after Ezra. These Writings included:

(a) Poetical books (Psalms, Proverbs, and Job)
(b) The Five Scrolls (Song of Solomon, Ruth, Lamentations, Ecclesiastes, and Esther)
(c) Prophecy (Daniel)
(d) History (Ezra, Nehemiah, and Chronicles)

These books received their canonical status individually on the bases of their popular support, their national flavor, their rational consistency with already canonized books, and their proof of pre-Ezra authorship. The book of Esther, for example, had great difficulty being accepted because it insisted upon a feast not already prescribed in the Law, and because it did not mention the name of the Divine. The Song of Solomon, if it were read literally, appeared to have no religious allusions in it. Indeed, selections from this book were sung by balladeers in the bistros of Alexandria. It remained for the Christians to endow it first with a "spiritual" message. In any event, in 90 A.D., at the Council of Jamnia, presided over by Johanan ben Zakkai, the present scripture of the Old Testament was fully accepted as authentic.

There were still books which had been presented for canonicity but which had not made the grade. These Apocryphal, or "hidden" books represented the contribution of the Alexandrian Jews, who were very simply outvoted at the Council by the Palestinian contingent. These books were preserved by the Christians, particularly after the formal separation of Christian from Jewish synagogues after Bar Cocheba's rebellion (132–135 A.D.). Long before this, however, the Christians had demonstrated their affection for these books by quoting from them in the New Testament.[10] The Roman Catholic church accepted the Apocrypha of the Old Testament at the Synod of Hippo (393 A.D.) and at the Synod of Carthage (397 A.D.) in spite of the objections of Saint Jerome. The acceptance of these writings as sacred scripture was again ratified by the Roman Catholic church at the Council of Trent (1546 A.D.). It was formally asserted that "if any man does not accept as sacred and canonical these books, entire, with all their parts, as they have customarily been read in the Catholic Church and are contained in the ancient common Latin edition . . . let him be anathema." [11] This Roman position was finally confirmed by the Vatican Council in 1870 A.D.

The Protestants, on the other hand, followed the example of Saint Jerome in rejecting the Apocrypha from the class of sacred scripture. Luther, for example, regarded the Apocrypha as uncanonical but "good and useful for reading." The Westminster Assembly formally rejected the Apocrypha. The British and Foreign Bible Society refused in 1827 even to print the writings. They called them "those unhallowed productions of the wisdom and folly of men that have been so presumptuously associated with the sacred oracles of God." [12] And in addition to these fourteen Apocryphal books there were still others, called Pseudepigrapha (works written under an assumed name), which the Council of Jamnia rejected. Like the Apocryphal works, these Pseudepigraphal writings reflected a period of intense nationalism in aspiration, lay devotion to religion, and millennialist hopes.

In view of the scholarly analyses of these various rejected scriptures it may seem strange that most of them were not accepted as canonical. Most of them reflect the same high moral tone, the same profound religious emotions, and the same imaginative creativity as the accepted books. [13] In part, it appears as if the very rejection of a portion of the available contenders for canonicity reflected the internecine struggles between Palestinian and Alexandrian Jews for leadership. By and large the rejected books were the surplus of the Alexandrian canon over the mutually accepted Palestinian canon. Thus the Council of Jamnia determined not merely canonicity but church leadership as well. While all of the Apocryphal and Pseudepigraphal books failed to satisfy the pre-Ezra authorship criterion, the theory that all of the accepted books were indeed pre-Ezra in date was not supported by biblical criticism. Do we put the final decision down to a matter of the success of Palestinian taste and custom? Did the members of the victorious group at Jamnia believe that all the canonical works were truly pre-Ezra? Such questions, aside from the lack of evidence to answer them, do not touch the contemporary concern with scriptural authenticity. Canonicity would not be determinable by a first-century Jewish vote, even though such a vote would shed light on first-century beliefs.

WHO CANONIZED THE SCRIPTURE? THE NEW TESTAMENT

What developments led to the felt need for still more scripture by religious persons whose roots were essentially in the Old Testament? Several historical accidents have probably contributed to the emergence of a New Testament canon. From 41 A.D., when Jews who accepted Jesus as the Messiah were first called Christian, until the Bar Cocheba revolt led to the formal separation of Christian and Jewish synagogues, there had developed grounds for the felt need for new scripture. When Paul, Peter, and Barnabas brought non-Jews into the movement, this did raise a question of serious consequence. Many of the orthodox Jews saw it clearly as an undermining of the importance of the Law with its ritual, health, and dietary practices. If the Law could now be evaded, what principle of unity was there left to keep Jews united? When the beginning of the second century ushered in a Christian sect composed primarily of Greek Gentiles, it was natural to wonder whether this movement was really Jewish in any significant sense. By the end of the second century the membership was roughly half Latin and half Greek, but in any event, completely non-Jewish. When this exclusive Gentile membership became a fact, it was clear that the new church was not identical with the Jewish synagogue movement. Indeed, these Christian Gentiles seemed to lack a sense of historic root in the Old Testament. Nonetheless the sacred book for most second-century Christians was still the Old Testament of the Jews.

The whole question of the relation of the Christian church to the Jewish synagogue was further aggravated by the presence of Gnostic Christians, such as Marcion, who insisted that the Christian movement had no Jewish elements whatsoever. Marcion was perhaps the first Christian to attempt a delineation of which of the extant writings deserved Christian canonization. He taught in Rome that the Old Testament differed radically from the Gospels and Epistles. Indeed, they were so radically different that they must have come from different gods. He indicted the Law as having come from an inferior god, while the extant A.D. writings with which he was impressed must have come from a superior god. He developed this thesis in detail in his book *Antitheses*. He was convinced that Saint Paul was the only Christian who had seen this clear difference between Judaism and Christianity. As a consequence, when Marcion gathered his putative New Testament (c. 150 A.D.) he included ten of the letters of Paul, but only one Gospel (Luke). In part it was because of his cabalistic claim to mystical insight that the more orthodox Christian bishops pronounced his views anathema, but perhaps even more because of his vehement rejection of the Old Testament as a book with an inferior message. The dominant view among the Christians was friendly toward the Old Testament. Not only had this book been the canon of scripture for almost a century of Christendom, but they believed that they could find in it predictions of the coming of Christ.[14] If Marcion did nothing else, he at least compelled the more conservative bishops to undertake the task of selecting a Christian canon.

Justin Martyr reported that while most churches used the Old Testament in the middle of the second century, some churches did have lists of Evangels and Pauline Letters which they considered inspired. Clement of Alexandria (150–220 A.D.) said that the Alexandrian churches had four Gospels which were inspired, although not so inspired as the Old Testament. They also had some Pauline Letters which were inspired, but not so inspired as the Gospels. Eusebius, Bishop of Caesarea (313–339 A.D.) summarized the available books into three classes: (a) the recognized books: four Gospels, Acts, Pauline Epistles, Hebrews, I John, I Peter, and Revelation; (b) the disputed books: James, Jude, II Peter, II and III John; and (c) the spurious books: Acts of Paul, Shepherd of Hermas, Revelation of Peter, Epistle of Barnabas, Teaching of the Twelve Apostles, and the Gospel of Hebrews. In addition, he mentioned some books "so unworthy" that they were not even to be classified as spurious. These books were the Gospels of Peter, Thomas, and Matthias, and the Acts of Andrew and John. Eusebius held a deep concern for the problems of the early church in the decision of a canon of scripture. He asserted that the early church had in fact used two primary criteria. On the one hand they had rejected any book which spoke slightingly of the Old Testament or its ideas. On the other hand, they had also prohibited all books which spoke of Jesus as a wonderworker. Since the Gospels which were canonized do speak of Jesus' miracles, it may be inferred that they did not see these as wonders of the distasteful sort. A perusal of the uncanonized Gospels may throw some light on this. In these we find Jesus, as a small boy, winning at the game of hide and seek because he can see out of the back of his head, or healing sick or dead animals belonging to his playmates, striking his fellow toddlers dead when they irritate him, and in deference to the pleas of his parents bringing them back to life. It was probably not only the fantastic element in such occurrences but also the questionable moral and psychic attributes which such a boy would have possessed which led the early church to eliminate these from canonical consideration. Irenaeus, Bishop of Gaul (180–220 A.D.), asserted three criteria for canonicity: (1) The books must have an apostolic authorship. The author must either be one of the original twelve or else a direct convert of one of the twelve. (2) The writings cannot be contrary to "the rule of faith." This "rule" was probably the creed which Irenaeus had originally composed and submitted to the bishop of Rome for approval, and which was finally ratified at the Council of Nicaea in 325 A.D. (3) The writings must be supported by one or more of the "leading" churches.[15] He doubtless had in mind the churches under the jurisdiction of Rome. Saint Athanasius, bishop of Alexandria, in his "Easter Letter" on the canon (367 A.D.), identified the present twenty-seven books as being the authentic scripture. Saint Jerome reasserted this in 420 A.D., and Saint Augustine supported this list in 430 A.D. It was, however, the Synod of Carthage (397 A.D.) that gave the official church sanction to the New Testament as we now possess it. This gave the Christians a book of scripture which included the present Old Testament, the present New Testament, and the Apocrypha.

THE BIBLE MUST BE INERRANT: SAINT AUGUSTINE

While a current movement among Catholic scholars would limit the inerrancy of the scriptures to matters of faith and morals, Saint Augustine insisted that the Bible was infallible from beginning to end. The history was absolutely correct; so also were the poetry and similes, the reports of miracles and speeches, as well as the assertions of dogma. Not only were the scriptures inerrant in their truth, but it was impossible that there could be any contradictions between books. It became a duty of the Christian scholar to see to it that in his interpretations he did not give the impression of contradiction. "There are two things necessary to the treatment of the Scriptures: a way of discovering those things which are to be understood, and a way of teaching what we have learned." [16] On both of these matters Saint Augustine assumed that adequate criteria could be humanly discovered. The fact of the matter was, however, that variant interpretations were in circulation. It became essential, therefore, that guides be postulated for proper understanding. Since the Bible was practically (although not theoretically) necessary for salvation, man's eternal destiny would be jeopardized if biblical interpretation were at variance with some Roman Catholic dogma. "Faith will stagger if the authority of the Divine Scripture wavers." [17] The possibility of such a shattering of the faith was complicated, Augustine noted, by the fact that some of the scriptural writing was simile, some metaphor, some literal history, and some simply so obscure that even erroneous interpretation was unlikely, since no interpretation at all could be imagined.[18] Since the Bible was essential for salvation in the sense that it contained the divine message, it seemed obvious to Saint Augustine that God would have provided man with an infallible interpreter to settle the finitely caused chaos. Since the church wrote the Bible, Augustine saw no reason why it could not in fact be trusted to interpret it. When this confidence was coupled with the Augustinian assumption of an infallible spokesman for this church, there was no real problem in theory; although, in fact, the differences of interpretation continued, and have not yet been resolved in the twentieth century. Augustine assumed that what was necessary for man's spiritual health must be clearly written. The obscure parts merely support the clear parts, and serve the function of testing man's ingenuity and scholarship.

The biblical scholar, Augustine insisted, must be familiar

with Latin, Greek, and Hebrew so that he may read the various codices in the original. He should be familiar with the attitudes among the Catholic churches both on the matter of interpretation and on the matter of what writings were canonical. Preference should be shown for those books which all, or most, churches accept. The vote of large churches should be preferred to the vote of small churches, and the vote of churches with "weighty authority" preferred to those of lesser authority.[19] In comparing various manuscripts, considerable ingenuity was required in order to determine which represented the intent of the author. Augustine preferred Greek translations to the Latin translations on the grounds that the "more learned" churches attested to the superiority of the Septuagint Greek codices.[20] In his analysis of scriptural variants we may note the seeds of nineteenth-century higher criticism. He urged, for example, that translators be familiar with the milieu in which the books were originally penned, so that the author's meaning will be related to his own era and not to modern times.

Augustine's analyses of the problem of time (both *chronos* and *kairos*) in the context of the creation story of Genesis indicated something of the ingenuity which he demonstrated in his quest for the infallible word. The problem was simply this: If creation occurred as Genesis asserted, then it should have occurred as soon as possible. A transfinite being would not have dallied in an act of creation which had cosmic import. How could this Being have created the world "as soon as possible" if the world were created at a moment of time such that there was a time before the world was made? The problem was to explain why a God who planned to make a world as soon as possible did not make it sooner than he did. Augustine's answer presupposed a view of time. All time was present in thought. This mental property of time resembled the later views of Kant and modern physics. Augustine spoke of "a present of things past, a present of things present, and a present of things future." The conclusion at which Augustine arrived was that there was no "sooner" than the act of creation, because time began with creation, and, hence, the world was created at the soonest possible time. Prior to creation God was all that there was. Since God was eternal, and since in the eternal there was no time, it followed that prior to creation there was no time.[21]

INERRANCY IS INVINDICABLE AND FUNCTIONLESS

The claim that the Bible is the infallible word of God has been held traditionally by Christian thinkers, particularly those of the Protestant persuasion. The Roman Catholic sages have had less difficulty with this issue, inasmuch as they held that their church was an infallible interpreter of the Bible. Men like Saint Augustine could admit the allegorical nature of much of the scriptural writing without undermining the absoluteness of the faith, since, after all, the interpretations given by the church were absolute. The Protestant movement, however, has always lacked any official arbiter of scriptural meanings, and hence it has tended to rely on the thesis that the words within the Bible were infallibly obvious. When John Calvin asserted the literal inspiration of the Bible authors by God, he entertained the question, "But how do we know all this? I answer, the selfsame Spirit revealed both to the disciples and to the teachers that the author of the Scriptures is God." [22] This may be all very well for the disciples and teachers referred to, but what does a religious person cite as evidence in the twentieth century as proof that the disciples were not in error in their assumption of divine inspiration? Calvin had no reply to such a query. Indeed, Protestants in the sixteenth-century tradition have never been in a position to defend any merely human interpretation of scripture. The existence of well over two hundred Protestant sects, each claiming scriptural support, has made the possibility of any human arbitrament impossible. It was the hope of the Protestants to circumvent this battleground of multiple interpretations by the simple claim that the Bible itself was the infallibly correct word of God, and trust that Christians would in fact agree in their interpretations (a view abysmally ignorant of sixteen centuries of debate over scripture). A number of theoretical and practical problems have attended this claim.

In the first place, the assertion that the Bible was infallibly correct could never be infallibly determined. If this matter were accepted as a dogma of faith, the practical problem still remained to decide which of all the contradictory human interpretations was the closest to the one infallible and correct meaning. This very claim to infallible scripture rested, as Kant had noted,[23] upon the lack of confidence in human reason, and hence by accepting the dogma men prevented themselves from having access to the only tool which could publicly substantiate their initial claim. This contention that the Bible was inerrant became a statement which could not be substantiated, led to no consequences, and shifted the epistemological problem to a no man's land. Suppose that the Old Testament were really infallible, as it is conceivable that it might be. From this we might at least conclude (though all too hastily) that the correct formulations were to be found in the translations which we possess. Our problem, however, was not merely one of correct words, but more important, it was one of the correct meanings of the words. As an example of the perennial nature of the question of meaning, let us consider a simple statement such as the Mosaic commandment, "Thou shalt not kill." The printed words are generally held to be the ones originally intended; and for our present purposes, let us assume that this has been a correct assumption. Even if this much were infallibly correct, we would still not be "off the ground" theologically. We would still be in doubt as to what the commandment meant. Indeed, the history of both Jews and Christians has demonstrated that even for such an apparently simple statement a wide diversity of meanings is possible. The fact that shortly after the commandment was purported to have been delivered to Moses he and his fellow Jews were engaged in a war over which they felt no pangs of conscience would seem to indicate that whatever "Thou shalt not kill" meant, it did not include wandering Bedouin tribes. What did the commandment "Thou shalt have no other gods before me" mean? Biblical critics drew the understandable inference that Jehovah admitted the existence of other gods, but he insisted that he was more important than they. From this it was inferred that Mosaic Jews were henotheists. Should we have interpreted "gods" metaphorically to mean things such as money, prestige, or power, which we are not to put ahead of Jehovah? It would make a considerable difference to the Old Testament message how we interpreted these apparently simple remarks. When we multiply these two phrases a thousandfold and conjure with the plethora of inconsistent interpretations, we then see what still confronts us as a problem long after we may have asserted that the scriptures are infallibly inspired and correct. To aver that the scriptures mean just what they say, as was commonly claimed, blurs the obvious fact that there has never been common agreement as to what the infallible word actually meant.

The claim of infallibility has usually resulted in an egregious claim that not only are the scriptures infallible, but so also are the meanings as interpreted by the claimant. Such a pretension must be thought through in the light of the fact that at any time there have been innumerable varieties of meaning interpretation for any given passage. Each of these interpretations has claimed to be the infallible meaning of the infallible word. To hold the infallibility theory with regard to the humanly assigned meanings is to make of the theory a hortatory crutch to lend weight to evangelical pronouncements. It is in the frame of such a presupposition that evangelists may then aver: "My meanings are God's meanings, and hence they are not to be challenged." The profusion of meanings assigned to any given scriptural statement has been a quagmire into which many a Protestant movement has sunk. What alternative does a Protestant have if he believes in the Priesthood of All Believers? When the Protestant movement rejected all infallible interpreters, such as church councils, bishops, or popes, it appeared to cut itself off from the possibility of any substitute.

There is a sense in which the claim for the infallibility of the scriptures has represented a human attempt to shift the responsibility for proof of authenticity to a power outside man, while at the same time reserving for man the right to give his own very human meanings. It has been clear that those who hold to the infallibility of the scriptures do not expect that mere human beings will be able to prove the truth of the claim. The infallibility of the scriptures has been a dogma of faith, while the belief in infallible interpretation has not. The net result of this has been that while the thesis of an infallible scripture has been psychologically comforting, it has not been epistemologically useful. If this infallibility thesis is to be held at all, it must be held as beyond explanation and hence beyond debate. If it is held to be truly undebatable, then, in all fairness to the nature of proof, it must not be held as true or false. Infallibility, as applied to the scriptures, has not been a fruitful thesis. It has obstructed biblical scholarship, distorted or made impossible biblical history, and in general removed the scriptures from the realm of human understanding. Strictly speaking, the issue of the divine inspiration of scripture has never been a philosophical problem. It has been, and still is, a theological problem. The dogma of scriptural inerrancy has functioned for Protestants in much the same fashion as the seven sacraments for Roman Catholics. None of these matters raise questions of truth or falsity, and consequently they should entail neither claims to truth nor claims to falsity.

Even where a Christian may have been willing to concede that the infallibility of the scriptures was beyond reason to establish, he still faced real problems. If he were to say, "Let us accept the scripture in the same sense in which a geometrician accepts a given set of postulates," he still found himself confronted by a kind of problem which geometricians have not had to face. In geometry there has been general understanding of the meaning of the postulates, so that persons of disparate backgrounds were all able to work out theorems and corollaries with the same results. The scriptures have faced men with a very different situation. Even men of common backgrounds have not understood common meanings, with the result that religious "theorems" have been conspicuous either by their absence or by their ambiguity. All of this lends support to the supposition that the real issue was not whether the scriptures were inerrant, but whether human meanings were.

Alfred Loisy, a Roman Catholic scholar, scrutinized the traditional Christian claim that the scriptures were infallible.[24] He began by raising a question concerning the assumption that God wrote books, an assumption peculiar to the Judeo-Christian tradition. "The idea of books entirely God-made, but written in the languages of men, in the native dialects of particular peoples and in the idiom of given times . . . is inconsistent and self-contradictory." [25] One would have expected that a God would not have expressed himself in the myth form of primitive culture if he had intended the remarks to be timelessly important. In view of the assumption implicit in the history of any other area—namely, that later civilizations have been superior in both knowledge and moral insight—it could at least be hoped that a divine book would somehow be able to avoid being culture-bound. This has not proved to be the case with the scriptures in question.

Loisy noted a second problem. "The books themselves make not the slightest claim to the divine origin attributed to them by the theologians, but are in fact made up in the human manner." [26] In the face of the understanding which biblical scholarship has given us of how the scriptures came to be written and how they came to canonized, it would be impossible on the basis of any evidence to hold that the original authors even held such claims for their own products. The stamp of infallibility was affixed at a much later date.

In the third place, the infallibility claim has led the church into compromising positions with regard to the facts of archaeology, geology, biology, and history. As a result of the Christian claim to infallible scriptures the church has run the risk of being in conflict with every advance of science. Since there has been little doubt but that rationality lay with the scientific accounts, the church has been pushed to deny science in favor of myths, and to engage in debates over issues which contain no essentially religious message. In the face of historical analysis of the Book of Revelation, for example, religionists have attempted to find meanings hidden between

247

the lines. It would have been so much simpler, and with no jeopardy to religion, to admit that the message of revelation, which foreshadowed the imminent end of the world, was proved false by the continuation of the world. A theologian has put himself in a harrowing situation when he feels called upon to predict anew each year the destruction of the world, for no other pressing reason than to save the putative inerrancy of the millennialist prediction. Predictions of the millennium have thus far all been ill-advised, and while there is a theoretic probability that some year some prediction will turn out to be true, this possibility is an unstable foundation on which to rest the criterion of significance for the scriptures.[27]

In the fourth place, biblical scholarship has established a historicity for the scriptures which, if correct, turns out to be an indictment of the intelligence of God when combined with the infallibility claim. The prevailing view of biblical scholars [28] has been that no serious student or theologian could possibly question the historical view that the scriptures were written by men (however inspired) and that they have undergone emendations in the process of cultural change and the mere process of copying. How can the divinely inspired thesis be maintained in the presence of the obvious error of attributing the Pentateuch to Moses' authorship, or of assigning the Book of Isaiah to a single prophet? In view of the conclusions of biblical scholarship that there are disparate and conflicting accounts in both the Old and the New Testaments, the divine authorship thesis would require that God have been confused as to what actually took place. A more reasonable historical thesis is that the church produced the scriptures, and that the original authors were speaking spontaneously of local problems.

The question of the validity, truth, or significance of the scriptures of any religion will be answered, if at all, by appeals to conventional scholarship. Inspiring as the theory of inerrant scriptures may be, it has not been able to be authenticated, nor has it served the cause of those who wish thereby to add stature to their holy writ. If the Gospels, for example, are both authentic and timeless, this matter will have to be determined by the best human creative study. If, on the other hand, some still feel that the dogma of an infallible scripture ought not to be given up so easily, let them assert their "faith," but admit also that no scriptural meanings will ever be decided by this strategy. Indeed, the human problem has never been whether what a book said was inviolable, but rather whether any given human interpretation was beyond dispute; and as we have seen, such a hope is beyond fulfillment.

XI

The Problem *of* Fixed *or* Evolving Religions

A PROBLEM peculiar to religions with established scriptures
is that of determining whether the insights of the movement in question emerged full-blown from the beginning, or
whether there was a long period of evolutionary development.
The very presence of a finished scripture lends the impression
that the religion always had the properties distributed throughout the written book. When this impression is coupled with a
lack of historic sense and an unawareness of how scriptures
developed, the illusion of a fixed and changeless religious
message becomes complete. Once this preliminary position
has been reached, it becomes standard procedure to seek for
the original and (complete) message implicit in the scripture.
It became an established and legitimate enterprise to search
for the authentic Moses or the historical Jesus, with the assumption that Moses had all the insights expressed from Genesis to Malachi, or that Jesus had ratified Matthew to Revelation
as a univocal message.

   The question whether any particular religion has increased in content since its genesis is strictly an empirical

question to be answered by archaeology, anthropology, and history. The data revealed by these disciplines must in turn be interpreted to determine whether common statements may not have undergone changes in essential meaning during the history of a religious movement. There appears to have been a general fear among many of the orthodox in both Judaism and Christianity that historical and critical analyses may reveal that these two religions betray the same tendency to acquire new ideas which all other movements have already been amply demonstrated to do. In part, this fear has been associated with the claim to uniqueness which has been a property of much Judeo-Christian theology. A religion which lays claim to ideas found in no other religion can ill afford to admit that it may have picked up some of its notions considerably after its genesis. A second basis for this fear has been rooted in the concern with authenticity. If a religion does indeed have a univocal message, then the discovery of its genesis should reveal this message in all its fullness and clarity. If, on the other hand, the religion in question has a history, then there will always be doubt as to the point (if there is any at all) at which the complete message may be said to have been presented. A third factor relates to the problem of the evaluation of the developing message. Most enterprises of man begin with simple myth, rudimentary knowledge, and chauvinistic morals. If a religion actually has a history, then the believers are confronted with the problem of determining whether all the parts of the contemporary accumulation are of equal moral value or of equal factual truth.[1]

Immanuel Kant distinguished between what he called ecclesiastical faith and real religion. The former rests upon a historical event in time and, hence, may be expected to have a history. The latter, being based upon "pure moral faith," and having no public status, could have no history in the strict sense of the term. If any changes have indeed been made in the moral faith of an individual, he would be the only one to know this, and the fact would be of no public importance.[2] Let us consider the evidence for the ineluctable conclusion that all religions, like all human processes, have a history, and that, as a consequence, there are developments and changes in any religion, so that it cannot lay claim to being complete or to have had a beginning in complete enlightenment.

HAS JUDAISM EVOLVED?

Two types of problems face the contemporary student of the Old Testament. The problem implicit in what has been called "lower criticism" is one of determining the correct literal translation of what the scriptures report. This task is clouded by the early Hebrew practice of leaving out the vowels in writing and that of running the words together. One can imagine what a task it would be if a book in English were to omit the vowels. The single letter *t* could mean three different words, depending on whether the omitted vowel was a preceding *a* or *i* or a following *o*. The problem for biblical students was, first of all, to determine exactly what had been said. This problem was already apparent to the devout in ancient times. The problem of "higher criticism" was more difficult. It included not only the question of the authorship of the various books, but also the thorny problem of what the literal sentences really meant in the age in which they were written. The ability to answer this semantic question required extensive anthropological and archaeological data which were not available until comparatively recent times. In order to understand what a given writing originally intended, it was necessary to penetrate into the cultural milieu of the time in which a book was composed. This has proved to be a possible, although by no means easy, task.

In 90 A.D., when the Old Testament was canonized at Jamnia by the Alexandrian and Palestinian Jews, there was no notion of a problem of higher criticism. This was not because the works were of comparatively recent formulation, but because the Jews had no idea of a progressive revelation through successive historical periods. These first-century Jews assumed that everything of importance was in Moses, and that the later portions of the scripture simply explicated

Moses. The problem of the new criticism arose over the question of the Mosaic authorship of the Pentateuch. Celsus, a second-century Mithraist, insisted that the Pentateuch could not have had a single author. Porphyry (233–304 A.D.) attacked the historicity of the book of Daniel and showed that it must have been written in the Maccabean period about the second century B.C. Thomas Hobbes had advocated biblical exegesis in 1651 in his *Leviathan* (3:33), and had doubted the Mosaic authorship of any scripture. One of the first men to carry out a scholarly defense of a higher critical nature was Spinoza, a Jewish layman. In a book, *Tractatus Theologico-Politicus*, published in 1670, he attacked the Mosaic authorship of the Hexateuch on the bases of shrewd biblical observations. He noted, for example, that the books in question described the death of Moses, and also events which clearly followed his death. There were reports of Canaanitic activity known to have occurred long after Moses. There were eulogistic descriptions of the virtues of Moses which would have been egregious coming from Moses himself. In addition to the problem of Mosaic authorship Spinoza noted conflicting accounts of the same events which seemed to suggest that many reports had been combined into one to form the Hexateuch. In 1678 Father Richard Simon, a French priest, published his *Critical History of the Old Testament,* in which he agreed with the results of Spinoza's investigations. He noted, for example, that there were two accounts of the creation. In one of these man was created first, then the animals, and finally woman was made out of Adam's rib and some dust. In this account woman appears as the clear inferior of man and not in the "image of God." In the second account man and woman were created at the same time, each in "God's image"; and this did not occur until after the animals had been created. Father Simon suspected in this latter account a reflection of the widespread primitive notion of male and female deities. He noted also that there were two conflicting stories of the Flood. Not only was there a difference in the number of animals admitted to the ark, but there was in one a distinction between clean and unclean animals. In this account there were seven pairs of each clean species and one pair of each unclean species admitted. In the other account two of each animal, regardless of cleanness, were admitted. In each instance there was an equal number of males and females. In one account the water came from the heavens, while in the other the water came from the earth, perhaps in a tidal wave. In one account Noah was in the ark 150 days, while in the other he was in the ark a whole year. In 1753 a French Catholic layman, Jean Astruc, published his *Conjectures on the Original Memoirs Which It Appears Moses Employed to Compose the Book of Genesis*. It was here that the idea first appeared of distinguishing two distinct Hexateuchal accounts on the bases of the use of the terms "Elohim" and "Jehovah" for God.

If we go back in time, we may note an early factor which contributed to the rise of the "higher criticism" approach. This was the awareness of the allegorical nature of some Old Testament passages. This was asserted to be the case by Philo (50 A.D.), Origen (254 A.D.), and Saint Augustine (in the fourth and fifth centuries). It was presupposed that the scholar or saint could read between the lines. This enabled the devout to avoid the apparent contradictions in the Old Testament. The only limit placed upon allegorical interpretation was the imagination of the reader, within the bounds of certain basic orthodoxies. While this approach did attack biblical literalism, it did not constitute the essential approach to higher criticism, since the reader interpreted the documents in terms of his own times, rather than in terms of the milieu in which they had originally been written.

The nineteenth-century contributions of anthropologists and archaeologists provided the current biblical critics with the essential tools of higher criticism. Works like Sir James G. Frazer's *Golden Bough* and his three-volume work, *Folk-Lore in the Old Testament,* gave the ancient writings a milieu in which they could be interpreted. In the latter book Frazer noted the widespread occurrence of certain common religious themes such as a creation story, a flood story, the tale of the basket in the bulrushes, ideas of blood sacrifice, and a host of taboos with regard to marriage and food. Put together, these indicated the setting in which ancient scriptures had been written and gave an insight into the possible meanings that may have been intended. In the context of such facts it became highly probable that the Old Testament contained many non-Israelitic writings, and that while some of the stories were fact, many were fiction or part of the vast myth accumulation of the race. Fictional characters would include Adam, Noah, and Samson. Factual characters would include Moses, perhaps three Isaiahs, and Ezra. Some of the fictional characters had fact woven around them, while some of the factual characters had myth associated with them. The more remote a book was from the actual incidents described, the less reliable it could be considered to be as a report of what was actually felt by the persons in a given age. As one scholar put it, "Their credibility decreases in the ratio of their distance in time from the narrator." [3] One relatively clear consequence followed from higher criticism: attempts to read modern issues and concerns into ancient biblical passages were now considered improper. Biblical literalism alone could not shed fruitful light on the ancient meanings. Even if the scriptures were to be considered infallible, the problem of original meanings still remained. The devout still faced the question, "What did the writer mean?"

One of the most radical consequences of higher criticism to Old Testament analysis was the thesis that the religion of the Jews did not appear full-blown in its inception, but developed and evolved from relatively primitive beginnings to the high moral insights of the Hebrew prophets. Frazer had drawn this inference from his anthropological findings. "All civilized races have at some period or other emerged from a state of savagery. . . . Despite the high moral and religious development of the ancient Hebrews, there is no reason to suppose that they formed an exception to this general law." [4] The distinguished biblical archaeologist, William F. Albright, concluded that although ancient Judaism was probably implicitly monotheistic, it spoke the language of explicit polytheism. He conjectured that "explicit monotheism could not fully emerge until after the dawn of the logical age about the sixth century B.C., since clear definition and logical formulation are necessary to change an implicit belief or concept into an explicit doctrine or idea." [5] One of the more popular presentations of this idea of a historical development in the religion of Israel is that of H. E. Fosdick, in which he presents the changing concepts held by the Jews with regard to God and immortality during the long history from Genesis to the great prophets.[6]

Biblical critics concluded, for example, that during the historical period leading up to the death of Moses and the entrance into Canaan, the language of the scripture taken in the context of the best archaeological data would seem to indicate that the Jews were perhaps at least henotheists. They spoke of other gods, but asserted that their god was superior in power for them. He was a tribal god unconcerned with the fate of other peoples than the Hebrew tribes with whom he had made a covenant. He was a war god, a storm god, and he resided on Mount Sinai. So restricted was his locale that the Hebrew peoples feared to travel far from the mountain home because they might then be too far away for their god to be of any effective help. The assurance that an angel of Jehovah would accompany them, plus the visual presence of the ark, sufficed to carry them all the way to Canaan in spite of their real fears. Even as late as the victory of Deborah Jehovah was still pictured as residing upon Sinai (Judges 5:4–5). Elijah was reported to have fled to Sinai to get in the presence of Jehovah (I Kings 19:8). In addition Jehovah was endowed with the anthropomorphic properties which the gods of neighboring tribes had. He walked with Adam, talked with Moses and Abraham, and wrestled with Jacob. On occasion Moses had to intercede with Jehovah on behalf of the Hebrew people so that his wrath would not be visited upon them. During this period there was no belief in immortality. This would be understandable in view of the "strong" argument for immortality which required belief in a transfinite god. Jehovah was clearly not omnipotent, omniscient, or omnigood.

Later, after Canaan had been occupied, Jehovah was represented as living in the new land, symbolized by the ark

in the temple of Solomon (973–933 B.C.), but he was still
thought of as confined in his sphere of influence. When David
(1050–973 B.C.) had to flee to the Philistine land scarcely
twenty-five miles from Jehovah, he assumed that he was
beyond the range of divine help (I Samuel 26:19). The
mythical character, Jonah, for very different reasons fled to
the coast to get away from Jehovah. If there is any moral on
this score in the Jonah myth, it was that Jehovah was effective even for distances beyond a day's journey. Perhaps this
tale indicates that Hebrew thinking on the limited domain of
divine effectiveness was undergoing a change. During this
period Jehovah is reported to have demonstrated his effectiveness as a god of war. The Hebrew peoples achieved such
success that they could well sing praises to their god while
passing the ammunition. There were times when Jehovah was
represented as being even more bloodthirsty than his followers. As the occupation of the new land was effected, their god
took on some of the fertility properties of the agricultural
Baal gods, and at some points became syncretized with them.

We find a new chapter in god speculation in the writings
of the great eighth- and seventh-century Hebrew prophets.
They saw Jehovah as an intertribal, universal, spiritual, transfinite, and moral being. For virtually the first time Jehovah
appeared distinctly better than any Hebrew leader. During
this period Jehovah demonstrated his new character by becoming a critic of Jews as well as Gentiles. The exiles through
which the Jews were forced to pass brought about radical
changes in thinking. In the Babylonian exile the Jews were
shut off from the Temple and from what had been assumed
to be the literal presence of their god. Events seemed to make
it clear that Jehovah was no mere tribal or localized god, for
on many occasions he appeared to the Jews to have helped
their enemies. It was during these exiles that the synagogue
movement emerged to replace the Temple. These lay study
houses were centers where the Jews could maintain their
traditions and rally their spiritual forces. The very idea of the
synagogue symbolized the degree to which the idea of a universal and immanent god had progressed. Out of this same

synagogue movement arose the need for writings which culminated in the canonization of a scripture.

While in the early period there was a popular belief that the dead can influence the living, there was no belief in immortality in any hopeful sense. What life there was after death was in a Sheol so undesirable that no anticipation or hope was connected with it. In addition, Jehovah had no jurisdiction over Sheol. Death was under the jurisdiction of Baal gods. In the later period the influence of Jehovah was reputed to reach even to Sheol for purposes of retributive punishment. The great prophets of the exile destroyed the cult of the dead and raised messianic expectations and millennialist hopes. When these became linked with the idea of a friendly and omnipotent god, the possibility of belief in a tolerable immortality arose. At the hands of these same prophets a conviction of a resurrection also emerged. The Jews now had the milieu for explicit monotheism and a hopeful immortality.

During the time when the Temple had existed it had been the rallying point for Judaism. Under the prophetic leadership devotion to the Law now replaced devotion to the Temple. The Law did for Judaism what Christ was to do for the Christians. They were both the media through which it was believed that the god revealed himself. This devotion to the Law became so strong that when the Temple was finally and irrevocably destroyed in 70 A.D., Judaism reorganized itself on the basis of a book. A number of events were taking place which indicated that this shift in importance was well established by the time of the Christian era. The Essene sect, for example, deliberately refrained from taking part in Temple sacrifices, and yet they were regarded by their fellow Jews as models of piety. The relative sympathy with which the attacks of Jesus on ceremonialism were received by first-century Jews made it increasingly clear that the shift from priest to prophet, from Temple to book, was well on its way.

A further indication of an evolution in Judaism may be found in the development during the second century B.C. of the great parties of Judaism. Most of these were led by laymen or prophets. The Pharisaical school arose as champions of the oral Law. They inspired the people to synagogue participation and brought religion to the homes. Like most of the "parties," they were nationalistic. Two schools of Pharisees developed, each from a popular rabbi of the time. There was the Hillel school, currently known through Hillel foundations on college campuses. These were a moderate, broad-minded group. On the other hand, there was the Shammai group, which tended to be exclusive, extreme, and bitter. This latter group is conjectured to be the one against which Jesus inveighed when he spoke about the religious sanctimony of the "whited sepulchre" variety. There were, in addition, the Zealots, spiritual descendents of the Maccabees who in 166 B.C. won national independence for the Jews in Palestine.[7] This national enthusiasm was not lost even when they were once again reduced to the status of an occupied country by the Romans. The week before Palm Sunday (commemorating Jesus' last entry into Jerusalem) a revolution of Zealots had been quelled by the Romans, and a thousand crosses with a thousand crucified Jews lined the streets leading into Jerusalem. This national hope flared up again in the unsuccessful revolt against Roman domination in 66–70 A.D., which resulted in the destruction of the Temple and the ruin of the sacred city of Jerusalem. From this time on the party of peace ruled, led by Johanan ben Zakkai. Rebellion broke out in 117 A.D., and finally, in the disastrous revolt of 132–135 A.D., led by Bar Cocheba, the Zealot hopes perished. After this time the Jews reconciled themselves to being a people of the Book, and the era of rabbinic or Talmudic Judaism flowered.

Also in the second century B.C., a "party" called Sadducees flourished and participated in the synagogue program. Unlike the Pharisees, however, this group denied the resurrection thesis, personal immortality, the millennium, fate, angels, and all the scriptures except the Law. Contemporary with these other parties, on the shores of the Dead Sea were gathered the Essenes, who lived in religious communistic communities. In closely knit fellowships they stressed personal purity and the rejection of ritual sacrifice. This was the group whose recently discovered writings, known as the Dead Sea Scrolls,[8] have created such a stir in religious circles.

Such a picture of a historically evolving religion has not met with universal approval among either orthodox Jews or Christians. The deep-seated suspicion of the relativism of historic processes has contributed to this rejection. It is not inappropriate to note that the Old Testament is probably the only religious scripture which combines the sweep of time and the sense of historic continuity which make possible a higher criticism of the type we have been discussing. The historical thesis has been most clearly set forth in the context of the Old Testament. Martin Buber, a distinguished contemporary Jewish philosopher, raised serious doubts concerning the legitimacy of the higher critical inferences of an evolving Judaism. His major thesis leading him to this rejection was that the Old Testament was not the result of the "historization of myth" but of the "mythization of history." [9] He assumed that if a saga assumed poetic form early enough it remained essentially unchanged by later emendations and accretions. He believed that this poetizing had occurred in the case of the Old Testament. He objected further to the higher critical assumption that a historical continuity could be formed out of the disparate sagas. Terms such as pantheism, henotheism, kathenotheism, and polytheism were, he averred, views of the world, not of god, and hence they were not relevant to any survey of the theistic position of Judaism. He concluded further: "It may be enough to mention at this point that I regard the prevailing view of the Biblical text, namely, as largely composed of 'source documents' (Yahvist, Elohist, etc.), as incorrect." [10] Buber denied as groundless the Kenite hypothesis, which had claimed that Yahweh had been unknown to Israel until the advent of Moses. He asserted that the god of Moses was the same as that of Abraham, and that the god of the prophets was the same as that of Moses. "At Sinai Israel does not go over to the God of the Kenites, yet equally the Kenites do not go over to the God of the Israelites." [11] Buber was not claiming that there had been no altering of the language in which the revelation of Judaism had been expressed, but rather that there had been no change in the basic message, particularly as it applied to god and to morals.

Are we, then, left with no suggestive information to determine the original question, "Has Judaism evolved or was its basic message fixed once and for all?" A summary of the present data would indicate that Judaism must have developed in some real sense, whether Moses is considered as being the founder of the faith or as a continuer of an already existing faith. In the first place, the tools of biblical criticism, which include both archaeology and semantics, argue for evolution in every area of human experience ever studied. A people would have to have been remarkably insulated and unimaginative to have continued for several millennia without an altered conviction or new data. Yet this is precisely what would have to have occurred if Judaism is considered as a single and final revelation. The historical reading of the Old Testament argues specifically for the evolution thesis. If a religion rejects the tools of scientific discovery for its own domain, it puts itself out of the realm of rational discussion. If it does this, then it can no longer lay claim to statements of truth, although it may still make its claim for significance. In the second place, much of the resistance to the evolution thesis rests on the unsubstantiated assumption that the value of a religion is somehow bound up in the determination that it did not evolve. If this thesis were pressed for the scientific disciplines, then astrology would have a higher status than astronomy, since the former has not evolved, while the latter has undergone the most radical developments. While it may be true that an evolving religion is more open to the vagaries of probabilities as they apply to the question of what is authentic for a religion, even a fixed and final revelation cannot escape these problems entirely. What has probably been of more urgent concern for proponents of the "fixed and final" thesis is the psychological feeling that a changing religion is not worth the effort required to support it. Such a position, however, is not of philosophic concern at this point. Unpleasant or not, the view that Judaism evolved has the support of the available facts, and it can be further asserted that this state of affairs

261

does not entail any invidious implication concerning the value of this religion. Indeed, if we have any confidence in the investigatory procedure, and in the ability of the mind of man to absorb new facts, we should imagine that, other things being equal, an evolving religion would have a more timely word to speak than any changeless religion.

HAS CHRISTIANITY EVOLVED?

The same sense of evolution or development may be noted in the New Testament, although the restricted period referred to (perhaps 120 years) and the relative contemporaneity of the authorship of the books offer less data for so grand a picture as the Old Testament reveals. Nonetheless, study of the Bible and of the extant writings of the Apologists, church fathers, and non-Christian contemporaries, led scholars to the same conclusion of flux and development for Christianity. Obviously this conclusion carried with it a host of questions concerning relative authenticity which have not been resolved. The existence of more than 250 sects would suggest something of the breadth of variance in interpretation which has actually occurred.

Since the Christian movement began in a Jewish environment and was led by Jewish thinkers, it can be understood only in the context of its religious roots in Judaism. In general, the post-exilic developments in Judaism were the context in which Christianity was born. The Jews met in synagogues for discussion and wrote books which provided the locus for their religion. Divergent opinions were to be found among the members of any typical synagogue. As a consequence there was nothing out of the ordinary in the debates in which Jesus was reported to have participated. Differences of opinion could be expected on matters such as the millennium, the messiah, immortality, resurrection, or the canon of scripture. In such a context of free, though heated, debate there was nothing especially heretical in the remarks of either Jesus or his disciples. If it is noted that Jesus spoke slightingly, on occasion, of the Temple liturgy, it should also be noted that the Essenes and Hillel Pharisees probably shared these feelings. When the Temple was destroyed in 70 A.D., it was not found important enough even to be rebuilt. The first Christian book was the Old Testament. The first Christian church was the Jewish synagogue. The first twelve disciples were Jews, and Jesus was hailed as a Jewish messiah.

The dominant spirit of the age was the Jewish expectation of the return of Elijah (Malachi 3:1, 4:4–6; Mark 9:11–12), the appearance of a messiah, and the imminent end of the world.[12] During the first century A.D. there was a tremendous revival in messianic speculations owing to the popular belief that the year 5000 in the Jewish creation calendar would usher in the millennium. Josephus, the first-century Jewish historian, expressed this expectation. Most of the New Testament, from Matthew to Revelation, was written in the firm conviction that the time was at hand. John the Baptist carried out his program of baptizing on this assumption. That the expectation continued into the second century was amply testified to by Church Fathers such as Polycarp, who found it difficult to sustain interest in maintaining a church at all because of the popular assumption that the world was going to end at any moment. It may be assumed that the error of this millennialist expectation, and the failure of the world to end, did far more than dampen Christian enthusiasm for eschatology.

In the early part of the first century the Christians met in the same synagogues with the rest of the orthodox Jews. Apparently these first twelve and their converts "had no idea whatever either of being, or of becoming, separatists." [13] The conversion of non-Jews, or Gentiles, by Paul, Barnabas, Stephen, Peter, John, and Philip aided in the ultimate separation. This circumstance compelled an early decision on the question of the relation of the new movement to the long tradition of Judaism. The headquarters of the Christian church was Jerusalem, where James, a brother of Jesus, was the head for a time. This first-century church was distinguished by a number of essentially Jewish practices and beliefs:

1. They gathered daily for common worship and discussion. It was a religious law that if seven Jews were unemployed, the synagogue must be open. Understandably this was always the case. The discussion centered on the available canon of scripture: the Law and the Prophets.

2. Although the early group led by Stephen preached that God did not dwell in temples made by human hands, the Jerusalem Temple was a significant rallying center. Stephen had traditional support for this thesis of a spiritual God from Hebrew prophets in the past.

3. They practiced baptism as a symbol of entrance into the fellowship. Since John the Baptist had done this by immersion, this was doubtless the way in which the early Christians performed it. It was an adult initiation into a group of repentant and expectant persons.

4. They participated in a common meal at which bread and wine were blessed. This had been a part of Jewish religious ceremony ever since the celebration of the Passover. This was continued by first-century Christians in the added context of the Last Supper. This common meal was early discontinued because of the social problems associated with rich and poor persons eating together. A symbolic love feast took its place, and this ultimately became the communion.

5. They passed on the mantle of authority to new missionaries in a symbolic "laying on of hands" ceremony. All of the disciples and the later apostles did this. Jews had performed a similar act at least as far back as the Elisha saga. When the issue of apostolic succession emerged, this ceremony became the guarantee of authenticity in ordination.

6. They said prayers for the dead and dying in the assurance that these were effective in helping the soul in its journey to the next life. In later organized Christianity this became the sacrament of extreme unction.

7. They collected food, clothes, and money for the needy churches, and in particular for that group known as the "needy saints" in Jerusalem. These were millennialists who had forsaken all their worldly possessions in the expectation that the end of the world was imminent.

8. While initially the membership of the Christian movement was entirely Jewish, the introduction of Gentiles into the
faith led, in the beginning of the second century, to a preponderance of non-Jews and a consequent lack of religious
leaders with roots in the past.

In addition to these essentially Jewish roots, the first-
century Christian movement inherited a milieu of Greek and
Roman mystery religion and philosophy. Plato and Aristotle
had cultivated a philosophic following alert to cognitive
issues. Both Stoicism and Epicureanism had lent a philosophic
skepticism to vital human problems. Ancestor worship played
a living role in official state religion. "Mystery" cults flourished.
The members of these cults were admitted or chosen through
certain rites rather than through citizenship or family ances-
try. These cults represented an escape from more ancient
tribal religion and had the affirmative objective of achieving
personal happiness both in this life and in the next. Divine
creatures such as Mithras, Cybele, Dionysus, Eleusis, Isis,
Aphrodite, and Orphic spokesmen all had their respective
devotees. Religious ceremonies centered on death (in the fall
of the year) and life (in the spring of the year). Both birth and
death were personalized in divine creatures who functioned
as god-men or god-women. The spring symbolized their belief
in ultimate resurrection from death. They experienced a
symbolic oneness with the gods in the ceremonies, notable
among which was the Tauroboleum, in which a bull was slain
and his raw flesh eaten and the raw blood drunk. The participants then felt themselves one with the god. In the famous
Mithra movement,[14] as in most of these cults, there was a
mediator (Mithra) who saved people from both sin and death.
Here the influence of Greek thought permeated. They had a
philosophic foundation and hence had the means for systematic theology. There is good reason to suppose that the Gospel
according to John and many of the letters of Paul were formulated with Greek ideas in mind. It does not follow from
this, however, that a structured theology underlies the New
Testament. As one scholar noted, "The fallacy lay in the
fundamental axiom of traditional thinking that a formulated

theology lies behind the New Testament writings, or, in fact, a theology of any kind, formulated or unformulated." [15] Theology was a Greek concept, not a Hebrew concept. Judaism did not bequeath theology to Christianity. Indeed, Judaism was ill disposed to accept any philosophic structures. Even the structured system of Moses Maimonides was never accepted as authoritative by Judaism.

This "higher criticism" account of the genesis of Christianity would indicate that initially there were no profound differences between it and first-century Judaism. In church structure, in belief (with the exception of their thesis that the messiah had come and, hence, was not yet to come), and in scripture the two groups were scarcely distinguishable enough to warrant a separation. Since this is no longer the case, it is clear that there must have been some evolution in Christianity. What were some of these developments in the budding Christian sect which led to the creation of a new and distinctive religion?

By the end of the second century the membership in the Christian synagogues was about half Latin and half Greek—in any event, exclusively Gentile. This historic development by itself was sufficient to indicate that the Christian and Jewish movements were not identical on the basic issues of ritual, health, and dietary practices, since Gentiles were not bound to obey them. One of the pressing issues which the second century witnessed was the question of the creed which would signify exactly what it was that Christians subscribed to. As Christians traveled around to various churches in the Roman empire, they discovered conflicting views on the Christian message. Vehement criticisms from both within and without the movement necessitated a decision on orthodoxy. Early traditions referred to rules of faith as composed of remarks of the early apostles. As early as 140 A.D. the church at Rome had a fixed creed associated with baptism. While similar creeds probably existed elsewhere, most churches had no creed and hence no universal dogma on which the faith rested. The church at Alexandria, for example, appears not to

have had any established creed. Following the example of the
Roman bishops, Irenaeus and Tertullian formulated a creed,
which was submitted to the Roman bishop. It was accepted
by the churches under the Roman jurisdiction, and a revised
form of this declaration of faith was ultimately adopted at the
Council of Nicaea (325 A.D.) and later at the Council of
Constantinople in 381 A.D. It was precisely at the point of the
interpretation of this statement of faith that the Eastern
orthodox churches (Greek Catholic, Coptic, etc.) parted company with the Western Roman orthodoxy. Thus from 325 A.D.
on there were at least two separate traditions as to the essential meaning of the Christian message.

In addition to the internal divisions which prompted the
need for a creed, there were external attacks upon both the
beliefs and the practices of the Christian movement. Some
clear and unified word was needed to counter these attacks,
and obviously the first century lacked the required univocality.
Men like Celsus, a Mithraist, had attacked the irrationality of
certain prevailing ideas in Christendom. Assuming the historicity of the Gospel accounts, Celsus concluded that Jesus was
an illegitimate son. If Joseph was not the father and if he
knew that he was not the father, he would scarcely have
been impressed by Mary's purported claim of a miracle or by
the claim that the Holy Spirit was the father. It seemed clear
to Celsus that the Christians had invented the conception
myth to cover their embarrassment over Jesus' illicit origins.
Further, Celsus inferred from the language of the communion
service that Christians ate flesh and blood, and hence were
cannibals. To add insult to these injurious accusations he observed that after all the movement was composed mainly of
old women and thus ought not to be taken seriously. The
church was also subject to attacks from business organizations on the grounds that the Christian message destroyed
trade. Paul had experienced some of this antagonism. Dealers
in animals for sacrificial purposes were affected because
Christians opposed animal sacrifice, and thus every new
Christian convert meant fewer animals sold. The silversmiths

were antagonistic to the Christians because they attacked the icon trade. All of these conflicts compelled centralization of church thinking.

The completion of an ordered clerical empire was furthered by the canonization of a new set of scriptures. While the first-century church had most of the writings which became canonical much later, they were not considered in the exalted role, noted in Chapter X, in which the third-century church held them. The Synoptic Gospels appear to have been originally essentially Jewish in content and spirit, while by the third century the Pauline letters, now read with the perspective of neo-Platonism, embodied an entirely new kind of explication of the whole set of New Testament writings. This marked contrast between the Synoptic Gospels and the Pauline letters provoked both Friedrich Nietzsche and Soren Kierkegaard in the nineteenth century to observe that Saint Paul had distorted and spoiled the original message. Paul had spoiled the movement by a combination of institutionalizing it and systematic theologizing about it. The development, for better or for worse, of Christianity appears to be a fact.

A further new element was introduced into the first-century Christian program with the ultimate adoption of the dogma of the apostolic succession of the clergy. The thesis that there was an unbroken succession of ordained clergy back to Christ through Peter aimed to prove that the church had the authentic spirit and authority of its founder. It served also to separate the heretics from the orthodox. Since the church already had bishops, they were the logical men to serve as the links in this succession. The first-century view of bishops may be seen in I Timothy and Titus. Here the bishops were essentially organization men. They were not consulted for their views on religious matters. In Ignatius of Antioch (50–116 A.D.) we find the first post–New Testament expression of episcopal supremacy. For Ignatius, obedience to the bishop was the same as obedience to God; in fact, prayer could not be effective save in the presence of a bishop. Yet, on the other hand, no bishop could decide policy issues until he had consulted the presbyters or elders of the church. Polycarp

(69–155 A.D.), bishop of Smyra, made no mention of the role of the bishop, and thus indicated that there was no unanimity of view within the Christian community. It was Irenaeus, bishop of Gaul, who made the first appeal to an apostolic succession grounded in the office of the bishops. It was he who asserted also the primacy of the Roman bishop in this succession. Tertullian, although rejecting this thesis at first, endorsed the apostolic superiority of bishops. His successor at Carthage, Cyprian (248–258 A.D.), reaffirmed the authenticity of the apostolic succession. In spite of this enthusiasm for apostolic authority, the ancient churches of Antioch, Alexandria, and Jerusalem do not possess to date any catalog of bishops earlier than the fourth century, when Eusebius wrote them down. The church at Constantinople cannot trace its episcopate back farther than the seventh century. Even for Rome the first historical series of papal biographies, the Liber Pontificalis, dates from the sixth or seventh century. While later historians refer to more ancient lists, these have not been preserved. Eusebius quoted from a purported list made by Hegesippus, a Syrian Christian in 150 A.D., but he does not give us the complete list. Irenaeus made an abridged list which was sufficient to note that Linus was purported to have been the second pope and the bishop referred to by Saint Paul in Timothy. Hippolytus, bishop of Porto, was said to have compiled a list of the popes in 235 A.D., but this is not extant either. Biblical scholars such as Mommsen, Lightfoot, and Duchesne have analyzed the Liber Pontificalis into two parts. From Peter to the seventh century they concluded that the list is "a mesh of veritable facts, romantic legend, deliberate fabrication, and heedless error." [16] However, from the seventh century on, the list is by and large historically supportable. In spite of the apparent lack of data to support even the list of names of Roman Catholic popes, there is little doubt that from about 200 A.D. on, the apostolic succession of Roman bishops was assumed to be true by churches under the Roman jurisdiction. Greek orthodoxy and Coptic orthodoxy, however, rejected this succession from the start.

We have seen in this historical pattern a clearly evolving

and developing religion. The Synoptic Gospels stand in contrast to the Gosepl according to John, and both are emended further by the Pauline letters. The whole document called the New Testament presents such an interwoven mesh of conflicting dogmas that the more the higher critics discover about the putative genesis of Christianity, the less it resembles what subsequently emerged. This has posed a host of conflicting theories with regard to what the genetic issues really were. Albert Schweitzer concluded that the historical Jesus was beyond scholarly discovery. Even the Gospel accounts were so encrusted with later elements that the original events were beyond recall. When this Protestant position is contrasted with the prevailing Roman Catholic view that the genetic Jesus was known to have commissioned Peter the first pope, established the seven sacraments, confirmed the immaculate conception, the virgin birth, the doctrine of papal infallibility, and a wealth of other Roman dogma, the only tenable position a historical scholar can take is to conclude that Christianity has undergone a most radical sequence of transformations. What knowledge we possess of what Christianity has been comes from the expressions of local groups preserved for us in historical documents. The data are univocal on the question of an evolving Christendom.

IS CHRISTIANITY UNIQUE?

We have seen that from the point of view of biblical criticism the claim that the Christian church began with a complete dogma which has not evolved is not supported by the facts. This has appeared to be true both of Judaism and of Christianity. In each instance a historical reading of the scriptures shows that the revelations were worked out over long periods of theoretical and doctrinal struggle. In the case of the Old Testament, there appeared to be an evolution of the idea of God and of immortality. In the case of the New Testament, the higher criticism of the nineteenth century exposed a clash between the teachings of Paul and the general spirit of the Synoptic Gospels.

While this has been the spirit of the nineteenth and twentieth centuries in religious studies, it has not been the dominant view through the majority of the history of Judeo-Christianity. For the first eighteen centuries of the Christian era the prevailing opinion of Christian theologians was that Christianity was unique when compared with other religions. While other faiths had evolved, Christianity began complete. It was, in addition, held that there were criteria which showed conclusively that Christianity was not only superior in degree but also superior in kind. It is this claim which we shall discuss in this section.

In the light of the available historical facts it is unlikely that the doctrine of Christian superiority was seriously asserted, and with emphasis on universality, much before the Council of Nicaea in 325 A.D. The Christian church had too limited a following and was too seriously challenged by rival sects ever to be in a position to make a claim to universality. What was required was supplied by the decision of Constantine to make Christianity the religion of the empire. This gave to the Christian church the political structure which an effective claim to universality required.

The thesis that the Roman Catholic Christian church, in particular, possessed a legitimate claim to universality and supremacy was effectively developed by Saint Augustine in the fourth and fifth centuries. According to Saint Augustine, the Roman Catholic church had been given the "keys to the kingdom" by Christ through Peter. It was, in addition, maintained that the complete revelation emerged at the time of the initial transaction between Christ and Peter. It is interesting, however, that although Saint Augustine asserted that the Christian church began with a completed dogma, he did not believe that there was a comparable completeness for the interpretation of the meanings of the dogma. This was due, essentially, to his thesis that while the revelation of complete dogma came from God, the interpretation of the meanings of dogma was a proper human function. Like all matters of human knowledge, it was expected that interpretations would evolve. This idea of a completed dogma and an endlessly evolving interpretation of

271

meanings has been a fundamental guiding principle of the Roman Catholic church since Saint Augustine. This explains the long history of theological conflict among Roman Catholic theologians. It also explains the situation described by Saint Abelard, that on 158 basic doctrines the church fathers disagreed. On the face of it, such a situation, where religious thinkers fail to agree on the meanings of religious dogma, might appear to be a most unhappy one; but it did not indicate any serious doubts on the part of Roman Catholic thinkers, at least as to the ultimate nature of the revelations. The dogmas were secure even if the meanings were not.

The Protestant tradition, on the other hand, has not fared so well. For Protestants, both the nature of the revealed dogma and its meanings have been topics for serious debate. In this sense, the very existence of Protestantism has argued against the claim of medieval Christianity to uniqueness.

Nonetheless, while there has been general agreement among Christians on the claim that their uniqueness rested upon their dogma and not upon their interpretations of meaning, it has not been easy for theologians to distingush clearly between dogmas and meanings. John Calvin, one of the cofounders of the Protestant Reformation, was particularly sensitive on this point. He agreed with the Roman Catholics that Christianity had genetic dogmas communicated by Christ in their completeness. He felt, on the other hand, that the Roman Catholic church had blurred the issue by their rites and ceremonies. Liturgy ought not to be confused with dogmas of faith. In this matter Calvin was sure that even if there had been no church history, an intelligent person would be able to see that the complex priestly practices of Roman Catholicism did not spring up in the genesis of Christianity, but that, on the contrary, these had been added over a long period of time. Hence there was an evolution of ritual. While Calvin insisted that ritual ought not to be confused with the fundamental Christian message, he suspected that the Roman church had not been consistently aware of this.

A review of the history of papal encyclicals would seem to support Calvin's contention. It does take a considerable amount of ingenuity to be able to show scriptural foundation for the doctrines of extreme unction, the medieval practice of penance, the theory of papal infallibility, or the doctrine of the immaculate conception and bodily ascension of the Virgin Mary. Religious Christians have been exceptionally fertile in their conjectures on meaning. If it is granted that the Roman Catholic doctrines have scriptural support, would we admit this also for the Christian Science metaphysics of the universal Mind or for the Protestant analyses of the meaning and significance of baptism? A simple reading of the Synoptic Gospels does not reveal much dogma, and what dogma it does present is indistinguishable from the long traditions of Judaism.

Something must be done about the difference in emphasis between the Gospels and the letters of Saint Paul. The Synoptic Gospels, on the one hand, breathe the air of the Old Testament Hebrew prophets. Saint Paul, on the other hand, exhibits the influence of both Greek philosophy and the mystery religions which were dominant at the time of the Roman Empire. From the point of departure of nineteenth-century biblical criticism, an evolution of Christian dogma is apparent even in the New Testament.

During the Middle Ages the chief claim of Christianity to uniqueness was centered in the revelation which Christ literally and symbolically demonstrated. While Judaism had its Moses, Buddhism its Buddha, and Islam its Mohammed, only Christianity had Christ. If the personality of Christ had been the only basis of the Christian claim to uniqueness, no persuasive argument could ever have been given to any except convinced Christians. With equal facility the Moslems and the Jews could claim supremacy for their respective leaders. The more important emphasis of Christians was on the meaning of the transformation of Jesus into the Christ. This meaning was avowed to be unique to Christianity. If occasionally Christian theologians were tolerant enough to recognize that God might have revealed something to Moses, Buddha, or Mohammed, two assumptions took the merit away from the recognition. Either it was assumed that the insight was really Christian, and hence gained its worth by virtue of being a vehicle for

Christianity; or it was asserted that there was something incomplete about the revelation—that while there might be a little truth in it, Christianity had the revelation in a more complete fashion.

Paul Tillich, the contemporary Harvard theologian, has pared away what seemed to him to be the husk of Christianity in an attempt to find the fundamental core of the Christian claim to uniqueness. This essence was not to be found in either ritual or systematic theology. In neither of these areas can Christianity claim universality or unconditional dogmas. Indeed, he remarked somewhat cryptically that although Christianity was not final, it did bear witness to what was final. This element of finality, however, was not to be confused with ecclesiastical structure or current theology. On only one item does Christianity have the final word. This is in its witness that Christ was "grace and truth."

He asserted further that Jesus, as a person, was culture-bound and caught in the petty interests of his historical time. As a consequence we ought not to become overly concerned either with Jesus' millennialism or with the peculiar moral requirements specified in the Sermon on the Mount. Jesus, as a finite person, had special interests and possessed the prevailing finite knowledge of his day. In the case of the millennialist expectation he was clearly mistaken. Jesus had all the limitations to which human beings are prone. Consequently, Christians ought not to attempt to follow Jesus' example—or, in the words of the title of Sheldon's book in the nineteenth century, they should not try to walk *In His Steps*.

On the other hand, Jesus the person was the medium of an ultimate incarnation. In this event Jesus played a passive role. The mystery which the term "Christ" symbolizes was determined by God and not by a conscious act of will of Jesus. While Jesus as a person had nothing to offer of cosmic concern, the meaning of Christ, which is of ultimate concern, is not dependent upon any temporal events.

Now the problem confronting the proponent of such a thesis has been to explain what all of this means in such a fashion that it does not sound like specious presumption to a non-

Christian. One of the simpler ways in which this was attempted was to shift the emphasis from what is basically a mystery and to concentrate upon the practical consequences to which Christianity was claimed to lead. George Berkeley, the eighteenth-century Anglican bishop, endorsed with enthusiasm the doctrine of the practical superiority of Christianity. While he recognized that other religions had produced some useful results, he credited this to the fact that these other religions happened to have some basic Christian truths. This was maintained even for religions which were in existence long before the birth of Jesus. In addition, he believed that an impartial survey of all religions would reveal that Christianity has these same truths and that it has comprehended them in a more complete fashion. It was as a consequence of this assumption that he avowed that Christianity was able to enforce basic human virtue by sounder authority and with a stronger motivating power than any other religion.

James Martineau, a nineteenth-century English theologian, expressed the same basic proposition. In 1845 he wrote:

> Such I regard as the leading principles, by which Christianity has exerted influence on human morality and civilization. By its sentiment of universal brotherhood it has nerved the arm of the oppressed seeking to be free, it has produced the benevolence of class to class, and rendered pure and affectionate the interior morality of churches. By the sentiment of the importance of speculative truth to the great mass of men, it has created the virtue of honest speech and commenced the education of the multitudes.[17]

He believed that an impartial survey of those nations of the world which do not profess the Christian gospel would show a social decay and a "triumph of violence and superstition."[18] Christian nations, on the other hand, show the fruits of a truly authentic religion. These fruits were exhibited not only in terms of high moral behavior, but also in terms of the benevolent institutions such as hospitals and schools which they possessed. He insisted, further, that no religion had ever produced so little human misery and so much common brotherhood as had Christianity. This claim of the moral superiority of Christianity was a distinguishing characteristic of nineteenth-century Protestant Modernism. Christianity was superior because of what it produced both in the life of the individual and in the society.

We in the twentieth century, with the advantage of historical perspective, may not be quite so confident as either Berkeley or Martineau that Christianity has had such unmixed advantages. After all, the social evils about which Charles Dickens wrote were the products of Christian nations. The Salvation Army, for all its Christian orientation, arose to protest and to attempt to ameliorate a kind of human misery which was a concomitant of a supposedly Christian society. The histories of the nineteenth century reveal that it was not uncommon for Protestant clergymen to justify child labor and unsanitary working conditions. While there were protests against the social evils, they were not made exclusively by Christians.

It has been equally evident that Christian nations have not been laggard in participating in and creating their share both of international war and of internal revolution. While Christian pacifism has been a perennial option, Christian militarism has been far more common.

Both Berkeley and Martineau would have been disturbed by the results of a recent investigation made by a subcommittee of the United Nations. This committee was concerned particularly with the degree and number of what are called crimes of violence. These included murder and rape, together with alcoholism as a potential cause. By an unfortunate coincidence, as far as Berkeley's thesis is concerned, the so-called Christian nations led the world. In addition, it appeared that the nations which call themselves Christian have more than their worldly share of neurotic persons and institutionalized patients. Such information, of course, needs to be taken advisedly, since many nations of the world do not have, and never have had, institutions for the care of the mentally ill. It may be that the excessive number of mental patients in the United States is simply due to the fact that we are more concerned with mental illnesses and that we have, as a consequence, more facilities for their diagnosis and care. In view of this real possibility, it would be difficult if not impossible to prove that there are more mental cases in the twentieth century than there were in the eighteenth century. The number of patients diagnosed and treated is hardly a necessary or sufficient datum.

In view of the wide disparity of practices all of which are claimed by someone to be derived from basic Christian beliefs, it seems unlikely that Christianity can ever be claimed to have any beneficial and univocal consequences. The general moral and emotional attitude expressed in Nathaniel Hawthorne's book *The Scarlet Letter* indicates that Christianity has had its low periods. Christian ideas of sin and predestination have contributed a large share to the production of human uneasiness, anxiety, and despair. Jonathan Edwards, the eighteenth-century New England clergyman, could conclude, however, that this whole dismal picture was simply a part of the ordinary facts of experience. Christianity, according to Edwards, had a word to bring to this situation. If the Christian message did not result in peace of mind, this was not through any shortcoming of the Christian gospel but was due rather to the evil in human nature and the illusory nature of the world. If the gospel made men miserable, it was because they deserved to be.

One of the dominant themes of contemporary Existentialism has been the attempt to make some sense out of this whole dilemma. If it is the function of Christian ministers to point out the abysmal anxiety which the facts of human experience produce, it is also the business of the clergy to indicate a way out. If from the point of view of an independent observer the way offered by Existentialism does not appear to be hedonistically satisfying, the Existentialists would still be able to reply that this was the best that could be expected.

IS CHRISTIANITY A RELIGION AMONG RELIGIONS?

There have always been religious proponents of the thesis that all religions are human products and are, hence, to be judged by common criteria. If any religion claims a superiority, the justification will have to be available to public inspection. When this assumption is granted, a case for any religion will always be limited to a particular range of facts. At no point will universality be likely to appear.

Part of the humanist critique of the Modernist claim for the unique superiority of the Christian message consisted in showing that all religions have had unpleasant consequences; and that, further, the Christian religion is in no better position to make good its claim for practical success than is any other religion. The humanists observed that all religions have, on occasion, been seriously and enthusiastically promoted by sensitive and intelligent followers. Where this has been the case, advantageous results sometimes occur. At the same time, every religion has had its callous and unwise spokesmen, who have contributed to the destruction of hard-won human values. The Modernist claim that Christianity is superior on psychological and sociological grounds was attacked by humanists on the ground that it is not supported by fact.

The theory that all religions have evolved and are evolving requires a degree of sophistication which religious scholars have only recently achieved. The evolutionary hypothesis as applied to religion needs a dispassionate historical outlook. History of religion as we know it is a recent arrival on the religious scene. Medieval theologians lacked the sense of history with regard to their religion. In the first place, the men in the Middle Ages lacked the necessary information concerning both the development of their own movement and the history of related movements. In the second place, there appeared to be a tinge of heresy in the idea of historical evolution. It seemed clear that if one religion was subjected to historical analysis, the result would be that the origins would always be less significant than the present. For a religion such as Christianity, which has maintained that its genesis was its high point, the consequences of a historical approach might destroy the faith.

It was in the nineteenth century that evolutionary theories were first being seriously pressed not only in biological and geological studies, but in the social field as well. G. W. F.

Hegel was the theoretic leader in the evolution movement. While Hegel maintained an endless evolution for the human spirit, with God as the motivating force behind it, Karl Marx proposed an almost endless evolution of societies with economic class struggle as the power behind the process. If, as both of these men maintained, the history of all society reveals a long, slow, and inevitable development from simple roots to a rich flowering, then why should it not also be true that Christianity was part of the same cosmic movement?

Adolf Harnack, a nineteenth-century German theologian, was a leader in this regard. He asserted:

> The claim of the church that the dogmas are simply the exposition of the Christian revelation because deduced from the Holy Scriptures, is not confirmed by historical investigation. On the contrary, it becomes clear that dogmatic Christianity (the dogmas) in its conception and in its construction was *the work of the Hellenic spirit upon the Gospel soil.*[19]

It was Harnack's contention that the Christian dogmas did not arise as a simple result of exposition of supposed Christian revelation. On the contrary, the task of formulating doctrine has been the function of theologians. In fulfilling this responsibility the theologian has always faced a dilemma. On the one hand, the theologian needed to show that the doctrines he was expounding were the authentic and genetic Christian ones. On the other hand, in order to make this claim secure, it was always necessary both for the theologian and for the church which supported him to minimize the task of the individual scholar. If the conclusions were considered to be the result of personal investigations, they would be subject to the same probabilities which all scholarly programs faced. The only simple solution to this problem was to assert that every theologian was the recipient of a divine revelation. But this had a double result. First, it robbed the scholar of the fruits of his labor; and second, it put the justification of the conclusions reached in an inaccessible realm. The history of dogma reveals a panoramic picture of this theological deception. The fact is that dogmas have evolved in Christianity, but churchmen have endeavored to hide this from the laymen, as well as from themselves. Harnack considered, for example, the obvious transformation in dogmatic emphasis between the Synoptic Gospels and the letters of Saint Paul and then observed that theologians ever since have attempted to conceal this change. As a further example, he mentioned the accretions to the ritual which may be historically documented. The evolution of ritual has had a concomitant manifestation in an evolution of dogma to interpret this ritual. Every church reformer from Saint Augustine to Martin Luther believed that he was returning Christianity to its real roots. The fact that there have been reformers would seem to support the thesis that there has been an evolution. Unless Christianity was evolving, it would be difficult to explain the protests of prophets and puritans.

Harnack saw his function of a historian of dogma as that of laying bare the processes of the origins and developments of the creeds as the best means of emancipating the church from excessive rigidity.[20] After his case had been made, his conclusions meliorated what might otherwise have been an attack upon the unity of the Christian message. On the one hand he did discover some basic dogma which had not changed essentially; but more important, he insisted that the essence of Christianity did not lie in its dogma anyhow.

Ludwig Feuerbach, a nineteenth-century German philosopher, pressed the evolutionary hypothesis further by changing the locus of what had evolved. According to Feuerbach, the history of the Christian church exhibited a tendency to imagine that the initial dogmas were objective facts. He saw that this had been particularly the case during the first few centuries of the Christian era. He asserted that as religions mature, as he believed that Christianity had done, religious thinkers see that the original dogmas were really subjective. These genetic doctrines explained the nature of man, his hopes, fears, and aspirations. They were not intended to be metaphysical descriptions of the nature of objective reality. They are, rather, a story of the development of the human race. The failure of contemporary religious movements to see that the essence of Christianity lies within the hearts of men, and not in external dogma, has been the primary cause for theological debate. Feuerbach was sure that it would be far better for the Christian movement to recognize and admit that it had a human origin and a human growth, and that its greatest contribution has been to explain what man is like. If religion is given these human roots, and this human orientation, then it follows that evolving religion will be a desirable state of affairs.

Friedrich Schleiermacher, a contemporary of Feuerbach, believed that to disclaim uniqueness was in the best interests of Christianity. He urged Christians to renounce both the claim to universality and the claim to distinctiveness. Indeed, it has been the case, and ought to continue to be the case, that Christianity thrives on multiplicity. Any one of the dogmas of the Christian tradition could become the basis for a new religious insight and a new religion. Christianity should look with appreciation on any religion which has produced ideas and practices that Christianity could not or at least did not produce. While this worldly tolerance of the contributions of other religions was not widely held in the nineteenth century, it was a natural consequence of biblical criticism and historical investigation. If religions do evolve, and if Christianity does fit into this category of evolution, then we would expect that all over the world there would be various manifestations of true and valuable ideas. The Christian religion cannot defend with evidence any claim to a corner on worthy consequences. It follows, therefore, according to Schleiermacher, that any expectations for a universal religion are presumptuous. If Christianity is to escape the stigma of presumption, it too must give up any aspirations for universal support.

The thesis we have been considering is that Christianity is, after all, but one more religion among religions. If persons of a particular culture find Christianity more vital and more appealing, this is due simply to the limiting nature of their milieu. Most people reflect the values of the society in which they have been reared. Most residents of Ceylon are Buddhists, most citizens of Spain are Roman Catholic Christians, and most Egyptians are Moslems. These preferences are not explained by any claims of cognitive or normative superiority for any religion. Each society has religious ideologies which are coherent with its social, political, and economic values. If there really were a superior religion for the world, the evidence for this fact would have to be super-empirical. So far, the shrewdest way in which the claim to uniqueness has been defended has been to appeal to intuitive insights or divine revelations. These, however, suffer from being inexplicable, incommunicable, and, from the perspective of an independent observer, indefensible.

IS CHRISTIANITY FINAL?

Paul Tillich has presented one of the most thoroughgoing alternatives to the findings of biblical scholarship. Since he was aware that higher criticism gave the clear impression of an evolving religion, and since he found such a position unacceptable, he endeavored to find a new basis for an element in the Christian faith which was fixed and final in its genesis. He contrasted two elements in the Christian genetic milieu: the "situation" and the "message." The situation was the scientific, artistic, economic, political, and ethical forms in which Christians of any age express their interpretations of the essentials of existence. We may consider the New Testament as a situation, and all of the varied remarks which it contains may be understood as interpretations of some essential reality. These interpretations are more important than any facts that may seem to be entailed. On the other hand, there was a message inextricably associated with the event of the incarnation. While the situation as expressed by the New Testament was a vehicle for the transmission of the message, the message ought not to be confused with the scriptures. The problem of the Christian theologian is not, "What do the scriptures say?" but rather, "What do the scriptures mean?" as they relate to the genetic and authentic message. In the explication of this thesis Tillich began with certain assumptions which he aimed to protect from any philosophic questions. Among these postulates were the following:

1. The Christian faith is unique.
2. This uniqueness cannot be explained to any who do not already admit it.
3. This faith is the expression of an ultimate concern. An ultimate concern is indefinite, unconditional, and independent of situations.
4. An ultimate concern is one that threatens the foundation of a person's being.
5. The only adequate basis for a theology is something which is absolutely concrete and absolutely universal.
6. Christianity is the only religion which can satisfy No. 5.
7. All other religions are, therefore, secondary to Christianity. Whatever value other religions have is directly proportional to the degree to which they anticipate or point to Christianity.
8. Philosophy has nothing to say against this theology, since philosophy deals merely with universal reason, while theology deals with an ultimate concern.
9. The Bible is the source book of the Christian message, but it is not the only source.
10. The biblical theologian does not give pure facts, he gives theologically interpreted facts.
11. The systematic theologian uses the historical data to support his thesis. If the historical data do not support his thesis, he attacks the historical data.
12. A genuine norm of the authentic message must not be the private opinion of a theologian but "the expression of an encounter of the Church with the Christian message." [21]

What does all of this mean for our question concerning the fixed or evolving nature of Christianity? If Tillich is correct, then, as he asserted, nothing can change the substance of the Christian answer, for an ultimate commitment cannot turn out to be a mistake. The Christian word must, then, be fixed and final. But what about the Christian religion as it occurs in fact? What about the historical data which revealed the multiplicity of sects and interpretations within the framework of Christianity? These are not final, Tillich insisted, although what they witnessed was final. The same state of affairs exists for dogma or doctrines, for there were no fixed and final doctrines, although, once again, what the doctrines meant or intended was fixed and final. What do we conclude when we are confronted with the long history of conflicting revelatory messages, particularly within Christianity? Tillich insisted that this does not support the evolution theory for Christianity, but that it does indicate the shortcomings of all rational attempts to explicate the basic message. What, then, does this mean for the problem of philosophy of religion? The only plausible conclusion seems to be the one which Tillich himself supports; namely, that this is not a matter of philosophy, but a matter of faith. The ultimately concerned Christian will assert the inerrant message and that will be the end of the matter. No question of truth or falsity, nor even of significance or insignificance, will ever be brooked. If this is the Tillichian word, then the position is, indeed, of no philosophic concern, however important it may be for religious faith or pedagogy.

Let us turn briefly to our original question: "Are Judaism and Christianity fixed and final in their origins, or did they evolve and develop?" If this is considered as a historical question, then the answer is highly probable from the available facts. These two religions, like all other human enterprises, have exhibited the changeableness of essentially human constructs. If the problem is to be considered as an empirical one, then we must conclude for the evolutionary hypothesis. Every claim of Christian theologians for an original and fixed message must be confronted by the historical fact that there has been an evolution of interpretative meaning as to what the supposed original message was. Since it is not vouchsafed to any human being to be able to demonstrate either that there was a complete dogma in the beginning, or that there has been any consistency in interpretations of meaning, we seem to be left with no other choice.

The problem before us, therefore, appears to be: "Will

the value and significance of any particular religion, such as Christianity, be seriously jeopardized by this conclusion of its evolutionary development?" There is no logical reason why it should. It will be necessary, however, to alter the evidential basis for any future Christian claim. Whether Christians will be able to make an effective argument for the utilitarian superiority of their religion will be determined, in part, by the actions of Christians themselves. Philosophically speaking, the traditional theological claims for Christian uniqueness are unprovable. Indeed, in a world of democratic latitude, it seems unlikely and unnecessary for any religion to be seriously concerned with any but its own subjective superiority. It may be sufficient, and many pragmatists have found it so, to be able to demonstrate the value, for us, of our particular religion without having to detract from the value of other religions for their devotees.

In any event, the justification, either for the truth of a point of view, or for the value of a religious position, cannot rest upon a mere matter of origins. As we have previously seen, the origin of an idea has no necessary bearing on either its truth or its value. If this is accepted, then in the future, Christians, and indeed any other group of religious persons, will have to be far more concerned with their present and their future than they have been with their past. As with other human efforts, it is not so much what a religion was as what it is and can be that counts.

It still remains an open question whether what has been said at any point in the development of religion is true or false, worthy or unworthy, significant or insignificant. Suffice it to say that these matters are not decided by the determination that a religion had a mature genesis, nor are they endangered by the thesis that a religion had a progressive revelation.

XII

The Problem *of* Fundamentalism

THE TERM "Fundamentalism" in its Protestant context has been associated with the doctrinal views which constituted the essence of the Protestant Reformation in the sixteenth century. Generally speaking, the term still designates a Christian position in which the dominant theological emphases of that period are of major importance. Since Fundamentalism has this Reformation orientation, some word about the genesis of the Protestant protest against Roman Catholicism is in order.

Protests against supposed abuses in the Roman Catholic church antedate considerably the emergence of the dominant Protestant movements. These forerunners illustrate the fact that at least some of the original protests were not intended to be separatist, but proposed instead to purify the Roman Church without creating schisms. The fact remains, however, that divisions in the otherwise impregnable front of Christendom did occur. John Wyclif (1320–1384), a professor at Oxford University, has been called the "morning star of the Reformation," for he seems to have initiated the series of movements of rebellion which culminated in the sixteenth century. Complaints about papal abuses had occurred long before Wyclif, but the election in 1341 of the first lay chancellor at Oxford provided a more compatible atmosphere for a heretical professor—at any rate, until 1382, when he was forbidden to teach further at Oxford. This movement toward lay leadership in institutions of power had been further aided by the Statutes of Provisos (1351), which had been issued to ensure that the appointment of clerics was made by Englishmen rather than by Roman decree. The seriousness of these Provisos is indicated by the fact that they provided for imprisonment of any papal choice for office which did not have English sanction. In 1353 the Statute of Praemunire forbade all appeals to Rome on the part of the English clergy. Prior to this time an English Roman Catholic clergyman could not be tried by a local civil court, and if he was challenged, he could always appeal either to a local clerical court or directly to Rome, even on matters of no theological concern.

Wyclif's attack came at several strategic points. In the first place, he redefined the nature of the church. The church was, he insisted, the whole company of the elect, and not merely the hierarchy at Rome. Indeed, Wyclif went so far as to recommend that when the current Pope Urban V died, he should not be replaced, but the administration of the Church should be handled by the whole body of the members. In the second place, his analysis of power (dominion) stipulated that the lordship of political and material things carried with it certain conditions. Prelates who committed mortal sins should have their lands and power taken from them. A third objection consisted of an attack upon the doctrine of transubstantiation. On the basis of an essentially realist philosophy he denied that the wafers and the wine could be transformed during the Mass into the body and the blood of Christ. In addition to challenging a basic religious dogma, his attack undercut the status of the sacramental function of the church. Finally, Wyclif's views concerning the Bible made it clear that here was a protest which covered the whole gamut of religious administration and doctrine. He asserted that wherever there was a conflict between the Bible and the church, one should obey the Bible. Wherever conscience and the church conflicted one should obey conscience. His translation of the New Testament was followed by an edict which banned it. The public sentiment in favor of Wyclif, however, was strong enough to defeat the measure. In spite of a parliamentary law in 1414 prohibiting the public reading of the Scripture, Wyclif's followers, called Lollards, continued unabated to make the Bible public property.

Across the English Channel, in Bohemia, the influence of Wyclif was expressed in the activity of John Hus. This fiery preacher insisted that preaching the Word was more important than the sacraments. When a papal crusade was initiated against the German emperor, and indulgences were offered to all who took part in it, Hus earned the disapproval of the church by attacking the whole enterprise. He was excommunicated, called to trial before the Council of Constance, condemned, imprisoned, and finally put to death.

The rise of Christian mysticism introduced a degree of individualism which constituted a more subtle protest against the Roman church. Although the German mystics Eckhart and Tauler and the Flemish Ruysbroeck were thoroughly Roman Catholic, their writings implied a tacit criticism of papal control. This was apparent in Eckhart's emphasis upon the nobility of the human soul and the importance of private experience. The same element was somewhat differently stressed by Tauler when he preached that the works which God demonstrated in the world were more important than religious contemplation, which had been an essential medieval emphasis. These mystics soon formed organizations, and some, like the Brothers and Sisters of the Free Spirit, were investigated by the Inquisition. Others, like the Brothers of the Common Life, attracted laymen who spoke as if they were clerics, and the church took action to silence these nonprofessionals. These trends concretized a growing lay movement in religion which militated against ecclesiastical authority.

The intellectual renaissance made a further contribution to the preparation for the Reformation. Dante, Petrarch, and

Boccaccio were symbols of a growing secularism and world-liness. Boccaccio, for example, treated priests and monks with utter disrespect by picturing them as an ignorant and fleshly lot. The humanism which these writers promoted revived interest in man and his life in this world for its own sake. There was a concomitant rise in pagan morality, whose keynote was naturalism: "Let nature be your guide." In this respect the Renaissance is understandable as an emotional protest of long-outraged fleshly desires. It is interesting to note that this intellectual revival had the support of a number of popes: Nicholas V founded the Vatican library in 1450; some popes, such as Alexander V, Alexander VI, Leo IX, and Julius VI, showed a marked degree of secularization. Even the clerical excesses of secularity aided the cause of reformation. Renaissance scholars adopted linguistic tools in order to examine the ancient documents and to judge them. Lorentius Valla, for example, claimed that the Donation of Constantine was forged, and that the apostles did not write the Apostles' Creed. Erasmus of Rotterdam made a bitter and satirical attack on the clergy in his book *In Praise of Folly.* Although he has been criticized as a petty-minded man, "descended from a long line of maiden aunts," and a rascal of intrigue, he did make a contribution to the reformation of the church through his writings. He edited the New Testament in Greek (1516) and made a new Latin translation which broke the monopoly of the Vulgate version. Using three different sources, he selected what seemed to him to be the most likely interpretation, and although his translation was not a work of profound scholarship, it did point the way for others to go back to more original sources. The frank admission that translation posed real problems of scriptural interpretation added to the disturbing quality of the intellectual renaissance.

THE ATTACK ON ROMAN AUTHORITY: MARTIN LUTHER

As one of two great founders of the Protestant Reformation, Martin Luther (1483–1546) deserves special attention in the investigation of the nature of Fundamentalism.

As a youth and young man he was a pious Catholic with no trace of the rebel in him. About the age of fourteen he came into contact with the Brothers of the Common Life, a group dedicated to voluntary poverty, social service, and the most rigorous self-mortification. His memory of the devout Prince Anheit, who died from self-inflicted flagellation, remained fresh enough in his mind so that two months after graduating with a law degree, he joined the Augustinian order. The Augustinian monastery at Erfurt was a strict and well-kept place, and there he applied himself diligently to the study of theology. He has recorded in his autobiographical writings the mental and physical sufferings he endured while in the monastery. He exceeded the prescribed austerities and wearied his superiors with his penances, all of which earned him the name of being the most strict and pious monk in the whole institution. He was plagued with the problem of the gulf between his own limitations and God's greatness. Through the Occamites, who held that God is will, Luther came to believe that an act of his own will was all that was needed to attain God. His study of Saint Paul, particularly the Book of Romans, gave him the idea of a gracious God, a view which was furthered by his study of the writings of Bernard of Clairvaux.

Three men helped him in the monastery: the Master of the Novices, who impressed on him the conviction that God was willing to forgive him his sins; the confessor, who chided him on his many trivial confessions of sin; and, most of all, Joseph Stampitz. Stampitz, seeing that Luther was worried about the doctrine of predestination, advised him not to ponder the eternal punishments of God, but to think about Christ, in whose person he would find the mercy and love of God. This man was influential in changing Luther's mind about penance and directing his attention toward repentance. It was while he was reading the Book of Romans that Luther had what he called his "tower experience." It was as a consequence of this conversion crisis that he embraced the Pauline mandate that "the just shall live by faith," and with a new sense of personal security about his own salvation, he set out to preach. Although he still regarded the church as the pope's house and the pope as the house father, he did attack scholastic theology with great vehemence. This by itself did not, however, make a "protestant" out of him.

The real issues which culminated in the Protestant Reformation were summarized in Luther's ninety-five theses which he nailed on the door of the church at Wittenberg in 1517. While these theses discuss penance, pardon, purgatory, and papal power, the basic theme is the sale of indulgences. During the Crusades, when indulgences were first instituted, an indulgence was intended to free the individual from the ecclesiastical penalty for essential ecclesiastical omissions or commissions. Originally they had no relation to absolution from guilt or punishment for mortal sins, nor were they intended to relieve the individual from his personal responsibility for righteous living. Through carelessness the indulgences had come to be considered, however, as capable of giving remission for sins, which in terms of church doctrine the church had no power to do. A first step in error occurred when indulgences were made effective to remit punishment for souls in purgatory. The next step was to free the sinner from all guilt. By the time that John Tetzel was sent to Germany to sell indulgences, there was the clear impression given that the purchase of an indulgence would remit sins both here and in the hereafter. The theory surrounding the practice of selling indulgences had powerful symbolic imagery. It was presumed that saints died with a surplus of merit which was deposited in a figurative bank called the Treasury of Merit. Average sinners could then borrow merit from this bank for their own use in assuring salvation. This practice had the obvious consequence of relieving men from personal moral responsibility and of permitting virtue to be transferable. This was the concrete issue which first led Luther down the road to rebellion against the Roman church. Luther insisted that indulgences could not prevail on behalf of souls in purgatory, and, indeed, the Christian who has true repentance needs no indulgence, for he is already forgiven by God.

Luther's theses enumerated five kinds of punishment for sin, and by the same token five kinds of sin. There are eternal punishments, which are brought about by God and can be remitted only by God. Second, there are purgatory punishments, which are also brought about by God and can be remitted only by him. Third, there are evangelical punishments, which refer to Christ's recommendation that Christians mortify their flesh. God accepts such mortification, and only his grace can determine that it may not be required. Fourth, there are corrective punishments, as in the case of disease, which are administered by God for human enlightenment. While prayers and penitence can assist man, they cannot frustrate God's educative intent in sending the disease in the first place. Fifth, there are canonical punishments, which relate to infractions of Church laws and chastisement by the popes and the councils for such sins. This was the only kind of sin which it was within the jurisdiction of the church to remit, but even here, good reasons had to be shown to justify remission. The only proper sphere of indulgences, therefore, was to remit the punishments for transgressions against ecclesiastical polity. An indulgence cannot remove guilt, nor can it remit the divine punishment imposed by God for sin.

Three political movements aided the emergence of a distinct Protestant church. First, many of the German nobility were eager to break connections with Roman taxation and therefore supported Luther in his rebellion. Secondly, sheer economic desperation had led to peasant revolts against the civil leaders, most of whom owed their allegiance to the pope. Both the nobles and the peasants looked to Luther as a symbol of their aspirations. Thirdly, the rise to power of the Turks and the near capitulation of Germany to them united the nobility and the peasants against the common enemy. This situation was complicated by the fact that the pope was at the same time attempting to raise an army from Luther's homeland to engage in a crusade against the Moslem infidels. While Luther opposed the papal crusade against the Turks, he did not oppose war against the enemy. Since he was against the papal plan, many assumed that he recommended giving Germany over to the Moslems, although his polemic pamphlets against the Turks should have removed any suspicion that Luther was indifferent on this issue of national security.

In his book *Freedom of the Christian Man* Luther preached in favor of spiritual emancipation from authority, which the peasants took to mean freedom from their political and economic overlords. Since they believed that Luther was on their side, they submitted their manifesto, *The Twelve Articles of the Swabian Peasants,* to him for correction. They were disappointed in Luther's response, for he approved only two of their articles: (a) People have the right to choose their own pastor, and (b) The death duty should be abolished. This had been a penalty exacted on the death of a peasant whereby his heirs were compelled to give up to the baron the deceased's most valuable single possession. The rest of the articles were rejected by Luther in two pamphlets, *An Exhortation to Peace,* and *Against the Thieving, Murdering Hordes of Peasants.* He opposed their wish to be free from serfdom and their recommendation that church tithes be divided equally between priest and poor, and, although he directed a tirade against the princes for their treatment of the peasants, he urged these same princes to quell the revolt. The peasant revolt was doomed to failure, and about a hundred thousand peasants were killed before the princes finally desisted lest there be no one left to run the farms. Because Luther had aligned himself with the princes, the Reformation became a middle- and upper-class movement. The Lutheran church paid the price of secular control by becoming a state church, supported by state armies, and forced to look to the princes for protection against the Roman Catholic church. The division of the country into factions as a result of the Peasants' War made the unity of the Protestants a necessity if they were to exist. Philip of Hesse hoped to settle the Protestant differences by arranging a meeting between Luther and Zwingli to talk these matters over. Although there were some fourteen doctrines on which the two men did agree, their disagreement over a fifteenth, the Eucharist, prevented any real Protestant unity.

Luther's position on the Eucharist was complicated. The

Catholic position was that the bread and wine were transformed into the body and blood of Christ at a certain moment in the Mass. This event occurred independently of the partakers of the elements. This position has been called the doctrine of transubstantiation. Luther's problem was to determine what did happen to the bread and wine. He concluded that the substance of the elements remained, but that to them were added the sacramental body and blood of Christ. To accomplish this latter transformation no priest was needed, since the promise of God assured men of the presence of Christ. This resurrected body and blood was equally distributed everywhere. The role of man was simply to pronounce the proper words with the proper faith: "This is my body which was given for you," and "This cup is the new covenant in my blood which was shed for you." Zwingli, on the other hand, insisted that the only dependent factor was the faith of the partaker. The bread and wine were only symbols, and no material or substantial change occurred in them during the Eucharist.

The term "Protestant" appears to have emerged as a consequence of a debate concerning the decisions of two diets. In the first, the Diet of Spires in 1526, Protestants and moderate Catholics combined forces in a declaration that each German state could conduct religious worship in accordance with the wishes of its prince. Within three years almost all the states became Protestant. In the second Diet of Spires in 1529, a Catholic majority declared that no more innovations in religion were to be tolerated, and that Catholic states were not bound to accept Protestants in their midst. A Protestant minority of the second Diet framed a protest against this majority edict, and from this document the term "Protestant," as we have used it, was born.

The historic Augsburg Confession in 1530 summed up the Lutheran position as "the priesthood of all believers and justification by faith." Melanchthon represented Luther at the Augsburg sessions, since Luther was in exile. The Emperor, Charles V, attempted to get national agreement on the religious platform, but even though he used force, he was unsuccessful. What did occur was a nine-year religious war which ended with the Peace of Augsburg in 1555. Under the terms of the peace, Lutheranism was to be accepted as a legal religion supported by law; however, each of the princes had the power to choose whatever religion he wished as the official one for his state. If the citizens did not like the monarch's choice of religion, they could always move to another state.

Lutheran ministers put special emphasis upon preaching. They denied the need for pilgrimages, asserted that the Bible was indispensable for salvation, pronounced that it was better to read the Bible and to pray than to do good works, permitted praying to saints but insisted that Christ was the only mediator between man and God, and branded the Mass as a sacrilege because Christ's death on the cross was the only necessary sacrifice. They did away with the authority of bishops, although in some areas the prince took over the bishop's function. Because the new movement was to be based upon the Book, it was necessary that the layman as well as the clergy know the Bible. Luther had already translated the Bible into German, and to this he added a catechism for both children and adults. Luther set the tone of the sect by his insistence that religion had to be understood by the people if it was to be of any effective value.

From this tentative picture it can be seen that the Protestant movement, for Luther, was directed primarily against church organization rather than against doctrine. He protested against religious authorities far more than he protested against religious dogmas, and this situation still marks the essential difference between liturgical Protestant churches and Roman Catholicism. The mere differences of opinion on the meaning of dogmas would not have constituted a Protestant church as distinct from the Roman church, since interpretative differences had characterized the Catholic church for centuries. The challenge to the authority of the pope, the bishops, and the church councils was, however, of a distinctly radical nature. Since Luther did not effect the Reformation alone, it is necessary that we see the nature of the Calvinist protest in order to comprehend what Fundamental Protestantism was all about.

THE RISE OF BIBLIOCRACY: JOHN CALVIN

John Calvin (1509–1564) was born at Noyon in Picardy, where citizens were known for their independence of mind. He began his studies in theology, but his father, as a result of a quarrel with the clergy, had him transferred to law. He was early acquainted with Renaissance humanism. While a student at Bourges he studied under Volmar, a Lutheran in all but name. After the death of his father he decided to pursue further study in humanism and literature in Paris. There he joined a humanistic society which spent its time discussing the doctrines of Luther. His association with liberals led to a premature departure from Paris, and sent him on a series of travels to Italy, southern Germany, and Switzerland. It was at Basel, in 1536, that he published the *Institutes of the Christian Religion*, which was probably the greatest Protestant document ever written. In his introduction he stated two purposes: (a) to enable theologians to study the Divine Word, and (b) to vindicate Protestant doctrines against the calumnies of the Catholic church and the persecutions of kings. He was called to Geneva, already a Protestant stronghold, to bring some religious order. In general he appealed to the early New Testament church for doctrine, discipline, and church organization. He proposed a disciplined excommunication, which excluded unworthy persons from communion. This effort led to Calvin's exile from Geneva, because the people wanted no religious authority over them. The turmoil in Geneva, however, led to his recall, and he rose to the occasion by organizing the Venerable Company among preachers. Its function was to promote the study of theology and to enable the clergy to exercise discipline over one another. New ministers had to be elected by the church, examined by the Venerable Company, and approved by the town council. He also organized a Consistory, composed of ministers of the city and twelve lay elders. It was their task to discipline the citizens. They carried out their function with seriousness by spying on neighbors to discover wrongdoing and by employing civil government to enforce church conduct.

Calvin's greatest doctrine was that of the sovereignty of God. In so far as this concept deals with the lives of individual persons it results in the doctrine of predestination. When it is viewed from the social perspective we have the rule of God in civil states on earth.[1] He created the "religious sanction" intended to establish a community of God in Switzerland. In a sense he tried for a world monastery with Calvinists as ascetic priests of the market place. Even the reprobates were to be compelled to high moral effort. The combination of compulsion with a citizenry zealous for freedom led to the early failure of the godly commonwealth. Calvin had asserted that both the church and the state were divine and were to serve divine purposes on earth. The state was not to meddle in church affairs, but since the state did exist to serve divine ends, it was bound to bring its force to bear on the securing of proper worship and the maintenance of public morality. It was the church, however, that decided what was true, so that in practice the state became the servant of the church. An element of disestablishmentarianism was maintained by the prohibition of ministers from holding political or civil office. In order to promote the cause, Calvin established a training school at Geneva which sent 161 pastors into France in one short year. Geneva became known as "the mine whence came the ore of heresy."

The doctrine of predestination was one of the most stirring dogmas promulgated by Calvin. It was this doctrine which led, several centuries later, to many of the denominational splits. Originally the thesis of predestination was to proclaim a doctrine of assurance. This may seem odd in view of its premise that God damns the overwhelming majority of men to eternal punishment. But it contained also the premise of a saved remnant whom God singled out for eternal blessedness. Since neither salvation nor damnation was a function of the kind of moral life one led or of the deeds performed, it was apparent that in theory predestination cut the nerve of moral effort. In fact, it did not work out this way. Calvinists were intensely preoccupied with the moral life and concerned that men assume responsibility for both private and public welfare.

Their involvement in the rise of both capitalism and nationalism, although of mixed merit, showed their willingness
to exert moral effort.

Although no man could be absolutely sure of his "election" by God to salvation, every man could assume that he was
one of the elect through certain suggestive evidences.[2] After
all, there was scriptural evidence that the Jews knew that
they had been elected. Romans 8:29–30 seemed to guarantee
that Christians might have the same assurance. The signs of
election were experienced internally by a divine calling, a
sense of justification, and an assurance of sanctification. Essentially the assurance claimed for the doctrine of predestination stems from the Pauline thesis of Calvin that all men are
innately and inevitably sinners. As such, they could by no
effort of will ever perform a righteous action. Creatures such
as this obviously deserve damnation with dispatch. Men cannot excuse themselves on the ground that Adamic sin was not
their creation, for the fact remains that all men sin and they
sin with approval of their deeds. Here, then, is the situation:
All mankind stands worthily condemned by God to damnation;
however, God in his infinite mercy does not permit all men to
remain in this depraved state. He elects some, though personally unworthy and undeserving, to salvation and everlasting bliss. Calvin raised the question whether predestination
should be taught, since it was a rather grim idea. He concluded: "Since the truth is of such a nature that, when we
speak of it, he becomes worse who cannot understand it, and
when we are silent about it, he who can understand it becomes
worse, what do we think ought to be done?"[3]

Calvin was basically an "interpreter of the Word" rather
than a theologian. It was not that he was unacquainted with
traditional theology, but rather that he felt that this approach
was religiously sterile. For example, he never felt any necessity for giving proofs for the existence of God. Such speculations he branded as "cold and frivolous." The existence of
God is no problem, since every person by instinct believes in
God. What problem there is concerning God refers to his
relations to men. These relations are spelled out in the scrip-

tures, which are the sole and sufficient guide to all religious matters. Calvin asserted the Athanasian view of the Trinity and the Augustinian view of the creation of the world *ex nihilo*. On all such matters Calvin assumed the sufficiency of scriptural answers. He assumed that no man needed an interpreter for Holy Writ. The devout reader, whether clerical or lay, could understand the scriptures through his own study. One of the fundamental differences between Luther and Calvin lay in their approach to the Bible. Luther emphasized the promises, while Calvin emphasized the new law which must be enforced. Luther let everything stand which was not contrary to scripture. Calvin said that anything not permitted in the scriptures was forbidden. As a result of this, Calvinism represented a more radical revision than Lutheranism. Calvinists, unlike Lutherans, removed images from the churches, advocated severe simplicity in ritual, and forbade clerical vestments other than a black gown. While Luther accepted the political organization which he had inherited, Calvin believed that he saw in the Bible a blueprint for a new society. Luther educed consubstantiation as the interpretation of the Eucharist, while Calvin assigned a purely spiritual or dynamic merit to the elements with no spatial properties.

THE FUNDAMENTALIST PLATFORM: SIXTEENTH CENTURY

The sixteenth-century Protestants accused the Roman Catholics, to borrow a modern cliché, of being soft on sin. The dogma, the liturgy, and the actions of the Roman Catholic church made it perfectly clear that they believed that men were sinners; but they also indicated that man could, by prayer and penitent deeds, and through the efficacy of sacraments, take away some of the stigma of human foulness. There was, in Catholicism, something men could do to improve their future lot. Men could freely perform good deeds. Protestants, in part because of their greater stress on predestination, and in part because of their belief that God's foreknowledge precluded man's free will, denied that man could do anything to improve his lot in the next life. Men were sinners, desperately and hopelessly. That some persons were to be elected to salvation was due solely to the grace of God. Man was too corrupt to be expected to aid in his own salvation. Protestants, therefore, felt that the Catholic Church gave men a kind of hope which the facts of man's nature denied. It was for this reason that Protestants attacked the sacraments as being unnecessary for salvation. For the same reason the Protestants opposed indulgences, penances, and pilgrimages. In spite of the differences, it is interesting to note that Catholics denied that a man could ever have assurance that his future life would be blessed, while Protestants admitted the possibility that a divine election could be known in this life by an undeserving sinner. Since Protestants maintained the utter sinfulness of human nature, they multiplied the list of sinful acts which men performed. This conviction of man's propensity to sin led Protestants to a brooding self-analysis. They found sin expressed in all acts which were symptomatic of man's search for pleasure and which nurtured his pride. Thus, the wearing of stylish clothes, dancing, card playing, drinking and eating to excess, and a host of other daily acts were all sinful. This multiplication of sinful deeds, beyond Catholic necessity, distinguished Protestantism.

The Protestant thesis of bibliocracy, that the scriptures contained all that man needed to know, added to the dogma of the priesthood of all believers, led to a second distinction in emphasis between Protestants and Roman Catholics. Protestants denied the Catholic claim that the church was a necessary, let alone the sole, guide to salvation. To the Protestant the church was merely a community of believers. No priestly functions were essential, no objective sacraments were effective, and no institutional stamp of approval was required to aid man in his quest for God. Every man was his own priest, and faith alone was all that was required. This denial of the place and power of the church in salvation constituted a serious break with papal authority. While the original debates of Luther over the indulgences had intended to raise a question only over the authority of church councils, the insistence of the Roman authorities that councils were also infallible led Luther willy-nilly to question papal authority. Perhaps if the church had pressed less for the correctness of councils, the break with papal authority might not have occurred.

Once the Bible-centered thesis became a firm Protestant doctrine, a series of lesser objections to the Roman dogma and practice followed. These sixteenth-century Protestants challenged the Roman claim that post-Biblical miracles occurred. If the Bible were, indeed, the sole guide for Protestants, all the miracles necessary for salvation and insight must be contained therein. It was, derivatively, obvious that the recognition of later miracles supported the Roman Catholic claim to being the only authentic Church. It still seemed that miracles did not happen to Protestants with anywhere near the frequency that they happened to Roman Catholics. It became necessary, therefore, for Protestants to deny that any miracles had really taken place after the New Testament era. Modern Protestant groups are not univocal on this score. Contemporary Protestant confidence in miracles of a postbiblical sort appears to be proportional to the degree of evangelical fervor displayed. Members of middle-class "intellectual" denominations commonly reject even biblical miracles. Indeed, it seems reasonable that the rejection of postbiblical miracles should lead to the rejection of all miraculous occurrences at any time.

A further consequence of the doctrines of biblical sufficiency and the priesthood of all believers was a distaste for theology. Calvin, in particular, had no patience with the "cold and frivolous" speculations of theologizing. If every man can be his own priest, obviously rational speculation is not essential. The mental incompetence of most persons would necessitate such a conclusion. In addition, if "justification by faith" ruled out works as unnecessary, it must clearly eliminate intellectual proofs as equally unnecessary. The idea of systematic theology is still looked on with suspicion by many contemporary Protestants. Paul Tillich, in spite of an imposing work called *Systematic Theology,* exhibits this same fundamental doubt as to its legitimacy or necessity. The intellectual incompetence of man seemed a natural corollary to his moral incompetence. Even where there were Protestant attempts to formulate doctrine, it was admitted that diversity of presentation was to be expected. Thus the multiplication of Protestant sects, each claiming to be interpreting the biblical Word, has been a natural consequence. The Catholic dream of theological unity was not even a remote thought in Protestantism.

THE FUNDAMENTALIST CONTROVERSY: TWENTIETH CENTURY

The antirationalism and the stress on biblical inerrancy led the Fundamentalist churches quite understandably into the heated conflict over biological evolution which was symbolized in the trial of John T. Scopes, a biology teacher in Tennessee, in the summer of 1925. Tennessee had already passed a law prohibiting the teaching of any scientific theory which was contrary to the Bible, but of all the possible points on which the law might have been enforced, biological evolution was the only one which actually reached the stage of serious debate. This was not a mere accident of history, for ever since Charles Darwin, Fundamentalism had raised its voice in protest against the "monkey" theory of human origins. It was beside the point that Fundamentalists, with few exceptions, had no idea what the theory of biological evolution was all about. They were even less literate than the age which condemned Gallileo and the Copernican theory of planetary motion. It was sufficient for the Fundamentalist Protestant to note that the Genesis story of creation, if literally interpreted, was contradicted by the theory of endless evolution from simpler forms of life.[4]

This phenomenon of the aggressive, emotional, and schismatic attack upon science as the foe of religion, typified by the clash between biological evolution and the Garden of Eden tale, was almost peculiar to the nonliturgical Christian sects. Roman Catholicism, Lutheranism, Anglicanism, and even Methodism were relatively uninvolved; the first three because they were still within the cognitive tradition of Saint Thomas and Saint Augustine, and the fourth because John Wesley had never held to a strict doctrine of inerrancy of the Bible. The attack came instead from the pentecostal, faith-healing, and small evangelical sects.

A number of characteristics seemed to typify this revolt of Fundamentalism against the encroachments of science. The adherents of this belief demanded and required certainty. To admit the findings of science raised doubts of the inerrancy of the Bible, and hence science was the Antichrist to be defeated at all costs. The movement was further characterized by an intense emotionalism coupled with a sense of militant urgency. Fundamentalists were going to war against the powers of darkness, and the issues were of the magnitude of life and death. In addition, the first thirty years of the twentieth century witnessed a rise of hatred and bigotry from which some of the movements have not yet recovered. The attack upon evolution was coupled with attacks upon Jews, Catholics, the labor movements, Negroes, and the whole emphasis on "social gospel." Fundamentalists joined and were joined by the Ku Klux Klan, anti-Semitic organizations, and scores of similar hatred and bigotry groups. While these pressure organizations were unsuccessful, they exerted a mighty effort to stir American Protestantism awake to the putative dangers of a host of demonic powers. Scores of such movements flowered and withered in short order. Added to all these characteristics of the Fundamentalist protest against evolution in particular and science in general, was a piously held ignorance of human intellectual accomplishments. Clerical leaders asserted that all necessary information could be found in the Bible, the hymnal, and the almanac. To advocate any other books than these was to nurture impious doubts and to undermine scriptural faith.

This twentieth-century Fundamentalist protest stemmed from a threefold platform. The Fundamentalists opposed science in education, the "social gospel" in religious practice, and communism in politics. Instances of these latter two trends they found in all social-service enterprises, labor criticisms of management, pacifist challenges of militarism, and the efforts of some to promote the integration of the races. These same devotees of biblical inerrancy gloried in their intellectual ignorance and fostered the thesis that stupidity was next to godliness. As in the case of William Jennings Bryan, most of these opponents of evolution had never read a scholarly book on the subject in question. It would, of course, be misleading to give the impression that all Fundamentalists, from Calvin to the present, have been illiterate; but the fact remains that the Fundamentalist stress upon certitude, personal enlightenment, biblical inerrancy, and Christian uniqueness has nurtured an intolerance in dealing with other ideas and a fear of science.

The chief theological ideas of Fundamentalism during this period were typified by the famous five points announced by the General Assembly of the Presbyterian Church in the United States in 1910. These points were: (a) the Bible is the inerrant word of God; (b) Jesus was born of a virgin; (c) Jesus died to pay the retributive price which God demanded by virtue of human sin (the Atonement theory); (d) Jesus was physically resurrected; and (e) during his lifetime he performed miracles. Other religious groups added to this list of basic dogmas such doctrines as these: (f) Jesus will come again (millennialism); (g) the whole Christian revelation had been effected by the end of the New Testament era; and (h) Christianity was a unique religion, and not the result of historical development. With claims of such magnitude coupled with the demand for absolute certitude and the denial of human reason, it has been little wonder that intolerant bigotry has characterized the Fundamentalist message.

PERSISTENT PROBLEMS OF FUNDAMENTALISM

Perhaps the greatest general difficulty which any Fundamentalist faces is the sharp contrast between his approach to the subject of religion and his approach to most other fields of thought. His methodology, or lack of it, puts his religion in such a light that no secular experience can ever shed any light on his religious experience. As a consequence, his intellectual life is schizophrenic, for his religion makes no contact with the rest of human effort. He may accept the findings of diagnostic and curative medicine, but these are divorced from his religious commitments. He may be a courageous and enthusiastic democrat, but he still idolizes scriptural stories in which medieval lords and tyrants are the heroes. If he studies biology, anthropology, and geology and accepts these disciplines as contributing to the store of human knowledge, then his religion, by contrast, will seem a pretty naïve affair with its six-thousand-year-old world, fixed species, and providential laws. If he rejects the findings of these sciences, then he puts himself in a most unfavorable light among scholars. All of these situations could be avoided; indeed, Roman Catholicism has demonstrated a convenient way of doing this —namely, by insisting that the religious explanation be amenable to the methods of science. While it is true that the Roman Catholic has revealed dogmas which transcend science, they do not conflict with science. The Protestant Fundamentalist, therefore, must be an intellectual anachronism if he is to hold his position seriously.

A specific aspect of this difficulty arises when biblical scholarship is admitted to be a possibility. Historical, critical, and philological analyses of the Bible make Fundamentalism, at the point of biblical inerrancy, a pretty indefensible position. The alternative which the Fundamentalist has is to reject all scriptural scholarship, but this option puts the Book in an area which makes it beyond both dispute and support. If the Bible is to be discussed at all, then biblical scholarship must be admitted. If biblical scholarship is to be rejected, then the Bible can never be cogently talked about. It is quite understandable that the Fundamentalist feels himself to be put in a dilemma, but this very fact suggests that there is at least one self-contradiction entailed in the position of Protestant conservatism.

A further problem that persists in the Fundamentalist point of view relates to the insistence upon the "priesthood of all believers" and the denial of all objective authorities. If

the Protestant Fundamentalist wishes to hold to the position
of individual inspiration and enlightenment, and still wants to
deny that any arbitration will ever be possible, then he must
consign himself to the anomalous situation of hundreds of
contradictory sects, each claiming apodictic certitudes. Unless
he holds to the position that all these contradictions are equally
true or insightful, which he does not, then he is caught by his
very inability to prove which sect has the most authentic
message. Exhortation is his only weapon in this predicament,
and this has not proved to be either fruitful or defensible. This
dilemma could also be avoided, as pragmatists like William
James have indicated, by emphasizing the consequences of
religious commitment rather than the theology of religious
belief. This shift in emphasis makes the issues of scriptural
inerrancy, doctrinal truth, or the reality of miracles quite secondary to the matter of the pragmatic fruits of religious commitment. The Fundamentalist, however, wants to talk like
Saint Thomas, but without any rational basis for doing so.

All of the foregoing has a bearing on the contemporary
religious theme that man is alienated from his fellow men,
from his world, and from God. This alienation has been expressed in terms of man's inability to find security in a world
of flux, to find a guiding Providence in a world with so much
natural evil, to feel at home in a world so indifferent to
human aspirations, or to find grounds for brotherhood in a
world of warring peoples. It is perhaps not inappropriate to
note that the Fundamentalist is alienated from the whole
intellectual history of man. Not only are his emotions frus-
trated in such a world as this, but his intellect is confounded
by his premise that rationality and religion are irreconcilable.
If we consider the positions held by Saint Augustine, Immanuel Kant, Ludwig Feuerbach, and William James, there is
an element of agreement here between the Fundamentalist
and the Modernist, as well as between the Roman Catholic
and the Protestant. The abyss is, however, unbridgeable in
Fundamentalism by virtue of its claim that science is a threat
to religion. The four men named above would agree that religion is not fundamentally a cognitive affair, but they would

not set religion and science at each other's throats. The religious man is in a desperate position when he declares science and religion to be enemies. The choice between them then becomes an exclusively disjunctive one where both science and religion are the losers.

The dominant elements in the Protestant Fundamentalist position stand out most clearly when contrasted with the correlates in Roman Catholicism. Four items have been crucial: (a) The Roman Catholic view was that, while man is morally a sinner, he is able with the assistance of the Church to rise above his sinfulness. This was ideally expressed in the lives of saints, but held also in the case of average parishioners who could by prayer and penance achieve some moral rectitude. (b) The Roman Catholic church assumed that man was intellectually competent to construct mundane theology and to understand the philosophic metaphysics which supported this theology. (c) The Catholic assumed that supernatural revelation had not ceased with the end of the New Testament, but that God had continued to manifest himself, particularly in the case of miracles. (d) Finally, the Catholic insisted that the church with its sacraments, its clergy, and its infallible authority was essential to salvation.

Protestant Fundamentalism, on the other hand, signified an attack upon all four of these conventional doctrines. (a) The Fundamentalist returned to Saint Augustine in his emphasis upon the depth of human sin. Apart from God, man was so corrupted by sin that he could do nothing to save himself. Salvation, if it came at all, was a gift of God. By implication, therefore, the complex Catholic system of sacraments and penances was superfluous and presumptuous. In this regard Protestant Fundamentalists had far less confidence in man's moral potential than did the Roman Catholics. (b) Fundamentalism represented an attack upon the possibility of rational theology. In part this attack was predicated upon the assumption of man's intellectual incapacity, and in part it rested upon an analysis of the nature of religion such that theologizing and philosophizing were irrelevant and contradictory. (c) The emphasis upon the Bible as the sole guide to salvation led the Fundamentalists to reject the possibility of postbiblical revelation. Their denial of postbiblical miracles was an instance of their confidence in the sufficiency of the scriptures. (d) The Protestant Fundamentalist attack upon all authority, save that of the Bible, led naturally to their rejection of the entire sacramental system of the Roman church. The Fundamentalist denied that the church had a necessary role in salvation, in the remission of sins, or in the fulfilling of godly requirements. If the Roman Catholic church had been admitted to possess infallible interpretative wisdom of the Bible, then clearly it would have been more necessary than the scriptures for salvation. The individualism of which Fundamentalism was a part prohibited the admission of any authority outside that of individual enlightenment. A consequence, however, of this Fundamentalist rejection of authority was the emergence of a host of sectarian differences which there were no means of reconciling. This has been the plague of Protestantism, for it has had to pay dearly for its individualism by accepting irresolvable religious differences of opinion as the desperate situation which is doomed to prevail.

XIII

The Problem *of* Modernism

THE NINETEENTH CENTURY bequeathed to the study of religion both an attitude and a set of data which created an intellectual revolution in the philosophic approach to the Judeo-Christian religion. The attitude was expressed as a confidence in the endless evolutionary development of the creations of human intellect. This century was characterized by a spirit of flux and change. The old absolutes collapsed and confidence was shaken in the old Aristotelian theory of fixed species, in the idea of a perfect and changeless political utopia, and in the belief that there were moral verities which would never change. The means of explicating this mood of dynamism was supplied by the German philosopher G. W. F. Hegel. He proposed a dialectical logic which would embrace all empirical statements, much as in induction. Hegel believed that his logic, unlike traditional induction and deduction, portrayed the world, and not merely grammar. Since he assumed that things in the world were in constant change, he doubted that a logic of fixed disjuncts would be adequate. Previous logical systems had presupposed the Law of Excluded Middle.

This had entailed that any field of discourse could be exhaustively characterized by a twofold classification of either-or. Statements were either true or not true, and disjuncts such as the following were assumed to be appropriate: "Either the sun is shining or it is not shining"; "Either there is a God or there is not a God." With such a dichotomy it was presumed that all possibilities were explained: clearly, if it was not the case that there was a God, then it must be the case that there was not a God. This whole logical pattern presumed a fixed and changeless situation. If, as Hegel believed, the world was in constant change, then a logic which took account of this change was required. While the old logic distinguished either-or situations, Hegel's logic proposed a both-and situation. In place of a grammatical logic, he supplied a metaphysical logic.

While there were serious doubts that Hegel's logic actually evaded the Law of Excluded Middle, or that his logic was really metaphysically true, the fact remained that Hegel influenced his age in favor of the evolutionary attitude. The nineteenth-century thinkers developed the implications of this evolutionary hypothesis in geology, biology, economics, politics, and ethics. As a consequence there were revolutions, both material and mental. Virtually all the empirical disciplines uncovered data which supported the thesis of endless change. Specifically for religion the crucial data were supplied by historians, philologians, psychologists, and sociologists. When the spirit of dynamic process was coupled with the data to support this spirit, a nineteenth-century consequence in religion, called Modernism, appeared. This new religious expression presupposed religious evolution and the denial of fixed absolutes.

The essential religious mood to which Modernism was contrasted was that passed on by Protestant Fundamentalism and Roman Catholic orthodoxy. Let us review the basic elements which these two emphases contained. Our survey of the problems of Fundamentalism indicated that in spite of its attack upon several Roman Catholic dogmas, its basic attitudes toward reason and faith remained in the medieval tradition. If we use Saint Thomas as the Roman Catholic archetype, it is clear enough that this religion rested upon faith. In spite of the stress upon reason in his *Summa,* thinking was at best a vehicle for the transmission of meanings. Reason did not claim to prove the articles of faith. Rational theology merely indicated that the results of reason were compatible with the pre-commitments of faith. Nor was it ever intended in either the Roman Catholic or the Protestant sects that reason could or should undermine faith. While it was a standard procedure to quote the position of the church fathers of the past to support a particular interpretation of the meaning of a dogma, and, further, to use reason to bolster the views of the church fathers, it was still not imagined that the dogmas of faith were ever in question. The scholastics knew the answers at the start. It was enough if philosophy could arrive at answers consistent with faith or consistent with intuitive theology. The simple fact that philosophy was dominated by the church precluded any other possibility. With all of this the Protestant Fundamentalist was in practical agreement. The medieval search for unity of knowledge and faith, when backed by an authoritative church power, led naturally to the view that reason is a poor country cousin whose function is to aid faith where it can and to keep silent otherwise.

After all the initial furor of the Protestant revolt had mellowed, we find the new movement in essential agreement with the old in this matter of the secondary role of reason. While the Protestants rejected the authority of the church councils, the church fathers, and the popes, their alternative was simply to substitute new authorities for the old. Most Protestants thought of the Bible as an authority whose word was not to be tampered with by fallible human reason. The Protestants, like their Roman Catholic ancestors, still considered it proper to quote men of the past to support dogma. While this commonly meant Saint Paul or Saint John, even Protestants were not averse to citing the opinion of St. Augustine, Martin Luther, or John Calvin. In spirit the Protestants still assumed a unity of authoritative knowledge about religion. Understandably, the lack of any Protestant body to provide the official position led to a Protestant disunity in fact. In spite of the Protestant protest against Roman authority, Fundamentalism did not intend to leave religion to the mercies of subjective interpretations. Nor did the Protestants intend to reconstruct religion on the basis of rational scholarship. This combination of medieval authoritariansim and ultimate reliance upon faith bound both Roman Catholics and Fundamentalists into a common although unadmitted alliance.

THE SPIRIT OF MODERNISM: CATHOLIC AND PROTESTANT

The movement called Modernism represented an attack upon the authoritarianism of both Catholics and Protestants. Since the members of the new movement were themselves Catholics and Protestants, it constituted for many of them a puritan emphasis rather than a new separatism. The spirit of the Modernist approach was characterized by an insistence that there should be no authority over the individual in his search for truth. Neither church nor Bible, pope nor apostle should fetter the free and objective search. The Modernists insisted that human freedom from the past had been a precondition to thoughtful investigation in all other areas, and that therefore religious scholars must be free to raise questions even concerning the most sacred dogmas and texts. Modernism represented a serious attack on the medieval presupposition of the unity of faith and reason as an axiom. What the Modernists proposed was a reassessment of the Christian traditions as found in the Bible in the light of scholarship using the methods of science. The typical credo of this new religious scholarship endorsed the freedom of thought and belief, the use of scientific tools in the study of the Bible, and the justification of the Christian faith as unique by the pragmatic study of the its psychological and sociological consequences.[1]

Modernism produced a threefold classification of the modes of scriptural investigation:

1. *Textual criticism,* which aimed first of all to get the documents of scripture correctly translated. The fulfillment of this task required manuscripts of sufficient age and variety,

scholars of linguistic skill, and men of sufficient imagination to be able to choose when faced with variant copies of the same passage.

2. *Higher criticism,* which proposed to determine the authorship, origin, date, and literary structure of the scriptures using the best available tools of modern literary scholarship. The success of this effort required archaeological data, historical knowledge of the times in which the respective books were written, and comparative data from other religious traditions.[2] Among the scholars in this emphasis may be mentioned S. R. Driver, A. F. Kirkpatrick, Marcus Dodds, G. A. Smith, and F. W. Farrar. While it was not the original intent of higher criticism to evaluate the truth of the statements of scripture, it soon became evident that inferences regarding truth did appear to be entailed.

3. *Historical criticism* aimed to determine the credibility of the documents. If, for example, it was discovered that the Pentateuch was written many centuries after the events described took place, then it would be natural to raise the question whether the facts reported were really correct. When, for example, some critics proposed the multi-document hypothesis of the origin of the Pentateuch,[3] and when the biblical scholar discovered that the same event may be described in variant accounts, then it was reasonable to question which account, if any, was the true one. While the problem of higher criticism was to discover, if possible, precisely what a given scriptural statement would have meant in the age in which it was written, the problem of historical criticism was to determine which scriptural variant was actually the authentic report.

One of the factors that compounded the seriousness of the critical approach to the scriptures was the moral quality of the actions and assertions of many of the biblical characters. The problem was not merely whether any particular statement was actually made, or even whether the statement was true. Both of these matters were secondary in emotional significance when matched with the obvious moral penury in the actions of hitherto important religious seers. Was Noah a drunkard, Jacob a thief, Lot guilty of incest, and Saul a murderer? If we take the stories about these men as correct reports, then they shrink in moral stature. If, on the other hand, we wish to save their character, then we must presume that at these points the Scriptures are incorrect. In the light of science it would be incredible that axheads would float on the water or that the sun would stand still (II Kings 6:6; Joshua 10:13). Taking the scriptures as authentic reports, we find very few of the Old and New Testament religious leaders worthy of emulation.

Some Modernists carried this spirit of free inquiry to the point where they doubted that there was any scriptural support for the pre-existence of Christ, the virgin birth, the miracles, or the Resurrection. Tolstoy, in particular, insisted that Jesus did not believe in the Resurrection, and that the whole idea of a future life was a heathen distortion. Both Catholic and Protestant Modernists concluded that there was no scriptural support for the authority of the Roman church, the infallibility of the papacy, the inerrancy of church councils, or the literal significance of the seven sacraments.

The conclusions of Protestant Modernism are well exemplified in the work of David C. Torrey.[4] His thesis was prompted by the assumption that religion was an affair of the mental processes, and that it followed that the only sanctions for religious faith lie in men's minds. Human reason and human science were the only legitimate sources of appeal. It followed, therefore, that both the existence and the nature of God had to make rational scientific sense. Torrey's defense for a God consisted basically in a teleological argument in which the assertion "God exists" was coherent with the other facts of human experience. This God had to be intelligent, good, immanent, and potent. It could never be held that this God would do what a man would be punished for doing. If we accept this analysis of the nature of the God, then a wholesale rejection of most of the Old Testament accounts of God would have to follow. While Torrey discussed Jesus as if he were, in some sense, divine, the meaning of "divine" appeared to be purely symbolic. The term "Christ" is merely an archetype of what all men could become. The incarnation is not a unique event, therefore, but rather something that could and should happen to all persons. Torrey rejected the miracles of Jesus as of no interest to men of intelligence. He dismissed predestination as unworthy of a God who was claimed to be both wise and good. Though the above comments may seem to be inimical to the Christian belief, Torrey maintained that when the balance sheet was totaled, Christianity still appeared as the best religion in the world.

Like most Modernists, Torrey appealed to the data of psychology and sociology as supporting the conclusion that Christianity worked best. It was, however, at this precise point that the Modernist faced a contradiction. If he were to be a firm advocate of modern science, and to let the facts speak for themselves, then it seemed necessary for him to recognize that other religions have just as good psychological and sociological support as does Christianity. If we study the facts, it should be obvious that Christianity cannot make any pragmatic claim to a sincere Hindu or to a sincere Moslem on the grounds that their religions lack some worthy quality which only the Christian message can provide. At this point, therefore, the Modernists appeared to be inconsistent: they claimed a practical superiority for Christianity which the facts did not support. Critics of Modernism have pointed out that the advances in a country such as the United States cannot all be laid to the credit of the Christian religion. There are economic, geographic, scientific, and political factors which may well account to a far greater extent for the advantages enjoyed in a particular land than the religious persuasion which happens to predominate. Since it is perfectly reasonable to draw this inference, this may be one of the reasons why Fundamentalists have felt that Modernists undermine the authenticity and uniqueness of the Christian religion.

Modernism has not, however, been a peculiarly Protestant movement. Contemporary with the Protestant manifestation there was a vital and driving Roman Catholic corollary. The seriousness of the Roman Catholic movement may be measured, in part, by the number of defections from the faith attributed to Modernism. In the short span of twelve years, from 1898 to 1910, it was estimated that over 75,000 Roman Catholics left the faith in Austria alone. It was further estimated that in the nineteenth century about a million Roman Catholics were lost in Europe and the United States.[5]

A further indication of the magnitude of Roman Catholic Modernism may be inferred from the encyclicals issued by the popes on the subject. On April 17, 1907, Pope Pius X issued some strong words of protest against the Modernist heresies, which were at this time apparently quite widespread among the clergy. On July 3, 1907, he issued the "Decree of the Holy Officium Lamentabili," which contained a list of sixty-five Modernist theological heresies. On September 8, 1907, the longest papal encyclical ever written was composed against Modernism, "Pascendi Dominici Gregis." Since the "Lamentabili" lists the heresies which many Roman Catholic clergy were asserting, it is simplest to refer to this document for the evidence of what Modernism meant to the Roman Catholic leaders.[6]

The Roman Catholic scholars were apparently insisting that the same scholarship which was being applied to the Bible should be applied also to all pronouncements of the church fathers and to the edicts of the church councils. These Roman clerics posited further that the pope was in no position to be the judge of scholarship in any area other than that of revealed truth. They claimed that much of what was proposed for the assent of the faithful was false, and hence that the church ought not to require agreement on these matters from its members. If scholarship warrants, the clergy ought to be able to criticize the church councils and to ignore the Index. So far as the Bible is concerned, it is clear from Roman Catholic higher criticism that many parts are historically incorrect, morally suspect, or factually false. The Bible must be studied as any other historical document would be. As applied to the New Testament specifically, it was noted that the Gospels showed indications of later reworking by additions and emendations until there was serious doubt whether they presented any clear picture of Jesus. The gospel according to John was the most unhistorical and factually unreliable of them all. In some instances Modernists insisted that the church held views which were unscriptural, and that, therefore, the position of the church ought to be rejected. Even some of the purported revealed dogmas were open to question by these critics. If, after all, faith rests upon a mass of probabilities, then the dogmas are at best preceptive rather than matters of inerrant belief.

It is interesting to note some of the specific items which Roman Catholic Modernists identified. For example, they observed that if the New Testament is authoritatively correct, then Jesus must have made a factual mistake when he supposed that the world would end in his time. The Gospels seem to indicate clearly that Jesus was a millennialist. Since the world has not come to an end, Christians face one of two options: either they save Jesus' intelligence by blaming the millennial report on a scriptural error, or they save the inerrancy of the scriptures by blaming millennialism on Jesus' ignorance. Christians are put into a difficult position when they have to choose between the Bible and Jesus on the grounds that one of them must be mistaken. In addition, they noted that neither the doctrine of the Resurrection nor the doctrine of the Atonement was supported by the Gospels. Interestingly enough, however, both of these ideas are supported by Saint Paul. This would appear to constitute a support for the thesis that the Christian religion had evolved. When it was pointed out by certain Catholic Modernists that the church sacraments were not to be found in the New Testament, the only obvious inference to be drawn was that they were part of the later accretions to Christianity. Odd as it may sound, some of these same Catholic thinkers questioned even the dogma that Peter received the keys of the heavenly church from Christ. The fact that the Roman Catholic church currently claimed cosmic dominion was due merely to political exigencies coupled with interpretative imagination. In no case did the authority of the church derive from any biblical sanction. The dominant thesis throughout Modernism has been to oppose authority and to favor objective scholarship.

In the encyclical called "Pascendi" the pope accused the Modernists of agnosticism, on the one hand, and of believing too much on the other. Their agnosticism prevented them from giving sufficient assent to the dogmas of the faith, while at the same time it led them to put too much confidence in reason. These Modernists preferred science to faith. Pope Pius X dismissed higher criticism as impious and inadmissible in view of the obvious consequences of ecclesiastical anarchy to which it led. Some Italian clerics went so far as to deny Christ's divinity, and yet they still claimed that they were Roman Catholic priests. Although Italian clerics produced their share of biblical critics, much of their criticism was directed toward freedom of conscience in the political area.

Pope Pius X was not the first to raise an official protest against this Modernist movement. On November 18, 1893, Pope Leo XIII had issued an encyclical, "Providentissimus," which attacked the "heretical" interpretations of the Bible.

In any case, by December 31, 1910, Pope Pius X issued an anti-Modernist oath which was required of all Roman Catholic clergy in Europe and America. There is no accurate check on the number of clergy who left the church rather than take the oath as compared with the number of Modernists who took the oath and stayed with the church. Among the leading spokesmen of this Modernist position, however, were men of the stature of Abbé Alfred Loisy of France, Father Tyrrell of England, Dr. Hugo Koch of Germany, and Father Hecker of the United States.

If we were to concentrate on the degree to which higher criticism plays a role in the major Protestant seminaries in this country, it would appear that Modernism is widely taught and endorsed. If it is the case that most Protestants in the present National Council of Churches of Christ in America feel unmoved by the concern which made the Scopes trial so heated, it may indicate the degree to which Modernism has become an established element. In addition, in spite of the papal encyclicals branding Modernism as a heresy, there has been no movement on the part of Catholic clergy to attack biological evolution or geological history. Indeed, it would seem most un-Thomistic to propose such an attack. After all, Saint Thomas had insisted that the findings of science and those of mundane theology could not possibly conflict. Since these two areas used the same inductive and deductive methods, they ought to arrive at compatible conclusions.

The specter of Modernism appears to haunt both Protestant Fundamentalism and orthodox Roman Catholicism. For both groups this movement understandably threatens both faith in the dogmas and in the literal interpretation of the scriptures. As long as there are Christians who insist upon a literal rendering of all biblical passages, Modernism will be heretical. As long as there are Christians who insist that every statement in the Bible must be an inerrant religious statement, so that, if the statement is shown to be false or mythically figurative, then all of the Bible collapses—just so long will there be Christians who oppose the Modernist attempts to apply the principles of scholarship to the works of religion. Let us turn now to a closer look at the meaning of higher criticism and historical criticism as they were developed by these Modernists.

THE QUEST FOR BIBLICAL TRUTH

Certainly one of the most contentious issues to arise out of the Modernist analysis has been the application of the methods of scholarly thought toward the criticism of the scripture. These higher critics discovered two facts of ultimate significance. First, they discovered that most of the biblical writings were composed long after the events which they described took place. Secondly, their philological analyses revealed that much of the scriptural writing was never intended to be factual description. Large sections of the Bible were figurative, mythical, or essentially in the spirit of poetry. If this was so, then one of the problems of the scholar was to decide first of all which parts, if any, were intended to be factually understood. If, further, it was assumed that the New Testament books were written considerably later than the events they interpreted, there was a problem of distinguishing the later accretions from what had been the original event. As a consequence of this, it became popular to speak of the "spirit" of the New Testament as opposed to the "letter" of the New Testament.

Adolf Harnack, one of the leading biblical analysts, distinguished what he called the "kernel" as opposed to the "husk" of the New Testament. The urgent question for Christians was: "What was the original and authentic message which is the essence of Christianity?" We discussed a related question in the chapter on inerrant scriptures—the question whether the Old Testament was to be read as if it were literally correct or divinely inspired. We noted in that context that serious problems of the coherence of the Old Testament within itself and with the secular historical data made it unlikely that any rational interpretation would be possible under the thesis of divine inspiration. A comparable set of difficulties confronted the New Testament scholars.

Do the Synoptic Gospels portray the authentic message? Do they reveal the historical Jesus? Albert Schweitzer, in his *Quest for the Historical Jesus,* presented an incisive survey of the theories which led to the obvious conclusion that the historical Jesus was lost to modern man. Are we to assume that the Gospel according to John added Greek philosophical ideas which were not a part of the original message? Schweitzer recommended that we dismiss this fourth Gospel as clearly unauthentic.[7] And what shall we do with the letters of Saint Paul? Should we conclude with Kierkegaard that Saint Paul spoiled Christianity, and that, hence, his writings ought not to be considered as authentic? Yet even where scholars limited themselves to the first three Gospels, conflicting views were possible. If we were to stress the Sermon on the Mount, then it might appear that Christianity was another ethical religion. This was a point which Schweitzer stressed in his *Psychiatric Study of Jesus.* Some scholars maintained that the ethics in the Sermon on the Mount presuppose the millennialist view that the world will end at any moment. This view would make them interim ethics. We would then assume that the requirements that we turn the other cheek, go the second mile, or give away our coats were intended only for a space of time of a month or two at most. Under no circumstances was it intended that this type of behavior was desirable for the long run. Alfred Loisy concluded that there were no Christian ethics in the New Testament, on the obvious assumption that the writers did not expect the world to continue.[8] This would mean that the contemporary Christian who wanted a guide to Christian moral living could not find it in the Sermon on the Mount. Indeed, Loisy insisted that the eschatological preoccupation of Jesus led him to ignore long-term ethical considerations. Christianity was not an ethical religion. While it did reveal truth about the nature of God, it did not prescribe rules for human conduct. Reinhold Niebuhr, on the other hand, maintained that the eschatological message was a consequence rather than a cause of the New Testament ethics.[9] But if Christianity was not an ethical insight, then what kind of insight was it?

A group of scholars led by the German professor, Bruno Bauer, emphasized the element of coloration which the writers of the New Testament books were assumed to have added to the original accounts which they were elucidating. Bauer, for example, accepted only four letters as authentically from Paul.[10] In addition, he admitted that the Book of Revelation was an authentic picture, although in the language of myth, of the events described. Bauer found even the Gospels distorted by both Jewish and Greek thinking.

When we assess the implications of all these ideas, we conclude that the historical Jesus is not crucial to the Christian message. It is sufficient if we can show that the New Testament expressed the tendencies of later interpretations. Implicit within these accounts is a running intellectual debate between the original twelve disciples and Saint Paul. In 1835 David Strauss published his famous *Life of Jesus*, which asserted that the Jesus of the Gospels was so overlaid with myth that the historical Jesus was undiscoverable. In his revised version of 1865 he presented the Gospel accounts of Jesus as conscious inventions on the part of the writers. J. M. Robertson, in his *Christianity and Mythology* (1900), developed the hypothesis that Christ was a wholly mythical construct from pre-Christian times, and that, while there may have been a historical Jesus, there was never a historical Christ.[11] In a recent account one author's reaction to biblical criticism asserted that "our knowledge of Christ is not dependent on what can be reliably known about the historical life of Jesus," "our knowledge of the authentic words of Christ does not depend on what can be established as Jesus' words," and "the truth about the meaning of Christ does not depend upon what was present in the self-consciousness of Jesus."[12] While this would make it appear that knowledge about Christ was impossible, the author did insist that there was an authentic meaning which no amount of Biblical scholarship could shake. Men of the caliber of C. H. Dodd and Martin Dibelius supported this position that while the historical Jesus was unknowable, the meaning of Christ was not. In all of these speculations the idea of myth in the New Testament had an ambiguous connotation.

While all of this might appear to pose a high degree of confusion in the analysis of the Christian Scriptures, there were men like Friedrich Schleiermacher who insisted that the spirit or feeling element was all that was required to understand the Christian message. The sacred book of Christianity would not be unraveled by logical speculation. If we chose this view, then, even the thesis of Bauer, which claimed that both Jesus and Paul were dramatic creations, would not turn out to be crucially disturbing; nor would we feel uneasy about Feuerbach's contention that anthropology was the key to theology.

MYTH AND CHRISTIANITY

A recent controversy, predicated on the assumption that the essential Christian message is couched in myth form in the New Testament, approaches the issue as if the very element of myth were advantageous to Christianity.

The issue has come to be called the problem of demythologiz-ing. Friedrich Gogarten [13] held that the demythologizing is-sue arose over the question of the meaning of the historical message of the Christian faith in the light of the assumption that the New Testament account is overlaid with myth. The ensuing controversy [14] has divided the disputants into two op-posing, but not completely irreconcilable, groups. On the one hand, it has been asserted that we must pare away the myth to find the historical facts that underlie this myth. The pro-ponents of this view held that the historicity of the events is the basic matter, though it maintained at the same time that there was a transhistorical element in Christianity which had no secular parallel. While these historical facts supported the faith, the faith was not dependent upon these facts for its authenticity. The second position held that the scholar must pare away the myth, not to find historical fact, but to gain the insight into the *kerygma* (message) of the Gospels. This message is revealed by understanding on the part of man of the "existential possibilities." [15] While the former view seeks for historical authenticity, the latter view proposes existential insight.

The Jaspers-Bultmann controversy sharpened the distinc-tion between these two positions. This controversy has been marked by a degree of emotional enthusiasm reminiscent of Fundamentalism. Jaspers and Bultmann both recommended demythologizing. This process involves the recognition that the language of myth is not the language of science, and hence that the tools of science are not appropriate for the understanding of this language. Where the two men differed was at the point of what to do after the myths had been recognized as noncognitive and hence as neither true nor false. Jaspers proposed that in spite of the scientific limita-tions of mythical language it was still the best medium for the expression of the essential faith. Bultmann, on the contrary, insisted that once the myths had been identified as noncogni-tive, Christians would have to seek for the meaning of the message in personal existential experience. The myths were of no help in the clarification of meanings, which are, after all, cognitive matters. Jaspers countered by insisting that philosophy was incapable of understanding religion either historically or as a faith. Myths being what they are, the nature, methods, and results of science are all improper for their study. Philosophy is in no position to criticize religion as Bultmann seems to do. For example, Bultmann insisted that the scientific view does not permit Christians to keep the idea of miracles. Jaspers replied to this by noting that science has no world view which would enable it to cancel the miraculous, let alone to enable it to find any religious convictions unjustifiable.

Bultmann felt that personal existential experience had to supply whatever meanings Christianity was claimed to possess. In response to this, Jaspers noted that existential experience and science are themselves at odds. The latter presupposes the possibility of universals, while the former prohibits this. We would never find any scientifically systematized data existentially. Indeed, according to Jaspers, mythical language is closer to existential meanings than it is to scientific meanings. Jaspers assumed that there was a necessary incomprehensibility in religion which the scientific approach ignored. Of course myths are scientifically implausible, Jaspers admitted, but this fact is irrelevant to faith. Bultmann's rejoinder to this was to assert that demythologizing was not intended to make religion palatable, but simply to make it clear. As soon as we refer to the transcendence of the myths, as Jaspers does, we cast the whole problem of religious meanings in a fog of ambiguity, and we make religious understanding impossible.

Bultmann asserted that the value of the New Testament lies in its "meaning" and not in the history which it presents. The Jesus of history, for example, is religiously unimportant. In fact, we know so little about the historical Jesus that it is just as well that the matter is unessential. It is clear, for example, that the New Testament world view was mythical, and also that the remarks concerning the pre-existent Jesus were also mythical. The problem Bultmann saw was to interpret the myths in such a way that religious faith would be possible without intellectual suicide. He favored a demytholo-

324

gizing which, in effect, destroyed the myth. Under this myth he aimed to find the meaning of human existence. He found this meaning in the framework of an existentialist ontology. The familiar existential terms, such as anxiety, dread, tension, the need to decide, and a living toward death were revealed as the meaning of the message.

Jaspers, on the other hand, recognized the mythical element in the New Testament, but insisted that the myth must remain. He approved the halo which surrounded myth, and he favored the essential ambiguity of the myth. The myths put the reader in the frame of mind to be receptive to insights. Further, he claimed that there was a necessary incomprehensibility in religion which Bultmann's approach ignored.[16] While Bultmann rejected the myths on the grounds that they were scientifically implausible, Jaspers accepted them for the same reason. Faith was to be grasped by the myth, but not by the scientific study of or the rejection of myth. For Jaspers, theological propositions would lose all meaning if they were in scientific language rather than in the language of myth. Jaspers admitted that the myths of the New Testament were scientifically implausible, but he insisted that this was irrelevant. Religious myths were never intended to be acceptable to science. Both Bultmann and Jaspers agreed that the New Testament myths were enshrouded by apocalyptic, gnostic, and prescientific imagery. Bultmann found these facts disturbing to his scientific temper, and he believed that he would find the real message of Christianity if the myths were removed. Jaspers, on the contrary, insisted that the mythical language was the only way in which the message could be communicated, and hence to destroy the myth was to destroy the message.[17]

What has been particularly disturbing to many Christian theologians was Bultmann's interest in the meaning of the message at the expense of any facts on which this message might rest. This had led Bultmann to assert that he was more interested in the meaning or significance of Christ for man than he was in Christ himself. In his rejection of concern with dogmatics Bultmann has been criticized by men like Edmund

Schlink, Professor of Dogmatics at the University of Heidelberg, who insisted that the New Testament message could not be understood without dogmatics, and that to replace dogma by existential subjective meanings would make Christianity incomprehensible.

The Modernist controversies sharpened a time-honored religious and philosophical problem relevant to the relation of faith and reason. Modernists tended to reject the Calvinist thesis that philosophy and theology were inapplicable to faith, and they returned to Saint Thomas in their conviction that a rationale of the Christian faith could be given. Much of the controversy centered on the kind of evidence which could be considered as being in support of a particular Christian view. Many "higher critics" believed that the authentic message would be revealed by a historical analysis which pared away the accretions of interpretations and laid bare the real, historical Jesus. In effecting this, many approaches were endorsed as adequate. Some sought for the "spirit" rather than the "letter" of the original meanings.[18] Others posed a type of "form criticism" which endeavored to interpret New Testament passages in the light of what a first-century man would have meant.[19] Some believed that a historical Jesus could be found; others insisted that the accounts were so enshrouded by myth that the real Jesus might just as well not have lived at all.[20]

Since a guiding purpose in genetic Modernism was the aim to be scientific about religion, the thorniest questions have revolved around the factual analysis of the Scriptures. Bultmann was so troubled by the element of myth in the New Testament that he recommended that it be abandoned altogether. Yet, even when this was done, we do not find Bultmann constructing authentic Christianity from establishable facts. The authentic element was revealed in an existential encounter with the meanings of the message. Jaspers, on the other hand, accused Bultmann of excessive preoccupation with science in his rejection of the myths, while at the same time Bultmann was most unscientific in his existentialism. Jaspers saved the myth as the only medium through which the real Christian message could be communicated.

Philosophically there are several positions implicit in the above controversies, even though the varied answers given are developed theologically rather than philosophically. In the search for the truth concerning what Jesus said and what Jesus was, a kind of linguistic analysis was employed. Assuming that the sentences we have in the Gospels are correctly translated, our problem is to determine what they meant to the persons who uttered them, and not what they would have meant if they had been expressed in the twentieth century. The analyst needed to decide whether the statements in question were ever intended as literal by the persons who spoke them, or whether they were mythical in their original intent. If they were literal, then the problem could be approached factually. If, on the other hand, they were originally myth expressions, then the existential analyses seemed most compatible with the quest for original meanings. But existential analysis was not consonant with the scientific temper, and hence not easily suitable to the determination of truth. Even where scholars could agree as to the existential meanings, there still remained the question of whether what was said was true. On this latter point most of the discussions remained in an inaccessible area of ambiguity. The meanings were private and fundamentally incommunicable to any neutral observer. Indeed, the neutral position was alien and inimical to the existential spirit.

In all of these investigations Modernism represented a spirit of independence and criticism which stimulated biblical study on the one hand and cast serious doubts on neat structured theologies on the other. On the assumption that a rationale of Christian inquiry is possible, Modernism appears to be the logical expression of this position. There is, however, a psychological dilemma entailed in the Modernist approach. If, as a result of scholarly investigation, we conclude that the Scriptures are not reliable history, then we are confronted with the question of whether any authentic message is contained in the book. If human thought is the criterion for biblical correctness, then all the dogmas contained in the

3 2 7

Bible will have, at best, a probability of truth. The whole apodictic tone which characterized Fundamentalism becomes unjustifiable. If, on the other hand, we want to keep the biblical ideas as irrefutable truths, then we must give up biblical scholarship. Biblical inerrancy and human reason do not support each other. This Modernist approach, therefore, makes it impossible that Christians will ever possess the assurance which the essence of their religion seems to require.

Modernism represented a valiant attempt to provide probabilities of a high degree that the "kernel" or heart of the Christian movement could be inferred from the writings, even though the literal remarks of the scripture were commonly factually false, morally suspect, or emotionally inconsequential. The sheer inability of scholars to agree on what the essential spirit was seemed to cast doubt upon the original assumption of the Modernists that they were going to provide a firmer foundation for authentic Christianity. While Modernism overcame the blind irrationalism of Fundamentalism, it lost by this strategy the sense of confidence which Fundamentalist Christians possessed. Reliance upon human reason was purchased at the price of lack of confidence in the truth of the Bible. If Modernism is correct in its assumption that there are no absolute axioms from which a neat and valid deduction could be made, and if induction from probable premises is the only avenue open to reasonable men, then religious probabilities are all that we will ever be able to discover.

Two questions persist in all of this controversy. To what degree of probability are the Modernist conclusions true? Are probability statements adequate for religious faith? The Fundamentalists answer the second question with a negative. The humanists, whom we will discuss in the next chapter, answer the first question with the contention that at least some of the Modernist claims are probably false, while others possess so low a degree of probability of truth that no reasonable person would commit himself to them.

XIV

The Problem *of* Humanism

THE GROUNDS for humanism lie in the earliest records of human history; indeed, the fact that this view is found so ancient in man's development might suggest that primitive man could as likely have been a humanist as a theist. Generally speaking, the position characterized by the designation "humanism" maintains that all problems are human both in origin and in solution. If any gods are admitted to exist, they are functionless as far as the destiny of man is concerned. With this essentially human orientation, it normally followed that man's potential was held to be adequate to man's dilemmas. Sometimes the element in man which provided the human hope was his emotions; occasionally it was his intellect. Probably most so-called humanists were confident that the combination of human intelligence and human feeling was adequate to provide man with a confident outlook on the future. Pessimism was not the dominant mood. Indeed, humanists in all ages have felt that theism was to be attacked, along with any supernaturalism, on the grounds that this perspective cut the nerve of human endeavor and left man fundamentally at the mercy of forces held to be outside his control.

We shall consider manifestations of this revolt against supernaturalism both in the Orient and in the Western world. Among the problems which will appear throughout this investigation will be the questions: Is humanism true? Is humanism adequate to the needs of mortal men? Is humanism a religion in any definable sense? Does the movement express a progress of human thought, or is it, in the final analysis, a retrogression which ignores a phase of human aspiration which only theism or supernaturalism can explain?

HUMANISM IN GENETIC BUDDHISM

The development of Hinduism for perhaps three or four millennia was the background out of which Buddhism emerged. The religion of the Hindus had passed through a Vedic phase, during which religion was led by laymen, without the assistance of either formal clergy or churches. It had then developed through a Brahmanic period, in which an established ecclesiastical hierarchy with its sacred temples provided the religious leadership and the spiritual continuity of belief. These priests engaged in liturgies which only the initiated could comprehend, and the spirit of the prayer wheel symbolized the lack of human participation in religion. A new rise of lay leadership marked the third, or Upanishadic, period. New spiritual leaders attacked the power of the clergy, the place of sacrifice and sacrament, and the status of the scriptures. This was a period, however, in which the sense of cosmic struggle and the practically endless cycle of birth and rebirth crushed the spirit of sensitive persons. Following this third period, there arose an aversion to religion and to the conventional morals of society. This anti-religious milieu has been preserved for us in the famous epic tales, the Ramayana and the Mahabharata. During precisely this period of general despair two humanistic religions emerged, of which Buddhism was the first.

Gautama Siddhartha, a member of the Kshatriya caste,

lived from 563 to 483 B.C. His father was a petty monarch, and Gautama was thus reared in luxury. As is common in religions, both ancient and modern, the origins of the founder of Buddhism are overshadowed with myth and mystery. His mother was said to have conceived following a vision in which she saw the future Buddha enter her womb in the form of a white elephant, a tale reminiscent of early Christian accounts of Mary's impregnation by the Holy Spirit. The event was accompanied by natural wonders—earthquakes, heavenly music, flowers blooming out of season, and the sea water losing its salt. A tradition relates that he was born with the thirty-two marks said to indicate Buddhahood. These included hands reaching below the knees and a ten-foot halo. Twenty-four persons are mentioned as having foretold his birth. He, personally, was said to have known of six Buddhas who had preceded him. His given name, Siddhartha, means "he who has reached his aim." "Buddha" means "the enlightened one" and carries a religious significance comparable to "Christ." Stories are told of the many wonders he performed in his youth. His father saw the signs of greatness in the boy and assumed that he would become either a great king or a wandering mendicant holy man. In the hope that he would be a king, the father surrounded him with all the allurements of kingly status, and chose for him a young woman of great beauty as a wife. Tradition relates that when Gautama saw four "signs" his Buddhahood was near. These signs were: an old man who had no purpose, a sick man racked by fever, a funeral at which mourners were suffering, and a holy man enduring profound suffering for the good of his soul. These four signs pointed to the blackness, misery, and despair of man's condition. They raised what has since been the chief Buddhist problem: Why do men suffer? At the age of twenty-nine, shortly after the birth of his first child, a son, Gautama left his home in search of the answer to this fundamental problem. According to legend he saw the four signs on the first day after leaving home. For six years he wandered from one Brahman priest to another seeking the answer to human suffering. The traditional method of gaining insight was the recommendation of each priest; namely, to practice austere ascetic living. He was, apparently, a worthy adherent of the ascetic mode, practicing the most rigorous self-mortification until his ribs stuck out from his body. He finally concluded that asceticism would not give him the insights he sought. We may note a parallel in the experience of Martin Luther, who had been a stern ascetic in the Augustinian Roman Catholic order, until he too concluded that this was not the way to salvation or to insight. When Gautama left the ascetic life his five disciples left him convinced that he had lost the faith. Shortly after, seated under a pipal tree (called the Bo, or knowledge, tree) he found the solution in the mystical experience of Brahma-Atman. The traditions report that Mara, the god of death, saw that Gautama had become Buddha and had learned the secret of existence, and that he therefore threatened Mara's hold on the world. Mara attempted by four temptations (cf. the temptations of Christ) to subvert Buddha. The first three temptations were Desire, Discontent, and Lust, symbolized by Mara's three daughters. When these temptations failed to lure Buddha, Mara's last effort was to convince him that the insight of Brahma-Atman was so elevated and incomprehensible that the masses would never understand it. It was his hope that Buddha would retire to a monastery and that the secret would die with him. Buddha did not succumb to this temptation either. Instead, he traveled to Benares and there delivered his famous sermon at the Deer Park to the original five disciples. They were ordained as Buddhist monks and went forth to carry the good news to all of India.

The substance of the sermon was the Four Noble Truths. The first Truth asserted that suffering is universal. No mortal man can live without suffering. It is the price for being incarnated as a human being. All events of human life are causes of suffering: birth, death, decay, growth. All give rise to sorrow, pain, grief, and despair. The second Truth asserts that there is a single universal cause for suffering. This cause is desire. It does not matter whether it is the desire for life, wealth, or even salvation. Desire causes pain.

The third Truth asserts that this cause, desire, can be removed, and that, hence, suffering can be obliterated. The fourth Truth is the famous Eightfold Path by which desires will be eliminated and the suffering abolished. This Eightfold Path is to be achieved or followed essentially by reason, by intellectual reflection. In this effort the gods are ineffectual. Man alone performs the task, if it is to be performed at all. No supernatural interference is required. Underlying this intellectual effort was the confidence that there existed a natural moral law which would make such effort successful. This would be the Buddhist analogue of the Judeo-Christian confidence that we live in a world where we reap what we sow. The expression of the Path was in the spirit of the Golden Mean of Aristotle's ethics. Moderation was the watchword, and the Path marked a point somewhere between self-mortification and indulgence. The eight steps in the Path were:

1. Right understanding
2. Right-mindedness
3. Right speech
4. Right action
5. Right living
6. Right effort
7. Right endeavor
8. Right concentration

According to tradition, Gautama Buddha established separate monasteries for men and women. Ten commandments were proposed for the monks and nuns. The first five of the commandments were required of all laymen. By and large the commandments are self-explanatory. They were:

1. Refrain from killing.
2. Refrain from stealing.
3. Refrain from unchastity.
4. Refrain from lying.
5. Refrain from intoxicants.
6. Refrain from solid food after midday.
7. Refrain from dancing, music, and the theater.

8. Refrain from using flowers, perfumes, and salves.
9. Refrain from using high, broad couches.
10. Refrain from accepting gold and silver.

The relation of Buddhism to Hinduism is comparable to that between Christianity and Judaism. In each case the founder was a member of the parent group, and in each case a cultural sequence of events led to a separation, even though puritanism may well have been the original intent. Buddhism is commonly called a heresy from Hinduism, but Radhakrishnan, for example, though a Hindu, maintained that the separation is not due to differences in belief. He felt that Buddhism was in the essential tradition of authentic Hinduism. We may find comparable analyses in the relation between Christianity and Judaism, for there are those who maintain that Christianity is in the tradition of authentic Judaism, and hence not really heretical.

Two major traditions of Buddhism developed at an early period. The Hinayana, or "lesser vehicle," branch has its current strength in Ceylon, Siam, and Indochina. The Mahayana, or "greater vehicle," branch is concentrated in China, Japan, Korea, and Tibet. They share certain general views. By virtue of the simple fact that Buddha was a member of the Kshatriya caste, it was apparent that non-Brahmans could achieve Brahma-Atman. While this in itself might seem heretical enough to warrant the establishment of a new religion, it would overlook the fact that such ideas had already been intimated in the Upanishads.

A first fact which made Buddhism seem more earnest and more radical than its predecessors was the obliteration of all caste distinctions in the monasteries. In the second place Buddhism represented a protest against all authorities, both priestly and scriptural, and an equal protest against prayers and sacrifices, as carried out by priests, as religiously nonessential. The spirit of the Old Testament prophet, Amos, is reflected in the Buddhist protest against formalized religion. It represented an equal protest against rationalism. It is not how we think, but how we feel, that is the essential root of the religious problem. In this emphasis, Buddhism is closer

334

to psychology than to logic. In the third place, both traditions make the traditional gods either functionless or non-existent. The gods are functionally "dead" in the Nietzschean sense, for lack of any excuse for existence. It is the Mahayana branch which retains polytheistic but functionless gods, while the Hinayana branch is non-theistic. Both, however, have Brahma, as an impersonal principle of unity. A fourth agreement relates to the common denial of the doctrine of the eternal soul, and a consequent denial of the transmigration of souls. They retained the reincarnation theory. While it may seem, at first, peculiar to assert reincarnation and deny transmigration, it must be remembered that the Hindu position with regard to the soul was twofold. There was the temporal aspect of the soul, corresponding more or less to the ego of which we are self-aware. Since there is evidence for such a soul aspect, the Buddhist admitted it. On the other hand, there is the eternal aspect of the soul. This was the aspect which Hindus had asserted to continue between incarnations. It was not that there were two souls, but that there were two aspects of this soul—the one of which we were aware, and the other which was predicated by faith. At this point the Buddhists reacted like empiricists, and asserted that if there is no evidential or experiential evidence for the eternal aspect, we ought not to assert it. It is sufficient that we are aware of the temporal aspect within any incarnation. Inasmuch as there had never been a claim that there were memory links between incarnations, it scarcely seemed a drawback to withhold judgment or to deny the eternal aspect of the soul. If this position raised the question as to what happened to the soul between incarnations, it could always be asserted that Brahma could provide for the re-creation of the soul in each incarnation if this proved necessary. As a concomitant to this idea Buddhists have maintained that Nirvana, which was achievable in this world, was not the annihilation of personality but rather the annihilation of desire. It was not the loss of self-awareness, but the loss of self-love or self-concern. Parinirvana, or final and complete oneness with Brahma, came only at death.

The differences between Hinayana and Mahayana Buddhism were more matters of emphasis than of concrete belief. While Hinayana had no gods at all, Mahayana had functionless gods. Both were noncognitive, but Hinayana pressed this more consistently. It had been a Hinayana view that Buddha spoke no words after his enlightenment, while the Mahayana scriptures abound in Buddha's sayings. It was the latter group which introduced the myths surrounding his birth, deeds, and death. Ultimately, however, both groups would agree that the ultimate insight is silence. Seng Ts'an's poem on "Trust in the Heart," [1] a Japanese Mahayana composition, reflects this ultimately noncognitive position:

"The Perfect Way is only difficult for those who pick and
　　choose;
Do not like, do not dislike; all will then be clear.
Make a hairbreadth difference, and Heaven and Earth
　　are set apart;
If you want the Truth to stand clear before you, never
　　be for or against.
The struggle between 'for' and 'against' is the mind's
　　worst disease;
While the deep meaning is misunderstood, it is useless
　　to meditate on Rest.
It is blank and featureless as space; it has no 'too little'
　　or 'too much.'
　　　·　　·　　·　　·　　·　　·
To banish Reality is to sink deeper into the Real;
Allegiance to the Void implies denial of its voidness.
The more you talk about It, the more you think
　　It, the further from It you go;
Stop talking, stop thinking, and there is nothing you
　　will not understand."

There is no need to seek Truth; one need only stop having views. Hinayana Buddhism resembles Christian monasticism in its stress on the individual search for salvation. Each man must save himself in true existential fashion. This tended to an asocial view remote from the pressing social, political, and economic problems. Mahayana Buddhism, on the other hand, missionarized the Eastern world preaching the socially compassionate Buddha. The familiar china figurines of Kwan Yin, the Mahayana goddess, reflect this concern for world problems, for tradition relates that she turned back from the gates of the western heaven and returned to earth because she heard the children crying.

In Buddhism we find an early expression of the attempt to reassert a dominant and participatory role for man in working out his destiny. Even where gods are admitted, they are yet functionless as far as man's pressing problems are concerned. If there is any hope at all, it lies within the power of man to assure it.

HUMANISM IN GENETIC JAINISM

The sixth century B.C. was one of social unrest and religious concern. The overwhelming weight of the proliferated caste system and the oppression of the endless cycle of rebirth that would be required before salvation could be achieved drove thousands of serious Hindus from their homes and jobs in search of religious peace and escape. Two of the great religious leaders of the time came from the Kshatriya caste—Buddha, the founder of Buddhism, and Mahavira, the founder of Jainism. Like Buddha, Mahavira was a reformer and a puritan, who, by virtue of social contingencies, became the founder of a new religion. Mahavira was grounded in Hindu tradition, although he rejected the authority of the Vedas and the claims of priests to special insights. It has become common to generalize about the relations of Hinduism, Buddhism, and Jainism by categorizing Hinduism as stressing thinking, Buddhism as stressing feeling, and Jainism as stressing acting. There is a restricted sense in which this is correct, but it would be an error to imagine that all three of these faiths did not touch on all three of these elements. The versatility and tolerance of Indian faiths has permitted their followers to stress thought, feeling, and action. Nonetheless there is some convenience in noting the emphases which are strong in these movements.

3 3 7

Mahavira ("great soul") was born in 599 B.C. and died in
527 B.C. His ministry overlapped that of the Gautama Buddha.
Like Buddha, he was born of politically powerful and economi-
cally wealthy parents. Like Buddha, he left home at the age
of about twenty-nine in search of religious insight. He became
a novice in a monastic group which followed the Rule of
Parsvanatha. This was an ascetic order with clear-cut requirements. First, the devotee must fast for two and a half days
without allowing himself to think of food or drink. If at any
moment during that period the thought of sustenance did
cross his mind, he would have to start all over again. Obviously
one could not repeat this renewal process very many times in
a row without dying of starvation. Second, it was required that
one give away all his worldly possessions. This was the easiest
requirement to meet, and Mahavira fulfilled this, essentially,
when he left home. Third, one must strip off his clothes and
pull all bodily hair out by the roots. He must then live in
society without a sense of shame. Nudity leaves one with no
shell of illusion. If one could live shamelessly under these
conditions, he was indeed a victor over human pride. There
is an interesting parallel here with the Genesis account of the
experience of Adam and Eve when their nakedness became a
source of shame and hence a sign of pride. Protestant sects,
such as the Quakers, Mennonites, and Shakers, have sensed
the degree to which clothes become signs of misplaced human
pride, and have, as a consequence, urged simplicity in matters
of dress. Henry Thoreau, the sage of Walden, was likewise
sensitive to the false stress of bodily dress. He remarked that
if one gets new clothes it should at least be the sign that one
is a new person.

In the thirteenth year of his ascetic vigil Mahavira gained
the supreme knowledge and became a conqueror (Jina) of
Karma. The term "Jain" comes from the same root as "Jina,"
and is the religion of overcomers or conquerors. When he had
achieved the insight of mystical oneness, he set out to preach
and teach this way of salvation. Since he appealed to all
persons irrespective of caste, his sermons and actions appeared anti-Brahmanic or antipriestly. Like Buddha, he or-

ganized monasteries and nunneries, the members of which came chiefly from the Kshatriya caste.

His essential message was summed up in the Nine Truths which explained the relation of man's soul to Karma and the path to release from the endless cycle of birth and rebirth. Jainism has had a particularly keen interest in Karma. Indeed, the Jains distinguish 148 different kinds of Karma. Occasionally Karma is discussed as if it were an abstract law of retribution, but in the famous Nine Truths it is presented as if it were a kind of entity which a man carried as a burden, and which he might shed through appropriate action. These Truths may be noted as follows:

1. All sentient creatures possess life or consciousness (Jiva). It is this that makes them of worth, and hence animals as well as human beings ought not to be killed. It is through this Jiva that Karma enters into human experience.

2. In contrast to the animate creatures are the inanimate ones, which do not possess Jiva.

3. The principle of consciousness is the author of evil thoughts, conceit, sense desires, and deceit. These drives lead one to acquire Karma.

4. Sin is expressed as wrong actions which are functions of wrong feelings. The idea of sin includes hypocrisy in meditation, dishonesty, destruction of life, and unchastity.

5. Karma may be blocked or deterred by disciplined living. These include the patient endurance of pain, gentle speaking toward others, and the eschewing of the unclean.

6. Karma may be destroyed through the study of doctrine, reverent meditation, and ascetic practice.

7. Certain acts of merit lead to peace of mind.

8. This truth analyzes the nature of the bondage of the soul to Karma.

9. The state of Moksa, or complete deliverance from Karma, can be achieved.

The essential emphases of these Nine Truths show the composite role of feeling and thinking in the Jainistic salvation scheme; they also show how Jainism is rooted in Hinduism. The Three Jewels of the Jain scheme of salvation indicate that knowledge, feeling, and action are all involved. It would be incorrectly one-sided to imagine that Jains stress only action. The first Jewel, of right faith, stresses the role of proper feeling in achieving Jinahood. The second Jewel, of right knowledge, indicates that understanding the nature of the world and the soul are important. The third Jewel, of right action as a means of stopping Karma, points to the fact that action is of strategic importance.

The gods are peculiarly functionless in Jainism. Although they are not worshiped, they are occasionally used as aids in getting rid of Karma. Some of the Jain scriptures speak of the gods as inferior to men, since, even though the gods are subject to Karma, they cannot achieve Moksa, or the ultimate insight. Even the gods are arranged in castes, and ninety-nine of these gods are in the untouchable caste. Not only are the gods functionless, but there is no Brahma, no principle of unity, and hence no Brahma-Atman experience. The result of Mahavira's encounter was the discovery that the ultimate insight is oneness with oneself. This lends a note of existentialism to the movement. Salvation is a private affair. Each person must win it for himself, and no man can help another in the task. There is the same sense of "dreadful freedom" here which has characterized so much irreligious existential writing. This metaphysical pluralism was bolstered by a logic of relativism. There are no absolutes, for all knowledge is limited. Every question can be answered by both "yes" and "no." No proposition is absolutely true or false. The familiar story of the blind men seeking to describe what an elephant is was invented by the Jain thinkers as indicative of the subjective nature of all truth. Salvation depends on the individual alone. Mahavira said, "Man, thou art thine own friend. Why wishest thou for a friend beyond thyself?" [2]

The Jain thinkers viewed matter as existing in grades ranging in density from solid rocks to Karma matter, which latter, like barnacles, forms incrustations on the soul. The more Karma matter there is on a soul, the heavier it is and the lower it sinks. The light souls rise, and may even achieve incarnation as a god. With the previous view of the function-less role of gods, there may be some doubt whether this would be an accomplishment of any great functional use.

An essential element in the Nine Truths refers to the consciousness or soul (Jiva) which all animate things possess. From vegetables to human persons, all growing things possess soul. It follows from this that all animate things are to be reverenced. Here the doctrine of Ahimsa, or nonviolent resist-ance as found in the Bhagavad-Gita, is applied to all living things. This is the reverence for life discussed by Albert Schweitzer, but carried to an extreme which few religions have ever attempted. If destroying life is brutalizing, then even pulling a carrot from the ground will harden your spirit until, perhaps, you beat animals. From here it is but a short step to human murder. Since sensitive spirits were desired and required for Moksa, no serious Jain would be a farmer, butcher, or soldier. By a natural inference banking was proper for Jains, and, for a time, they held a preponderance of positions in this enterprise. Mahavira was so concerned with the sacredness of all living things that he carried a broom to sweep the path before him lest he unwittingly step on some tiny insect. He would not walk on the grass, nor pluck apples from a tree. He wore a cloth across his nose and mouth so that he would not accidentally breathe in tiny creatures. He strained his water, carefully removed the lice from his body and his bed so that he would not kill and thus go on the down-ward path to brutalization. Although he would not pluck any raw food, he would accept it from another. Although this is an obvious inconsistency, he can scarcely be blamed for it. Every religion draws the lines of its orthodoxy at some place short of absolute consistency. To survive, a person needs to eat. In terms of the gradation of soul substance, at least vegetables were at the bottom. If eating must be done, let it be done at the metaphysically lowest order. Clearly he admonished all to refrain from eating meat. Most religions of the West have found it necessary or at least desirable to limit the scope of moral absolutes. Some Christian priestly orders forbid their members to touch money or to own private property, but they do accept the results of both from others. The renunciation of killing any living thing is the first vow of Jain monks.

The second vow requires the renouncing of lying. This mandate was carried to a degree which few religions require, for they included the telling of jokes in the category of lies. Any person who laughs at a joke is expressing sympathy with falsehoods, for everyone knows that jokes are distortions of the truth. If one can be casual with the truth in small things like jokes, very soon one may become indifferent in large things. The early Christian Puritans in the United States had a similar suspicion of jokes and like merriment. They were not so opposed to laughing, in itself, as they were to the general casualness with the truth which such pleasantries seemed to symbolize and to promote.

The third vow required the renunciation of the taking of any thing, animate or inanimate, unless it was given by another. A Jain monk could not, in principle, go out for a stick of firewood for the stove unless there was a non-Jain monk to give the stick. The monk could not pull rhubarb, but he could accept it if someone else had pulled it. He could not accumulate private possessions by the standard economic practices. Indeed, the primary reason for the mandate was doubtless to discourage economic competitiveness, private ownership, and material possessiveness.

This was in the same spirit and letter as the Order of Saint Francis of Assisi. The New Testament commission found in Matthew 10:7–10 urged nonownership and voluntary poverty, and this Saint Francis advocated for his followers. This spirit was so alien to the economic competitiveness of his time that the Bishop of Assisi begged Francis to permit his followers to own property, but the Little Friar saw that this was the source of wars, lawsuits, and divisiveness among men. One of his followers, Brother Bernardo, was approached one day by a man who wanted to give him money. " 'Why,' the man asked, 'since you are poor, will you not accept like the others?' 'It is true that we are poor,' replied Bernardo, 'but poverty does not weigh upon us as upon other poor people:

for by the grace of God, whose will we are accomplishing, we have voluntarily become poor.' " [3]

The fourth Jain vow was the renunciation of all sexual pleasures. Mahavira had said, "The greatest temptations in the world are women." Indeed, they cannot win salvation until they have been reincarnated as men. The requirement of sexual continence has been standard in monastic movements in most of the major religions of the world.

By the fifth vow the Jain monk relinquished all personal attachments. This precluded the having of wives or friends. While the necessities of monastic life required some contact with other persons, at least such contact could remain emotionally cool and detached. In something of the spirit of the ancient Stoics in Greece, they urged dependence on none but oneself. This, too, is in the tradition of existentialism in ethics. The message of Jean-Paul Sartre's play, *No Exit*, carries this essential idea: there is no escape from the personal responsibility for our moral acts. The "Hell is other people" idea to which Sartre refers carries this precise meaning. To depend upon others for moral sanction and moral support is Hell, and it leads to the damnation of character. The Moksa ideal of Jainism is so ruggedly individualistic that even in the ultimate insight we find only ourselves.

THE PIONEERS OF HUMANISM

The humanism of the nineteenth and twentieth centuries took its intellectual nourishment from Renaissance humanism, although the content of current humanist writings could be traced all the way back to Protagoras, who had asserted that man is the "measure of all things." Western expressions of the humanistic approach generally represented a belief in the importance of man, a confidence in his powers of reason, and a conviction that he was capable of moral greatness. This approach, therefore, opposed the traditional preoccupation with original sin, predestination, and general human incompetence. Renaissance humanists, such as Petrarch and Erasmus, for all their emphasis upon human worth, still maintained belief in the supernatural. While they might be accused of fostering immorality, they could not be accused of advocating impiety. Contemporary humanism, however, has been open to the accusations of both immorality and impiety.

We may take the point of departure for this current humanism from David Hume (1711–1776), who had insisted that the study of religion ought to entail the same scientific caution which was to be found in the natural sciences.[4] Hume felt that progress in any area in the past had been a direct function of the degree to which supernaturalism had been banished by reason. He assumed, therefore, that the same progress would follow in religion if nature were to be the arbiter, and by this thesis he laid the foundation for the scientific study of religion. We should begin with experience, eliminate supernatural presuppositions, and see what man alone can reconstruct. When Hume had applied these procedures, he discovered that primitive religions began as polytheism and only later became monotheistic. He conjectured that the reason for this was that early man was first impressed with the "events of life," such as disease, floods, tornadoes, and drought. Concentration on these fortuitous misfortunes (tychisms) led naturally to a view of plural gods. Much later, when the "works of nature"—that is, the orderly processes which give birth to natural laws—engrossed man's attention, the sense of unity in the world prompted monotheism. As we have noted in an earlier chapter, even if Hume's explication is correct, he has not discussed the question of whether a God or gods actually exist, for the origin of an idea is not what certifies its truth or falsity.

It seemed apparent to Hume that the average man cannot think in terms of a perfect God, and yet men are equally incapable, because unwilling, to impute imperfections to God. This double limitation has produced in theology contradictions within the putative character of God. On the one hand, men are afraid of their God, and on the other hand, they insist that he has the noblest virtues. Hume believed that this dilemma was what had prompted Judeo-Christians to be more impressed with the power of their God than with his goodness or intelligence. A consequence of the preoccupation with the power attribute of God was that the same locus of importance became crucial in their ethics. Religious persons tended to identify religion with those acts which are farthest from human ideas of goodness and rightness, which gave support to the apothegms that "ignorance is the mother of devotion" and that "barbarity and caprice are the dominant qualities of religion." [5]

Hume contributed two items to the attack on supernaturalism. In the first place he supplied a logical analysis which appeared to vitiate all attempts to give cognitive arguments for God. If Hume was correct, then the defense for the God element had to be other than rational. In the second place, he gave a devastatingly critical portrayal of the emotions prompting supernaturalism which made the whole theistic outlook suspect. Indeed, he found religion such an irrational mess that he recommended replacing reason with emotion when dealing with the ethical implications of religion in particular.

Immanuel Kant (1724–1804) accepted from Hume the theses that we can know only what we can come into immediate contact with in sense experience, and that we can know only such sense experiences as we can rationally interpret. Within the limits of these assumptions reasonable religion must operate. The results of analyzing religion within the limits of reason led Kant to reject the conclusions of all rational theology. All the arguments for the existence of God were fallacious; indeed, religion alone could defend no religious claims. While Kant proposed the hypotheses of God and immortality, the fact remained that they transcended experience and hence could not be known to exist. While Kant did not intend to subscribe to humanism, and in fact was not emotionally attracted to it, the fact remained that his attack on the possibility of a religion defended by reason provided intellectual support for the humanist sentiment.

A psychological sanction for the humanist position was provided by the deism of the eighteenth and nineteenth centuries. Since the God of deism had left the world to its own

345

devices, men could not expect any assistance from the supernatural; thus, even if it were granted that a God existed, he turned out to be otiose for the task of human survival. In such a situation religious persons could not afford to debase man with ideas of original sin or intellectual incapacity. If God was of no help, then man had better rise to the occasion. One of the results of deism, therefore, was to exalt confidence in man, and this attitude was basic for humanism. Such an amplification of human powers to resolve human needs was enthusiastically made by men like Newton, Voltaire, Lessing, Benjamin Franklin, Thomas Jefferson, and Thomas Paine.

When these attitudes encountered the nineteenth-century Modernist attempts at the scientific study of the Judeo-Christian religion, a new link was forged in the chain leading to humanism. What Kant and Hume had done for arguments for God and immortality was now furthered by the Modernist analyses of the Bible. While Modernism, to be sure, intended a defense of theism, or at least not an attack upon it, there seemed to be radical inconsistencies which remained if scholars stopped with the Modernist position. Humanism in the United States functioned as a gadfly for Modernism by attempting to press for what seemed to be the logical outcome in the denial of all supernaturalism. Humanists saw Modernists as inconsistent and incomplete through their attempts to be scientific and yet at the same time to maintain supernaturalism.

WHAT DO HUMANISTS BELIEVE?

Contemporary American humanism has combined two basic ideas which the eighteenth- and nineteenth-century liberals contributed. On the one hand, they accepted the Humean and Kantian abandonment of any scientific or experiential attempt to support supernaturalism. Secondly, they endorsed the confidence in human powers which characterized the nineteenth-century social scientists. If man is capable of solving his economic, political, and social problems, why should he not be equally capable of solving his religious problems? Since scientific solutions have not required any supernatural presuppositions, there should be no reason for religion to require any transcendent element. The march was on to banish gods from the skies and evils from the earth. The humanist endeavors were marked by a concern for a mature attitude of man toward his religious aspirations, and by a scientific attitude toward the world in which he lives. In keeping with these aims the humanist identified himself with the personal and social ideals which contributed to human welfare. He stressed the natural world, and denied that there was any world outside of it.

One of the more distinguished contemporary humanists, Charles F. Potter, defined his position as "faith in the supreme value and self-perfectibility of human personality." [6] He assumed that the universe had a meaning which man could discover within the range of experience alone and without any supernatural presuppositions. If we start from experience, then we begin without a God, a messiah, a body of authenticated scripture, or any established religious dogma. If these are to be reinstated at all, then experience must support them; and if Hume and Kant are correct, the whole enterprise is a lost cause.

It seems to be the general view of American humanists that humanism is not a sect of Christianity. Its conclusions are much too radical to be classified with any existing Christian sect, and, further, its aims are such that it does not consider any Christian title as appropriate to itself. Humanists do, however, consider that their movement is a religion. They appeal to what we have previously called the pragmatic definition of religion—religion being defined as that which promotes personal integration in a society conducive to this end. While some of the Roman Catholic Modernists, such as Alfred Loisy, approximate the humanist position, it is essentially a Protestant phenomenon. Renaissance humanism, however, is another matter. Jacques Maritain [7] has insisted that Roman Catholicism is consistent with the Renaissance ideal, but this is a far cry from the religious humanism which has emerged in the United States of America.

347

A first thesis of the humanists was expressed in their attack upon Modernism on the grounds that the Modernist contention that Christianity is unique and superior is not supported by the social-scientific data. According to the humanist, the data support many diverse religions, all of which produce emotionally healthy members. The Modernist is simply distorting the evidence when he draws the conclusion that Christianity is unique in its production of beneficial results. If whatever promotes integrated personality is religious, then Judaism, Hinduism, Buddhism, and Islam (to mention just a few) can all lay claims equal to that of Christianity. The humanist is not claiming that Christianity has had no worthwhile consequences, but only that it must recognize that most religions can claim as much. This matter of the emotional value of a religion is very important to the humanist, since he rejects any cognitive truth for religion.[8]

A second thesis of humanism has been expressed in its markedly unorthodox views on the question of a God. Gods are functionless and diversionary, according to most humanists, although whether humanists are thus atheists remains to be seen. Many humanists have contended that atheism is as untenable as theism, since neither position has sufficient evidence to support it, and they have preferred to reserve judgment by holding the agnostic view. C. F. Potter classified four senses in which one could be a nonbeliever in theism: (1) *Agnostic atheism.* Members of this option assert: "I do not know whether there is or isn't a God." This is the position which Potter accepts for his humanist emphasis. (2) *Negative atheism.* The proponents of this view state: "I don't know whether there is or isn't a God, and I don't care." The only difference between this view and the first is that the negative atheists add an emotive reaction of indifference to the epistemological situation. Even if we assume, however, that agnostic atheists do "care" about the God question, the distinction now leads to a new complication in distinguishing categories. Epistemologically the first two positions are indistinguishable, and hence it is not clear what the second stand would mean as opposed to the first, since the simple fact that one holds the latter view would seem to indicate that he does care at least that much. If emotive approval is to become a distinguishing property, then we should be able to have a long continuum of positions from "deeply caring" to "not caring at all." (3) *Dogmatic atheism.* Those who hold this view assert, "I know that there isn't any God." Potter does not indicate whether these persons are happy or miserable, or somewhere in between happiness and misery, with their stand, although it is quite obvious that a range of emotional reactions is both possible and likely. (4) *Moral atheism.* The defender of this alternative asserts, "I do not like the moral attributes associated with the idea of a God." Such a person could be agnostic, negative, or dogmatic in his atheism, and what is more confusing, the moral atheist appears not to care about the epistemological issue at all. Indeed, the moral atheist could be a firm believer in God, and reject a God whom he believes to exist, but whose moral properties are reprehensible. This objection to the God idea on moral grounds is what Ludwig Feuerbach called "true atheism." Whether this position is really "true" or not, moral atheism probably has a more devastating impact than any of the other grounds for opposing belief in a God. While the view held by Jean-Paul Sartre is not precisely that of moral atheism, it has something of the same emotional shock to theists. Sartre held that the very gesture of turning to a God was a sign of "bad faith" on the part of man quite independently of the moral attributes which were assigned to the God. No matter how good the God is predicated to be, the act of using him to validate moral choice constitutes an immoral act on the part of man. Now, while these four distinctions of Potter's are confused, unclearly disjunctive, and not exhaustive, they still suggest some meaning for the positions of humanism on the God issue.

The term "atheism" has had a long and multivocal usage. Commonly the term was a mere epithet and carried with it no clear designation of a point of view. On the contrary, any person was an "atheist" who held views contrary to those of some believer. For example, in 155 A.D. Polycarp, the Christian church father who was bishop of Smyrna, was called an atheist by some of his agnostic contemporaries. Deists have commonly been called "atheists" by those who believed in a personal God. In our own day, even Paul Tillich has been given the "atheist" label by evangelical Fundamentalists. The appellation "un-Christian" has had a similar undiscriminating use. Theistic Unitarians and Universalists were considered to be "un-Christian" and hence unworthy of admission into the former Federal Council of Churches of Christ in America. It is not out of the ordinary for lay Catholics to suspect that lay Protestants are not really "Christian," and vice versa. Kierkegaard had insisted that if Jesus was a Christian, then Saint Paul was not, and if Saint Paul was, then Jesus was not. In the heat of a debate Henry Sloane Coffin had called humanism "the scourge of Christendom." As a matter of fact, humanism very probably has been a thorn in the flesh and a threat to conventional Christianity, although it has not been incontrovertibly established in what tone of voice this observation should be made.

In 1933 Roy Wood Sellars, a professor of philosophy at the University of Michigan, was asked to write a humanist manifesto.[9] The manifesto he produced contained fifteen theses which have since become the catechism of the humanist position in the United States of America. It asserted that since the universe is self-explanatory as far as science is concerned, there is neither evidence nor incentive for any inference of a creator or sustainer God. It posed further that the universe did not appear to be either purposive or ideally suited to human aspirations and that, as a consequence, there did not appear to be any evidence, teleologically, for the idea of Providence. The manifesto indicated further that available scientific knowledge had made it clear that man was part of a long evolutionary process, and that he would very likely pass away like the woolly mammoth in the long struggle for survival. When this thesis is accepted, the chief argument for immortality, which rested upon human worth, appears to be groundless. Whatever immortality man may actually have would have to be limited to immortality of influence or to biological immortality, and even this kind of immortality would last only as long as the human species. Prayer was recommended as having possible psychological advantages for self-examination, and worship was identified with an honorific attitude toward man's capacity to achieve the good life. These humanists found no unique religious emotions, nor did they find any tenable distinction between the mind and the body, and, as a consequence, they denied any distinction between what had traditionally been called the secular versus the religious. A classic instance of this elimination may be seen in John Dewey's *A Common Faith.*

Some humanists carried their criticism of both Fundamentalism and Modernism to the point of analyzing the defects of Jesus with the result that he does not appear to have very much value to offer to modern men. On the assumption that the Sermon on the Mount is a faithful report of what Jesus actually said, it should be possible to determine just what kind of person Jesus really was. As is obvious, this assumption would be branded as presumptuous by the Modernists, who saw insuperable obstacles in the way of recapturing the historical Jesus. Humanists, however, have frequently presumed to interpret the real Jesus, and on this point have been closer to Fundamentalism than to Modernism, except in the matter of the tone of voice in which Jesus' character was explained. For example, the Sermon on the Mount puts a premium upon childlike faith and trust. If this is pressed to its extremity, and if this was Jesus' opinion also, then might we not conclude that Jesus did not value intelligence as the most dependable human faculty? Information would appear to be a disadvantage, and ignorance would be bliss. Jesus' purported comment that we should take no thought for the morrow, and his apparent unwillingness to commit himself on any social, economic, or political issues, led humanists to accuse him of being indifferent to man's predicaments. Jesus' putative belief in Providence led them to conclude that he was, after all, unscientific. Both by precept and example Jesus appeared to hold the family and the marital bond in low esteem. On the further assumption that Jesus claimed to be the messiah, he was judged to be presumptuous, immodest, and perhaps a victim of delusions of grandeur.[10] In spite of criticisms of this magnitude, some humanists still insisted that Jesus was, if not a paragon, at least a person worthy of study if not of emulation. Like Nietzsche, they could recognize the sincerity of Jesus, however ill-informed and misdirected he might otherwise be.

It would be futile to engage in debate over whether humanism is or is not a Christian movement, or even whether it is a religion. Fortunately for the record, most humanists prefer not to be associated with the Christian movement, and this saves what would otherwise be an embarrassing situation. It may be that humanists feel that Christianity cannot be purified to the required degree and still have anything distinctive left, or that supernaturalism is so deeply ingrained in the Christian message that it is alien to the humanist concern. On the grounds that this latter is the case, some humanists have maintained that a radical opposition to everything Christian is required, and that for humanists to claim to be Christian would be deceptive, misleading, and inappropriate.

The humanist critique of the role and character of Jesus appears to be on tenuous grounds. If humanists accept higher criticism—and there are consistent reasons why they should —then they should be aware that the reports presently comprising the Gospels reflect considerable emendation and influence by later Christianizers. It is a moot question whether textual quoting can be any more defensibly used by humanist critics than by Fundamentalist believers. The whole quest for the historical Jesus which has occupied so much attention by devout Christians has at least raised the probability that the New Testament in its present form does not give an authentic picture of the founder of the Christian movement. If this is so, then the humanist criticisms are ill founded or at least unprovable. On the other hand, the humanist might still point out that the conventional Christian construction of Jesus portrays a character with serious limitations for thoughtful and sensitive persons.

The Problem *of* Humanism

SUMMARY

The case for humanism appears to be strongest in its analysis of the confusion of systematic theologies which Christians have produced. The sheer bulk of conflicting and irreconcilable ideas, all of which are claimed to be derived from the same slim scriptural premises, supports the humanist claim that confusion does reign in so-called reasonable approaches to Christianity. Not only does this fact raise a question concerning the reasoning which occurs in Christian theologies and philosophies, but it sharpens the equally thorny question of the plethora of presuppositions from which theological conclusions are drawn. If we were to subtract all the unestablished premises from these theological systems, there is serious doubt that there would be anything left to theologize about, or that there would be sufficient bases to draw any conclusions at all. Theologians have begun their efforts, in fact, by assuming to be true all that they later give the appearance of having proved to be true.

There is little doubt that man's confidence in his own abilities and his conviction that his concerns are significant have provided an emotive sanction for much that has gone by the name of progress. This much cannot be taken away from the humanist. It is, however, quite another question whether humanism exhausts man's idealization of either himself or his world. Humanists have certainly claimed that their presentation was adequate for man, and that it went as far as reason could warrant, but this is not the same as having proved that people either will or should find humanism sufficient. If, however, humanism did nothing else, it could serve as a spur to serious Christians to strip away the needless aura which has accumulated around Jesus in the sense that it has produced invidious sentiments attributable to Jesus, so that he might appear to modern persons as a live, worthy, and compelling figure.

XV

Psychology *and* Religion

I N THE SECOND CHAPTER we discussed a number of theories
to account for the origin of religion. Some of these explanations seemed particularly unfavorable to the case for
religion. The conclusion we reached then was that the origin
of an idea has no bearing on the truth of an idea. Psychological, sociological, or economic motivations for having a religion are interesting to explore, but they do not touch the
epistemological question of whether any of the claims of religion are true. While it may have seemed unpleasant to
contemplate the possibility that religion was invented with
tongue in cheek, or that it was an expression of primitive
fears, the fact remained that even if these speculations were
demonstrably true, the cognitive status of religion was still
unaffected.

IS RELIGION NORMAL?

The classic work in the relation of psychology
to religion is still William James' *Varieties of Religious Experience*. James had psychical and intellectual talents which
set him apart from most writers in this field. He had medical
training, was a distinguished psychologist, became a philoso-

pher, and at the same time had warm religious sentiments of his own. These intellectual and emotional attributes, combined with a real gift of expression, enabled him to speak forcefully and effectively on both psychology and religion to the learned in both spheres, as well as to make these abstruse issues meaningful for the discerning layman.

His first and foremost problem was to show that there is a variety of religious experience which cannot be fitted into any neat philosophic system of unity. Further, he aimed to show that while much religious experience can be diagnosed as neurotic and psychotic, this fact does not settle any real religious or philosophic question. Indeed, the origins of religion, psychologically speaking, have no bearing upon the questions of religious truth or religious value. He was quite willing to admit that preoccupation with religious matters did tend to make the devotees eccentric. This was particularly apparent in the lives of the so-called religious geniuses, who commonly showed signs of nervous instability and were frequently the recipients of abnormal psychic visions. He commented concerning George Fox, the Quaker mystic, that from the point of view of his emotional make-up he "was a psychopath or detraque of the deepest dye." [1] If this sort of psychoclassification of religious saints had been thought to be either complete or religiously significant, however, James would have been the first to raise a protest. This oversimplification of man's religious life he called "medical materialism," and he categorized it as much too simple-minded for an intelligent person to accept. He commented on this naïve procedure: "Medical materialism finishes up Saint Paul by calling his vision on the road to Damascus a discharging lesion of the occipital cortex, he being an epileptic. It snuffs out Saint Theresa as an hysteric, Saint Francis of Assisi as an hereditary degenerate. George Fox's discontent with the shams of his age, and his pining for spiritual veracity, it treats as a symptom of a disordered colon. Carlyle's organ-tones of misery it accounts for by a gastro-duodenal catarrh." [2] If this sort of analysis is pressed, it appears that all religious persons are simply victims of some glandular, nervous, or organic disorder, and that with proper medication the chimera of religion would disappear. It is not surprising that such approaches to religion as James here questions should give serious and dilettante spiritual seekers something of a nightmare, and lend support to the popular assumption that psychology is indeed the Antichrist which aims to explain away all religion as sick and morbid.

This whole procedure, however, shows a lack of intellectual sophistication and honesty, which James sturdily attacks. Unless the psychologist has already proved a causal relation between physiology and spiritual values, he is quite illogical if he infers anything to the detriment of religion from such genetic accounts. And even should it be proved that religious sentiments are colonically generated, it would still be an invalid inference from this fact to conclude that religion has been demeaned. When we compare other value areas and our responses to them, it should be obvious that we never judge their worth on the simple basis of their causal antecedents. Instead, as James observes, we approve whatever we do either because we take an immediate delight in what is involved or because it leads to consequences which we find worthwhile. It would never occur to us to judge the general theory of relativity by Einstein's autobiography, or to raise any question about biological evolution on the grounds of some psychic peculiarity of Charles Darwin. Relativity and evolution must be judged by empirical investigation, and the fact that proponents of these doctrines may have neuroses is quite beside the point. Why, therefore, should we tolerate any attempt to judge religious values by the neurological types to which the authors belong? James's insistence that truth is judged by consequences is, as a matter of fact, far closer to what we actually do than any preoccupation with psychic genesis.

What is religion as James saw it? While he was impressed with the fatuity of arguments over the definition of religion, he still saw that it was important for his discussion that some stipulated meaning be accepted. More than this, he did believe that his investigations revealed some common elements in what has been assumed to be religious experience. He postulated that religion meant "the feelings, acts, and experiences of individual men in their solitude, so far as they apprehend themselves to stand in relation to whatever they may consider divine." [3] There appeared to be no single elementary religious emotion, nor any essential kind of religious object. In religion, pluralism is the case. The consequent diversity in religion is a function of "differing susceptibilities of emotional excitement" and "differing impulses and inhibitions." [4] Uniformity in religion, or a grand synthesis of all religions, is not to be expected.

The historically first task of a psychologist in religion is to determine the psychic origins of the religious sentiments and to trace the psychic consequences of these sentiments when they are seriously held. James discovered in his investigation of these two matters that religious persons may be conveniently divided into two groups: the "sick souls" and the "healthy-minded souls." These two classifications do not pretend to cover those for whom religion is little more than a form or a front, since their motivations are usually quite irrelevant to religion as such. Such persons echo the experience of others, never having experienced religion personally, and their promptings are usually of the most extraneous sort: prestige, convenience, or sheer dull habit. For those who have vital personal involvement in religion, however, the case is quite different. On the assumption that religious experience must precede religious concern, these are the only persons whose experience can shed possible light on the genesis of religion. Now the "healthy-minded" religious person sees life as good, and looks optimistically on the whole ongoing process. James felt that the Roman Catholic church was the most congenial soil for optimists, while Protestantism in its more Fundamentalist version catered to pessimists, or "sick souls." Liberal Protestantism, however, shares with Roman Catholicism the healthy perspective which avoids the morbid hell-fire theology which was so much a part of Reformation Protestantism. The "sick souls" require orgiastic revival services replete with the biblical emphasis on bloodshed before they are moved to reform. The very stress of these "sick" ones upon the bitterness and the evil of the world prevents them, however, from ever becoming quite comforted by their conversion experiences. As James observed: "They will always inhabit a universe two stories deep." [5] The evil and the good will remain in deadly combat, and the psychic uneasiness of the convert will be a psychological reflection of this metaphysical split in the nature of things. The assurances of the healthy souls that all is really well with the world will always strike the sick souls as not merely emotionally unpersuasive, but naïve and illiterate. The despairing cries of the sick souls, on the other hand, merely fill the healthy ones with consternation at the inability of some people to be happy. Both types of souls, however, find release in their respective outlets. There are, in addition, persons for whom either response is quite impossible. "There are," said James, "men anaesthetic on the religious side, deficient in that category of sensibility . . . so the nature which is spiritually barren may admire and envy faith in others, but can never compass the enthusiasm and peace which those who are temperamentally qualified for faith enjoy." [6]

If, as James insisted, the roots of religious experience lie in the subconscious, nonrational, and immediate reactions of man, where does this leave the so-called objective observer of religion? He, poor fellow, is out of touch with what it is all about, and is hence unqualified emotionally either to approve or to disapprove of religion. The inability, therefore, of some persons to appreciate religious excitement derives from this simple fact; they have had no religious experience, or they are psychologically incapable of reacting to it. Those who have the soul-stirring experiences, called religious, normally have emotive needs for the pomp and panoply of mystical, noumenal, aesthetic imagery, for a religion of empirical data is a pretty cold and unmoving affair. For this reason, James found it quite incomprehensible that Protestantism ever got any converts at all. Roman Catholicism, on the contrary, has saved the color and the spice of sensuous ceremonies and will always be superior to Protestantism in its emotive appeal. [7]

It was at this point of recognition of the basically emotive and noncognitive nature of religious experience that James's contribution to the psychology of religion was most constructive. Let us admit that religious saints are strong on feeling and weak on intellect, but this is no ground for despondent conclusions about religion. As James noted, "feeling is the deeper source of religion," and "philosophic and theological formulas are secondary products."[8] No mere philosopher can hope either to construct theological dogmas or to criticize existing dogmas unless he has had the emotional genesis of religious experience. If he has had these experiences, then he will know that reason alone can never establish either the existence or the attributes of entities such as gods. The so-called objective data alluded to in religious statements are always insignificant when compared to the rich and stirring private experiences which religious persons report. Indeed, if a religious person finds that a god works well for him, he will never raise such cold and frivolous questions as whether the god exists.

There is a form of intellectualism in philosophy of religion to which James took particular exception. This approach presumed to be able to construct religion from the meager resources of logic alone. Those who claim to have been able to do this put forth the most dogmatic and absolute theologies, which fail because they are so indefensible and so irrelevant to the religious life. The most that philosophy can hope to do with religious doctrines is to identify the contradictions implicit in them and to show which various formulations are at least logically possible. There is a chasm, however, between the logically possible and the existentially real, such that we can never move from the former to the latter, and if we have the latter, we shall never need the former. Religious belief will not be created out of whole cloth, but only out of religious experience. The question still remains open as to what, if any, elements there are in the basically religious sentiment. Perhaps James Henry Leuba's claim that religion means the desires associated with the sense of sin and the manner of release from sin is a case in point, but it is scarcely the only case in point. There are religious emotions, but there is no one and only religious emotion; and to suppose that religion is nothing but the emotions associated with sin would be contrary to the kinds of facts which James discovered. The Jamesian conclusion remains clear: religion will not be determined to be valuable or valueless on the grounds of its psychic origins or its manner of expression, but rather in terms of the consequences for human peace of mind to which religion leads.

James' message was directed to two groups of persons: psychologists who thought that the relation of neurosis and religion vitiated religion, and theologians who thought that the origin of their religion was a factor in the demonstration of the truth of their religion. To both of these groups James showed the ineluctable emotional component in all religion, and the fact that any belief seriously held may be diagnosed as obsessive or neurotic. Interesting as this may be to a psychologist, and disturbing as it may be to a religionist, the fact remains that the origins of religion can neither add to nor detract from the worth of religion, let alone affect the truth status of the claims of religion.

Gordon W. Allport [9] shared this Jamesian concern with the psychology of religion as opposed to the psychopathology of religion. He admitted that most psychologists who mentioned religion at all gave the impression that it was a pathological phenomenon rather than a function of healthy personality, and he deplored this situation as not quite fair to religion. In contrasting the cultural milieu of James with the present, Allport noted that while James spoke frankly about religion and bypassed sex, present-day psychologists speak frankly about sex and bypass religion. This situation reflects, in part, a change in attitude with regard to what it is safe to discuss and what it is indecorous to mention. Allport saw religion as having its roots in two related tendencies. On the emotional side, religion is rooted in desire, temperament, and the held values. On the cognitive side, it is rooted in the pursuit of meaning for life. Both of these roots are inextricably embedded in the cultural milieu of the believer. In his discussion of the relation of religion to mature personality he reported that as a matter of fact enlightened adults find a commitment to probabilities sufficient in religion. After all, these same persons bet their lives on probabilities in everyday matters involving life and death all the time, and thus they demonstrate that they live without absolutes in some areas where death may be the penalty. This does not prove, however, that they ought to be willing to do this in religion as well. When all is said, Allport concluded that religion and psychotherapy can be partners and need not be opponents. Each approach has its advantages, and each has its Achilles heel. For example, "Religion, we conclude, is superior to psychotherapy in the allowance it makes for the affiliative need in human nature. But when it comes to a question of implementing this insight we are confronted by the age-long failure of religion to turn doctrine into practice." [10]

It is particularly relevant to reassess this conclusion in the light of Sigmund Freud, who has been considered such an iconoclast in matters of religion.[11] Few men have conjectured about the origins of religion with more apparent antipathy than he. If Freud is correct, the beginnings of religion are mired in confusion, neuroses, and stupidity. Is it still the case that the origin of an idea has no bearing on the truth of an idea? Can man still avow religion even when he suspects that its origin is under such a cloud?

One of the tales concerning Baal Shem, the founder of the Hassidic movement, relates that when the master was faced with a particularly difficult task, he used to go to a certain place in the woods, light a fire, and pray; and his problem would be resolved. His successor, Maggid, followed the master's example and went to the same place, but said: "The fire we can no longer light, but we can still say the prayer." According to tradition, what he asked was granted nonetheless. Another generation passed, and Rabbi Mosh Leib of Sassov went into the woods and said: "The fire we can no longer light, the prayer we no longer know; all we know is the place in the woods, and that will have to be enough." What he asked was done also. In the fourth generation Rabbi Israel of Rishin stayed at home and said: "The fire we can no longer light, the prayer we no longer know, nor do we know the place. All we can do is tell the story." According to tradition even this proved to be sufficient. The last generation said: "The fire we cannot light, the prayer we do not know, and the place we do not know. We can still tell the story, but we no longer believe it. We might be able, through research, to rediscover the place and the prayer, but we doubt that the information would do us any good."

There is a suspicion that this tale represents the mood of modern man in relation to his knowledge of the origins of religion. The old tales can only be read with at best a sense of humor. The humor is, however, so grotesque and cynical that we are no longer sure whether to laugh or to cry. There would appear to be a practical limit to the ability of man to recognize the subjective roots of religion and at the same time maintain a sense of respect or awe in the presence of religion.

IS RELIGION NEUROTIC?

Freud discussed the origins of religion in a context so antagonistic to pious sentiment that even today psychology appears with the horns of a devil to most religious laymen. The conclusion to which his theories led was that religion was basically a sign of neurosis. If one were to infer from this that healthy persons would eschew such an infantile crutch, then it seemed clear that psychology was the mortal foe of religion; and religious writers were quick to draw this inference. The general situation since this Freudian insight has followed a more or less consistent pattern. Few persons of repute in religion dared suggest that psychology shed any fruitful light on religion. Psychology marked religion with the brand of infantility and neurosis. Virtually no one in psychology cared to modify Freud's analysis of religion, perhaps because there were safer areas still unexplored. Even Freud admitted that he had withheld *Moses and Monotheism* from publication for some years for fear that the repercussions would be damaging to the public acceptance of his psychoanalytic theory.[12] With some notable exceptions, the pattern has been relatively simple. From the religious point of view, psychologists were a stiff-necked, hard-nosed lot. From the psychological point of view, the religiously minded were weak-kneed and muddleheaded. All of this lent an aura of credibility to the assumption that there is an impasse between psychology and religion. There are two aspects of this to be noted. First, in Freud's religious writings the origins of religion were cast in such shadows of mental sickness that the dignity of religion appeared to be undermined. Secondly, psychoanalysis seemed to usurp the role of religion in the lives of its adherents. The real question, however, is whether this impasse need exist.

In *The Future of an Illusion* Freud analyzed the essence of religious belief and the primary motive for religious commitment to be essentially illusion (or delusion). He noted, "These, which profess to be dogmas, are not the residue of experience or the final result of reflection; they are illusions, fulfillments of the oldest, strongest, and most insistent wishes of mankind." [13] Indeed, to say that a dogma is an illusion is essentially to say that it is derived from wishes. If this were the major thesis of Freud's investigations, religious persons might not have felt threatened. Apart from terse formulas in the tables of chemistry or mathematics, there is very little that engages us that is not derived from the wishes of mankind. Even the former could be attributed to the original drive for order and plan in this world. What is more to the point is his claim that these very wish illusions, called religion, are incompatible with the world as it really is. That is to say, the world is not of the sort to prompt such fictionalizings. It could, however, be noted that the theories of economics, politics, aesthetics, and ethics are in a significant sense equally incompatible with the world as it really is. The theories of the social sciences differ from the religious theory, however, in that the former are not the sign of a sick personality, while religious illusions are, for Freud, comparable to what we find in Meynert's amentia, "a state of blissful hallucinatory confusion." [14] Thus religion arises not only from wishes, but from unhealthy wishes. While in Freud's terminology "illusions" are not the same as factual errors, religious daydreaming appears as a subclass whose nature is such that error is necessarily the consequence. Error in this sense means not merely that a dogma fails to describe what in fact is the case, but that its assertion by adults is inimical to a healthy personality. This last item is not so easily passed off, particularly if all other value enterprises are equally sick.

What are the religious ideas, according to Freud? What is their primary motive, and more important, what is their consequential worth? What prompted the invention of these violent supermen of the ethereal spheres whom religious persons have labored to bribe, appease, emasculate, or exorcise? Several explanations are successively asserted and rejected. At one point in *The Future of an Illusion* Freud suggested, "Now when the child grows up and finds that he can never do without protection against unknown and mighty powers, he invests these with the traits of the father-figure; he creates for himself the gods, of whom he is afraid, whom he seeks to propitiate, and to whom he nevertheless entrusts the task of protecting him. Thus the longing-for-the-father explanation is identical with the other, the need for protection against the consequences of human weakness; the child's defensive reaction to his helplessness gives the characteristic features to the adult's reaction to his own sense of helplessness; i.e., the formation of religion." [15] If the child becomes the symbol for the proto-primitive man, certain oddities emerge for Freud. Such an account suggests that primitive men were shrewd enough to see where their spiritual bread was buttered and to invent their own gods. What a rational giant genetic man must have been compared to modern man, who even today finds reasonable explanations no match for passionate impulses! To counter this supposition, it must be noted that Freud suspected that if religion had rested essentially on reason, if moral commands had gained stature solely from their instrumental usefulness, we would long since have slaughtered one another without inhibition. It was not a rational inference that prompted primitive man. It was an unconscious emotional subterfuge that gave rise to religion.

The theory to which Freud attaches the greatest explicatory usefulness in accounting for religion is developed at some length in *Moses and Monotheism*. In his research on neuroses he conjectured that the symptoms or phenomena of neuroses were the consequences of traumata in early childhood. The memory of these was repressed through a long latency period, and emerged in adulthood when the emotional situation was similar to the childhood situation, but with the roles reversed. These childhood experiences belong to the period of "infantile amnesia." [16] As Freud expressed it, "they concern impressions of a sexual and aggressive nature and also early injuries to the self (injuries to narcissism). It should be added that children at that early age do not yet distinguish between sexual and purely aggressive actions so clearly as they do later on (the 'sadistic' misunderstanding of the sexual act belongs to this context)." [17] Now when these long-slumbering memories return from the miasma of the past, they do so with cyclonic force. So great is the emotional component that all logical objections are helpless to disprove the claims of the emotions to be believed. This characteristic of such memories is compared by Freud to the delusions in a psychotic case, though without their hermitic character.

The birth of religion is likened to this individual history. In the prehistoric past the early tribes challenged the power of their chiefs. The tribal fathers were in fact killed. The tribal sons did in fact have incestuous relations with the tribal mothers. The traumata of their deeds were so great as to result in a repression of the facts through a long period of latency. The experience of Moses and the Jews is considered to be a case in point. In accordance with a tradition, with which Freud is in agreement, the Jews murdered Moses on Mount Nebo. It was not God who ordered Moses' death, nor was it Moses' sin which gave the warrant. The Jews repressed the memory so well that the scriptures give no hint of the deed. During the period from Joshua to Malachi, the recollection of the deed lay latent but seething. The murder of Jesus brought the ancient deed to light. What was more fitting than that the crime of patricide should be atoned for by the sacrifice of the son? After all, the primal father was slain by the son. The Christian could now say, "We have been delivered from the Adamic sin and guilt because the father-slayer has himself been slain."

Patrick Mullahy has suggested that "his [Jesus'] resurrection is connected to the incest wish by an old and typical idea of dying as a return to the mother's womb. . . . Beneath the elaborate symbolism of the religious phantasy, therefore, is to be found the phantasy of the incestuous rebirth from the mother." [18] In the many facets of the dogmas of religion one can retain his childish feelings of love and dependence upon the father, and, if one felt intense sexual rivalry with the father, he may find refuge in the mother figure of the Virgin Mary. God is the primal father with whom believers wish to re-establish the primal child-father relation. All the sacred prohibitions and holy beings were originally "nothing but the perpetuated will of the primeval father." [19] In order that this religious drama should not be claimed to originate anew in each person, Freud suggested that "it seems to me convincing enough to allow me to venture further and assert that the archaic heritage of mankind includes not only dispositions, but also ideational contents, memory traces of the experiences of former generations." [20]

Twenty-five years earlier, in *Totem and Taboo* (1912), Freud had come to the same essential conclusion. He asserted then that religious phenomena are to be understood as analogical with the neurotic symptoms of individuals who actually repress early traumata, slumber through latency periods, and in maturity grapple with awakened obsessions. In looking back on all of this it seemed Freudianly clear that religious persons think the world is a child's playroom in which they gently babble childish fairy tales because they are too infantile to face the world as it really is. Consequently, religion is "the universal obsessional neurosis of humanity," [21] which, if accepted, at least spares one the effort of forming a personal neurosis of his own.

To suppose from this that it necessarily follows that re-

366

ligious concerns and psychological investigations are antithetical would miss an important point. Even if Freud were right in his conjecture of the birth of religion, the truth status of religion would not be affected. Freud could well have noted this himself and replied, "You are quite right. Nothing I have said suggests that religious statements are false, but, after all, as a psychologist I am not interested in the truth of religion. I am only interested in its psychic origins and its psychic use." There is reason to believe that this is what he would have said. In addition, it could be noted that Freud did doubt that religious statements were true independent of the fact that they were motivated by man's neuroses. When we find combined in the thinking of one man the suspicion that religious statements are not true and the claim that the origin of religion is in neurosis, it is not surprising that some incorrectly inferred that it was because of the origin of religion that religious statements were false. This is not, however, what Freud said, nor would it be correct even if he had said it. That Freud was aware of the limitations of psychological studies of origins was indicated in his remark that "it does not lie within the scope of this inquiry to estimate the value of religious doctrines as truth." [22] Freud was not analyzing the truth status of religious statements, for this is not a psychological problem. Furthermore, the modern temper in theology, expressed by Paul Tillich, eschews the traditional search for religious truth. Religious security is still a live issue, but it is not to be found in empirical or deductive analyses of religious doctrines. It was traditionally found in a personal experience, such as that of Saint Paul or Saint Augustine. Even Freud's claim that the religious mood has an etiology of neurosis need not have threatened persons who seek religious comfort. Freud expressed some suspicion that this might be the case when he remarked, "Perhaps the effect of the religious thought-prohibition is not as bad as I assume; perhaps it will turn out that human nature remains the same even if education is not abused by being subjected to religion. I do not know, and you cannot know either." [23]

In another volume Freud observed, "How we who have little belief envy those who are convinced of the existence of a Supreme Power, for whom the world holds no problems, because he himself has created all its institutions! How comprehensive, exhaustive, and final are the doctrines of the believers compared with the laboured, poor, and patchy attempts at explanation which are the best we can produce!" [24] All of this might, however, seem to be a slim concession to religion from a man who thought that the experiment of irreligion was worthy of being tried. Because of these theses of Freud the illusion remains that psychology is a threat to religion, even though, as we have noted, the origins of an idea do not lend probability for the truth of an idea. Even if Freud were completely right, which is doubtful, the truth or falsity of religious doctrines remains untouched, however psychically disturbed we might be by his theories.

IS RELIGION A MIXED BLESSING?

There is an additional matter that ought not to be overlooked. Freud did not speak for all psychologists— not even for those who were influenced by him. Carl G. Jung differed sharply with Freud on the matter of the emotional value of religion for psychic health. For Jung, not only is modern man in search of a soul, but for the health of his psyche he ought to be in search of a soul. "Whoever cannot see this aspect of the human psyche is blind, and whoever chooses to explain it away, or to 'enlighten' it away, has no sense of reality." [25] Again, in a chapter entitled "Psychotherapists or the Clergy," Jung remarked, "It is no reproach to the Freudian and Adlerian theories that they are based upon the drives; the only trouble is that they are one-sided. The kind of psychology they represent leaves out the psyche, and is suited to people who believe that they have no spiritual needs or aspirations." [26] In looking back over those of his patients who had been over thirty-five years of age, Jung reported that the problem of every one of them was, in the last analysis, that of finding a religious orientation toward life. He maintained that they all fell ill because they had lost what live religions in every age have given to their followers, and they were not really whole again until they had regained the religious outlook. What compounds the chaos is that modern man has so little confidence in organized or unorganized religion when it comes to emotional health. The very persons who, in Jung's terms, suffer most for lack of a religious basis have the most cynical suspicion that the clergy are incompetent in all areas, and that to consult them for the answers to vital questions is preposterous. It is interesting in this regard to note the results of a survey made by Jung as to whether persons facing spiritual crises would consult first a clergyman or a doctor. Of the Protestants 57 per cent chose the doctor, 8 per cent chose the clergyman, and 35 per cent were undecided. Of the Roman Catholics, 25 per cent chose the doctor, 58 per cent chose the clergyman, and 17 per cent were undecided. All the relatives of clergymen, however, chose the doctor.[27]

A view which was not completely alien to that given by Freud, but which contained less of the invidious implication than Freud's doctrines, was given by Jung in his *Answer to Job*. His discussion was predicated upon the premise that there are psychic truths which cannot be explained or proved by any empirical procedure. The statements of religion are of this psychic type, and consequently they cannot be affected by any physical facts. Since the data of religion have this nonphysical property, their expression must always be in symbolic form. The biblical literalism of some Protestant Fundamentalists, for example, betrays an abysmal failure to understand the essentially symbolic meanings of events such as miracles. All rational attempts to accept or to explain the miraculous simply fail to recognize both the nature of religion and the nature of religious language. To the unlettered the obviously empirically incredible events reported by Scripture seem to be signs of human credulity, while to the informed these merely emphasize that spiritual insights are autonomous and that the psychic phenomena are to some degree not dependent upon physical occurrences. It would be irrelevant to wonder whether the psychic experiences should be more firmly rooted in the physical. The fact is that they are not.

The essential issue with which Jung was concerned was the picture of God implied by the story of Job as reported in the Old Testament. Out of the somewhat incomprehensible dialogues between God and the Devil, the Devil and Job, God and Job, and Job and his friends a panoramic picture of a Yahweh torn with inner contradictions was revealed. Here was a God who expressed no moderation in his feelings and who suffered through his own excesses. Here was a divine being who seemed so unself-conscious that he did not know that he was omniscient, while he behaved as if he were a typical irrational and irresponsible person. Job and his contemporaries were familiar with, even though they do not appear to be reconciled to, this divine arbitrariness. Yahweh was presumed to be both just and unjust simply because he was everything. The experience of Job appeared as an archetype of human awareness that there are antinomies within the divine character, and that at the point of this human insight, man transcends the knowledge which God has of himself. As Jung summarized this: "The unconscious mind of man sees correctly even when conscious reason is blind and impotent. The drama has been consummated for all eternity: Yahweh's dual nature has been revealed, and somebody or something has seen and registered this fact." [28] This dual nature may be seen in the deliberate connivance of Yahweh with Satan against the good Job, and, further, in Yahweh's amazing lack of conscious awareness as to what is happening in the world and of what his own actions clearly entail morally. As a consequence, it is no wonder that man saw fear of God as the beginning of wisdom. After all, God incorporated two warring tendencies. On the one hand, he aspired to perfection, which is necessarily incomplete; while on the other hand, his feminine nature longed for completeness, which is necessarily imperfect. The contemporary counterpart of this divine antinomy is the dogma of the Roman Catholic church of the Assumption of the Virgin Mary. While she certainly does not function as a female goddess, she does symbolize this other side of God which stands as a check against the masculine urge for perfection. At this point, Jung observed that there is a lacuna in Protestantism, for although it has the forceful and fearful perfection-seeking masculine side of God, it lacks the warm and friendly completion-seeking feminine element.

Jung felt that the Assumption of Mary was the greatest single religious event since the Reformation,[29] for it symbolized that the incarnation of God was only partially completed with the coming of Christ, and that there was this other side of God which was as yet not consciously expressed. The care which the Roman church took in preparing for Mary's Assumption seemed, to Jung, an indication that they were aware of the ancient and timeless antinomy in God. "Remarkable indeed," he noted, "are the unusual precautions which surround the making of Mary: immaculate conception, extirpation of the taint of sin, everlasting virginity. The Mother of God is obviously being protected against Satan's tricks. From this we can conclude that Yahweh has consulted his own omniscience, for in his omniscience there is a clear knowledge of the perverse intentions which lurk in the dark side of God. Mary must at all costs be protected from these corrupting influences." [30]

On the other hand, the character of Christ seems to express some of the masculine lack of self-reflection and urge toward perfection of the cosmic being. Jung saw Christ as a somewhat irascible person, a type often found among people of high and uncritical emotions coupled with a marked lack of self-awareness. Speaking of the Christ portrayed in the Book of Revelation, Jung observed: "The apocalyptic 'Christ' behaves rather like a bad-tempered, power-conscious boss." [31] His very irritability, moodiness, and emotional outbursts are simply symptomatic of his perfection-seeking chronic virtuousness. Yet it is this symbolic contradiction incarnated in Christ which provides the great insight which Christians incorporate in the Christ myth. The fact that it is myth does nothing to detract from its importance. Indeed, those who seek to capture in empirical language the historical personality of the man Jesus contribute only a culture-bound religious teacher.

If we keep in mind this cosmic clash within the meaning of God, then so-called Christian ethics makes sense. The very incomprehensibility of the demands of the Sermon on the Mount and the consequent conflicts of duty which they engender are their chief claim to fame, for they make man aware of the opposites and the insoluble conflicts in God's character. With this assumption in mind, it becomes much clearer that the purpose of the Atonement was not to make reparation for wrongs which man had done to God, but rather for wrongs done by God to man.[32] To be sure, this is not the conventional Christian interpretation of the Atonement, for the Christian interpretation presumes that God was so unforgiving that only a human sacrifice would appease him. But where in all this does the Holy Spirit fit? We have the perfection of Christ and the completeness of Mary, and there does not seem to be any reason for a third element. Jung maintained that the Holy Spirit symbolized the endless incarnation of God in human form, while Christ and Mary appear to stand for two events in time. The problem of the Holy Spirit, however, has been that it has appeared to have no controls. It moves wherever it pleases and in whatsoever fashion it pleases. The emphasis upon the Holy Spirit in Protestantism gave the movement its individualistic and heretical bent, and by virtue of this, the Roman Catholic Church has had to minimize the role of the Spirit in favor of the roles of Christ and Mary.

What does all of this mean for religion? Quite apart from the psychological interpretations which Jung gives of the meaning of Christian dogmas, the general mood of his comments is not inimical to religion. Religious experience is authentic, not in its objective descriptive capacity, but in its portrayal of real human feelings in a world of contradictions. In this sense religious statements are true, for they do assert what is the case with man. If man does find his world teeming with irrational opposites, then the symbolic language of religion is the only authentic way in which these facts can be effectively and adequately portrayed. It is quite beside the point that these symbols and sentiments are produced by the unconscious, although developed by the conscious mind, for after all, religious experience is psychic, not physical, and hence religious facts can be established only psychically. This fact, far from detracting from the significance of religion, is the very basis for its authenticity.

We ought not to infer from this, however, that religious conviction functions as an unmitigated good. The very involvement of the religious enthusiast may bring with it penalties which cooler heads might have avoided. In discussing, for example, the Communist techniques of conversion, Richard L. Walker observed that "the cynics and those with a sense of humor seem to survive best; those with strong emotions or deep religious or other convictions frequently break first." [33] This same thesis was proposed by William Sargant in his *Battle for the Mind*. He too recommended caution to religious enthusiasts. "One should not carry such an analogy too far; but it serves to emphasize the fact that some persons become converted against their will because they insist on doing what they consider the 'right thing' and go out to fight what is more wisely avoided or ignored. Their energies should be devoted instead to maintaining a policy of total non-cooperation, despite their pride and a natural inclination to test their courage and strength against those trying to provoke them." [34]

DOES PSYCHOLOGY THREATEN RELIGION?

The supposition that psychology threatens religion may well be an instance of the age-old fear on the part of some religionists of the discoveries of science. This fear might be explained by the similarity of the quest of scientists and theologians, on the principle that men of common interests are most likely to be in crucial disagreement. Both psychology and theology attempt to explain the world for purposes of security and control. Each is motivated by the desire to bring some order out of the basic chaos. If one wishes to raise doubts about the religious orderings, he could do so as well with the psychological orderings. In neither case would he be casting doubts on the empirical consequences which either discipline may claim. There is, after all, ample evidence that the accounts of theologians may threaten the accounts of psychologists, and vice versa. It has, however, proved more fruitful in the history of man's attempts to understand himself to consider both psychology and religion as grounded in human desires for security. This does not mean that we should waive the questions of empirical truth and falsity, but rather that we would do well to recognize what these two efforts have in common, independent of their descriptive accuracy.

Instead of this recognition of common aim, Saint Thomas in the thirteenth century proposed to delineate the domains of competence of science and religion in such a way that no conflict could occur. This separation accomplished at least a truce between the two areas, so that internecine battles need not be waged. Thomas had noted that both science and religion (mundane theology) used induction and deduction. If each discipline made no errors, they ought to come to similar conclusions. Since revealed theology was beyond reason, it was clear that no conflict was possible with science in this area either. The biblical literalism of the sixteenth-century Protestants, however, reasserted the possibility of a live conflict between science and religion. With the rise of biological evolutionary theories, which appeared to contradict a literal reading of the Genesis story, the Protestants reawakened a fear of science among religious persons. This was symbolized in the classic Scopes trial over the teaching of the theory of biological evolution in the public schools. This Protestant fear of evolutionary theory still crops up on the educational horizon. Only the respect generally accorded to science prevents these religious zealots from banishing biological evolution from the school curricula. All of this contributed to the equal suspicion with regard to psychology. It was not merely that psychology predicated human origins of

374

religion, but that some psychological theories found no support for original sin, predestination, or the "devil theory" of mental disturbances. The New Testament story of the Gadarene demented man and the swine [35] is still considered by some Protestants to be a phenomenological account of how mental derangement occurs and how it should be cured. "Beating the devil out of one" is still more than a colloquialism in certain religious circles.

There is some indication, however, that the Fundamentalist views on the reality and importance of sin are not to be canceled out in consequence of a hasty inference from Freudian psychology. In a recent book by O. Hobart Mowrer a case is made for the abandonment of psychoanalysis in general and Freud in particular.[36] While he cites Felix Adler, Carl Jung, and Otto Rank as pioneers in the break with Freud, the crisis which Mowrer has in mind is better expressed by men like Wilhelm Stekel [37] and Anton T. Boisen.[38] Boisen felt that "the real evil in mental disorder is not to be found in the conflict but in the sense of isolation and estrangement. It is the fear and guilt which result from the presence in one's life of that which one is afraid to tell." [39] While Freud had felt that the problem of man was rooted in the repression of feelings which he was afraid to express, Boisen saw the problem as a consequence of feelings which man had already expressed. Man was anxious, therefore, because he felt guilty for deeds committed, and not for deeds merely contemplated. This means very simply that the sins which cause mental disturbance have actually been committed.

Mowrer uses the term "sickness" as typifying the essential psychoanalytic view of man's neuroses, and since this term is ethically neutral, it follows that psychoanalysis denies the existence of any real moral issues. Mowrer saw this rejection of the moral as productive of pessimism on the part of the patient and confusion on the part of the analyst. The concept of sin, on the other hand, in spite of its harshness and apparent brutality, carries with it a hope of redemption and the promise that man can reform. "Just so long as we deny the reality of sin," Mowrer held, "we cut ourselves off, it seems, from the possibility of radical redemption." [40] Since earliest historic times it has been assumed that human beings know the difference between right and wrong, and this premise is still part of our psychic heritage. Psychoanalysis, on the contrary, has insisted that either there is no right and wrong, or else even mature persons cannot possibly know the difference and hence be responsible for their actions. Sin, Mowrer insisted, was "the lesser of two evils." [41] If we must choose between guilt and guilt feelings, then let us choose guilt as the root of man's anxiety. This choice is grounded in two facts: first of all, the history of man supports guilt as a fact consequent from committed sins, and second, the hypothesis that guilt feelings are the root of man's neuroses has not been very fruitful in effecting man's cure. Indeed, Mowrer leaves us with the impression that religious institutions have been more effective in both diagnosis and cure than have Freudian psychoanalysts. Unfortunately, the clerical implementation of Mowrer's contention is not very likely, since his impression is that leading American clergymen are even more enamored of psychoanalysis than are psychologists.

The thesis of Mowrer stands or falls on his claim that guilt is real rather than imaginary. He summarizes the data in support of his contention as follows: The Freudian thesis, that guilt is imaginary rather than real, does not accord with what we know about human behavior. In addition, this Freudian assumption gives false comfort to those very persons whose guilt rests upon real commissions. [42] While Mowrer did not intend to claim that no one is ever in the position of uneasiness over imaginary guilt, he did mean to show that these represent a fraction of the total number of anxious persons. While the acceptance of this position does not prove religious truth, it does lend pragmatic support from clinical psychology for the usefulness, for personal freedom from neuroses, of the religious emotional insights.

This position of Mowrer is both supported and tempered by Erich Fromm. [43] It is supported in the sense that Fromm conceded a potentially honorific role for religion. After all, the goals of psychoanalysis and religion are the same. Both want to get the patient to feel love and to accept his personal responsibilities, and if these can be achieved, it really does not matter what the symbolic representation or the metaphysical systems are. The real threats to religion, according to Fromm, do not come from psychoanalysts but derive from man's alienation from himself, from his love experiences, and from the ideals which he professes but does not practice. Most men go to church because they feel this profound alienation and because in church they find a haven of refuge, but the plain fact is that this churchgoing does not serve as an adequate incentive to become integrated.

The Roman Catholic demarcation of domains of competence and the predication of a basic similarity in method between science and religion has a modern Protestant counterpart in the systematic theology of Paul Tillich. The old fear of the threat of science is no longer supportable, according to Tillich. The domain of theology is ultimate concern, and hence theology is not concerned with science or the results of science. Further, theology should not pretend to be informed on matters of psychology, sociology, physics, or history.[44] No results of science can possibly affect the ultimate concern of religion. Tillich holds a similar view with regard to the relation of theology to philosophy. Not only is no conflict possible between them, but no synthesis between them is possible either. Theology and philosophy can neither disagree nor agree, for they do not talk about the same things. Those who talk of a "Christian philosophy" misunderstand both philosophy and religion. Those who are concerned for a "Christian science" make the same mistake. This has not prevented Tillich from being sympathetic with the efforts of certain existential psychoanalysts, whose views of man are not inimical to religious commitments.[45] Psychology of any sort, however, can hold no threats for religion. Even though he holds that Freud's theory of the superego is inadequate because it negates norms and principles and talks the language of the "father image" in accounting for norms, he believes that it is still possible to interpret Freudian psychology in such a way that it is not inimical

377

to authentic faith. "Real faith, even if it uses the father image for its expression, transforms this image into a principle of truth and justice to be defended even against the 'father.'" [46] On the other hand, the polarity of the ego and the superego, which is explicit in Freud, is consonant with the existential facts of man's search for an ultimate commitment. Since everything that happens in the personal life is a possible object of psychological inquiry, Tillich admits the possibility of a psychology of faith. Any psychology which attempts to ground faith in something other than an immediate encounter, such as fear or human ignorance, errs, however, for nothing can be more basic than the faith encounter. In this initial assumption of the absolute originality of faith, Tillich protects religion from any invidious interpretations from psychology, and hence removes any real threat to religion from the science of man.

There has been a suspicion that there is a danger in resolving the supposed threat of psychology to religion by such a radical separation. Psychology gives the descriptive analysis of man in his environment, while religion gives the prescriptive apologetic of man in his environment. Might this not result in unfortunate consequences to both disciplines? Psychology could then deny any interest in values, while religion could deny any need for validating its claims. Might this not support the popular impression that while psychologists are indifferent to moral standards, theologians are indifferent to verification standards? The popular impression, however, may well be correct. The hope of being able to combine in one grand discipline proofs of truth and verification of values may not in fact be possible. If psychology is a science, then its concern should be with what is the case, not with what should be the case. If religion is concerned with the ultimate commitment as to what should be, then it ought not to be concerned or troubled by whatever may turn out to be the case in fact. If science and religion are so blended that the "is" and the "ought" become the same, both fields would lose the many gains made over the centuries by the drawing of sharp distinctions. There is still a larger sense in which both of these areas represent man's attempts to find answers to crucial questions. If some are answered by psychology, perhaps others are answered by religion. The analysis of the human condition and the search for human security are the intent of both psychology and religion. If, as happened in Freud's writings on religion, the motivation for religion is invidiously explained by terms such as "neurotic," "illusory," "delusory," or "infantile," it can always be the function of religion to indicate the strictly descriptive nature of these terms. What value components they may appear to have can scarcely derive from psychology, but must, rather, derive from ethics or religion.

It should be obvious that the psychological study of religion has consequences for religion, just as the historical and sociological studies of religion have had consequences. It can scarcely be of no interest to a religious person to know, for example, that denomination X has primarily white-collar workers as members, or that the snake-handling sects do not appeal to college presidents. These facts are of interest even though they do not affect either religious truth or religious value. The contributions of the psychological study of religion ought to be of even more interest to persons who take religion seriously. Psychology seems to touch more pertinently upon the question of the value of religion than does any other science of religion. If, for example, some persons are so anxious about predestination that they become neurotic, no religious leader can afford to evade the implications of this fact. Obsessive concern with some religious dogmas is apparently harmful to healthy personality. On the other hand, if Jung is right, the ignoring of some religious issues may also be harmful to the psyche. While it must be granted that neither of these facts affects the truth or falsity of the religious dogmas in question, both of them do affect any judgment we may wish to make about the pragmatic value of religion. This does not mean that we would be warranted in concluding that psychology is a threat to religion just because the psychologist has found a neurosis-producing element in some dogmas. Similarly, when Copernican astronomy proved the Ptolemaic view incorrect, there was no reason to conclude, because the church favored Ptolemy, that astronomy was a threat to religion. The Modernists saw that the simple solution to this state of affairs was for the church to give up the old geocentric view. Might it not be equally obvious that religion can profit from this new science of psychology without having to stage a new Scopes trial? If the authors of ancient scripture erred on matters of geology, astronomy, and biology, may they not also have erred on some matters of psychology? If we would not accept Noah's account of the scope of the ancient Flood, or the Adamic report of the genesis of the human race, why should we accept the Gospel report that the young psychotic of Gadarea really suffered from demons? If we are suspicious of the morals of King David, or of the bloodthirstiness of Jael, why should we accept the judgment of Saint Paul that preoccupation with sin is "good for the soul"? While there is no real reason why anyone should imagine that psychology destroys religion, it seems inescapable that the lessons of psychology should bring about some changes in religious perspective. Just as the study of logic can teach a theologian what it means to be logical, so the study of psychology can teach religious persons what it means to be mature.

XVI

The Church *and the* State

THE ISSUES related to the problems of church and state
have aroused enthusiasm among pious and impious
alike. This is one of the few areas relevant to religion on
which even the religiously indifferent have opinions. The
Christian sects, both Protestant and Catholic, have historically
stood on most of the possible sides of resolution. The picture is
so confused that there is no agreement even on the question
of whether the problem is religious or political. For many
Christians, both Catholic and Protestant, the matter is a
political one. It is to be decided by appeal to political traditions and commitments and not to religious traditions or
dogmas. It would be reasonable to suppose that for the average uncommitted American citizen the assumption that the
problem is basically political is sound. There are, on the other
hand, Catholics and Protestants who feel that the issue is essentially religious, and that political considerations must bow
before the superior weight of theological tenets. Though it has
become common in this country to assume that all the Catholics are on one side and that all the Protestants are united on
the other, there is little evidence either from the past or from
the present to support this myth. In order to see the contemporary struggles in perspective it will help to review

some of the early Catholic and Protestant positions on the relation of church and state. Such a survey should at least dispel any illusion that the facts show that Protestants favored separation of church and state while the Roman Catholics favored the integration of the two. One common theme runs throughout—that the secular rulers are ordained of God in some sense. Both the Old and the New Testament appear to confirm this view. Christians through the centuries may have differed on the necessity of a state or on the relation of the religion to the state, but they have agreed that the rulers of the several states have some kind of divine commission. The differences emerge in the interpretation of where authority lies for certification of this commission.

THE PENDULUM OF HISTORY

The ancient Greek state prior to Socrates had a tolerance of religion and a faith in reason. It has been asserted that this very tolerance, which commonly approximated state indifference to religion, accounted in large measure for the great contribution which these ancient Greeks made to political philosophy.[1] The Jews and the Hindus took the world as it was, on trust, so to speak. Their interests were "not of this world." The Greek, on the contrary, was little attracted by religious motives and put his interest in the hurly-burly of the social and political milieu. These Greeks thought of the state as an ethical association for the attainment of virtue on the part of the citizens. The state thus assumed the obligations now commonly assumed by the churches—namely, of curbing sin and of pointing the way to virtue. Such a notion is alien to the modern man who criticizes the Greeks (as Hegel did) for failing to distinguish between "society" and "the state." As Hegel noted, when the state assumes social motives, then pressure groups will rule. To be sure, this prevailing Greek sentiment in favor of a state which assumed all of the functions, both normative and executive, was not uncontested. The existence of Cynics and Cyrenaics (of whom Diogenes was a shining example) indicated that there were some who rebelled, not only against a morally motivated state, but against the whole idea of law and order. These dissidents were mendicant beggars and anarchists; they have been regarded as predecessors of the early Christian Fathers.

Aristotle was a traditional Greek in his views on the state and religion. He could not conceive of any allegiances higher than the state, such as the religions have commonly pretended to be. He had no interest in allegiances to all mankind (such as the Judeo-Christian ideal) or in aspirations toward a world community (such as in Kant's *Perpetual Peace*). What religion there was existed by the grace of the state, and outside of this political permission, religion had no warrant of its own. While it is true that Aristotle averred that "the expense of religious worship should likewise be a public charge," [2] he never thought of religion as other than a function of state authority. The thought of religion setting itself off from the state, as a critic of the state, was inconceivable. The prevailing view was, thus, that religion existed by state permission, and both Judaism and Christianity fitted neatly into this dominant scheme. With few exceptions, during the Pax Romana religions existed through the grace of political authority, and it was not imagined that religion had any function as a political gadfly.

This situation changed with the adoption of Christianity by Constantine (313 A.D.) and with its establishment as an official state religion in 383 A.D. It was not merely that the political structure of the Christian church resembled so closely that of the Roman Empire, but also that within twenty-seven years after the official sanction of Christianity Rome fell. It was suggested that Christianity was the cause of the fall of Rome, for, after all, Christians were poor citizens, pacifists, and persons who held allegiance to institutions higher than the state. When a religion became as important as Christianity appeared to be to its followers, then the power of the state was undermined and the unity of political effort was destroyed. Previous to this era, religion had not been taken seriously enough to make men torture, kill, and be unpatriotic in its name. The subsequent Crusades, the Inquisition, the Protestant religious wars all justified the Greek unwillingness to permit any group to assume powers comparable to those of the state. Saint Augustine's *City of God* (413–426 A.D.) was composed to reply to the current charges that Christianity had undermined the Empire, and he had countered the charge, in part, by placing the blame on the barbarian hordes and the prevailing secularity of Roman culture. If Saint Augustine was right, then the Roman Empire was clearly not similar to Greece, for apparently it had not assumed the obligation of being the mentor of morals and the teacher of virtue.

If the Roman Empire did, indeed, reject its moral role, and if the subsequent developments up to the thirteenth century followed in this vein, then it can be understood why the Roman Catholic philosopher, Saint Thomas, insisted that the Church must exist as a companion in power with the state to keep the state aware of moral responsibilities. Indeed, for Saint Thomas, the state received its warrant for existence from God, and indirectly through the Roman Catholic church power was given to the political ruler that he might realize justice upon the earth. While the early Greeks had been aware of a real conflict of interests between individuals and the state, the medieval Christians saw the conflict as one between the church and the state. Absolute power resided with the Pope, and only relative power resided in the secular prince. The question of political obedience was now considered to be one that it was within the province of the church to answer, and we find Saint Thomas recommending that "existing infidel rulers are to be obeyed, but no new infidel kingdoms are to be established." [3] This was a far cry from the Greek ideal, in which the churches had existed through political permission and were never conceived to be in the position of acting as judges of the state's legitimacy. This medieval emphasis on the superiority of the church over the state, in which the state existed through the grace of the church, persisted with little serious revolt up to the sixteenth century. To be sure, there were a few, like Marsilio of Padua

(1275–1343 A.D.) who insisted that observation, not theology, should determine what is right in politics.

The first half of the eighteenth century saw the dissolution of clerical power in politics with Jean Jacques Rousseau as a chief advocate of this accomplishment. He noted:

> What the pagans had feared actually came to pass. The entire face of affairs was altered; the humble Christians changed their language, and soon this pretended kingdom of the other world became, under a visible chief, the most violent despotism in this. However, as there had always been a prince and civil laws, the consequence resulting from this double power has been a perpetual conflict for jurisdiction which has made any system of good polity impossible in Christian states; and men could never certainly inform themselves whether it was the master or the priest they were bound to obey.[4]

Where Christianity has erred, in addition, is in that it has failed to link itself properly to the body of the state. While the leaders of the church were trained in matters of an unworldly nature, they still presumed to legislate, and the result has been that in England, Italy, Russia, and the Moslem states the incompetent clergy have been the masters. Rousseau believed that Hobbes saw this danger clearly, but that Hobbes had erred in imagining that the two could be fruitfully joined with the secular princes as the heads. Rousseau observed of Hobbes that "he ought to have seen that the dominating spirit of Christianity would defeat his system, and that the interest of the priesthood would always triumph over that of the State."[5] Rousseau's position was an attempt to steer a course between the view that religion was of no use to the state and the view that it was essential to the state. In referring to these two options (and to Pierre Bayle, who held the former position, and William Warburton, who held the latter), he stated: "We should prove to the first writer that no state has ever been established without having religion for its basis; and to the other that the Christian law is at bottom more injurious than useful to the constitution of the State."[6]

385

Rousseau considered three kinds of religion, all of which he found injurious to a properly functioning state. The first was what he called "the religion of man." He identified this with the religion of the Gospels and found its distinguishing characteristics to be an absence of churches, ritual, and priests. Religion was the private affair of the individual. While this religion has a glorified view of all men as brothers, it never has any particular connection with the body politic. It robs laws of their moral force and social duties of their appeal, and leads the attention of men to otherworldly concerns. Of this religion he said, "I know of nothing more destructive to the social spirit." [7]

The second was a kind of national religion, whose distinctive characteristics were local gods, dogmas and rites, and priests. This religion tends to be intolerant of unbelievers, chauvinistic, and warlike. While such a religion does produce a love of local laws and an admiration for one's own country, it errs "because, as it is founded in error and falsehood, it deceives mankind, renders it credulous and superstitious, and clouds the true worship of the Divinity with vain ceremonies. It is likewise evil, when becoming jealous and tyrannical, it makes a people sanguinary and intolerant to such a degree that they breathe nothing but massacre and murder. . . ." [8]

The third type of religion (typified by the Lamas, the Japanese, and Roman Christianity) requires two allegiances, the one religious and the other secular, and carries with it the assumption of two masters. This religion confuses man and sets him in contradiction with himself. This third type he found "so evidently bad that it would be losing time to demonstrate its evils." [9] Indeed, the errors of all three of these types of religion stem from the evils implicit in Christianity, which thinks of nothing but heaven, and lacks the basic sense of worldly concern. "Christianity preaches only servitude and dependence. Its spirit is too favorable to tyranny not to be always taken advantage of. True Christians are formed to be slaves. . . ." [10]

Rousseau ends with several minimal requisites of what

he called a "purely civil profession of faith." The dogmas of this civil religion are simple: belief in a transfinite divinity, heaven for the good, and hell for the wicked, the sanctity of laws, and a conviction that the just shall be happy. The state ought to tolerate only those religions which tolerate all religions. Those religions which are not so broad-minded should be driven from the state. If any religion at all is to be permitted by the state, it must be because the religion in question leads citizens to love the laws of the state. Beyond this, the state has no concern or right in what religious persons wish to believe.

In this brief survey the relations between church and state fall into two general categories. On the one hand, as in the case of ancient Greece, the church is used by the state, and possesses warrant only to the degree to which it contributes to law and order. This was the position to which Rousseau gave allegiance. In this view the church has no moral rights inherently its own. It possesses no insights superior to those promoted by the secular princes, and hence is never in a position to be the judge of what is politically right. On the other hand, as in the medieval Roman Catholic position, there are two rival authorities, each with its proper domain of competence. In accordance with this position, there are areas in which the church is warranted in judging the state. Let us turn now to an analysis of the views of some of the major Christian spokesmen, both Protestant and Roman Catholic, with regard to the proper church-state relations.

MARTIN LUTHER AND THE STATE CHURCH

The variety of views attributed to Luther on this subject leaves the interpreter in something of a quandary in determining what is to be considered the authentic one. Some maintain that Luther paved the way for the secular control of religion which reached its culmination in the modern fascist state. Others have asserted that he paved the way for the democratic separation of church and state. Still others have held that he was a medievalist at heart and that his position reflected no change from the prevailing Roman Catholic one of his day. A review of Luther's writings would seem to indicate that he held successively several different views. Which of them is chosen as being essentially the one to be assigned to Luther would appear to be a matter of taste, unless one assumes that his last view was the one properly his. In 1520, when he issued his *Address to the Christian Nobility,* he was confident that an appeal to the German nobility would protect the Lutheran church against Roman Catholicism. At this period in his thinking he favored integration of church and state as being in the interests of religious freedom. In 1523, when he issued his book, *Concerning Secular Authority,* he was disillusioned with integration and advocated a separation of the church from the state. This disillusionment came after the judgment against him issued at the Diet of Worms in 1521. While he was suspicious of entrusting matters of religion to the emperor, he did assert that religious persons ought to be obedient to the rulers. He later proposed that under special circumstances rebellion against the emperor might be warranted, even to the point of war. His fourth position reasserted the sanctified status of the secular ruler. He appealed to the fourth Mosaic Commandment in support of all secular power as divine and holy. Every secular officer ruled as an ambassador of God. Since Luther agreed with Plato, Aristotle, and Cicero that the state is responsible, not only for enforcing the laws, but for making the citizens moral, improving their character, and curbing their passions, he presumed that secular government may be considered the Kingdom of God. It was on this point that Troeltsch linked Luther with Machiavelli and fascism, while others noted that Luther reserved for the church a domain of competence which was not subservient to the state. In this last position Luther was intolerant of all sects except the Lutheran. It is true that in 1523 Luther had said that there must of necessity be sects and differing opinions, but after the Peasants' War he rejected this tolerant position. By 1526 he advocated that members of faiths other than Lutheran be banished from the country. In 1530 he endorsed the death penalty for Anabaptists, a view lightened only by his wish that they might emigrate before the penalty became necessary. In 1535 Luther expressed the wish that there were more English kings to kill cardinals. When it came to dealing with blasphemers, Luther appealed to the Mosaic law in defense of the precept, "Don't dispute them, kill them." With regard to the Jews he recommended burning the synagogues, making them slaves, or banishing them. He added insult to injury by the unfortunate comment that he would rather be a pig than a Jew. While Luther broke with the papacy, at least in part because of the claim of infallibility on the part of church councils, it was also the case that after 1526 he endeavored to rebuild the German Lutheran church on the pattern of the old Roman Church under Constantine. His willingness to let the ruler aid and abet the Lutheran cause led to the submission of the church to the state. What Luther took away from the Roman Catholic church, he gave to the secular state.

JOHN CALVIN AND THE CHURCH STATE

The same ambiguity evident in Luther's positions is found in John Calvin's discourses on the relations between the church and the state. In Calvinism there is, however, much more skepticism about the secular authorities and their capabilities in church affairs. In part, this followed from his criticism of the Roman Catholic church's attempted role in secular matters. Calvin maintained that the proper sphere of the church is spiritual affairs. In principle, Calvin held rigidly to a clear separation between church and state, but in fact the Geneva churches had political connections. The consistories which he organized were partly clerical and partly secular in their responsibilities and in their membership. Unlike Luther, however, Calvin made the church the real leader of the two. At least after 1555, there was no doubt in Geneva which group called the tune: the church ruled the state. Both the state and the church were divinely instituted. Both had authority for their task from God. The office

of the ministry was, without doubt, higher than the office
even of a king. Once a pastor of a church had been elected,
he enjoyed a supreme position. His word was the law.
Yet the fact that congregations had a role in the selection of
the minister provided a measure of democratic control in an
otherwise tyrannous system.

Calvin's genius lay in the organization of the church as
an instrument of spiritual discipline. The function of this discipline was threefold. (a) The church was to see to it that
those who called themselves Christians lived in such a manner as to be worthy of the name. (b) The church tried to
make sure that the good people were not contaminated by
contact with wicked persons. (c) The church endeavored to
convict sinners of a sense of shame and to start them on the
road to repentance. Calvin felt that the early Christian
church had been unduly harsh in its excommunication procedures. The goal of punishment should be to bring lost
souls into the bosom of the church rather than to banish them
forever.

He considered that the secular state had its origin and
warrant in three causes. There was a provocative cause—
namely, human sin. If men had remained in the bliss of
Eden, the state would have been unnecessary. Secondly, there
was an efficient cause—namely, the grace and goodness of
God in providing for a curb on human sin. Thirdly, there was
a final cause—namely, the preservation of law and order and
the elimination of anarchy. Just as the church had its domain of competence and jurisdiction, so the state had its
duties for which it was ideally fitted. The secular powers
were to preserve public worship. They were to protect the
existing churches and to establish new churches where they
were needed. The rulers were to maintain law and order. In
all things the secular magistrates were considered accountable to God; and as a consequence, Calvin did not entertain
the possibility that citizens would be entitled to revolt. While
Calvin did inveigh against unscrupulous and profligate rulers
and courts, he assumed that God would take care of the problem. If rulers were evil, then God must be punishing the citi-

zenry for great moral offenses. While he held strictly to the position that the revolt of citizens was always unjustified, he did consider that lesser magistrates could, by virtue of their office, bring harsh pressures to bear on higher magistrates. In spite of the division of labor between church and state, Calvin hardly rated as a strong defender of what modern men consider as the doctrine of separation. The church was expected to exert pressure and censure on the magistrates; the magistrates were expected to give financial and legal protection to the churches. Nor was Calvin any more tolerant of other sects and faiths than Luther had been. The church Calvin had in mind was only the one which adopted Calvinism. Other sects were as abhorrent in Geneva as in Lutheran Germany. In neither Luther nor Calvin do we find clear separation as the doctrine. This idea came from other sectarian movements.

Some tentative observations may be made on the basis of what we have so far studied with regard to sixteenth-century Protestantism and the issue of the separation of church and state. Neither Luther nor Calvin endorsed the hands-off policy which characterizes the thinking of many in America today. They did not propose to keep the state out of religious affairs. Because each had an exclusive view of proper religion, each assumed that the state would block all religious movements except his own. There seems to have been a pattern since the sixteenth century which can be formulated as follows. The more keenly a religious movement feels its uniqueness and its consequent claim to sole possession of the divine insight, the more deeply will the members of that movement be committed to state interference in religion. The movements favoring the least state interference in religion appear to have been those with the least claims to uniqueness. There is an understandable thesis underlying this fact. A religious movement which feels that it possesses the sole insights which men need cannot afford to advocate a laissez-faire policy. If man's eternal salvation is at stake, then both a morally aggressive church and a state which implements religious legislation are warranted. Protestant Fundamentalism had this claim to uniqueness to no less a degree than did Roman Catholicism, and hence we would not expect to find the separation doctrine enthusiastically held by either group. A recently established pressure group presumes that Protestants and Catholics can be divided clearly on the church-state issue.[11] Not only is there no historical support for such a generalization, but there is no contemporary evidence that either group fits neatly into either category. Members of the aforementioned organization in one breath accused the Roman Catholics of influencing their parishioners on political and economic issues and in the next breath proceeded to influence the members of their own congregations on the same matters. In order to see the heritage of these two branches of Christianity, we will look at developments within Protestant sects in the early history of the United States of America and then consider the latitudinarianism found in the Roman Catholic church.

IS THERE AN AMERICAN TRADITION?

Medieval Christianity had, in general, advocated obedience to the civil magistrates. In return the state supported the church by punishing heresy and promoting religion. It had been the secular authorities that performed the executions, by burning or hanging, for religious dissent. The church courts had merely pronounced the sentences. It was generally assumed that the decision to be religious was a community affair, and hence the sixteenth-century churches, by and large, both permitted and urged the state to interfere in religious matters. The history of this relation indicated that it was an uneasy one at best. Secular princes early assumed the power which the churches seemed only too willing to give them. This gave rise to conflicts, which the secular princes usually won. In the alliances between church and state, the latter tended to assume the major power. The Act of Supremacy in the sixteenth century gave the English crown jurisdiction over all spiritual affairs. This included the appointment of the clergy and the determination of the dogma. This meant, in effect, that Parliament directed the national church. Even today changes in the Book of Common Prayer theoretically require the consent of Parliament. The defense of this state of affairs was classically presented in Thomas Hooker's *Of the Laws of Ecclesiastical Polity*.[12] The question of the relation of the church to the state, raised in the Reformation, was generally solved by giving the state jurisdiction. In the states where Reformed churches first settled (Scotland, England, Geneva, Holland, northern Germany, and the Scandinavian countries) the state assumed the right to determine religion. State or national churches emerged. In England, for example, to be a member of the state was to be a member of the state church. The enthusiasm for separation was supplied by those Protestant, Catholic, or Jewish sects which happened to be in the minority in a particular state. Since they did not wish to assert anarchy, and since they were persecuted by the state, the simple and obvious alternative was to advocate separation of church and state. In most instances where these same sects happened to be in the majority, they were as antidisestablishmentarian as any. Since Protestantism centered its authority in the Bible rather than in the pope or the church, the general result was characterized as a "Bible despotism." [13]

The New World illustrated this dichotomy of separation versus nonseparation. Where a sect was in the majority, it advocated integration of church and state. The pendulum had swung many ways in Europe before American traditions were ever established. In England after 1660 there was no real danger that any church would be able to rule the state. This was so even though church membership (Anglican) continued to be required of all members of Parliament and even though it was not until 1871 that the old universities of England were open to all, independent of religion.

The religious persons who first settled America were agreed that the state should support religion. The only disagreements among them were at the point of the form this support should take.

In New Holland religious homogeneity was not severely pressed. Calvinists, Lutherans, Mennonites, Quakers, Catholics, and Jews were all welcome. However, the Dutch West India Company issued in 1640 a mandate that no other religion than the Reformed as taught in the United Netherlands should be publicly recognized. Private conscience was respected, but dissent in public worship was not permitted. When the issue of public meetings did arise, Peter Stuyvesant, the Dutch Reformed leader of the colony, imprisoned and fined unorthodox preachers and congregations. The Dutch West India Company chided Stuyvesant for his intolerance and suggested that he ignore religious dissent. On the issue of religious toleration for the Jews the Company was also more liberal than either Stuyvesant or the New Holland residents.

In Virginia, which was established as an Anglican mission project, the royal charter of 1606 required all emigrants to the new land to take an oath of religious fealty to the Anglican church. Catholics were forbidden to hold public office. The parents who had scruples on infant baptism (Baptists) were subject to penalties for not presenting their children for this sacrament. The absence of any resident bishop in Virginia for the first years enabled the state to usurp religious authority more quickly. Secular magistrates administered even the ordination and confirmation of the clergy.

A similar limited bibliocracy existed in Connecticut under Thomas Hooker, in Rhode Island under Roger Williams, and in Pennsylvania under William Penn. Connecticut had no religious prerequisites for the franchise, even though Protestantism was clearly in the political saddle. There were no religious requirements for citizenship in Pennsylvania; all Jews, Catholics, and Protestants could live there. But only Christians could vote or hold office. The most liberal attitude toward other faiths than the dominant one was to be found in Rhode Island under Roger Williams, the Baptist. With few exceptions even Jews and Catholics could vote. Although Williams hated the Quakers, he never persecuted them.

The debate between John Cotton, representing the Massachusetts Bay Colony, and Roger Williams led to striking changes in perspective on the relations between church and state. Williams wrote *The Bloudy Tenent of Persecution for*

Cause of Conscience, Discussed in a Conference between Truth and Peace. Cotton replied with *The Bloudy Tenent Washed and Made White in the Bloude of the Lambe.* Williams contended for a number of points on the matter of religious liberty from the point of view of both state and church. The state has no jurisdiction over faith, discipline, worship, or church polity. The churches, on their side, must not expect state support. Religious liberty is the right both of individuals and of groups. If there is to be any religious progress, it must come as a result of voluntary activity on the part of interested persons. Churches should be built and maintained by their members. In the event of a real threat to the public peace, the civil authorities may intervene in the affairs of religion; but real cause must first be established.

It was in the Massachusetts Bay Colony that all of the deficiencies of religious intolerance were most completely and clearly expressed. The state and the church were identified, and citizenry and churchmanship were synonymous. One could not be a citizen unless he was a Puritan. The franchise was limited to members of the Puritan church. The tests for church membership were so strict that many persons who were otherwise Puritans remained outside the membership fold. This did not excuse them, however, from church attendance. A law of 1635 made church attendance compulsory under penalty of fine and imprisonment. The church effectively implemented both excommunication from the religious group and banishment from the colony. Such clerical judgments were carried out, with the assistance of the state, against Quakers, Presbyterians, Baptists, and Catholics. Those not actually banished from the society were commonly killed. The Cambridge Platform of 1648 laid down the responsibilities of clerics and civil magistrates. While each had his own domain of authority, it was assumed that the state would back the decisions of the church in the matter of punishments and in the matter of taxation for the support of the church. In Massachusetts, unlike many other areas, clergymen held political posts, and they administered affairs on the assumption that the Bible alone was a sufficient guide, since the state was in fact theocratic. There was a notable absence of democratic theory and practice. Even though the Puritans were at all times a small minority, they exerted an influence and assumed powers out of all proportion to their numbers.

Political differences were no more tolerated than religious differences. John Winthrop, the governor, said: "Democracy is accounted the meanest and worst of all forms of government." [14] If we accept the theory that religious liberty thrives best under secular laws, we can understand why there was so little liberty in Massachusetts under the Puritans. The local parson was charged not only with the care of souls, but also with attendance at public whippings. The wardens of the church not only looked after church attendance and church property, but also administered poor relief, game laws, and vagrancy laws, enforced regulations concerning weights and measures, and administered punishments for drunkenness. Massachusetts was the home of public education, but it was also the home of censorship of education.

What is intriguing about all of this is that as soon as Puritans became the political minority, they endorsed with great enthusiasm the principle of a nonclerical state. This raises an interesting question of fact. Do Protestants support the separation of church and state because they are in the minority, or is it a matter of principle which would hold even if they were the overwhelming majority? There is at least one factor which might favor the latter view, and that is the congregational element which is prominent in most Protestant sects. The individual congregation is autonomous in its selection of clergymen, in its choice of dogma to be emphasized, and in its administration of church polity. These sects fear the control of a national religious headquarters and might, therefore, be expected to be equally suspicious of any help that might be proffered from the secular state. On the other hand, any Protestant sect which believes that religion ought to play a part in everyday affairs will be prompted to bring pressure to bear upon the secular magistrates and thus break down the separation between the two powers.

The Church *and the* State

The American Revolution marked a turning of the tide from bibliocracy to separation. In part this movement toward religion free from state control was led by the minorities in each state. In part it was prompted by the issue of freedom of speech, which seemed closely linked to freedom of religion. In 1776 the Virginia Presbyterians announced that civil preference for any Christian denomination implied a claim of papal infallibility on the part of the state. They urged, therefore, that the state be shut out completely from all religious matters. The Virginia Declaration of Rights in the same year was *avant garde* with respect to most of America. It guaranteed complete religious liberty with no state interference. The Pennsylvania constitution declared religious liberty of worship and conscience, but required of all who would hold office a religious test which banned non-Christians. The New York constitution allowed complete freedom of worship, but all citizens had to renounce all allegiance, whether spiritual or political, to foreign powers. This, in fact, eliminated sensitive and sincere Catholics from citizenship. It was announced that no clergymen of any denomination could hold political office. The Massachusetts constitution permitted freedom of worship but levied taxes to support the Congregational church and required an oath of office which banned conscientious Catholics. No Jew could hold office in any case. New Hampshire, New Jersey, and North Carolina required office holders to be Protestants. South Carolina required this for the governor. Delaware and Pennsylvania restricted office holding to Christians. South Carolina declared that the Protestant Christian religion was the official one of the state.

While most of these constitutions marked an increase in separation, there was still no doubt that the states would enforce Protestantism where they could. The thorny question of Roman Catholicism was untouched until Congress found that it needed the support of Canada, which was primarily Roman Catholic. If Canada was to be an ally, some tempering of anti-Catholic laws was required. Benjamin Franklin went on a special mission to Quebec and took with him two Roman

397

Catholics: a layman, Charles Carroll, and a priest, Father John Carroll. By this time there were Catholics high in the army and in Congress. The prevailing position was typified by John Adams, who had asserted that Congress should not meddle in religion, but if the states wished to do so, that was their prerogative. James Madison argued that the churches would gain if the federal government were to stay out of religion altogether. In 1785 an act for religious freedom was drafted by Thomas Jefferson and passed by both houses. It guaranteed religious freedom from federal control.

IS THERE A ROMAN CATHOLIC TRADITION?

Where in all this debate over the role of church and state has the Roman Catholic church stood? A short review of its varied positions will indicate that it has by no means presented a univocal front. Much of the fear of Roman Catholicism on the part of Protestants rests on the assumption at the grass-roots level that modern Roman Catholicism is the same as medieval Roman Catholicism. It is further nurtured by the myth that the Roman church is homogeneous and was always so, while the Protestant sects indicate clearly all the heterogeneity implicit in them. The history of the Roman church would indicate otherwise. Like the Protestant sects, the Roman Catholic movement has always been riddled with differences of opinion.

For seventeen centuries the Roman church opposed usury; it now accepts it. Roman Catholic leaders have embraced Montanism, Arianism, Athanasianism, Jansenism, and Modernism. There have been bishops who objected to each and every one of these positions. The Catholic Encyclopedia reports that Pope Marcellinus was accused of having given up the Bible and offered incense to the gods of Diocletian in order to escape persecution. Jerome related that Pope Liberius was an Arian. Popes Innocent I and Gelasius I sent all infants who died without communion to hell; the Council of Trent declared that this notion was absurd. At one time the church asserted that heresy dissolved the marriage vows; Pope

Innocent III annulled this view. The dogma of the virgin birth of Jesus and the ceremony of the purification of Mary after becoming a mother are both celebrated in the Catholic church. For centuries Catholic mothers were considered to have been defiled by childbirth and had to be readmitted into the church; present Catholic ceremony blesses mothers. The Council of Trent asserted that Jerome's text of the Bible was official. Pope Sixtus V in 1590 published this text as pure and genuine and announced that it should not be altered under threat of excommunication. Yet in 1592 Pope Clement VIII introduced a new text with the same claims. More recently a commission was appointed to return to the text of Jerome, even though Jerome himself had said that his text was highly doubtful. The Jesuit order, formed under Pope Paul III, was abolished by Pope Clement XIV, and re-established by Pope Pius VII. In spite of all these discrepancies the modern impression still is that Roman Catholics present but one view, and that this view has never altered. Doubtless the manner of papal pronouncement has contributed to this illusion.

An even more striking heterogeneity may be seen in the views of the roles of the pope and the secular princes. Pope Gelasius in 494 addressed the Roman emperor on the thesis that church and state were two authorities and not two societies. Historically the Roman Catholic church has been in agreement with Pope Gelasius. In the sixth century the Emperor Justinian gave the church the right to share in the selection of government officials and to be in control of weights and measures. Pope Stephen III in 756 became the first temporal prince who was at the same time a pope. The degree of power entailed was so impressive that Roman Catholic authorities predated the event to Constantine to give to the idea the support of a long tradition: toward the end of the eighth century Pope Hadrian cited the forged "donation of Constantine" to prove that the first Christian emperor (Constantine) had given Pope Sylvester the palace and property in Rome, plus earthly dominion over the whole empire. The coronation of Charlemagne by Pope Leo III completed in 800 the impression that the state was the handmaid of the church. The

Bull of 1302 by Pope Boniface III gave classical expression to
the thesis that the pope deserved the secular obedience of all
men everywhere. During this same century, however, kings
began to revolt against church control. In 1365 Pope Urban
was refused the annual taxes, then thirty years in arrears,
owed by the king of England. In 1269 France announced that
elections would be free of any papal control, and the plan was
carried out even though most of the citizens were Catholic.
While Boniface VIII excommunicated the king of France for
this gesture of revolt, Clement V countermanded the order. In
1523 Pope Hadrian VI asked his legate to make a statement
before a diet in Nuremberg admitting that there had been
both stupidity and cupidity in the papal office in the past, and
that he would attempt to rectify this. In 1682 King Louis XIV
published a charter of Gallic liberties which, in effect, legalized nationalism in religion.

By 1870 no pope could in fact claim to have any political
power. Yet this was the year the doctrine of papal infallibility
was announced. It was remarked: "Thus impotence was coupled with infallibility." [15] The doctrine of the infallible office of
the pope was not, contrary to popular Protestant and lay
Catholic assumption, received with open arms by all Catholic
leaders. Professor Doellinger, a Roman Catholic German theologian, called it "a revolutionary innovation . . . begotten
in forgeries." [16] Archbishop Kenrick of St. Louis asserted that
since only God is infallible, no church or pope ought to lay
claim to such powers. On July 13, 1870, when the issue of papal infallibility was up for council vote, 88 delegates were opposed to the doctrine of infallibility and 66 had serious reser-
vations. The dogma was finally ratified by 533 votes. A series
of pacts entered into between the Vatican and Italy in February 12, 1929, resulted in the limitation of the pope's temporal power to an area of less than one-sixth of a square mile,
and thus ended the secular rule of the popes in fact.

A thorny issue of the twentieth century was raised by the
appointment of Myron Taylor, during the Franklin D. Roosevelt administration, as the diplomatic representative to the
Vatican. Many Protestants saw this move as entailing govern-

mental approval of Roman Catholicism, even though it was clear that diplomats in the past had commonly visited countries whose policies were not approved. The practice of appointing papal diplomats probably dates from the middle of the fifteenth century. During the centuries since that time it has been assumed that the Vatican was a sovereignty, and that, therefore, diplomatic relations with it were proper. From the point of view of a Roman Catholic, papal diplomacy was considered to be merely a gesture of acceptance of the sovereignty of the Vatican in a world of nations.[17] Diplomatic relations with the Vatican are political, and it is coincidental that the sovereign of that state happens to be the Roman Catholic pope. The delegates themselves have represented the whole gamut of possible religious persuasions. While some national papal delegates were Roman Catholic, others ranged through the major Protestant sects, Judaism, and all the way to Voodooism.

Only in the United States of America does the church-state issue function as an argument for not having diplomatic relations with the Vatican. What has the situation been with regard to the religious dominance of the nations which have papal legates? Thirty-five, mostly from Central and South American countries, have been traditionally Roman Catholic. Seventeen concordat states maintain diplomatic relations with the Vatican. These are states with special agreements specifying the role of the pope in their countries. Seventeen states have implicit or explicit separation of church and state and yet maintain diplomatic relations with the Vatican. These include Japan, Belgium, the Netherlands, Poland, Luxembourg, and the German Federal Republic. What seems to have troubled so many non-Catholics about diplomatic relations with the Vatican has been the suspicion that it entailed both a recognition of the spiritual authority of the papacy and a status elevation of Roman Catholicism not enjoyed by other religious groups. The feeling that diplomatic relations entail moral approval of a nation has contributed to a general unwillingness in the United States to recognize Red China. If the primary motivation in objecting to Vatican diplomacy were the separation principle, would it not be consistent to object also to diplomatic relations with any country having a state church or to resist any fraternization of the government, in its official capacity, with the dignitaries of any religious sect? It is not clear whether the situation would be aggravated if all major sects had titular heads with whom diplomatic relations could be maintained.

The matter of the stand of the Roman Catholic church on secular citizenship is also historically revealed as heterogeneous. At the time of the settlement of Spanish America and New France (Canada), both Spain and France were already politically and religiously freed from papal interference. This freedom was expressed in a number of areas in which the secular monarch could, and frequently did, overrule both local ecclesiastical and papal authority. The secular powers had control over the selection of bishops as well as parish priests, and they did, on occasion, prevent bishops from firing local priests. State approval was required before churches or convents could be built, and before church conferences could be held. No papal bull or brief could be circulated unless the monarch had read it and given it his approval. No excommunications were effective unless they had state approval. Having achieved these victories at home, the Spanish king assumed the role of pope in the new country and compelled religious homogeneity. The French king, Louis XIV, held the same power in New France, where church and state were united, even though in France the opposite was the case. In 1826 Bishop England of the see of Charleston (South Carolina, North Carolina, and Georgia), a Roman Catholic, was invited to speak before the United States Congress. His remarks ruffled the pope but found wide support among the Roman Catholic hierarchy in America: "Let the Pope and the Cardinals and all the powers of the Catholic world united make the least encroachment on that Constitution, we will protect it with our lives. Summon a General Council—let that Council interfere in the mode of our electing but an assistant to a turnkey of a prison—we deny that right, we reject the usurpation." [18] This view was in later years firmly supported by Father Hecker, founder of the Paulist Fathers; Cardinal Gibbons; Archbishop Ireland of Saint Paul; Archbishop Keane of Catholic University, Washington, D. C.; Cardinal O'Connell of the American College at Rome; Monsignor O'Gorman, Bishop of Sioux Falls, South Dakota; and Archbishop Kain of St. Louis. In a recent Roman Catholic pronouncement it was asserted that "the Church is superior to the State only in the dignity of its nature and end, and not in those matters that are the peculiar province of the State." In the face of popular contentions that Roman Catholics made poor citizens because they owed a primary allegiance to a foreign potentate, Father Doyle defended the position of the Catholic church on American citizenship with the insistence that "the Catholic citizen of the United States will never be in conflict with the Constitution on the one side and Church authority on the other, for the reason that these two jurisdictions are not only distinct, but are, as a matter of fact, separated jurisdictions, made so and preserved so by the Constitution which the Catholic citizen is or may be bound by oath to support, and which the Church authority at the very least, does not disapprove of in permitting him to take and observe such an oath." [19] On November 1, 1895, in an encyclical letter, "The Christian Constitution of States," Pope Leo XIII asserted the thesis that all Roman Catholics are bound to their several constitutions in their respective states. This same position has from time to time been reasserted, and most recently in 1949 by the Roman Catholic Welfare Council.

It may be readily understood why John Milton and John Locke held that Catholics had allegiances to the papacy inconsistent with complete loyalty to the state, but it is not so easily understood what prompted the discussions of 1928, when Alfred E. Smith ran for the Presidency, and again in 1960, when John F. Kennedy ran for the same office. A great many would-be defenders of the separation principle argued in both campaigns that a Roman Catholic was somehow disqualified for conscientious high office. Resident Roman Catholic leaders have been as clearly in favor of separation as have resident Protestant leaders. While there has been a temptation, to which Protestants have succumbed, to cite medieval cases to prove the Roman Catholic position, such a procedure would prove equally unfair to Protestantism, which has, in the past, enthusiastically endorsed state control of churches as well as church control of states.

Some authors [20] have cited cases from Roman Catholic church practices in Central and South America as evidence that the Roman church is subversive in the United States. Such data need to be seen in the perspective of two other equally authentic areas of fact. When in the fall of 1960 Puerto Rican bishops commanded their congregations to oppose the election of Marin under threat of committing sin, American Roman Catholic bishops branded such episcopal letters as nonsense. It is equally evident that Protestant data from contemporary England, Germany, or Scandinavia would not substantiate the American Protestant claims to being the torch bearers for disestablishmentarianism. Most churches have, in both past and present, reflected the society in which they find themselves. In conservative countries they are conservative, in democratic countries they are democratic, in monarchic states they are monarchic, and in totalitarian states they have been totalitarian. It has been a long time since any church played a serious role in the political life of a nation. At best, contemporary churches have played a conciliatory role; but equally often they have sided with reaction and the past against the progressive movements. Calvinistic ethics gave wings to capitalism, American Protestantism aided and abetted the Prohibition amendment, Roman Catholics have been active in curtailing information on birth control, and both Catholics and Protestants have fought divorce legislation and the secularization of the education system.[21] This merely substantiates the fact that neither Christian movement advocates that the church be indifferent to what happens in the political state.

THE CURRENT CONTROVERSY

The trend in the American Protestant sects toward attempting to effect reforms by influencing the state began during the first two decades of the nineteenth century. Lyman Beecher (1775–1863) was the outstanding Protestant clerical leader in this regard. Both religious organizations and individuals exerted potent influence on a number of social, economic, and political situations. At few of these points was it ever imagined that the separation of church and state was entailed. After the death of Alexander Hamilton at the hands of Aaron Burr (1804), reforms were pressed by religious sects to curtail and ultimately to abolish the practice of dueling. Among the clergymen prominent in this reform were the Reverend Timothy Dwight (president of Yale College), the Reverend Eliphalet Nott (later president of Union College), the Reverend Lyman Beecher, and the Roman Catholic bishop, John England. The early laws resulting from their efforts prevented any dueler or second in a duel from holding any public office. The laws were extended to deny the franchise to participants in any duel. As a direct consequence of religious pressures, twenty-six out of fifty states have laws against dueling.

The forces of religion made a second attempt to influence the course of social life by stopping the Sunday delivery of the mail. Many Protestant sects attacked the practice of mail sorting on the Sabbath day as an infringement of religious liberty. The problem was complicated by the Seventh Day Adventists, who opposed those Protestants who objected to Sunday mail sorting on the grounds that the real Sabbath day was Saturday anyway. Following a decision of the General Assembly of Indiana (February 15, 1830), it was generally conceded in Protestant circles that the attempt to eliminate Sunday mail service had failed. At a third point, the holding of lotteries, Protestants again attempted to influence both social and legal practice. This situation was complicated by the fact that many churches and schools had operated lotteries for generations. Harvard, Yale, Union College, Hamilton College, and the New York College of Physicians and Surgeons all operated lotteries at the time. Faneuil Hall, the cradle of liberty in the United States, was rebuilt with money gained from a lottery. In spite of the divided sentiments of religious sects, the religious pressures were great enough to lead to the enactment of state laws against lotteries in a number of states by 1834.

The enactment of the Constitution imposed certain prohibitions upon the federal government with regard to religious requirements. There were to be no religious tests required of office holders, and Congress was not to make any laws which established any religion, nor any which limited religious worship. By tradition this has been interpreted as a "hands off" policy on the part of the government toward religion. The issue has not been nearly so clear on the question of religious intervention in governmental matters. The concept of the separation of church and state has come to mean that the state should stay out of religious affairs, but emotions are mixed on the question of the church staying out of governmental affairs. Most sects approved the lack of governmental control. What they were not so sure about was whether they still had unlimited right to control the government. Legislative decisions on birth control, on the teaching of matters of fact contrary to Scripture, and on divorce and marriage have all been both supported and attacked by religious groups. Some claimed that the state was interfering with religious conviction, while others insisted that the state was within its rights in promoting the public welfare. Christian Scientists have objected to legal controls over public health. Roman Catholics have protested against legalized distribution of birth control information. Mormons protested against state interference with marriage practices. Jehovah's Witnesses objected to the legal requirement of a salute to the flag in schools. Quakers objected to taking oaths in courts of law. The degree to which complaints have been leveled against the state, with appropriate pressures brought to bear, would seem to indicate that many religious persons have thought of the separation principle as a one-way affair, which prevented the state from coercing religion, but which did not prevent religion from coercing the state. On December 8, 1864, Pope Pius IX issued an encyclical letter containing a syllabus of some eighty propositions which Catholics were expected to support. Among them were Proposition 45, which maintained that the secular state should not conduct public education without religious guidance, and Proposition 55, which insisted that the church and the state ought not to be separated. Many Catholic leaders protested against Proposition 55. On the other hand, many Protestant sects supported the spirit of both propositions. Much of the debate which has ensued over the role of the state in education has depended upon which religious group was bringing the pressure to bear. If the Roman Catholic church exerted a lobby influence, some Protestant sects have objected. Where Protestants have brought pressure to bear upon the government, there have been some Roman Catholic protests. In cases such as these, the issue was not really state versus church, but church versus church.

There have been a few points at which all religions tend to approve of what might otherwise be construed as state interference. It has been generally agreed that property used for essentially religious purposes should be free from taxation. The differences of opinion centered on the question of what was an essentially religious purpose. In some states educational plants and even religiously owned factories have been included in the tax-free category. When the remission of taxes was applied to buildings used for Sabbath worship, few religious bodies have made any protest. Most religions approve of the references to God in the federal and state constitutions, on the currency, and in inaugural ceremonies of government officers. Most religious groups have no objection to taking oaths in courts of law using the Bible and appealing to God. While some states bar atheists from giving testimony in courts of law, others, such as Washington, permit simple secular agreements to tell the truth without reference to either God or the Bible. The branches of the military service all utilize chaplains who are paid from public funds. Indeed, they are both supported and retired on government funds. In general, religious sects have not protested against this as a breakdown of the "wall of separation" between the church and the state. Why has this been so? Some have averred that facts of this type indicated that the United States of America is a "Christian nation," and that therefore chaplains, the swearing in of officials on the Bible, and the mention of God in prayers at the opening of legislatures are all beyond dispute. Such a conclusion would seem to be both naïve and unwarranted. In the first place, Jewish chaplains are also on the government payroll, and this would not seem to be consistent with the hypothesis that Christian influence in government has the status of a legal mandate. Quakers and Mennonites do not have to swear on the Bible if they do not find it within their religious conscience to do so. Indeed, if there were even a handful of Hindu congressmen, we would expect to find a Swami giving the opening prayer for Congress on some occasions. It seems most likely that such minor vestiges of religion continue essentially through sheer habit, rather than through any design or plan. In the second place, the genuflections which these practices express are capable of a wider interpretation than the "Christian nation" one. The Bible is, after all, a sacred book to the Moslems, and the first half of it is the sacred book of Jews. When this simple fact is coupled with the great number of biblical translations, it seems highly doubtful that much can be inferred from scripture with assurance. Indeed, there is no translation of the Bible which has the unanimous support of all Christians.

The state and federal governments have conceded that religious lobbies are legitimate functions of the various sects, but, in each instance, the churches are on their own. They do not speak with any legal sanction or support for what they say, but only for their privilege of saying it. Roman Catholics may advise their parishioners against birth control, and they may lobby in Congress for the same end, but this does not mean that there is any governmental sanction for the content of their program. Quakers may urge pacifism, within certain legal limits, but this obviously does not mean that the United States is a pacifist nation. Mennonites have been permitted, during wartime, to refrain from paying taxes which would go for military purposes, provided that they paid a comparable sum for some nonmilitary national purpose. The Episcopal church may advise against divorce, and Protestants may put on pressure for anti-alcohol laws. In none of these instances, however, is the governmental sanction other than permissive. We would not imagine, for example, that even the setting aside of the Christian Sunday indicates anything other than the general approval that one day a week be set aside for vacation from one's job. While the various sects do disagree with each other on the matter of what is worthy of lobby action, they all agree generally that the state is right in granting the lobby concesssion to religious groups. The states have been notably tolerant of religious convictions, even where state laws might be expected to compel other action from religious persons. For example, even after the enactment of the law prohibiting common drinking cups in public places, no real pressure was brought to bear against churches which used the common communion cup.

The range of causes defended by religious sects indicates that there is little agreement among them as to what practical affairs do or do not follow from the fact that a religion is espoused. Some clergymen have found the economic system of capitalism essentially "Christian." Others have endorsed communism or socialism. The Religion and Labor Foundation lobbied for the union movements and for greater understanding between management and workers. Spiritual Mobilization and Moral Rearmament appeared in defense of laissez-faire capitalism and states' rights. The Ku Klux Klan had its roots in Protestantism and received its impetus from Protestant clergymen in the defense of white, Protestant, capitalistic Americanism. Religious leagues for the censorship of books, magazines, movies, and television have commonly contradicted one another. The local, state, and national legislative bodies have varied, depending upon the pressures and the nature of the constituents, in the degree to which they have bowed to such religious lobbies. Here again it would seem that the defenders of the separation of church and state meant only that the state should not interfere in the assertion of religious ideas, and not that the state should support these programs. It has usually been an implicit assumption of religious bodies that they had every right to interfere with the state if they had enough power to get away with it. Even at this point, however, some religious persons have deplored the use of the church for the purpose of providing a tonic for the state. A distinguished Roman Catholic defended the position thus: "The greatest service the Church can render to Western civilization at the present time is to keep her own inheritance intact and not to allow her witness to be obscured by letting herself be used as the instrument of secular powers and politics." [22]

The crucial contemporary issues over the relations of the churches to the state have arisen in the field of education. Here, as elsewhere, the problems are complicated by the lack of a univocal religious opinion. Take, for example, the relatively simple question with regard to the use of the Bible in public education. Ever since Benjamin Rush (1745–1813) wrote his *A Defense of the Use of the Bible as a School Book,* questions have arisen over its proper use in tax-supported schools. Clearly the assumption has been that the Bible would be read in the schools, but the problem was which version was the nearest to nonsectarian. Until Roman Catholics and Jews issued protests, the King James Version was in common use. Roman Catholics, however, preferred the Douay version, while Jews preferred the Leeser version. In some states pressures were brought to bear to prohibit certain versions even from being in the school library. To be sure, a few Protestant denominations have opposed Bible reading from any version whatsoever. These include the Unitarian-Universalist church and occasionally the Lutherans and the Baptists. Such objections were, however, minor whispers compared with the general clamor of American public opinion. Even after the rise of the secular public schools it was still generally presumed that daily Bible reading was not inimical to the principle of the separation of church and state. The rise of Catholic parochial schools was stimulated in part by the fact that these early secular schools were run by Protestants and hence used the King James Version. Beyond the matter of the choice of biblical translation, Catholics shared with Protestants the conviction that secular education completely divorced from religion militated against the public good. The contentious issues have arisen over the points at which religion was to be related to education. For example, both Protestant and Catholic groups have brought pressure to bear on what is taught in the schools, and on what texts are used to further education.[23]

The current focus of concern is the question of financial assistance from the public treasury for religious education. The problem has arisen in the context of the existence of parochial schools which aim to replace the public schools. These schools purport to teach the same courses as those required in public schools, with the addition of specifically religious subjects. While the Roman Catholic church has been the undisputed leader in the establishment of parochial schools, they have not been alone in parochial education. From 1845 to 1870 the Presbyterian church (Old School) experimented with parochial education. At one time they had 264 schools in 29 states. The experiment was generally discontinued after 1870 in favor of secular public schools. Both the Reformed churches and the Episcopal church have attempted parochial schools, but in both instances the plan was discontinued. There are a few Jewish parochial schools, but they do not reflect the general opinion of Judaism. The German Baptist Mennonites (Amish) still have their own parochial primary and secondary schools, but they represent a very minor fraction of the school population. The nearest competitors to the Roman Catholic religious schools are those of the Lutheran church, especially Missouri Synod. The specific point at which the public financing of religious education has arisen has been in the transportation of children by public tax money to parochial schools. As of 1946 the following summary indicates the trends of practice:

1. In 18 states and one territory parochial-school students were transported at public expense.
2. In 6 states the courts had declared the practice unconstitutional.
3. In 2 states the courts had upheld the practice.

4. In 5 states free textbooks (when they were the same as those used in the public schools) were furnished to parochial-school students.

5. In 34 states laws permitted the use of public-school buildings for religious purposes after school hours.[24]

While only the first three apply specifically to the problem of transportation, the remaining items indicate something of the breadth of practice on related matters. This whole problem came to general public attention as a result of the Everson case. The New Jersey law, passed by the state legislature in 1941, permitted the transportation of parochial students who lived remote from their school by school-district buses. The constitutionality of this law was challenged by a taxpayer, Arch R. Everson. The state supreme court held that the payment of transportation for parochial schools was not authorizable under the New Jersey constitution. The New Jersey Court of Appeals reversed this decision, contending that such payment was consonant with both state and federal constitutions. On February 10, 1947, the United States Supreme Court, in a 5 to 4 decision, supported the decision of the New Jersey Court of Appeals. Interestingly enough, seven states have in the past held invalid the payment of similar transportation costs: Delaware, Kentucky, Oklahoma, New York (prior to a 1938 law which now permits such payment), South Dakota, Washington, and Wisconsin. Briefs in support of the New Jersey practice were submitted by six states which permit payment of parochial transportation (Illinois, Indiana, Louisiana, Massachusetts, Michigan, and New York). Justice Hugo Black wrote the opinion for the United States Supreme Court. He contended that payment of such funds did not constitute either support of a religion or the establishment of religion. Justice Black stressed the fact that the state must not hamper its citizens in the free exercise of their religion. Since the parochial schools in question satisfied state accreditation criteria, and since it was a matter of religious preference to attend these schools, the state would be interfering with the religious exercises if it refused to finance transportation. The court recognized that the "wall of separation" ought to be maintained, and that this case was an instance where the state "approaches the verge" of its constitutional power, yet it insisted that the practice was constitutional. Justice Robert H. Jackson wrote a dissent in which Justice Felix Frankfurter concurred. Justice Jackson reduced the whole problem to a simple question: "Is it constitutional to tax this complainant to pay the cost of carrying pupils to Church schools of one specified denomination?" [25] He answered with a clear negative. He contended that if parochial schools are public enough to warrant financing the transportation of students to them, they were then public enough to have their curricula set by the state. If this were done, then there would be no difference between public and parochial schools. A further dissent was written by Justice Wiley Rutledge, and concurred in by Justices Frankfurter, Jackson, and Burton. He insisted that the line could not be drawn between direct and indirect financial aid to religion, and that there was no difference in principle between public tax for transportation to parochial schools and public tax for parochial teachers' salaries. [26]

Roman Catholic leaders were not united in their position on the issue of the Everson case. Indeed, the prevailing sentiment in both Catholic and Protestant circles seems to be that to press for financial aid of any sort for religious purposes would be both tactically and morally unsound. As an instance of a counter opinion from a Protestant group which has parochial schools, we may note the action of the Missouri Synod as far back as 1890, which declared: "We . . . condemn all demands upon public funds for the erection or maintenance of parochial schools." [27] In 1938 the Albany, New York, District Evangelical Conference (Lutheran) refused to accept any money for parochial-school transportation even though it was permitted to do so by state constitutional amendment.

A related problem was given national publicity in the decision of the United States Supreme Court on the case of McCollum *vs.* the Champaign Illinois School Board (1948). In this situation students were permitted released time for religious instruction, which was, in turn, carried out in the public schools. Although the court ruled against the Champaign released-time program, the wording of the decision indicated that released time for religious instruction in buildings other than public schools was still an open matter. A variety of related issues have been discussed, and the final word is a long way from being spoken. What, for example, should the position of church or state be on the question of religious garb for public-school teachers, free textbooks for parochial schools, free lunches for parochial schools? Should parochial schools be used as public schools if there are no local public schools in existence? Is there such a thing as a nonsectarian religious instruction which could be provided by the public schools?

There is considerably less furor over comparable issues when they apply to the colleges and universities. Some state universities permit clergymen to teach courses in religion for college credit. In some colleges associated schools of religion have been established. These schools offer courses taught by ordained Jews, Roman Catholics, and Protestants. Such programs have been effective where charter and legal conditions permitted and where a religious school could be located physically near to an established school.[28] In some instances state-financed nonsectarian chairs of religion have been instituted.[29] Some institutions have even accepted courses taught by local clergymen off campus for college credit.[30] A report of the National Education Association in 1949 revealed that about 27 per cent of the public school systems have religious education programs.[31] Essentially Protestant movements such as the Edward Hazen Foundation, the Danforth Foundation, and the National Council on Religion in Higher Education have seriously investigated and promoted programs to further religious awareness at the college level.

All such efforts raise once again the question of separation of church and state. The issues have not provoked protests at the college level of the magnitude found directed toward primary and secondary schools. In part this has been due to the presumable maturity of the students and to the

The Church *and the* State

principle that colleges are centers where all kinds of issues may be freely raised. There has been far more agreement among Protestants, Catholics, and Jews that higher education is in some sense an affair of religious denominations than there has been concerning the lower grades. The presence of Y.M.C.A., Y.W.C.A., and Hillel Foundations on college campuses all indicate that when it comes to higher education, most religious groups are less decisive on the matter of the separation of church and state. For most of the above-mentioned programs, however, the only objective is to see that religion is studied as part of the cultural heritage of man. It is assumed that every religion has the right to announce its views publicly. To deny this public pronouncement is considered to be a denial of religion.

Kant held a peculiar view on this matter of religious freedom, primarily because of his belief in the private nature of moral religion. He remarked: "When a government wishes to be regarded as not coercing man's conscience because it merely prohibits the *public utterance* of his religious opinions and hinders no one from *thinking* to himself in secrecy whatever he sees fit, we usually jest about it and say that in this the government grants no freedom at all, for it cannot in any case hinder thinking." [32] Those acts which are public and hence could be either permitted or prohibited were considered to be mere matters of "ecclesiastical faith" and not essentially germane to rational religion. While this is perfectly understandable, from a Kantian view, the fact remains that most contemporaries who are concerned about religious freedom base their case precisely on these matters of public expression.

We have discussed some of the present issues confronting church and state relations, and we have contrasted these with the histories of both Protestant and Roman Catholic churches. The general picture, as we have seen, is far from univocal. If we take the long view—and there may be a serious question as to whether this is a relevant procedure—we find that both traditions of Christianity have favored both close

4 1 5

integration and clear separation of church and state. Both traditions have urged separation when they were in the minority, and both have urged establishmentarianism when it seemed possible to implement it. The stronger the claim to uniqueness which a sect makes, the more strongly and consistently has the desire for state assistance for the church program been pressed. At no point, however, has it ever been seriously maintained by any religious movement that the church ought not to attempt to influence the state and society in which it resided. Every organization which promotes some set of values has assumed the rightful role of moral and spiritual gadfly in the society.

XVII

———◆◆———

Religion *and* Science

I N ITS LONG HISTORY religion has had occasion to engage
in verbal and physical conflict with many specters which
have appeared like Banquo's ghost to haunt its peace of
mind. The most ancient and enduring conflicts have been
those between religious groups. These conflicts have been
peculiarly sharp and divisive primarily because they involved
two groups each of which claimed uniqueness, infallibility,
and certitude. Religious institutions have also had their battles with other social, political, and economic organizations.
The church-state issue has been typical of this type of controversy. In this instance, however, the battle was more one
of power than one of metaphysics. But of all the wars religion has waged upon infidelity and heresy, few rival the
controversy between religion and science. Since the sixteenth
century, this has been the key struggle. Each has appeared
as the foe of the aims and interests of the other. This conflict
arose concomitantly with the emergence of both Protestantism and modern science. Roman Catholicism has escaped
most of the serious aspects of this controversy, for two reasons. In the first place, pre-Reformation science was primarily the work of clerics. The scientists themselves had
good reason to present their views in such a way that no real

conflict could appear. This was apparent even for the revolutionary views of the clergyman Copernicus. He did not appear to imagine that his astronomical theory constituted any real jeopardy to biblical literalism or to ecclesiastical orthodoxy. In the second place, the analyses of mundane theology prescribed by Saint Thomas precluded any serious dichotomy between religion and science. Both areas used the same inductive and deductive methods and the same Aristotelian appeal to general principles, and found their evidence in the same world. Theoretically, at least, religion and science complemented each other. In the area of revealed theology it was presumed that science had nothing to say. Revealed theology was beyond science in any sense of the term. This theoretical amity between the two areas did not, however, prevent the inquisitorial treatment of both Galileo and Copernicus, a treatment which has been explained by Protestants [1] as indicative of a Roman Catholic repudiation of science, and by Roman Catholics [2] as due to the essentially religious doctrines of the two men in question. Independently of our solution to the question of the cause of the suppression of both Galileo and Copernicus, the fact remains that their scientific doctrines were declared heretical and factually false.

What have been the loci of the controversy between religion and science? Why have there been periodic revivals of attack by religious leaders upon scientists and their theories? Why did the emergence of each new science pose the threats anew? We shall consider some of the focal points on which the religious attack has been centered and some of the major reasons why religious persons have felt threatened.

THE LOCI OF THE CONTROVERSY

Probably the most ubiquitous and harassing element in all of the controversies has been that science appeared always to have been the victor. This fact, quite apart from any question as to who was right, has provided an irritant in every battle. It is not, however, so much a locus of explicit debate as it is an emotional stimulant to keep the controversies alive. The fact is that wherever science and religion have been opponents, religion has had to retreat; and this has been the case even where specific scientific formulations turned out to be incorrect.

A first point at which the controversy has been waged was over the authoritarian procedure which had characterized the medieval approach. It had been standardly accepted by the church fathers that doctrinal issues would be ultimately resolved by finding appropriate clerical support. If there was a question of the meaning of the dogma of the Trinity, this would be solved by appeals to Saint Augustine, Saint Jerome, or Saint Thomas; or if these approaches failed, the medieval scholar could always quote from the Council of Nicaea. The same procedure was followed for the resolution of all matters of biblical interpretation and of ecclesiastical polity. The emergence of Protestantism cast this whole method into disrepute, at least among the new dissenters. When it became clearly specified by scientists that no matter of fact could be logically settled by authority, this had an inevitable consequence. If matters of fact required observations and if these observations contradicted church authorities, then the gauntlet was down. Where should the church draw the line? If the reliability of the great religious writers of the past was doubtful on matters pertaining to geology, astronomy, or biology, was there any reason to believe them on matters of faith? At this point, the Thomistic blending of science and mundane theology now gave rise to doubts concerning any issue which had previously been resolved by appeal to authority. If the methods of science and religion were, indeed, so antagonistic, was it still possible to keep the medieval confidence that the two fields could not possibly conflict? Could any field, such as religion, which admitted revelatory data really be compatible with a science which rejected such evidence as inadmissible? It is quite understandable that this should have prompted live and compelling concern to all medievally minded religious thinkers. To be sure, this could have been resolved without capitulation to science by the simple expedient of separating the two areas, but this would have meant giving up the Thomistic thesis of compatibility, which most Roman Catholics were not willing to do.

Protestants faced the same issue. While they rejected many of the church councils and most of the church fathers on doctrinal matters, the Protestants still followed the medieval method of appeal to authority. Their authority was the Bible, which they held to be inerrant and complete. The Protestants shared with Roman Catholics the confidence that the clergy were competent to answer all questions. There was no separation of domains of competence, so that the Bible would be found to be either lacking in information or silent on matters that required answers. In spite of the fact that appeals to scripture had been used to support contradictory conclusions, the Protestant still clung to the dogma of biblical adequacy for all questions. The clear attack on the appeal to authority which scientists had launched could not help but challenge Protestant and Catholic alike.

A second locus of controversy involved a matter of epistemological procedure. The medieval Catholic thinker followed Aristotle in beginning with general principles, assumed to be true without proof, and from these principles drawing conclusions by deduction. The magnificent scheme of Saint Thomas remains a paradigm of this method. The Protestants were protected from entering into this point of the debate by their rejection of Saint Thomas and of reliance upon human metaphysical systems. The method of science, on the other hand, required observational data as the starting point of all rational investigation. If there were any general principles, they had to be inferred inductively from the particular facts. But induction provided, at best, only probability. If religion wanted and demanded certainty, then deduction from putatively true general principles had to be the method. If religion used the inductive methods of science, then all conclusions would be mere probability estimates as to what might be the case. This point of the controversy still engages the concern of medieval theologians. Logicians, if not scientists, have clearly struck a severe blow at religious assurance by branding the method of deduction inadequate for the discovery of factual truth about the world in which we live. Protestants have been driven more than ever to take refuge in revelation, even though these same Protestants never had much confidence in rational deductive systems. The scientific attack upon certitude, however, affected both traditions of the Christian faith.

A third locus of the controversies between science and religion was the Bible. While both Roman Catholics and Protestants had traditionally maintained that the scriptures were infallible and divinely inspired, the former tradition had an inerrant institution, the church, which could always provide the meaning of the biblical accounts. They possessed both the absolute book and the absolute interpretation of the book. Dating back at least as far as Saint Augustine, Roman Catholics had been accustomed to characterize some scriptural passages as purely figurative or metaphorical. This had meant that if a scientific discovery appeared to contradict a biblical tale, the church fathers could always hold that the Bible was intending a mere poetic account, and hence there would be no need to feel that science and the Bible were in contradiction. The Protestants had no such simple recourse. Since they denied that there was any infallible interpretive institution, their claim for an inerrant scripture was unsupported by any practical human agency. The Protestant assumption that the Bible was so clear that its message was obvious to all had already run aground on the schismatic divisions into which Protestantism had been split. The obvious scriptural message already had fifty-seven conflicting interpretations, each one of which claimed to be authentic. Imagine, therefore, the dilemma of the Protestant when a fifty-eighth interpretation was added by the scientists. Here was an attack upon Christendom of the proportions of an Armageddon, and Protestants armed quickly for the battle against this new Antichrist.

The rise of biblical scholarship had already prepared for the debacle by casting doubts upon the internal reliability of the scriptural tales. It had been determined that even the oldest Gospel, that of Mark, was written at least thirty years after the events described in it. Would it not be remarkable if Mark had still been able to record literally the conversations between Jesus and his disciples? Harmonies of the Synoptic Gospels (Matthew, Mark, and Luke) had been composed early in the nineteenth century, and these had revealed disparities in the various Gospel accounts of the same events. Christians had already objected to the biblical analyses which demonstrated that Moses had not written the Pentateuch and that David had not written the Psalms. This whole atmosphere of uneasiness which higher criticism and historical criticism had provoked among Bible-quoting Protestant Fundamentalists was further muddled by the appearance of the physical scientist in the arena. For a movement which had traditionally placed utter reliance upon an inerrant Bible, these new dissident facts were bound to create chaos.

One of the oldest points at which scientific theories and biblical narratives had come into conflict was the so-called Copernican revolution. Ever since 130 A.D. Christians had accepted the Ptolemaic view that the earth was the center of the universe, and that the sun and all the planets revolved around our fixed and immovable earth. The Ptolemaic view, to be sure, had rather thin scriptural support, but it had, nonetheless, the weight of centuries of acceptance. For all its limitations, the Copernican idea of a universe which was heliocentric rather than geocentric gave Christians the feeling that if the earth itself moved, nothing remained steadfast. John Wesley (1703–1791) opposed the Copernican position precisely on the grounds that it made God too far off and the world of human experience too unstable for human peace of mind. Both Martin Luther and John Calvin rejected the Copernican theory as unscriptural, and as late as 1835 books teaching the Copernican system remained on the Roman Catholic Index.

What were the reasons for the threat which Christians felt in the face of this new theory? The most obvious and immediate source of anxiety stemmed, of course, from the fact that, if Copernicus was correct, then the church had been mistaken for well over a millennium. Catholics and

Protestants alike had rested secure in their Ptolemaic universe, and they were ill prepared for the flux and size of the new view. The Ptolemaic universe, for all its scope, was still quite small enough for the wonder-working God to seem close to every man. In addition, the old view provided a stable universe, which seemed compatible with the assumption of a changeless deity. The vast increase in the size of cosmic spaces compelled both a radical increase in the size of the God as well as a dynamism in the character of the God. The old universe had been cozy enough for Joshua, with the help of God, to command the sun to stand still. The new universe extended to such incredible distances that the old tale of Joshua seemed quite beyond reason. The old slow-moving astral bodies now became so speeded up and so complex in their motions that man could not fit his contemplative deity into the new tempo. If even the earth moved, then the changeless God might have to find another footstool on which to rest, and the feeling of a far more remote God emerged. In these obviously anxiety-producing data Christians saw a new threat to their religion and to their sacred book.

A further expression of this instability was seen in the new theory with regard to comets. In the former little Ptolemaic universe these heavenly bodies were assumed to appear within the earth's atmosphere, or at least within the spaces between the earth and its moon. When the paths of comets had been traced to infinitely greater distances from this earth, and when the theory of their continuing creation had been proposed, Christians saw a clear attack upon their old doctrine of a fixed and final creation. If the new theory of comets was correct, God had not finished the task of creation in the first six days. Either he was endlessly at work creating, or else there were processes over which he had no effective control. In either case, the character of the Old Testament God was being contradicted. The new science must, therefore, be the work of the Devil or of human unbelievers.

According to the traditional interpretation, the Creation was a brief six-day *fait accompli*. The rise of geology as a science cast insuperable doubts upon this simple explanation.

While even the ancient Greeks had thought in terms of a world of great age, Christians had held to the Jewish theory that the age of the earth was coextensive with the span of human history. Both began at the same time. The Reverend John Lightfoot (1602–1675), an English Hebraist and rabbinical scholar at the University of Cambridge, had asserted in all seriousness that biblical exegesis supported the date of 4004 B.C. for the creation of the universe. His exegesis was so precise that he felt able to pin creation down to a Friday, October 23, at 9:00 A.M., 4004 B.C. Neither astronomy nor geology supported this thesis of a universe so dewy fresh and new, and hence the Christian believers felt a new threat from science toward their religion.

Even up to the beginning of the nineteenth century, biological speculation was still carried on within the framework of this six-thousand-year span of time. The discovery of fossils in prehistoric rock strata posed a real problem for biologists who accepted biblical chronology. As late as the nineteenth century, Philip Henry Gosse (1810–1888), an English naturalist, asserted that God had created all the rocks with the fossils planted in them. This interesting, logically possible, but empirically unlikely theory proved quite unacceptable, however, to thinking men, and a further challenge to the parochial biology of the Bible had proved religiously unassailable. According to the biblical account of the Flood, members of every animal species climbed aboard Noah's ark to be saved from a watery extinction. This story remained credible as long as there were no more species than the average layman was actually aware of. By the time scientists were talking in terms of millions of species, this posed an ark too crowded even for the most imaginative believer. Consider further what a cosmic task poor Adam must have had, since according to scriptural tradition he named them all. Biological exploration complicated the biblical story of creation still further. If all species had been on the ark of Noah when the Flood receded, then how did all the three-toed sloths, slow-moving as they are, get to South America, while all the kangaroos ended up in Australia? What is equally remarkable, none of these species left any of their members along the way. In addition, the traditional Christian had held the view that before the fall of Adam and Eve all animals and insects were friendly. John Wesley had insisted that before the Adamic fall, spiders did not catch flies and tigers did not eat lambs. The data of biological evolution cast grave doubts upon the thesis that every species had at some time been vegetarian.

By far the most serious threat to religion from biology came from the theory of human evolution. If God had made man in his own image, then the long, slow process from simpler forms of life to *Homo sapiens* could not be accepted. Biology animalized man, and this seemed a horrible jeopardy to man's spirituality and to the assumption that he possessed an immortal soul. The trial of John Scopes, the Tennessee schoolteacher, in 1925 climaxed a long and hotly contested battle for authority between religion and biology. Here also science has won the battle, and religion has had to retreat. Christians must now think in terms of creation as a long process, and of the arrival of man on the earthly scene as quite recent. While this new perspective has been achieved, consistently with the faith in a creator God, the old biblical chronology has had to go. The scriptural accounts have had to be reassessed as metaphors with a spiritual message rather than as empirical accounts with scientific status.

The science controversy has also been waged in the field of medicine, both mental and physical. In spite of the remarkable developments in the area of human biology, the majority of religious persons still attributed disease to divine punishment and mental illness to demonic possession as late as the seventeenth century. It would be incorrect to assume that the medieval clerical schools had no interest in human medicine, for they had made significant contributions in this area; what sharpened the controversy was the issue of the application of this medical knowledge. As long as Christians held that natural evils were punishment for moral evils, or that they were goads to spiritual maturity, it was difficult to inspire much clerical enthusiasm for health programs. This was the case in spite of the long-standing Franciscan ministry to the lepers. In the Middle Ages plagues were generally assumed to be punishments for personal and social sins. The cure for such catastrophes, therefore, was far more often considered to be repentance than medicine. The Old Testament mandate (Exodus 22:18) on exterminating witches governed much of the approach toward mental disease. The problem, as in the case of the young man on the Gadarene slopes, was to exorcise devils and to placate the deity. Medicine seemed to constitute a heathen approach to what were basically sicknesses of the soul. Spurred primarily by this doctrinal analysis of disease, religious institutions and religious leaders denied the theory of the circulation of the blood, forbade operations, opposed the use of vaccination and anesthetics, and stood staunchly against both birth control and abortion. If smallpox could be considered divine punishment, it was not surprising that the pregnancy of women too ill to bear children was also judged in the same light. But here also science has won the controversy, and the few healing sects which remain to obfuscate medicine are exceptions to the general rule. Where science and religion have entered the arena of debate, science has emerged victorious.

In all of these controversies biblical literalism has lost status, and all sects which depended upon an inerrant scripture have suffered correspondingly. When the ledger is added up, the result seems inescapably to destroy traditional faith in the Bible. Science has accomplished this end, at least. It has demanded re-analysis of the sacred books and a reformulation of their significance. Modernism stands as a testimony to the fact that science need not prove inimical to scriptural commitment, provided Christians are willing to consider the Bible as a book of faith rather than a book of science.

A fourth locus of the science-religion controversies was found in the creeds and dogmas of church traditions. To be sure, science did not attack these creeds directly, inasmuch as their content was in principle unprovable. However, the success of science in bringing doubt to biblical narratives had a concomitant effect upon the revealed dogmas of the faith.

Historically, religious persons have had the greatest success in maintaining their revealed dogmas in spite of all the advances of science. This was due, no doubt, to the simple fact that these dogmas had no practical or empirical consequences, and hence nothing which science might assert could conceivably shake confidence in the doctrines. In spite of this, there have been psychic consequences of the rift between religion and science. If science does not support the biblical account of creation, of the Flood, of the Exodus from Egypt across the Red Sea, and a host of other firmly held beliefs, might this not mean that the revealed dogmas are themselves open to question? There is no great leap involved in moving from a six-day creation to a virgin birth, but there is an abyss between the sciences of biology and geology and the virgin birth. There is no doubt that many religious persons have been influenced by the incongruity of this latter disparity, and hence there has very probably been a decrease of confidence in revealed dogma commensurate with the increase of successful science. It is not that science forbids belief in a Trinity, the Resurrection, the Incarnation of God in Christ, the virgin birth of Jesus, or the miracle of the Eucharist. It is, rather, that the temper of science makes such commitments emotionally difficult, and when they are made, they stand remote from the rest of experience.

Since it does not seem likely that religion will be able to reject science in any persuasive way, what alternative means does religion have of rising above the controversies? The most fruitful achievements seem to have been made as a result of the strategy of drawing a new line of demarcation between religion and science in such a way that each retains its own peculiar domain of competence without threat from the other. Let us consider some of the ways in which this division has been made.

MUST RELIGION BE THREATENED BY SCIENCE?

One of the ways in which this duality has been expressed has been to let science take care of the description of the kind of world in which we live, while religion has the task of prescribing an ultimate meaning for this same world. This twofold task has been reflected in the thesis that while political science describes the kind of society in which we live, ethics prescribes the kind of society in which we would want to live. Furthermore, if ethics can determine what would be a worthy society, political science can at least specify whether such a society either does or could exist. Let man's moral ideals indicate what he prefers. Let social science show how such ideals can be made effective and real. In such a joint enterprise there may never be any real conflict of domains of competence, unless the ideal state turns out to be impossible. Even here, there need be no such battle as has been waged between geology and religion, for if the perfect society is humanly impossible, it is scarcely the fault of science. In addition, there are ancient traditions in Christianity which take account of just such a contingency. Perhaps the Kingdom of God can never be a reality in a world of sinful men. Indeed, the likelihood that this really is the case was asserted by Emil Brunner.[3] Man's reach will always exceed his grasp in these matters of the spirit, and this is simply the condition which must prevail. Part of the very difference between religion and science may lie at this point of impossibility. Let science talk about what is, was, or could be, while religion will have eminent domain in the area of unfulfillable dreams.

To put the issue in this way, however, does not do justice to either area. A more gracious interpretation was suggested by Henry N. Wieman when he identified "efficiency" as the task of science, while "appreciation" was the function of religion.[4] Man needs both areas in order to fulfill these two aims. Science gives man the knowledge of the world in which he lives which permits him to make predictions successfully. The systems of science and the methods by which these systems are corroborated give men a sense of law and order, of causal contingency, and of the kind of inexorable interrelations which prevail to enable men to choose alternatives with reasonable confidence. Science provides men with knowledge which serves as an antidote or corrective to sentimentality in religion. By sentimentality Wieman means the well-meaning, vaguely defined wishes of mankind which stand no chance of success because the world is what it is. Wieman held that God can be known in two ways: as any other fact is known (i.e., by experience), and by intuition. He rejects the latter alternative on the grounds that it makes religion unscientific. The basic experience which bears the essential meaning of the religious appreciation is the experience of God. For Wieman the term "God" refers to a process which can be observed. This process is evidenced whenever events occur which promote human values. He believed that we live in a world which supports man in the sense of supplying man's needs. Man needs food, clothes, and health. The world has the means of satisfying these basic wants. This tendency of the world to conserve these human values is called God. Wieman spoke as a naturalist and not as a personalist. In spite of this difference in the meaning of God, Wieman's remarks still serve to indicate a useful dichotomy between science and religion. If we wish to know what the experience of God denotes, we must turn to science. Now science, at the moment, has no word to speak about God, for we have not developed a science of God; however, if we keep religion grounded in experience, such a science may develop in the conceivable future. Religion needs science, therefore, if it is ever to have statements which are provable as true. Now it is quite problematical what kind of God science will be able to establish, but religion will at least not be unscientific if it lets the term "God" mean "that object . . . which will yield maximum security and abundance to all human living, when right adjustment is made." [5] This security is the item of religious appreciation which shows that, in principle at least, religion is not antithetical to science. Science will not establish that men ought to want security; but if they do want it, science can show what events produce it and what events destroy it. Religion, in this scheme, is not based upon science, even though science has a word to say about the practicability of religion. Arthur S. Eddington, the English physicist, shared this conviction that religion ought not to be based upon science, but, at the same time, ought not to be anti-science.[6] The two areas combined permit man to fulfill his two most universal desires: knowledge of his world and appreciation of his world.

J. Arthur Thomson, a Scottish biologist who has expressed great concern for religion, insisted that the science-religion controversy was a pseudo-conflict, and that it should cease immediately. The aims of these two areas are dissimilar, although they are related by virtue of being pursued by the same human beings. The scientist wishes to know what a thing is, how it behaves, where it came from, and how it got to be the way it is. In the pursuit of the answers to these questions the scientist observes, measures, and systematizes until predicted results are verifiable. He discovers in this pursuit that there are generalized laws of nature which explain the vast sets of impersonal data. Religion, on the other hand, deals with ethical considerations and aims at emotional satisfaction. To be sure, science can explain the origins of religion, but these are of no religious concern. In its ethical aims, religion is beyond science, or at least quite other than science. Thomson deplored the thesis that religion was man's attempt to plug the gaps of science with God, so that whatever is incomprehensible is religious. This does religion the disservice of making God incoherent. The whole attempt to erect a scientific basis for theism Thomson branded as a mistake.[7] Religion interprets the world; it does not intend to describe the world. However, if religion asserts an orderly, reasonable God, then, at least, science cannot be antagonistic to theism. Thomson considered arguments for the existence of a God based upon empirical data to be presumptuous, for they entail a reading into nature of properties which really are not there. The kind of fallacy which this leads to was best expressed in the remarks of the opponents of the teleological argument for God. John Stuart Mill, for example, felt that there were so many events inimical to man and illustrative of bestiality in nature that there couldn't be a good God. William James also read into nature a combination of cosmic horror and beauty, and T. H. Huxley saw nature as a battle of beasts on a cosmic scale. These judgments, however, reflect the emotions of the observers and not properties implicit in the events. Nature is what it is, and evaluations of nature will always be artificial appendages. This separation of religion and science performs a double service to religion. In the first place, it forestalls any future conflicts between religion and science. In the second place, it prevents opponents of religious dogmas from using scientific data as support. Thus what religion may seem to lose by way of scientific arguments in its favor, it gains by virtue of being protected from scientific arguments against it.

A good many of the elements of both Judaism and Christianity can be interpreted fruitfully if this dividing line is drawn. The Ten Commandments of Moses, the rhapsodic emotions of some of the Psalms, the dreams of Isaiah, and the Sermon on the Mount can all be explained as man's attempt to evaluate, appreciate, and idealize his world. These scriptural accounts do not tell us what kind of world we have; they prescribe the attitude we should take toward this factual world. These religious idealizations show man how he fits into the scheme of things, and are, therefore, attempts to provide man with feelings of security and worth, with a sense of purpose and direction, and with a background for making moral distinctions. These same religious expressions give man a sense of cosmic destiny in relation to the whole dialectic of history and prehistory, and thus serve the same function that a man's personal ethics does for his relation to his fellow men. The Bible, therefore, would be looked upon as a panoramic history of man's attempts to provide himself with a normative basis for appreciation of his cosmos. Those parts of the scripture which simply describe the world would then be seen as superfluous to the religious concern, although they would be of interest to anyone who was writing a history of science. If the Genesis tale were read as if it were science, then it would, at the very least, be designated as naïvely prescientific. If, on the other hand, the Genesis story were understood as an attempt of men to prescribe a divine origin and destiny for their world, then this evaluation could remain no matter what new developments took place in the description of the origin of our earth. The modern religious person, armed with modern geology, astronomy, and biology, could still assert his appreciating judgment of divine destiny. Thus the religious prescription could endure through all the changes in the scientific account of creation. By the same token, if religious persons did not get bogged down in the absurd calculations as to whether Jonah could or did enter the belly of a fish, usually interpreted as a whale, and concentrated instead on the religious message that man cannot escape from "God," they would avoid all the harassing embarrassments involved in learning that a whale's throat is not big enough to swallow a man and avoid also having to predicate the unparsimonious thesis that God got Jonah alive out of a shark by a miracle. After all, a man-swallowing whale is scarcely any more of a "holy" phenomenon than a man-swallowing shark. Preoccupation with such events is more properly left to the curious scientist, since, after all, it would only constitute a description of the world in which we live. Religious persons would seem to have an unduly tenuous faith if their religious insights would be shaken if it turned out that a man cannot get into a whale's stomach through his throat, and that it is quite improbable that a man could live as long as Jonah was supposed to in a fish's stomach.

The Fundamentalist has compounded his own problem in the science-religion battle by his insistence upon the adequacy of the Bible for every problem. This self-inflicted limitation reached its extreme when the biblical literalist maintained that no book other than the Bible needed to be read. This put him in the compromising position of having to find his botany, geology, physics, chemistry, and psychology out of this same little book. He was required, further, to credit Moses with possessing a Ph.D. in every field known to man. Even if Moses had been as well read as this, the history of science would have made it clear that refresher courses in a modern university would certainly be in order. If the religious person wishes to hold to the view that his religious insights are timelessly important, he would do well not to ground them on science, which is always time- and culture-bound. The Protestant Fundamentalist who wants an inerrantly authoritative Bible will have to decide on a more limited area of authoritative domain if he is not to lose the whole book as a consequence of advances in science. A comparable set of problems has confronted the biblical literalist in the area of the social sciences. On the misguided assumption that the Bible solves all problems, the devout Fundamentalist has had to support the medieval economic theory implied in the New Testament story of the workers in the vineyard, the Pauline blessing of slavery, and the politics of patriarchal tribes. This has made him the unwitting tool of reactionaries in a world of progressive democracy. In all of this the Fundamentalist has battled windmills with a religion which grows progressively less tenable and less appealing to persons of moderate intelligence. What is so sad about the situation is that it could have been avoided, not by denying the authority of the Bible, but by limiting the domain of its authority. The religious beliefs in a God or an immortality could enjoy a relative timelessness if they were divorced from empirical matters, and constituted, rather, human normative judgments which lend meaning and direction.

There is, however, a strong current of objection to the dichotomy which we are discussing. This current is expressed, in part, by the interest in the writings of L. Ron Hubbard, Madame H. P. Blavatsky, and Immanuel Velikovsky. These books typify the irrepressible desire of many religionists to solicit the aid of science in the defense of religion. Velikovsky, for example,[8] aimed to show that Joshua's account of the sun standing still was a literal report of an actual event when a large comet passed near our planet and disrupted its movement. Basing his reasoning upon passages from the scriptures of widely different religions, he conjectured that this comet was our present planet of Venus. Hence, about 1200 B.C. there was no planet Venus, but instead a vast comet which came close enough to our earth to cause a slowing of the earth's rotation, which in turn was experienced from an earthly point of view as a stopping of the sun. Some six or seven centuries later, the planet Mars passed through the tail of the comet Venus, shattering it and contributing to the present position of Venus as a planet in our solar system. This latter catastrophe was used by the author to explain the reports of dire omens made by Amos and Isaiah. Prior to both of these events our earth had years of 360 days each, and since these events our years have increased to 365¼ days each. A phenomenal hurricane and a series of earth tremors were predicated as the cause of the Red Sea incident when the children of Israel were enabled to walk across the sea with a wall of water on either side of them, whereas the Egyptian pursuers perished when these walls collapsed. Velikovsky entertained the question: "Why have both of these events been forgotten?" His answer was that the events were so gruesome that the whole human race experienced a kind of collective amnesia, and the only vestiges of memory are to be found in the religious literature of mankind expressed as if the events were metaphorical rather than real.

We may, for our purposes, waive the question as to the likelihood that this account is true and concentrate, rather, upon the relation of science and religion which it presupposes. What makes Velikovsky's book important for our problem is that it typifies the attempts to find scientific foundation for religious myths. The average religious person had long since lost interest in such an obviously poetic account as that of the sun standing still when Velikovsky's book spun a web of probability around even this unlikely event. The problem here is not so much that the events described have such a low degree of probability as that occurrences which seem to bear so little relation to the basic message of religions should be elevated to the status of ultimate concerns. This emphasis was matched by the claims of the old school of Bishop Ussher that the world was created in 4004 B.C. It was not simply that the evidence was all against the Ussher hypothesis, but that people had become vitally concerned over a matter of dating which made no religious difference. If the religious person wanted to assert that his God had created the world, the matter of the amount of time involved was clearly irrelevant. For the religious person to worry about whether Joshua's axhead had floated on the water, whether Aaron's rod could bring water out of a rock, or whether Adam had a navel was to distort the historical religious concern with meaning and evaluation by making it into a mere issue of whether empirically unlikely events did or did not take place. This not only put religion in the unfavorable position of opposing science, but transformed the religious God into a capricious and humanly incomprehensible creature. That religion which sets itself up as the foe of science must take its stand in intellectual absurdities and empirical cabalism. Constant opposition to science leaves a religion with no practical message and, what is more important, with no unique message.

The attempt of some religious enthusiasts to discover in the Judeo-Christian scriptures either a reflection or a fulfillment of more ancient gnosis or wisdom belongs in the same category as the search for a scientific basis for religion. The gigantic two-volume work by H. P. Blavatsky [9] represents probably the most energetic and "scholarly" attempt to find empirical wisdom in religious scriptures. While at least a part of her conclusions lie in the area of "appreciation" or evaluation, much of what she discovers is essentially pseudo-science. The enthusiasts for her point of view are compelled to fight conventional science in a battle in which religion has always come out the poorer. In much the same spirit as the Protestant Fundamentalist who insisted that the Bible contained all knowledge, Madame Blavatsky contended that the sum of all religious scriptures contains the sum of all knowledge. Since the scriptures of the Hindus, Zoroastrians, and Moslems contain the same kind of empirically incredible reports as are to be found in the Bible, the essential result of this approach is to put religion in unnecessary conflict with science and to blur the historical distinctions which have existed between these two human concerns. William Kingsland, an English member of the Blavatsky association,[10] followed in the same tradition when he attempted to show that the Judeo-Christian scriptures contain vestiges, albeit abbreviated and confused, of far more ancient wisdom. Since much of the wisdom involved is quasi-scientific, the clear assumption on which Kingsland operates is that primitive men possessed more adequate knowledge of the world in which they lived than most modern men. This conclusion is one of the unfortunate consequences of the attempt to make religion into a descriptive science and, hence, to make religion a competitor with science.

In all of this, the dichotomy between religion and science has had a significant word to speak. If science is given the domain of description, and if religion is given the domain of prescription, then there need never be any conflict between the two areas. Indeed, within the framework of this division, good cases have been made for the assistance which each area can give to the other. Religion needs to know what kind of world man faces, and for this information it depends upon science. Science, on its side, needs to know how sensitive and imaginative persons have reacted to the world as it is. Furthermore, in view of the high degree of control which man has over his world, he cannot escape concern with prescriptions for the future. Long after man has discovered what kind of world he lives in, he will have to make decisions as to what he proposes to do in such a world. The world as it is always confronts man with a range of possibilities from which choices may be made, and religion may persist as the basis for such choices.

RELIGIOUS MEANING AND SCIENTIFIC TRUTH

We began our investigations with the premise that philosophy of religion has been concerned with two questions: Which religious statements are true? and Which religious meanings are ultimately worthy? If we distinguish, as we did in the previous section, between science and religion, does it not follow that there can be no real philosophical question of truth in religion, since truth applies only to those statements which describe the world of experience? The dichotomy we have discussed presupposes that this descriptive function is the domain of science, and that, hence, there is no real question of religious truth. Religious meanings, however, remain untouched by any inability to specify truth. The Ten Commandments of Moses or Buddha and the Sermon on the Mount of Jesus have not historically been dependent upon factual truth. These have been value expressions of what is worthy in the sight of men, and it has usually been presumed that these value judgments are unaffected by science or by any empirical state of affairs. Let us consider some of the implications of the separation of science and religion as seen from the point of view of truth as opposed to value.

The position of Paul Tillich [11] reflects an attempt to resolve this specific problem. On the assumption that religion is man's expression of "ultimate concern," and on the assumption that such a concern is not a consequence of an empirical induction, then it should follow that truth is not really of any religious importance. This should be the case whether we are talking about truths of science or truths of religion. Tillich accepts this inference as proper for religion, and he avers that neither the truth of religious statements nor the existence of the referents of religious statements is of religious concern. Specifically this means that the religious person ought not to be concerned either with the truth of the statement "God exists" or with the existence of a God. Religious assertions express a normative, or value, meaning; they do not intend any descriptive content. In the writings of Tillich we may see a live and current expression of the view that there is a dichotomy between religion and science, such that each neither threatens nor assists the other. It is in this sense that we could maintain that there is really no conflict between religion and science.

One of the prices which must be paid for this methodological division, however, is that religion appears to have no communicable procedure even for the determination of its meanings. Independently of the question of whether Tillich's inference is valid, he does draw the conclusion that the ultimate meanings which are the Christian revelation are incommunicable to those who have not already experienced the revelation personally. Since those who have already had the revelation scarcely need enlightenment, it may be concluded that communication, after all, is of no religious concern. In the conventional sense in which communication involves the transmission of objective data, the irrelevance of such communication would seem to be obvious, if for no other reason than that such communication misinterprets the nature of the Christian meanings. If, as Tillich avers, there are no objective Christian data, then explanation to an unbeliever would be impossible. As a minimum, the unbeliever might be informed that a revelation has occurred to someone, but he could not be enlightened either as to how such revelations occur or as to what the meaning of such revelations is. In part, this impasse in communication has given the impression to the objective observer of the Tillichian scheme that the whole presentation of the "ultimate concern" is couched in narrow sectarian meanings, and is assigned far more certainty than the evidence would warrant. It might be expected that a message as basically incommunicable as that of Tillich would be posed more cautiously and hypothetically. It would seem that Tillich's assurance that Christianity is both unique in its message and unsurpassable in its ideals does not fit in well with his admission that this whole affair is beyond demonstration and outside of human cognition. But whatever one may feel about this, the fact remains that science can never be a threat to religion so defined. Let science have its truth; religion will at least be the sole possessor of unique meaning. While Tillich does speak of a "truth of faith," [12] it is clear in context that this expression bears no recognizable relation to what truth means in academic disciplines.

What is there about the term "truth" as it has been used in the sciences which has produced this abandonment of the term in some religious circles? Why do some feel so strongly that if religion is to be saved at all, it must relinquish all hope of being descriptive and settle for the more tenuous goal of ultimate meaning?

In the first place, the scientific meaning of "cause and effect" has appeared intimidating to traditional religion. If, for example, the assertion that some X is caused by some Y means that X and Y have, in the past, had a contiguous, time-ordered relation, it should be sufficient, in order to explain the causal factors for some event, to make a coherent list of the contiguities. This Humean view has had considerable contemporary appeal, primarily because it does not require the predication of any secret connection between events. To say that X causes Y is merely to say that X has always been contiguous to and prior to a following Y. Even where other meanings of causation have been employed by the scientist, the result has been that causes have been considered to be explained when a system of consistent and predictable relations has been produced. Now what does this mean for the traditional religious concern? Precisely this: the theologian has sought for a First Cause believed to lie behind all temporal contiguities and all coherent patterns. To the theologian the scientific account of causation seems particularly truncated and incomplete. From the scientific point of view, however, this contiguous and structured notion of causation is quite sufficient for answering all questions of the why and wherefore of experienced events. What creates the friction between the religionist and the scientist is the assertion, not merely that a First Cause is scientifically undemonstrable, but that it is scientifically irrelevant. The scientific analyses of the universe are all formulated as if the universe were self-explanatory; in any case, the theories of science do not require any God hypothesis for their completion. The reports of the scientist remain the same whether there is a God or not. For a religious person who believes that religion is all-encompassing, this state of affairs is scarcely acceptable. If man can understand his world descriptively without religious doctrines, then a vast area of human interest seems to have been removed from the domain of religious relevance. This situation is not saved, as we have noted, by bringing in religion to fill the descriptive voids of science, for this reduces religion to magic and chaos.

In the second place, the whole religious concept of First Cause seems to require both beginnings in time and a fixity of creation which the facts of science do not support. Science does not speak in terms of First Cause, but rather in terms of processes. The scientific understanding of biological evolution illustrates this thesis. In the light of the information we now possess, which is admittedly incomplete, we are able to trace regressively the origin of species back through a long period of time. As new information is discovered, we expect to make the evolutionary story longer still. In this whole panorama, there is no mention of a First Cause. There are, instead, hosts of secondary causes traced regressively. For every newly discovered event, some newly discovered cause is also specified. In none of this do we find the scientist asking, "But what was there before there was anything?" Nor does he raise the query, "But what was the absolute beginning?" While these are of religious concern, they have not been of any scientific concern, for science has no way of interpreting or handling such questions. If religious persons wish to ask these double questions, then at least they should know that they will get no support from any science. If there were some evidential support for the assumption that there was a time when there was "nothing," science might get concerned over the question, but until such support is found, it remains a begging question and out-of-bounds scientifically. Science operates within the realm of, in principle, observable processes. The idea of a First Cause does not fit into this pattern. It is because of this methodological situation that science does not support either theism or atheism. The whole religious assumption of a First Cause is beyond science. Furthermore, scientific explanations of causation are set into a dynamic, fluctuating context which offends some religious devotees of cosmic stability. Religious philosophers in the tradition of Alfred N. Whitehead, however, expect no fixity, and hence are not bothered by this element in science.

In the third place, science, for all of its achievements, has never been able to produce more than probabilities, and these seem incompatible with the traditional religious commitments to certainties. It would be alien to the religious mood to assert a God as a probability, or to hold to the Christian Incarnation as having better than a fifty-fifty chance of having occurred. Science must talk in terms of probabilities, but these do not satisfy the needs of religious commitment. When it was determined, further, that deduction from absolutely true premises was the only logic which could give apodictic answers, and yet that such absolute premises were beyond science, then it must have seemed even more obvious that the procedures of science could not contribute to religion. The only kind of truth which science can contribute is probable truth. Furthermore, to say that any statement is probably true presupposes that appropriate inductions have been made and that successful predictions follow from the probable truths. Religion, however, has had no success either in inductions or in predictions in support of its most precious beliefs.

This scientific milieu may be summed up in what has been called the mechanistic-teleological disjunct. The findings of science portray a mechanistic universe in the sense that its operations can be understood within the universe itself, and in the sense that the causal sequences have an inexorable quality, which is expressed in the idea of physical laws. Bodies which are heavier than air fall toward the gravitational field when they are released from support, supersaturated clouds under the appropriate temperatures release their burdens as rain, hail, or snow, and the ocean tides move with predictability in close relation to the phases of the moon. The scientific picture appears to have no room for Providence. What is more, the scientific analyses of our world possess a self-containment which expresses part of the meaning of mechanism. Each part of our world is explicable in terms of other parts of our world, in much the same way as the location of one cog in a machine explains the locations of all of the other cogs in the machine. Now religion, on the other hand, is concerned with the purpose of the cosmic machine. While science investigates the creation of events, religion investigates the creator of events. Science seeks an explanation of the plan of nature, while religion seeks for a planner of nature. While science develops theories to account for nature as we find it, religion develops theories to give meaning and normative purpose to this same nature.

These two aims, while not contradictory, appear to be independent of each other. The mechanisms of science require no planner for their explanation. The thesis of a religious planner of nature is equally independent of all scientific accounts. While religion speaks the language of teleology, science speaks the language of mechanism. From the religious point of view, scientific mechanism is not a threat because of any attack which it could make upon teleology, but simply because mechanism ignores teleology as an expendable frill. Science does not show that there could be no purposer. It simply operates as if it made no difference whether there were or were not such a deity. The religious person who insists upon bringing a God into the scientific picture is in the same category as the artist who insists that the beauty of molecular action be considered as necessary for an adequate scientific explanation.

In the face of all this, what can the religious person do? Should he insist that the literal Genesis account of creation is true in the face of all scientific evidence to the contrary? Should he oppose all medical knowledge as sophistry and illusion in order to save the first-century notion that disease is caused by devils? No, if he divides the domains of competence of religion and science, he would give the task of explaining both creation and disease to the appropriate scientists on the grounds that these are, after all, matters of description, while religion is concerned with judgments of worth or value. The religious person could assert his conviction that there is a divine planner without difficulty as long as he permits the scientist to explain the plan. This division of intents between science and religion puts the latter in the same general category as ethics and aesthetics. These three areas, then, express the human evaluation of the world, and they portray both the fertility and the complexity of the human imagination, as well as the needs of the human psyche. For religious persons to attempt to substitute for the growing body of predictively useful scientific knowledge the pathetic myths of bygone scriptures is to do religion, science, and the hope of human progress a disservice. No real harm has been done by those religious thinkers who have perennially pointed out the limitations of science, but when these same religious spokesmen have used the limitations of science as a basis for disparaging the whole program of science, the matter stands much differently. After all, it is the limitation of a field which provides it with its significance. The weakness and ineffectiveness of Fundamentalist religion are due, primarily, to the unwillingness of this movement to limit itself to a domain which does not presume to be everything. Religious thinkers of the stature of Saint Augustine and Saint Thomas did not assume that religious doctrines could provide men with all the information there could be about the world. To be sure, religion discussed metaphysical answers to questions which science could not answer because of its own self-limitations. Religion, further, provided an emotional and evaluative milieu which gave to men a sense of their worth and destiny, and this was also beyond the scope of science. Neither of these men, however, doubted that pure secularists could discover truths of science and mathematics. The realm of description was the proper domain of science, and it ill behooved religion to lay claim to descriptive insights. Theoretically, therefore, religion and science touched borders, but did not overlap; nor should they ever conflict. In fact, however, neither religion nor science has been quite so pure or quite so aware of its limitations. The temptation of religious persons to establish the dominance of religion by claiming that it answers every type of question has been difficult to overcome. As we have seen, theologians, whose message gives no insights into the empirical processes of the world, have set religion up as a kind of super-physics, -chemistry, -geology, -biology, -psychology, and -political science. On the other hand, scientists have not been immune to the same temptation to presume a completeness for science which it cannot possess. Not only is science no substitute for religion, but it is equally silent in the areas of aesthetics and ethics.

However dreamy the speculations of religionists and ethicists may seem from the point of view of empirical science, these conjectures express a facet of the human creature which cannot be ignored, nor can they be subsumed under either the heading of pseudo-science or super-science. Just as the science of religion is not religion, so also the religion of science is not science. These expressions are attempts, which at best symbolize the fact that both efforts may be promoted by the same person. At worst, they typify the presumption that man must choose between science and religion as if the world of intelligent creatures could not hold them both.

To be sure, when religious believers measure science by the normative criteria of religion, science is seen to leave a great void of human concern untouched. Likewise, when scientifically minded men measure religion by the precise criteria of science, religion appears as a vast web of myth and fantasy. The unity and common agreement which pervades the structures of science will not be found to prevail in religion. We have seen this to be the case by virtue of the plain fact that there is no one philosophy of religion which has ever commended itself to all men of good will. There are philosophies of religion, and there would seem to be no reasonable basis for assuming that this patchwork quilt will ever be remade into a blanket of solid color. Each individual, to be sure, will probably choose one philosophical approach to religion and ignore the other possibilities. This seems as likely and as psychologically necessary as that each person will decide on a mate or on a personally approved scale of values. The enterprise of looking at this vast mesh of approaches to religion requires a philosophic detachment and an emotional neutrality which are alien to the spirit of religious commitment. But this merely supports the conclusion reached by millennia of religious thought: philosophy of religion is no substitute for religion, just as philosophy of science is no substitute for science.

Summary Questions

•

What Is Philosophy of Religion?

1. If we imagine that truth is the major problem in philosophy of religion, does this mean that, except for its subject matter, religion is like physics or biology? If we do not wish to link religion so closely to science, do we then have to give up the claim for religious truth altogether?

2. William James and others have claimed that significance and practical value are more important for religion than mere rational truths. Would you feel that this Jamesian view puts religion in an embarrassingly weak position when compared with the disciplines of science? Since James redefines truth so that true religion is that which is practical, do you feel that this gets around the problem?

3. What if Sigmund Freud were correct in his evaluation of religion as an infantile neurosis? Would this have any bearing on the quest for religious truth or religious value? Would Freud's invidious hypothesis still permit us to maintain that the origin of an idea has no bearing on whether it is true or not?

445

4. William James asserted: "To plead the organic causation of a religious state of mind, then, in refutation of its claim to possess superior spiritual value, is quite illogical and arbitrary. . . ." Does this mean that the psychology of religion has no bearing on its truth or importance?

5. According to Rudolf Otto, the essence of religion is a noumenal experience, which is incommunicable, incomprehensible, and ineffable. Would such a definition of religion seem to make questions as to both the truth and the value of religion irrelevant?

6. Are there any inferences to be drawn from the fact that there is so little agreement among religious persons as to what philosophy of religion really is? Does the fact that there are philosophies of religion rather than a generally agreed upon philosophy of religion mean that there is, after all, no possibility of either truth or value being established for religion?

7. Hocking asserted that our wills do have a strategic part to play in determining what is the case religiously. Since he does not mean that we can will a God into existence, nor will immortality into effect if there really is no immortality, what can he possibly mean by the role of the will?

8. William James insisted that "if your heart does not want a world of moral reality, your head will assuredly never make you believe in one." James has the support of both Saint Augustine and Saint Thomas in this thesis. If this is true, then what function could philosophy of religion serve for unbelievers?

C H A P T E R   I I

The Definition of Religion

1. If religion needs to be defined to be understood, and if definitions are neither true nor false, does this mean that religion is neither true nor false? Try this same question substituting the word "physics" for the word "religion."

2. If definitions are inadequate to determine truth issues, then how are matters of truth to be determined? Since it would be very peculiar if we were to try to prove a statement true before we had defined what it meant, doesn't this mean that the use of definitions is inescapable?

446

3. Many years ago the former Federal Council of Churches of Christ in America voted that Universalists and Unitarians were not really Christian. Is there a way in which this conclusion can be drawn without appealing to definitions? How would one prove that it is true that some denomination is not Christian?

4. Suppose that all persons in the world who call themselves religious did, in fact, mean the same thing by religion. Would there be less reason to complain about inferring truth from definitions in such a case than there is when we confront multiple and conflicting definitions? Would a consensus on a definition make it legitimate to infer truth from the definition?

5. If each of the three definitional types which we considered has the same problems—namely, that they include those who wish to be excluded, and that they exclude those who wish to be included —would some combination of the definitions avoid the difficulties? Or is preoccupation with the definition of religion merely a waste of time?

6. Would we arrive at the same truth statements no matter what definition of religion we were to use? Could there be a definition which disallows the truth enterprise altogether, or which makes religious value impossible?

C H A P T E R   I I I

Why Do We Have Religion?

1. If the origin of an idea has no bearing on its truth, is there then no philosophic problem over the question of religious origins? Does this mean that the psychology, sociology, and history of religions are not relevant to the problems of philosophy of religion?

2. Is the fact that religions have been used by power-hungry monarchs and calculating politicians for devious ends of religious concern in the sense that this use constitutes a judgment of the worth of religion? Is this merely an illustration of the cliché that the best of things can be used for the worst of ends? If Marx were correct in his analysis that religion has been an opiate of the people, would this be of religious concern?

3. According to the history of religions, all of the faiths of mankind began with confused, naïve, and often normatively question-

able ideas. If this is true, should religious persons be concerned? Would these data make it impossible to hold that a given religion is unique or complete in its message? Does the common Christian claim to uniqueness fail if doubts can be raised concerning the adequacy of the genesis of Christianity?

4. Does the fact that children tend to hold the religious convictions of their parents support the contention that religion survives through inertia, or that it is transmitted through a kind of unconscious osmosis?

5. The most ancient pictures we have of primitive gods show them with horns. The common picture of the Devil also shows horns. When the horns gave place to halos, we find gods of most religions possessing these new signs. Do such facts have any bearing on the meaning of gods in human experience?

6. All of the theories which we have studied presupposed that religion was invented. Are there any implications for religion from this idea? Must religions rise to their defense and pose the counterthesis that men really had no part to play in the birth of religion?

C H A P T E R   I V

The Idea of God: to What Does the Term Refer?

1. James Leuba noted forty-eight definitions of the term "God" which have been in use. Our own observation has been that there have been widely divergent meanings assigned to this term. In view of the fact that there have been such disparate meanings for "God," would it be safe to conclude that the term never functions as a designating name?

2. If the meaning of the term "God" is a matter of definition, then it would seem to follow that no definition of the term could be true. Suppose, however, that the meaning was a report of a personal experience. Would it then be possible to argue for the truth of the meaning?

3. Tillich's explication of God as the "ground of being" has led to the accusation that his God lacks the essential Judeo-Christian personal properties, and hence is not even a Christian option. How would you evaluate this objection?

4. David Hume suspected that primitive peoples asserted polytheism because they were scientifically illiterate, and that with the rise of science, monotheism became a tenable thesis. Does it follow, if Hume was right, that monotheism represents a defensibly superior interpretation of deity? How could this be explained plausibly to a polytheist?

5. Most of the great Roman Catholic thinkers from Saint Augustine to Saint Thomas felt that it was impossible to explain what God was. The explanations most commonly offered were all in the negative; that is, they asserted what God was not. Is there a logical problem in the assertion that they know what God is not when they do not know what God is?

C H A P T E R   V

Arguments for the Existence of God

1. The data on which the teleological argument rests are facts of order, design, or purpose. These data have had to change as man's knowledge of his world changed. Would you agree with Eddington that no matter how much order man discovers, the inference to an orderer is scientifically unwarranted?

2. Historically the ontological argument for God has made the most apodictic claim of all arguments for the existence of God. In spite of this, the ontological argument has probably had the fewest supporters. Is this due to the nature of the intuition which it entails? Is it a function of the lack of any evidence to support it, or are there psychological reasons why this approach has been the least compelling?

3. Protestant Modernists share with Roman Catholic Thomists an enthusiasm for the cosmological argument for God. It has been held that this argument is the only one which combines metaphysics, physics, and religion. How should we react to the remarks of physicists like J. A. Thomson and Arthur Eddington that science does not need, and does not entail, a doctrine of First Cause? On the other hand, Thomists assert that the account of our world is incomplete without an answer to the question of metaphysical causation. Is there some shrewd way to reconcile this discrepancy?

4. Tillich has maintained that arguments for the existence of God are irrelevant, misleading, and unprovable. He illustrates this by

the remark that all objectors to the arguments to prove the existence of God have attacked the form of the arguments, while all supporters of such arguments have stressed the meaning of the inference. Is this a real distinction?

5. Ludwig Feuerbach remarked that "there is merely an illusory distinction between divine revelation and so-called human reason or nature. . . ." As a consequence, he saw the essence of theology to be anthropology. Suppose he were correct, as well he might be. Would such a fact affect the status of arguments for the existence of God? If religion were really a matter of subjective feeling, would it then follow that no argument for God really touches true religion?

6. Suppose we were to decide that all arguments for the existence of a God were invalid, or at least that they involved appeals to evidence of so weak a nature as to be insufficient. Would this pose any serious problem for religion? Does religion have to have arguments?

7. How would you account for the paucity of arguments for the nonexistence of God (atheism)? Do you imagine that this is due to social pressure, to the lack of any prime psychological motivation toward atheism, or simply to the lack of data to support the atheist conclusion?

CHAPTER VI

The Problems of Religious Knowledge

1. Throughout the history of the Christian churches there has been a variation of answers to the question, "Is religious knowledge possible?" By contrast, the major tradition of Buddhism has univocally denied religious knowledge. Part of the dilemma seems to have been prompted by the feeling that if there were no religious knowledge, then religion was somehow jeopardized. Do there seem to be bases for this fear?

2. Hegelians have insisted that the coherence theory of truth was the one that could be applied most effectively to religion; pragmatists have countered by the claim that the pragmatic theory of truth best saves religion; while throughout the chapter we have presupposed the correspondence idea of truth. Would this diversity

of preferred meanings of "truth" tend to undermine all claims that there is a definition of "truth" which is most suitable for religion? Would a change in the definition of "truth" lead to the discovery of any different conclusions?

3. If the conclusions of induction are, by virtue of the nature of the method, probable at best; and if religion aims at conclusions which are certain, does this mean that religious arguments ought not to be inductive? Would you expect, as a consequence of this, to find that most religious thinkers have preferred deduction?

4. It is always possible in induction that upon later investigation the conclusions previously reached may turn out to be false. If religious persons find this to be an impossible situation for religious claims, are the grounds for the meaning of "impossibility" psychological or logical? Kierkegaard, for example, found the probabilities of induction incommensurate with the very essence of Christian certitude.

5. If we denied the possibility of religious knowledge, would we have to give up the claim for religious truths? Would the denial of religious knowledge also entail the inability to establish religious value or significance?

C H A P T E R   V I I

The Problem of Natural Evil

1. What implications are there for the problem of natural evil if we take the position that the question, "Why is there natural evil?" is purely existential? Are any of the solutions which we have considered consistent with the existential thesis that both the question and the answer pertaining to natural evil are purely personal?

2. Is the question, "Why are there natural evils?" a double question, in that it appears to presuppose that the evils were caused or intended, and, hence, that it is proper to ask "Who did it?" or "Why do they exist?" Since the problem of natural evil could not arise for a non-theist, or for a theist whose God was less than transfinite, would it be better to shift concern to the nature of the God rather than to remain preoccupied with the nature of the world?

3. Do the data summarized by John Stuart Mill in his essay on *Nature* entail that there is a limited God, a malicious God, or no

God at all? Mill infers that a God cannot be both omnipropertied and loving, that he cannot be both just and loving, or that if he is all-powerful he must be immoral. Is there a contradiction between the Christian claims that God is good and that God is just?

4. In what sense does it seem proper to say that neither the Christian Science solution nor the limited-God solution really faces the original problem? If there really is a problem, then it would seem that the two answers given above completely miss the point.

5. Some Christians have claimed that their God operates in terms of radically different moral laws from those by which men are judged. On this assumption these Christians have dismissed all solutions to the problem of natural evil as presumptuous. But if morality for God and man is so different, doesn't this make theodicy incomprehensible and philosophy of religion impossible?

C H A P T E R   V I I I

The Problem of Immortality

1. There seems to be a division in the ranks of Christian theologians on the matter of the importance of the belief in immortality. Idealists like Bradley and Royce are unimpressed with the claims that immortality must be personal. William James admitted that he really had no strong feelings on the subject either way. Spinoza considered the whole question unworthy of an intelligent man, while existentialists find it the only ultimate issue. Are there some facts implicit in particular religions which explain why there must be more time, or is the whole question really a function of personal taste?

2. Oriental religious views of immortality seem to stress the impersonal nature of the experience, while Occidental religions tend to stress the personal elements in immortality. Would this be a case where we should decide that one of the two traditions is mistaken on the thesis that one of them must be correct? Or do we entertain the possibility that both of them are mistaken on the thesis that the terms "personal" and "impersonal" are inappropriate for this state of affairs?

3. The only scientific supports which have been claimed for the belief in immortality have been pseudo-scientific in the unparsi-

monious "Bridey Murphy" tradition. Does the lack of any reputable scientific argument for immortality constitute a fact of any religious significance, or is this really irrelevant?

4. Suppose that the cultural theorists were right in the hypothesis that the idea of immortality had its genesis in reactions to dream experiences or because primitive man was unwilling to accept death for himself. When we add to this the obvious biological fact that all other living creatures die, would this evidence have any bearing on either the truth or the value of the immortality claim?

5. The Jamesian pragmatists recommend that we forget about the truth or existence of immortality and emphasize instead the emotional value which the belief has. Doesn't this reduce the whole question of immortality to psychology instead of religion? Would men be willing to believe in an immortality because it gave them peace of mind, even though they were not able to prove statements about immortality to be true? Are there any correlates to this same situation in other human commitments, such as love, ethical or moral sanctions, or the devotion to democracy?

C H A P T E R   I X

Is Religion a Matter of Knowledge?

1. If we were to emphasize the Roman Catholic tradition from Saint Augustine to Saint Thomas Aquinas, would we conclude that, for Roman Catholics at least, religion was not at any time considered to be a matter of knowledge? If faith is given logical and psychological priority, does this mean that the roots of religion are noncognitive?

2. Does religion lack intellectual status if it is determined that there are no knowable facts about it in the sense in which truth and falsity are normally considered? Is Tillich's position that authentic faith is noncognitive inimical to the emotional life of religious persons, or is it the case, as he avers, that real religion will be saved by divorcing it from all rationales of logic? Is the ability of Kierkegaard and Tillich to appreciate a religion so divorced from reason a matter of the psychic biographies of these two men, or are there pragmatic grounds for the separation such that it can appeal to religious persons on its own merits?

453

3. If we were to be impressed with the majestic rational structure of the *Summa* of Saint Thomas, do we conclude more than that the mind of man is a fertile and imaginative machine to have constructed so complex a systematic of religion? What problems do we have to face in view of the "analytic" nature of many of the Thomistic premises? Is it not the case that, whether Thomas uses induction or deduction, or some combination of the two, analytic premises entail that the conclusions must also be analytic?

4. If, as Saint Thomas appears to have held, the *Summa* does not intend to prove the truth of faith, but only to show the compatibility of faith with reason, would religion lose anything important if we were to decide that faith and reason were not compatible? If faith can begin without reason, are there any reasons for concluding that it would be in any way jeopardized if it turned out that reason could not be related to faith in any significant fashion?

5. What consequences must we accept if we take the option of the pragmatists to redefine truth in such a way that religion becomes true by virtue of the consequences to which it leads, and not by virtue of the events which it purports to describe? Or is it the case that if we accept pragmatic criteria, we should then consistently agree with Tillich that the existence of the referents of religious statements is not of religious concern?

6. If religion is claimed to have a rationale, in the sense of a cognitive defense, do we not then have to face the possibility that reason may dispense with religion? Or, on the other hand, if we accept pragmatic results as significant, ought we to discard religion if psychologically it produces neuroses or if sociologically it disrupts the stability of society?

CHAPTER X

The Problem of Inerrant Scripture

1. If inerrant interpretation is unprovable, as it appears to be in the Protestant tradition, what is gained by still asserting the claim for an inerrant message? How does this relate to the existential thesis that we can never know the *what* of revelation, even though we can know the *that* of revelation?

2. Can any conclusions which might seem provable be drawn from the fact that in science all claims are fallible and probable, while in certain Biblical matters inerrancy is claimed? Is there an inconsistency in holding that human thought cannot arrive at certitudes, and yet that man can know that the Bible is inerrant?

3. There is an apothegm in pragmatism to the effect that a distinction which makes no difference is not worth making. Is the doctrine of scriptural inerrancy a case in point in the sense that it has no practical use and leads to no practical consequences? Of what use is inerrancy to a finite creature who cannot know certainty anyway?

4. When we apply the doctrine of biblical infallibility, do we raise the status of the assertions of scripture? If we were to deny that the Bible had absolute insights, would this lead naturally to a demeaning of the book? Since this does not occur for books in science, why should it be expected to occur for books in religion?

5. Some Fundamentalists have felt that if the Bible were found to be errant at any point, then it would be useless at every point. Why should this follow? Is this a case of throwing out the baby with the bath water?

6. We have noted that the origin of an idea has no bearing on the truth of an idea, and yet we have seen that the researches of biblical scholars on the origins of the scripture have affected the claims for inerrancy. Is there some mistake in the inference at this point?

C H A P T E R   X I

The Problem of Fixed or Evolving Religions

1. Why should the authenticity of a religion be considered as a function of the completeness of the origin of the movement? Is an evolving religion necessarily less worthy than one with genetic completeness? Since an evolving science is assumed reasonably to be preferable to a fixed science, why should we expect anything different for religion?

2. There are striking similarities between the religion of Mithras and that of Christianity. If it could be shown that Christianity inherited symbolism from the Mithraists, would this fact take away some of the uniqueness which some Christians claim to possess?

455

3. Sir James Frazer has noted a large number of myths which the Old Testament shares with more ancient scriptures. What inferences might be drawn from the commonality of these stories? Would the Bible be any less "inspired" if the form of many of its accounts were borrowed from other traditions?

4. According to biblical criticism, the Old Testament reveals an evolution of Jewish thinking about God. This evolution began with polytheism and ended with monotheism. Martin Buber, on the other hand, insisted that polytheism, henotheism, and kathenotheism are theories about the world and not about deity, and that, hence, the Jews were not polytheists in the sense of admitting the existence of many gods. If the Jews really were henothists during the Mosaic period, for example, would this be a fact which would undermine contemporary Judaism?

5. Would you consider the rise of an Old Testament late in the history of Judaism or the rise of a New Testament late in the history of Christianity to be evidence that both religions had been evolving? Suppose, further, that the biblical critic were correct in his thesis that there is a dichotomy between the Gospels and the letters of Saint Paul. Would this raise the probability that Christianity has changed its emphases during its history?

CHAPTER XII

The Problem of Fundamentalism

1. If the Fundamentalist eliminates postbiblical miracles on the grounds that the Bible is the sole guide to salvation, would it not be consistent for the Roman Catholic to reject biblical miracles in favor of postbiblical miracles on the grounds that the church is the sole guide to salvation? How should we interpret the fact that the Church has not done this?

2. The Fundamentalist insists that the Bible is the sole and sufficient guide to salvation, and yet he denies that there are any infallible authorities for the interpretation of the Bible. Doesn't this mean, in effect, that every person is his own authority, and that hence there is no universally comprehensible Christian message?

3. If Protestant Fundamentalism is actually noncognitive, then doesn't this mean that a philosophy of Protestantism would be a

contradiction in terms? Does the fact that John Calvin was not enthusiastic about theology support this inference?

4. Since Protestant Fundamentalism seems to thrive upon diversity and even to demand it, is there any hope for Christian unity which this movement can offer? Is unity, after all, a Roman Catholic doctrine which is inimical to the spirit of Protestantism? What possible hope for a divided world could an equally divided religion have to offer?

5. There seems to be a clear contradiction in the following Protestant claims: the Bible is the sole guide to salvation; the message of the Bible is inerrant and complete; there are no human interpreters who can determine what the message really is. If Protestants insist on all three of these dogmas, don't they have to admit that the first two are functionless?

CHAPTER XIII

The Problem of Modernism

1. Is it possible in a complex society to determine with any assurance that the Christian religion has had certain beneficial consequences? Do we attribute the miseries in Christian nations to the sinfulness of particular believers, or do we consider these gruesome events to be the natural results of the Christian religion? If we deny Christian responsibility for the evils in the world, must we also deny Christian responsibility for the blessings?

2. Modernism applies the findings of the social sciences in the evaluation of religion, and yet at the same time it asserts the superiority of Christianity. Can it be shown, for example, that Christianity is psychologically superior to all other religions? Humanists answer this question with a negative. Is there a contradiction if the claim to uniqueness is related to the evidence of the social sciences?

3. How can we reconcile the moral depravity of many of the biblical characters with the position that the Bible is the sole guide to salvation? Isn't there a problem, in view of the immorality of King David, in crediting him with the authorship of the Psalms? If we answer this question by claiming that God, after all, wrote the Psalms, don't we still have to conjure with the moral stature of David?

4. One of the consequences of Modernist scholarship was to cast doubts upon the authenticity of miracles and the historicity of Jesus. These data led Albert Schweitzer to conclude that the quest for the historical Jesus was a lost cause. Does this lacuna jeopardize Christianity in any way? Does Christianity require authentic data about the man Jesus? Can doctrines about the transhistorical Christ supply Christianity with enough content to distinguish it from other religions?

CHAPTER XIV

The Problem of Humanism

1. It has been a conviction of humanists that the importance of man in any religion has been inversely proportional to the seriousness with which the God concept has been held. In the light of religious history does this seem to be a supportable hypothesis? Do religious persons face a dilemma in which they must choose between human worth and divine significance because they cannot have both without contradiction?

2. It was the claim of David Hume that supernaturalism in religion had been a fetter on religious progress. If we were to assume that religions have progressed, would an analysis of religious beliefs indicate that there has been a steady decline in supernaturalism? Are there any indications that the least supernatural religions have been the most progressive?

3. Would you suppose that the humanist concern with anti-supernaturalism demonstrates that humanists believe that religion can be, and ought to be, scientific? In the Kierkegaardian plan science plays no role in religion, and supernaturalism appears as the essence of piety. On what points do these two emphases diverge so that they come out with opposite preferences?

4. How should we explain the apparent lack of social concern which the New Testament report of Jesus expresses? Should we conclude that, after all, ethics is not essential to the Christian message, that the "interim ethics" is a consequence of Jesus' misguided millennialism, or that the real social message of Jesus has been lost?

5. Can any significant inferences be drawn from the fact that there have been no claimants for the position of "ademocrat" or

"ahumanist," while there have been supporters for a position called "atheist"? This seems to be the case in spite of the fact that there have been persons opposed to both democracy and humanism. Is this a function of the difference in claims of these three emphases? Neither democracy nor humanism makes the claim that something exists, but rather assert their positions as value commitments. Theism, on the other hand, is more than a value stand; it has asserted the existence of a referent of the term "God." If theists intended no referential claim, would this vitiate the atheist position?

CHAPTER XV

Psychology and Religion

1. In Chapter I of *The Varieties of Religious Experience,* William James discusses the thesis that the origin of a religion has no bearing on either the truth or the significance of religion. Is this the case even for a hypothesis as negative as that of Sigmund Freud? If religion were really a product of neurosis, wouldn't this affect the status of religion?

2. Carl Jung claimed that the doctrine of the bodily assumption of the Virgin Mary was the most important religious event in Christianity since the Reformation. Why should this be so? Since Protestantism generally does not accept this doctrine, does this leave Protestants without some essential component? What do Protestants lack by their rejection of Mariolatry?

3. In terms of sheer numbers of books written, the history of religion leads the list, while sociology and psychology of religion lag far in the rear. This can scarcely mean that there are fewer data in these two latter fields. Is there some reason implicit in the nature of sociology and psychology why the religious data should have been ignored? Is it because these two fields pose threats to religion which history does not pose?

4. The observation has commonly been made that the psychopathology of religion has been more often studied that the psychology of religion. If we assume that this has been true, who is responsible for the greater stress on the sick elements in religion than on the healthy elements in religion? Are there actually more neurotic elements in religion, or is it simply that psychopathology is a more interesting field for study?

5. Would it be proper to credit psychology with the decrease in revivalism in religious ceremony on the grounds that this highly emotional method has been shown to be inimical to psychic health? Is the degree of revivalism directly proportional to the lack of intelligence or is it due to the psychic anxieties of the revivalist himself?

CHAPTER XVI

The Church and the State

1. What is the warrant for the general assumption in the United States that the state should maintain an attitude of neutrality toward all religious programs? The state does not maintain this attitude toward all programs of public health, housing, or salary. Is this because there is some basic difference between the two kinds of values entailed? Since the state has assumed some responsibility toward the mental health of its citizens, why ought it not to assume a responsibility toward the spiritual health of its citizens?

2. Is the "wall of separation" doctrine an indication of a property of religion which is peculiar to this area? Would we endorse the same separation on matters of the branches of the military, on political parties? Is there, in fact, and should there be in theory, the same "wall of separation" between the state and every value enterprise? Is the justification of the "wall" a function of the special nature of religious statements? Is this because religion is a matter of a special act of faith entailing no publicly provable facts? Does the espoused neutrality rest on the simple fact that religion deals with issues whose truth or falsity cannot be determined, and that, hence, the neutrality of the state is a public demonstration of the impossibility of proving that any religious program really ought to be promoted?

3. If this is the case, why should we so zealously urge the right of all groups to promote their programs? Is there some contradiction in the position which maintains that every religion can rightfully promote its values, while the state must not, by any legal machinery, assist in the fulfilling of these values? Since the state does not maintain neutrality where it can be determined that there is a "clear and present danger," does this mean that the pro-

motion of religious values rests upon a limited right? Wouldn't it then be the case that any limit constitutes an interference of the state in the due exercise of religion?

4. If religion is, on the other hand, really pertinent to this world and if it has the clear, univocal, and true word to speak on the affairs of man, then why shouldn't a church-controlled state be the logical outcome? Is the fear of denominational preference a sufficient warrant for disestablishmentarianism? If, instead of 265 sects in America, we had but one or perhaps two, would we then take a different view toward the question of the "wall of separation?" Does the "wall" rest upon the multivocal nature of religion?

5. Is there a religious view of human nature which calls for one form of government more than any other? A perusal of the positions held by Roman Catholic, Jewish, and Protestant thinkers would appear to militate against this possibility. Is there evidence that the interest of a religious organization in government is directly proportional to the degree of confidence in "human nature" which the religion possesses? (This would mean that the more a religion asserted the original or innate sinfulness of man, the more the religion would insist upon inviolate state power, while a religion which held that man is capable of moral behavior would be more likely to challenge the adequacy of a purely secular state.) Or is the case the reverse?

6. It has been generally assumed by religious organizations that the "wall of separation" doctrine is consistent with the right of religions to assert their values and to urge others to do the same. This holds equally where the religious lobby is pressuring the state and where it is attempting to influence elements in the society not under immediate governmental jurisdiction. Does this mean that the separation principle applies merely to the organization of religion and not to the causes which it seeks to promote? Once a religiously promoted value becomes part of the constitutional rights of citizens, the state does, in fact, enforce and promote these values. At this point do we consider it coincidental that church and state cooperate on the same cause? Is the real question one of keeping a religious hierarchy out of legally preferred positions? Does the issue also apply to keeping religious values out of legally sanctioned rules? Can Congress actually refrain from making *any* laws with respect to religion? Where shall the line be drawn?

CHAPTER XVII

Religion and Science

1. According to Soren Kierkegaard, no matter of science can ever aid or harm an authentic religious issue. Both Arthur S. Eddington and J. Arthur Thomson shared this view. Does this radical dichotomy between the two fields leave religion without any data for its support?

2. Do the basic theses of Christian Science demand that physics, chemistry, biology, and psychology ought to be usable for the support of special Christian claims? If no empirical science can aid Christianity, could there still be a Christian Science?

3. The facts show that in the science-religion controversies science has consistently emerged the victor and religion has had to retract its "scientific" claims or else reject the whole field of science. Is there any lesson which could be learned from this long and unsuccessful warfare of religion against science?

4. The Fundamentalist Protestant wanted his scripture to be inerrant in its message, its syntax, its history, and its science. The tradition of religious Existentialism has consistently recommended that Protestants give up inerrancy in all areas except the message. Does this seem to truncate religion or dwarf its significance?

5. Does it really follow that if religion and science are separated into distinct fields, there can then be no religious truth? Does the possibility of truth in religion depend integrally upon the existence of scientifically demonstrable facts? Suppose it turns out that the only relation between religion and science is psychological. Suppose, further, that the data of neither field supports or harms the other. Would this prove to be disastrous for either religion or science?

Notes

CHAPTER I

What Is Philosophy of Religion?

1. E. S. Brightman, *A Philosophy of Religion* (New York: Prentice-Hall, 1940), p. 116.

2. *Ibid.*, p. 121.

3. William James, *Essays in Pragmatism* (New York: Hafner, 1948), p. 105.

4. *Ibid.*, pp. 88–109.

5. W. E. Hocking, *The Meaning of God in Human Experience* (New Haven: Yale University Press, 1912), p. 139.

6. *Ibid.*, p. 141.

7. *Ibid.*, p. 156.

8. Among the classics contributing to our understanding of the data of the religious past are: Max Muller, *Sacred Books of the East* (1876); James G. Frazer, *The Golden Bough;* George F. Moore, *History of Religions* (1913); and C. H. Toy, *Introduction to the History of Religions* (1913).

CHAPTER II

The Definition of Religion

1. See Chapter 25 in Henry S. Leonard, *Principles of Right Reason* (New York: Henry Holt, 1957).

2. Friedrich Schleiermacher, *On Religion* (New York: Harper, 1958), pp. 31, 36, 93, 101, 162.

3. Josiah Royce, *The Religious Aspect of Philosophy* (Boston: Houghton, Mifflin, 1885), pp. 3–4.

4. Rudolf Otto, *The Idea of the Holy* (Oxford: Clarendon Press, 1950), pp. 12–24.

5. H. Richard Niebuhr, *Radical Monotheism and Western Culture* (New York: Harper, 1960), p. 16.

6. Durant Drake, *Problems of Religion* (Boston: Houghton Mifflin, 1916), p. 129.

7. William E. Hocking, *The Meaning of God in Human Experience* (New Haven: Yale University Press, 1912), p. 3.

8. *Ibid.*, p. 238.

9. Ludwig Feuerbach, *The Essence of Christianity* (New York: Frederick Ungar Publishing Co., Milestones of Thought Series, 1957), p. 65.

10. Micah 6:8 (American Standard Version).

11. Luke 4:18 (American Standard Version).

12. Matthew 10:7–10 (King James Version).

13. Paul Sabatier, *Life of St. Francis of Assisi* (London: Hodder and Stoughton, 1904), pp. 281–282. See also *The Mirror of Perfection*, Chapter 69 (New York: E. P. Dutton, Everyman's Library, No. 485, 1910).

14. H. Richard Niebuhr, "The Disorder of Man in the Church of God," in *Man's Disorder and God's Design* (New York: Harper, 1948), p. 85.

15. *Ibid.*, "The Witness of the German Church Struggle," p. 99.

16. *Ibid.*, "Rival Secular Faiths," Vol. II, p. 43.

17. *Ibid.*, "The Involvement of the Church," Vol. III, p. 98.

18. *Ibid.*, "The Christian Citizen in a Changing World," Vol. IV, p. 91.

19. *Ibid.*, "Our Responsibility in the Post-War World," Vol. IV, p. 129.

CHAPTER III

Why Do We Have Religion?

1. Niccolo Machiavelli, *The Prince* (New York: Random House, Modern Library, 1940), pp. 41–42.

2. Niccolo Machiavelli, *The Discourses* (New York: Random House, Modern Library, 1940), p. 151.

3. *Ibid.*

4. *Ibid.*, p. 150.

5. Thomas Hobbes, *Leviathan* (Oxford: Clarendon Press, 1909), p. 85.

Notes

6. *Ibid.*, p. 249.

7. *Ibid.*, p. 287.

8. *Ibid.*, p. 362.

9. *Ibid.*, p. 432.

10. R. H. Tawney, *Religion and the Rise of Capitalism* (New York: New American Library, 1950), p. 230.

11. *Ibid.*, p. 20.

12. *Ibid.*, p. 226.

13. *Ibid.*, pp. 234–235. Note also Max Weber, *The Protestant Ethic and the Spirit of Capitalism* (New York: Charles Scribner's Sons, 1958) for a development of the thesis that Protestantism has served the cause of capitalism.

14. Karl Marx, *The Civil War in France* (New York: International Publishers, 1940), p. 57.

15. Karl Marx, *The Eighteenth Brumaire of Louis Bonaparte* (New York: International Publishers, 1940), p. 56.

16. Karl Marx, "The Jewish Question," in *Selected Essays* (New York: International Publishers, 1926), p. 62.

17. Gerald Heard, *Social Substance of Religion* (New York: Harcourt, Brace, 1931), p. 85.

18. *Ibid.*, pp. 90–91.

19. *Ibid.*, pp. 96–97.

20. Sigmund Freud, *The Future of an Illusion* (New York: Doubleday, 1957), pp. 25–26.

21. *Ibid.*, p. 34.

22. *Ibid.*, p. 51.

23. C. J. Jung, *Modern Man in Search of a Soul* (New York: Harcourt, Brace, 1933), p. 259.

24. *Ibid.*, p. 237.

25. Ludwig Feuerbach, *The Essence of Christianity* (New York: Frederick Ungar Publishing Co., Milestones of Thought Series, 1957), p. 11.

26. *Ibid.*

27. George Santayana, *The Life of Reason* (New York: Charles Scribner's Sons, 1954), p. 182.

28. Henri Bergson, *The Two Sources of Morality and Religion* (New York: Doubleday, 1954), p. 122.

29. *Ibid.*, p. 212.

30. George Berkeley, *Alciphron: Or, the Minute Philosopher* (Oxford: Clarendon Press, 1901), Vol. II, p. 151.

31. William E. Hocking, *The Meaning of God in Human Experience* (New Haven: Yale University Press, 1912), p. 20.

32. *Ibid.*, p. 28.

33. *Ibid.*, p. 31.

34. Jung, *op. cit.*, p. 244.

35. See Albert Schweitzer, *The Psychiatric Study of Jesus* (Boston: Beacon Press, 1958).

CHAPTER IV

The Idea of God: to What Does the Term Refer?

1. Margaret Murray, *The God of the Witches* (New York: Doubleday, 1960), p. 13.

2. Clarence A. Beckwith, *The Idea of God* (New York: Macmillan, 1924), pp. 16–17.

3. Margaret Murray, *The God of the Witches* (New York: Doubleday, 1960), Chapter 1.

4. Martin Nilsson, *Greek Folk Religion* (New York: Harper, 1960), pp. 3–21.

5. Franz Cumont, *Oriental Religions in Roman Paganism* (New York: Dover, 1956).

6. Both Arthur Schopenhauer and Friedrich Nietzsche revived European interest in Zoroastrianism. Nietzsche's *Thus Spake Zarathustra* reflected the element of eternal struggle believed to be grounded in the metaphysical nature of things.

7. Cf. Robert H. Pfeiffer, *Introduction to the Old Testament* (New York: Harper, 1941), p. 404; and Harry E. Fosdick, *A Guide to Understanding the Bible* (New York: Harper, 1938), pp. 5, 20, 62.

8. Murray, *op. cit.*, pp. 6–7.

9. David Hume, "The Natural History of Religion," in *Essays Moral, Political, and Literary* (New York: Longmans, Green, 1907), Vol. II, p. 314.

10. Benedict Spinoza, *Philosophy of Benedict de Spinoza* (New York: Tudor, 1936), p. 39.

11. *Ibid.*, p. 53.

12. John Calvin, *On the Christian Faith* (New York: Liberal Arts, 1957), p. 18.

13. Emil Brunner, *Revelation and Reason* (Philadelphia: Westminster, 1956), p. 23.

14. Emil Brunner, *Philosophy of Religion* (New York: Charles Scribner's Sons, 1937), pp. 55–56.

15. Emil Brunner, *The Divine-Human Encounter* (Philadelphia: Westminster, 1943).

16. This seems to have been the motivation behind Nietzsche's comment, "God is dead."

17. Henry N. Wieman, *Normative Psychology of Religion* (New York: Thomas Y. Crowell, 1935), pp. 51, 137.

18. Samuel Alexander, *Space, Time and Deity* (New York: Macmillan, 1920), Vol. II, p. 361.

19. Saint Bonaventura, *The Mind's Road to God* (New York: Liberal Arts, 1953), p. 35.

20. Etienne Gilson, *God and Philosophy* (New Haven: Yale University Press, 1949), pp. 51–52.

21. Paul Tillich, *Systematic Theology* (Chicago: University of Chicago Press, 1951), Vol. I, p. 156.

22. *Ibid.*, p. 205.

23. *Ibid.*, p. 211.

24. G. W. F. Leibniz, *Discourse on Metaphysics, Correspondence with Arnaud, and Monadology* (New York: Open Court, 1902), p. 261.

25. E. S. Brightman, *A Philosophy of Religion* (New York: Prentice-Hall, 1940), pp. 157–161.

26. William James, *A Pluralistic Universe* (New York: Longmans, Green, 1909), p. 311.

27. H. G. Wells, *God the Invisible King* (New York: Macmillan, 1917), pp. 98–99.

28. Jacob Boehme, *Six Theosophic Points* (Ann Arbor: University of Michigan Press, 1958), p. 203.

29. Borden P. Bowne, *Personalism* (Boston: Houghton Mifflin, 1908), p. 319.

30. Henri Bergson, *The Two Sources of Morality and Religion* (New York: Doubleday, 1954), p. 214.

31. William E. Hocking, *The Meaning of God in Human Experience* (New Haven: Yale University Press, 1912), p. 332.

32. Ludwig Feuerbach, *The Essence of Christianity* (New York: Frederick Ungar Publishing Co., Milestones of Thought Series, 1957), p. 33.

33. *Ibid.*, p. 23.

34. Sigmund Freud, *The Future of an Illusion* (New York: Doubleday, 1957), pp. 39–40.

35. Immanuel Kant, *Religion within the Limits of Reason Alone* (New York: Harper, 1960), p. 157.

36. *Ibid.*, p. 158.

C H A P T E R   V

Arguments for the Existence of God

1. Aristotle, *Metaphysics* (London: Oxford University Press, 1942), Book B. 4, 1001, A, p. 20.

2. Cf. Martin Heidegger, *An Introduction to Metaphysics* (New Haven: Yale University Press, 1959), p. 19; and Jacques Maritain, *A Preface to Metaphysics* (London: Sheed and Ward, 1945), p. 44.

3. Saint Anselm, *Proslogium* (New York: Open Court, 1939), Chapter 2.

4. René Descartes, *Meditations and Selections from the Principles of Philosophy* (New York: Open Court, 1950), pp. 215–223.

5. Saint Anselm, *op. cit.*, Appendix, Chapter 1.

6. Benedict Spinoza, *The Ethics* (New York: Tudor, 1936), p. 45.

GOD, MAN, AND THE THINKER

7. *Ibid.*, p. 46.

8. Paul Tillich, *Systematic Theology* (Chicago: University of Chicago Press, 1951), Vol. I, pp. 204–207.

9. Etienne Gilson, *God and Philosophy* (New Haven: Yale University Press, 1941), p. 88.

10. A. S. Eddington, *The Nature of the Physical World* (New York: Macmillan, 1948), p. 72.

11. Peter Bertocci, *The Empirical Arguments for God in Late British Thought* (Cambridge: Harvard University Press, 1938).

12. Immanuel Kant, *The Critique of Pure Reason* (New York: P. F. Collier, 1901), Transcendental Dialectic, Book II, Chapter 3, Section 6, p. 464.

13. Saint Bonaventura, *The Mind's Road to God* (New York: Liberal Arts, 1953), p. 21.

14. George Berkeley, *Alciphron: Or, the Minute Philosopher* (Oxford: Clarendon Press, 1901), Vol. II, p. 160.

15. Kant, *op. cit.*, Section 7.

16. Friedrich Schleiermacher, *On Religion* (New York: Harper, 1958), p. 15.

17. *Ibid.*, p. 99.

18. David Hume, *Dialogues Concerning Natural Religion* (New York: Hafner, 1951), p. 22.

19. *Ibid.*, pp. 34, 48.

20. *Ibid.*, p. 39.

21. *Ibid.*, p. 87.

22. Moses Maimonides, *Guide for the Perplexed* (New York: Dover, 1956), p. 147.

23. *Ibid.*

24. *Ibid.*

25. *Ibid.*, p. 148.

26. *Ibid.*, p. 151.

27. Saint Thomas, *Summa Theologica*, Part I, Question 2, Article 2, Reply to Objection 1.

28. *Ibid.*, Article 3.

29. Job 37–41; Psalms 8, 19, 104.

30. Acts 14:15–17; Acts 17:24–28; Romans 1:30.

31. Cicero, Seneca, Epictetus, Cleanthes, and Marcus Aurelius all discussed the cogency of the appeal from order or design as well as from motion.

32. Edmund Whittaker, *Space and Spirit* (Chicago: Henry Regnery, 1948), p. 46.

33. Immanuel Kant, *op. cit.*, Book II, Chapter 3, Section 5.

34. Cf. Plato, *Laws*, Book X.

35. Immanuel Kant, *The Fundamental Principles of the Metaphysic of Ethics* (New York: Appleton-Century-Crofts, 1938), p. 84.

468

36. George Berkeley, *op. cit.*, p. 155.

37. John Calvin, *On the Christian Faith* (New York: Liberal Arts, 1957), p. 9.

38. *Ibid.*, pp. 7–8.

39. Cornelius Jansen (1585–1638), was a Dutch theologian who held to the view that man was totally corrupted owing to original sin. He denied that man possessed freedom of will and that Christ died for all without exception. Port Royal, a Cistercian convent in Paris, became the center of this sect.

40. Ludwig Feuerbach, *The Essence of Christianity* (New York: Frederick Ungar Publishing Co., Milestones of Thought Series, 1957), Chapter 13.

41. *Ibid.*, pp. 54–55.

42. Thomas H. Huxley, *Science and the Christian Tradition* (New York: D. Appleton, 1896), p. 245.

43. Chapman Cohen, *A Grammar of Free Thought* (London: The Pioneer Press, 1921), p. 101.

44. Charles F. Potter, *Humanism* (New York: Simon and Schuster, 1930), pp. 46–48.

45. *The New Humanist*, February, 1929.

46. Potter, *op. cit.*, p. 50.

47. Cohen, *op. cit.*, p. 11.

48. Jean Meslier, *Superstition in All Ages* (New York: The Truth Seeker Company, 1950), pp. 242–243.

49. *Ibid.*, pp. 58–110; and Woolsey Teller, *Essays of an Atheist* (New York: The Truth Seeker Company, 1945), p. 300.

50. Teller, *op. cit.*, Chapter IV.

51. Potter, *op. cit.*, p. 58.

C H A P T E R   V I
The Problems of Religious Knowledge

1. William James, *Essays in Pragmatism* (New York: Hafner, 1948), p. 147.

2. *Ibid.*, p. 154.

3. Immanuel Kant, *The Critique of Pure Reason* (New York: P. F. Collier, 1901), p. 474.

4. Saint Bonaventura, *The Mind's Road to God* (New York: Liberal Arts, 1953), pp. 20, 21, 28.

5. *Ibid.*, pp. 23–24.

C H A P T E R   V I I
The Problem of Natural Evil

1. David Hume, *Dialogues Concerning Natural Religion* (New York: Hafner, 1951), p. 66.

2. John B. Noss, *Man's Religions* (New York: Macmillan, 1956), p. 118.

3. John Stuart Mill, *Nature* (Eugene: University of Oregon Philosophy Reprints, No. 1), p. 13.

4. *Ibid.*, p. 13.

5. Moses Maimonides, *The Guide for the Perplexed* (New York: Dover Publications, 1956), p. 270.

6. John Laird, *Mind and Deity* (New York: Philosophical Library, 1941).

7. Niccolo Machiavelli, *Discourses* (New York: Random House, Modern Library, 1940), p. 108.

8. G. W. F. Hegel, *Lectures on the Philosophy of History* (London: George Bell & Sons, 1894), pp. 411 ff.

9. Laird, *op. cit.*, p. 178.

10. Maimonides, *op. cit.*, p. 269.

11. Josiah Royce, *The Religious Aspect of Philosophy* (Boston: Houghton Mifflin, 1885), p. 457.

12. F. R. Tennant, *Philosophical Theology* (Cambridge: Cambridge University Press, 1928), Vol. II, p. 198.

13. William James, *Talks to Teachers on Psychology: and to Students on Some of Life's Ideals* (New York: Henry Holt, 1902), p. 270.

14. John Calvin, *On the Christian Faith* (New York: Liberal Arts Press, 1957), pp. 72–77.

15. Jacob Boehme, *Six Theosophic Points* (Ann Arbor: University of Michigan Press, 1958), p. 167.

16. Saint Augustine, *The Confessions*, Book VII, Chapter 5.

17. *Ibid.*, Book VII, Chapter 13.

18. Maimonides, *op. cit.*, p. 266.

19. G. W. Leibniz, *Discourse on Metaphysics, Correspondence with Arnauld, Monadology* (La Salle, Illinois: Open Court, 1902), pp. 5, 10, 271.

20. John M. E. McTaggart, *Some Dogmas of Religion* (London: Edward Arnold, 1906), p. 278.

21. *Ibid.*

22. William James, *Essays in Pragmatism* (New York: Hafner, 1948), pp. 16–17.

23. Job 13:15.

24. Josiah Royce, *The Religious Aspect of Philosophy* (Boston: Houghton Mifflin, 1885), p. 451.

25. Saint Augustine, "The Enchiridion," in *A Select Library of the Nicene and Post-Nicene Fathers of the Christian Church* (New York: The Christian Literature Company, 1887), Chapter 14.

26. Rabindranath Tagore, "The Problem of Evil," *The Hibbert Journal*, Vol. II (1913), p. 705.

27. *The Sacred Books and Early Literature of the East* (New York:

Notes

Parke, Austin, and Lipscomb, 1917), Vol. I, "Babylonia and Assyria," p. 218.

28. Benedict Spinoza, *Ethics* (New York: Tudor, 1936), p. 74.

29. *Ibid.*, p. 75.

30. *Ibid.*, p. 73.

31. Maimonides, *op. cit.*, p. 279.

32. John Stuart Mill, *Nature* (Eugene: University of Oregon Philosophy Reprints, No. 1), p. 16.

33. *The Little Flowers* (New York: E. P. Dutton, 1938), pp. 10 ff.

34. John M. E. McTaggart, *Some Dogmas of Religion* (London: Edward Arnold, 1906), p. 219.

C H A P T E R   V I I I

The Problem of Immortality

1. Miguel de Unamuno, *The Tragic Sense of Life* (New York: Macmillan, 1926).

2. A. Seth Pringle-Pattison, *The Idea of Immortality* (Oxford: Clarendon Press, 1922), p. 486.

3. Immanuel Kant, *Religion within the Limits of Reason Alone* (New York: Harper, 1960), p. 117.

4. *Philosophy of Benedict de Spinoza,* translated by R. H. M. Elwes (New York: Tudor, 1936), p. 237.

5. S. Radhakrishnan, *Indian Philosophy,* Vol. 1 (London: George Allen & Unwin, 1929), p. 140.

6. Chand. 5.10.7. in *The Thirteen Principal Upanishads* (Oxford: Clarendon Press, 1934), p. 233.

7. S. Radhakrishnan, *op. cit.*, p. 244.

8. John Donne, "Devotions: Meditation, XVII," in *Tudor Poetry and Prose* (New York: Appleton-Century-Crofts, 1953), p. 1176.

9. Leo Tolstoy, *My Religion* (New York: Thomas Y. Crowell, 1885), p. 151.

10. A. Seth Pringle-Pattison, *The Idea of God* (Oxford: Clarendon Press, 1920), pp. 348–349.

11. A. Seth Pringle-Pattison, *The Idea of Immortality* (Oxford: Clarendon Press, 1922), p. 147.

12. Josiah Royce, *The Religious Aspect of Philosophy* (Boston: Houghton Mifflin, 1885), p. 478.

13. George Santayana, *Reason in Religion* (New York: Charles Scribner's Sons, 1905).

14. *Ibid.*, p. 518.

15. Sigmund Freud, *The Future of an Illusion* (New York: Doubleday, 1957), pp. 143, 151–156.

16. August Weismann, *Essays upon Heredity* (Oxford: Clarendon Press, 1892), Vol. II, p. 79.

17. Fred Hoyle, *The Nature of the Universe* (New York: Harper, 1950), p. 139.

18. C. D. Broad, *The Mind and Its Place in Nature* (New York: Humanities Press, 1951), p. 525.

19. Ashley Montagu, *Immortality* (New York: Grove Press, 1955), p. 27.

20. *Berkeley's Complete Works* (Oxford: Clarendon Press, 1901), Vol. II, p. 128.

21. William James, "The Will to Believe," in *Essays in Pragmatism* (New York: Hafner, 1958), pp. 106–109, and particularly the footnote on p. 108.

22. F. H. Bradley, *Ethical Studies* (Oxford: Clarendon Press, 1927), p. 280.

23. William E. Hocking, *The Meaning of Immortality in Human Experience* (New York: Harper, 1957), Part 3, Chapter V.

24. *Ibid.*, p. 139.

25. *Ibid.*, p. 206.

26. *Ibid.*

27. William James, *Human Immortality* (Boston: Houghton Mifflin, 1899), p. 3.

28. Saint Augustine, *On the Immortality of the Soul* (New York: Appleton-Century-Crofts, 1938), Chapters I and II.

29. A. E. Taylor, *The Christian Hope of Immortality* (New York: Macmillan, 1947), pp. 19–20.

30. C. D. Broad, *The Mind and Its Place in Nature* (New York: Humanities Press, 1951), p. 515.

31. F. H. Bradley, *Essays on Truth and Reality* (Oxford: Clarendon Press, 1914), p. 440.

32. Rudolf Hermann Lotze, *Microcosmus* (New York: Scribner and Welford, 1890), Vol. II, p. 390.

33. C. D. Broad, *The Mind and Its Place in Nature* (New York: Humanities Press, 1951), p. 515.

34. Abraham Edel, "Context and Content in the Theory of Ideas," in Roy Wood Sellars, V. J. McGill, and Marvin Farber (editors), *Philosophy for the Future* (New York: Macmillan, 1949), p. 444.

35. Cited in Ashley Montagu, *Immortality* (New York: Grove Press, 1955), p. 23.

C H A P T E R I X

Is Religion a Matter of Knowledge?

1. Saint Augustine, *Concerning the Teacher* and *On the Immortality of the Soul* (New York: Appleton-Century-Crofts, 1938), pp. 59–61.

2. Saint Anselm, *Proslogium* (New York: Open Court, 1944), p. 7.

3. Frederick Copleston, *A History of Philosophy* (Westminster, Md.: Newman Press, 1955), Vol. II, p. 303.

4. For detailed investigation of the philosophy of Saint Thomas two recent books by Roman Catholic thinkers deserve mention: Etienne Gilson, *The Philosophy of Saint Thomas Aquinas* (London: B. Herder, 1937); Jacques Maritain, *St. Thomas Aquinas* (London: Sheed and Ward, 1945).

5. Saint Thomas, *Summa Theologica*, Vol. II, Chap. II, Question 2, Article 4.

6. *Ibid.*, Article 10, Reply 2.

7. A. J. Ayer, *Language, Truth and Logic* (New York: Dover Publications, 1950), p. 13.

8. Soren Kierkegaard, *The Sickness unto Death* (Princeton, N. J.: Princeton University Press, 1941), p. 166.

9. *Ibid.*, p. 167.

10. Soren Kierkegaard, *Fear and Trembling* (New York: Doubleday, 1954), p. 45.

11. Soren Kierkegaard, *Concluding Unscientific Postscript* (Princeton, New Jersey: Princeton University Press, 1941), p. 55.

12. *Ibid.*, p. 26.

13. *Ibid.*, p. 31.

14. *Ibid.*, p. 115.

15. Karl Jaspers, *Reason and Existenz* (New York: Noonday Press, 1957), pp. 110–111.

16. Paul Tillich, *Systematic Theology* (Chicago: University of Chicago Press, 1959), Vol. I, p. 12.

17. Paul Tillich, *The Dynamics of Faith* (New York: Harper, 1958), p. 31.

18. *Ibid.*, p. 35.

19. *Ibid.*, p. 38.

20. *Ibid.*, pp. 42–43.

21. Paul Tillich, *The Protestant Era* (Chicago: University of Chicago, 1957), pp. 95–96.

22. Karl Jaspers and Rudolf Bultmann, *Myth and Christianity* (New York: Noonday Press, 1958).

23. Sigmund Freud, *The Future of an Illusion* (New York: Doubleday, 1957), pp. 43–53.

24. Friedrich Paulsen, *Immanuel Kant, His Life and Doctrine* (New York: Charles Scribner's Sons, 1902), p. 7.

25. Immanuel Kant, *Religion within the Limits of Reason Alone* (New York: Harper, 1960), p. 3.

26. *Ibid.*, p. 5.

27. *Ibid.*, p. 130.

28. *Ibid.*, p. 142.

29. *Ibid.*, p. 156.

30. *Ibid.*, p. 102.

31. *Ibid.*, p. 100.
32. *Ibid.*, p. 43.
33. *Ibid.*, p. 16.
34. *Ibid.*, p. 35.
35. *Ibid.*, p. 162.
36. *Ibid.*, p. 167.

C H A P T E R   X
The Problem of Inerrant Scripture

1. See, for example, the discussion in this vein given in L. W. Munhall, *Anti-Higher Criticism* (New York: Hunt and Eaton, 1894), p. 332.

2. Daniel J. Saunders, *Reason to Revelation* (London: B. Herder, 1949), Chapter VII.

3. Swami Prabhavananda and Frederick Manchester, *The Upanishads* (New York: New American Library, 1957), p. x.

4. Swami Prabhavananda and Christopher Isherwood, *Bhagavad-Gita* (New York: New American Library, 1954), p. 26.

5. E. A. Burtt (ed.), *The Teachings of the Compassionate Buddha* (New York: New American Library, 1955), p. 24.

6. Alan Watts, *The Way of Zen* (New York: The New American Library, 1959), p. 55.

7. William F. Albright, *Archaeology and the Religion of Israel* (Baltimore: Johns Hopkins Press, 1941), p. 176.

8. Note the discussion of this in Immanuel Kant, *Religion within the Limits of Reason Alone* (New York: Harper, 1960), pp. 151–155.

9. For a careful analysis of one of the more popular theories as to the compilation of the early part of the Old Testament see Robert H. Pfeiffer, *Introduction to the Old Testament* (New York: Harper, 1941), Part II, Chapters 1–6.

10. Note references to the Apocalypse of Elijah in I Corinthians 2:9 and Ephesians 5:14; to Ecclesiasticus 5:11 in James 1:19; to II Maccabees 6–7 in Hebrews 11:35; to the Assumption of Moses in Jude 5:9; and to the book of Jannes and Jambres in II Timothy 3:8.

11. Julius Bewer, *The Literature of the Old Testament* (New York: Columbia University Press, 1940), p. 429.

12. *Ibid.*, p. 429.

13. Charles F. Horne, *The Great Rejected Books of the Biblical Apocrypha* (New York: Parke, Austin, and Lipscomb, 1917), pp. 1–6.

14. The view of cabalism persists in both Jewish and Christian circles. An extreme expression of this numerological interpretation of scripture may be seen in E. W. Bullinger, *Number in Scripture* (London: Eyre and Spottiswoode, 1913). Cf. also Abba Hillel Silver, *A History of Messianic Speculation in Israel* (Boston: Beacon Press, 1959).

15. For a discussion of this canonization process the following books may be consulted: Ernest F. Scott, *The Literature of the New Testament* (New York: Columbia University Press, 1932); and H. F. Sparks, *The Formation of the New Testament* (London: SCM Press Limited, 1952).

16. Saint Augustine, *On Christian Doctrine* (New York: Library of Liberal Arts, 1958), p. 7.

17. *Ibid.*, p. 31. Note, however, that a man who already has an unshaken faith, hope, and charity does not need the scriptures save for the instruction of others.

18. *Ibid.*, pp. 27, 98.

19. *Ibid.*, p. 41.

20. *Ibid.*, p. 49. Note that Augustine believed the world to have been made from nothing as Genesis seemed to assert. This view was alien to the Greeks and to pantheist Christians, such as Spinoza.

21. Saint Augustine, *The City of God* (New York: Random House, 1950), p. 350: "Time does not exist without some movement and transition, while in eternity there is no change."

22. John Calvin, *Commentaries* (Philadelphia: Westminster Press, 1958), Vol. XXIII, pp. 84–85.

23. Kant, *op. cit.*, p. 103.

24. Alfred Loisy, *The Origins of the New Testament* (London: George Allen and Unwin, 1950).

25. *Ibid.*, p. 10.

26. *Ibid.*

27. See Abba Hillel Silver, *A History of Messianic Speculation in Israel* (Boston: Beacon Press, 1959), for a studied account of the consequences of two millennia of errant predictions.

28. Note, for example, the remark of Friedrich Gogarten, *Demythologizing and History* (New York: Charles Scribner's Sons, 1955), p. 12: ". . . what the Bible says is said by men and does not derive its authority from the fact that it is written in the Bible. It is rather the Bible which derives its authority simply and solely from what is said in it."

C H A P T E R   X I

The Problem of Fixed or Evolving Religions

1. Immanuel Kant, in *Religion within the Limits of Reason Alone* (New York: Harper, 1960), p. 122, asserted: "If now one asks, What period in the entire known history of the church up to now is the best? I have no scruple in answering, *The present.*"

2. *Ibid.*, p. 115.

3. Robert H. Pfeiffer, *Introduction to the Old Testament* (New York: Harper, 1941), p. 27.

4. James G. Frazer, *Folk-Lore in the Old Testament* (London: Macmillan, 1919), Vol. I, p. vii.

5. William F. Albright, *Archaeology and the Religion of Israel* (Baltimore: Johns Hopkins Press, 1953), p. 177.

6. Harry E. Fosdick, *A Guide to Understanding the Bible* (New York: Harper, 1938).

7. The celebration of Channuka commemorates the temple-cleansing ceremony which followed the victory of Judas Maccabaeus over Antiochus Epiphanes.

8. For an objective and open account of these documents see Millar Burrows, *The Dead Sea Scrolls* (New York: Viking Press, 1956).

9. Martin Buber, *Moses: The Revelation and the Covenant* (New York: Harper, 1958), p. 17.

10. *Ibid.*, p. 8.

11. *Ibid.*, p. 98.

12. Abba Hillel Silver, in *A History of Messianic Speculation in Israel* (Boston: Beacon Press, 1959), p. ix, observed: "Three factors contributed to the spread of the Messianic belief in Israel: the loss of national independence and the attendant deprivations, the will to live dominantly and triumphantly as a rehabilitated people in its national home, and the unfaltering faith in divine justice by whose eternal canons the national restoration was infallibly prescribed."

13. H. F. D. Sparks, *The Formation of the New Testament* (London: SCM Press, Ltd., 1952), p. 22.

14. Franz Cumont, *The Mysteries of Mithra* (New York: Dover Press, 1956) and *Oriental Religions in Roman Paganism* (New York: Dover Press, 1956).

15. Frederick C. Grant, *Early Christianity* (Greenwich, Conn.: The Seabury Press, 1954), p. 146.

16. Louise Ropes Loomis, *The Book of the Popes* (New York: Columbia University Press, 1916), Volume I, p. x.

17. James Martineau, *The Rationale of Religious Enquiry* (London: E. T. Whitfield, 1853, Fourth Edition), p. 100.

18. *Ibid.*

19. Adolf Harnack, *Outlines of the History of Dogma* (Boston: Beacon Press, 1957), p. 5.

20. *Ibid.*, p. 7.

21. Paul Tillich, *Systematic Theology* (Chicago: University of Chicago Press, 1951), Vol. I, p. 48.

C H A P T E R   X I I

The Problem of Fundamentalism

1. See John Calvin, *On God and Political Duty* (New York: Library of Liberal Arts, 1956).

Notes

2. John Calvin, *Institutes of the Christian Religion*, Vol. II, Book III, Chap. 21, pp. 176 ff.; and Vol. II, Book III, Chap. 24, pp. 217–226.

3. John Calvin, *The Christian Faith* (New York: Liberal Arts Press, 1957), pp. 94–95.

4. See Norman F. Furniss, *The Fundamentalist Controversy, 1918–1931* (New Haven: Yale University Press, 1954), Chapters I–V; and Henry F. Osborn, *Evolution and Religion in Education* (New York: Charles Scribner's Sons, 1926).

C H A P T E R   X I I I
The Problem of Modernism

1. Shailer Matthews, *The Faith of Modernism* (New York: Macmillan, 1924), pp. 180–181.

2. See especially T. W. Doane, *Bible Myths and Their Parallels in Other Religions* (New York: Charles P. Somerby, 1882); and James G. Frazer, *Folk-Lore in the Old Testament* (New York: Macmillan, 1919).

3. Robert H. Pfeiffer, *Introduction to the Old Testament* (New York: Harper, 1941), Chapter 4.

4. David C. Torrey, *Protestant Modernism* (New York: G. P. Putnam's Sons, 1910).

5. Adam J. Loeppert, *Modernism and the Vatican* (New York: Eaton and Mains, 1912), p. 147.

6. Anne Freemantle (ed.), *The Papal Encyclicals* (New York: New American Library, 1956), pp. 202–207.

7. Albert Schweitzer, *The Psychiatric Study of Jesus* (Boston: Beacon Press, 1948), pp. 45, 54.

8. Alfred Loisy, *The Origins of the New Testament* (London: George Allen and Unwin, 1950), pp. 39 ff.

9. Reinhold Niebuhr, *An Interpretation of Christian Ethics* (New York: Meridian, 1956), pp. 58 ff.

10. Galatians, I and II Corinthians, and Romans.

11. For a critical analysis of opposing views of the New Testament myths see Thomas J. Thorburn, *The Mythical Interpretation of the Gospels* (New York: Charles Scribner's Sons, 1916).

12. John Knox, *Criticism and Faith* (Nashville: Abingdon-Cokesbury Press, 1952), p. 47. See also E. P. Booth (ed.), *New Testament Studies* (Nashville: Abingdon-Cokesbury Press, 1942), pp. 115–138.

13. Friedrich Gogarten, *Demythologizing and History* (New York: Charles Scribner's Sons, 1955).

14. Cf. Rudolf Bultmann and Karl Jaspers, *Myth and Christianity* (New York: Noonday Press, 1958).

15. *Ibid.*, p. 89.

16. *Ibid.*, p. 29.

17. Cf. Nicholas Berdyaev, *Freedom and the Spirit* (New York: Charles Scribner's Sons, 1935), pp. 70–71, for support for mythical language over factual language.

18. F. D. Gealy, "The 'Ipsissima Verba' or the 'Ipsissimus Spiritus,'" in E. P. Booth (ed.), *New Testament Studies* (Nashville: Abingdon-Cokesbury Press, 1942).

19. F. V. Filson, "Form Criticism," in Thomas Kepler (ed.), *Contemporary Thinking about Jesus* (Nashville: Abingdon-Cokesbury Press, 1944); and T. S. Kepler, "The Jesus of 'Formgeschichte,'" in E. P. Booth (ed.), *New Testament Studies* (Nashville: Abingdon-Cokesbury Press, 1942).

20. Cf. David Strauss, *Life of Jesus* (New York: C. Blanchard, 1860).

CHAPTER XIV

The Problem of Humanism

1. Edward Conze (ed.), *Buddhist Texts through the Ages* (New York: Philosophical Library, 1954), pp. 295–296.

2. *Sacred Books of the East*, Vol. XXII (Oxford: Clarendon Press, 1884), p. 33.

3. Paul Sabatier, *The Life of Saint Francis of Assisi* (London: Hodder and Stoughton, 1894), p. 85.

4. David Hume, "The Natural History of Religion" in *Essays Moral, Political and Literary*, Vol. II (New York: Longmans, Green, 1907).

5. *Ibid.*, pp. 281–283.

6. Charles F. Potter, *Humanism a New Religion* (New York: Simon and Schuster, 1930), p. 139. For a similar position see also Corliss Lamont, *Humanism as a Philosophy* (New York: Philosophical Library, 1949).

7. Jacques Maritain, *True Humanism* (London: Centenary Press, 1941).

8. This may be observed in a lively exchange of letters between Arnold Tunn, who defended conventional Christian beliefs, and C. E. M. Joad, who attacked them. *Is Christianity True?* (Philadelphia: J. B. Lippincott, 1933).

9. "A Humanist Manifesto," in *The New Humanist*, Vol. VI, No. 3.

10. See Albert Schweitzer, *The Psychiatric Study of Jesus* (Boston: Beacon Press, 1958).

CHAPTER XV

Psychology and Religion

1. William James, *The Varieties of Religious Experience* (New York: The New American Library, 1960), p. 25.

Notes

2. *Ibid.*, p. 29.

3. *Ibid.*, p. 42.

4. *Ibid.*, p. 208.

5. *Ibid.*, p. 155.

6. *Ibid.*, p. 168.

7. *Ibid.*, p. 350.

8. *Ibid.*, p. 329.

9. Gordon W. Allport, *The Individual and His Religion* (New York: Macmillan, 1951).

10. *Ibid.*, p. 82.

11. The pertinent books by Freud on the subject of religion are: *Totem and Taboo, The Future of an Illusion,* and *Moses and Monotheism.*

12. Sigmund Freud, *Moses and Monotheism* (New York: Vintage, 1958), pp. 66–71.

13. Sigmund Freud, *The Future of an Illusion* (New York: Doubleday, 1957), p. 51.

14. *Ibid.*, p. 78.

15. *Ibid.*, p. 40.

16. Freud, *Moses and Monotheism,* p. 93.

17. *Ibid.*

18. Patrick Mullahy, *Oedipus: Myth and Complex* (New York: Grove Press, 1955), p. 101.

19. Freud, *Moses and Monotheism,* p. 156.

20. *Ibid.*, p. 127.

21. *Ibid.*, p. 78.

22. Freud, *The Future of an Illusion,* p. 57.

23. *Ibid.*, p. 86.

24. Freud, *Moses and Monotheism,* p. 157.

25. Carl G. Jung, *Modern Man in Search of a Soul* (New York: Harcourt, Brace, 1933), p. 140.

26. *Ibid.*, p. 259.

27. *Ibid.*, p. 265.

28. Carl G. Jung, *Answer to Job* (New York: Meridian, 1960), p. 55.

29. *Ibid.*, p. 191.

30. *Ibid.*, p. 77.

31. *Ibid.*, p. 145.

32. *Ibid.*, pp. 112–113.

33. Richard L. Walker, *China under Communism* (New Haven: Yale University Press, 1955), p. 70.

34. William Sargant, *Battle for the Mind* (New York: Doubleday, 1957), p. 23.

35. Mark 5:1–17.

36. O. Hobart Mowrer, *The Crisis in Psychiatry and Religion* (Princeton: Van Nostrand, 1961).

37. Wilhelm Stekel, *Technique of Analytical Psychotherapy* (New York: Liveright, 1950).

38. Anton T. Boisen, *The Exploration of the Inner World* (New York: Harper, 1936).

39. *Ibid.*, p. 268.

40. Mowrer, *op. cit.*, p. 40.

41. *Ibid.*, pp. 44–45.

42. *Ibid.*, Chapters 5 and 8.

43. Erich Fromm, *Psychoanalysis and Religion* (New Haven: Yale University Press, 1950).

44. Paul Tillich, *Systematic Theology* (Chicago: University of Chicago Press, 1951), Volume I, p. 18.

45. Rollo May (ed.), *Existence* (New York: Basic Books, 1958).

46. Paul Tillich, *Dynamics of Faith* (New York: Harper, 1958), p. 6.

C H A P T E R   X V I

The Church and the State

1. Cf. Ernest Barker, *The Political Thought of Plato and Aristotle* (New York: Dover, 1959).

2. Aristotle, *Politics* (New York: Random House, 1943), p. 298.

3. Dino Bigongiari (ed.), *The Political Ideas of St. Thomas Aquinas* (New York: Hafner, 1960), p. xxxvi.

4. Jean Jacques Rousseau, *Social Contract* (New York: Hafner, 1947), p. 117.

5. *Ibid.*, p. 118.

6. *Ibid.*, p. 119.

7. *Ibid.*, p. 121.

8. *Ibid.*, p. 120.

9. *Ibid.*

10. *Ibid.*, p. 122.

11. Protestants and Other Americans United.

12. Cf. R. A. Houk (ed.), *Hooker's Ecclesiastical Polity* (New York: Columbia University Press, 1931), Book VIII,

13. Ernest Barker, *Church, State, and Education* (Ann Arbor: University of Michigan Press, 1957), p. 117.

14. *Ibid.*, p. 122. Cf. also Evarts B. Greene, *Religion and the State: The Making and Testing of an American Tradition* (New York: New York University Press, 1941).

15. Conrad H. Moehlman, *The Catholic-Protestant Mind* (New York: Harper, 1929), p. 66.

16. L. W. Bacon, *An Inside View of the Vatican Council* (New York: American Tract Society, 1871), p. 228.

17. Robert A. Graham, S.J., *Vatican Diplomacy* (Princeton: Princeton University Press, 1959), p. 12.

18. Moehlman, *op. cit.*, p. 129.

19. *Ibid.*, p. 278.

20. Cf. Paul Blanshard, *American Freedom and Catholic Power* (Boston: Beacon Press, 1958).

21. Cf. G. J. Heering, *The Fall of Christianity* (New York: Fellowship Publications, 1943).

22. Christopher Dawson, *Beyond Politics* (New York: Sheed and Ward, 1939), p. 21.

23. For specific data on the problems of church-state relations see Howard K. Beale, *Are American Teachers Free?* (New York: Charles Scribner's Sons, 1936); and the three-volume work by Anson Phelps Stokes, *Church and State in the United States* (New York: Harper, 1950).

24. Stokes, *op. cit.*, Vol. II, p. 720.

25. *Ibid.*, p. 706.

26. *Ibid.*, pp. 707–708.

27. *Ibid.*, p. 673.

28. This arrangement has been effective in conjunction with the University of Missouri, the University of Iowa, the University of Texas, and Montana State University.

29. This has been done at the University of Virginia, the University of Oregon, Oregon State College, North Carolina State College, Miami University, and the University of Connecticut.

30. Such a program has been operative at the University of Tennessee, Montana State College, and the University of Alabama.

31. States leading in this program were Utah, New York, Minnesota, North Carolina, Rhode Island, and Oregon. Five states have not had any program at all—Maryland, New Hampshire, Wyoming, Alaska—and neither has the District of Columbia.

32. Immanuel Kant, *Religion within the Limits of Reason Alone* (New York: Harper, 1960), p. 124.

CHAPTER XVII

Religion and Science

1. A. D. White, *A History of the Warfare of Science with Theology* (New York: D. Appleton, 1903), Volumes I and II.

2. James J. Walsh, *The Popes and Science* (New York: Fordham University Press, 1911).

3. Emil Brunner, "And Now?" in *Man's Disorder and God's Design* (New York: Harper, 1948), Volume III, p. 180.

4. Henry N. Wieman, *Religious Experience and Scientific Method* (New York: Macmillan, 1926), Chapter I.

5. *Ibid.*, p. 381.

6. Arthur S. Eddington, *Science and the Unseen World* (New York: Macmillan, 1929), p. 73.

7. J. Arthur Thomson, *Science and Religion* (New York: Charles Scribner's Sons, 1929), p. 144.

8. Immanuel Velikovsky, *Worlds in Collision* (New York: Doubleday, 1950).

9. H. P. Blavatsky, *The Secret Doctrine* (Los Angeles: The Theosophy Company, 1925).

10. William Kingsland, *The Gnosis or Ancient Wisdom in the Christian Scriptures* (London: George Allen and Unwin, 1937).

11. Paul Tillich, *Systematic Theology* (Chicago: University of Chicago Press, 1951), Volume I, and *Dynamics of Faith* (New York: Harper, 1958).

12. Paul Tillich, *Dynamics of Faith* (New York: Harper, 1957), Chapter V.

Bibliography

C H A P T E R   I

What Is Philosophy of Religion?

Archer, J. C., *Faiths Men Live By* (New York: Ronald Press, 1958), Chapter 1.

Bertocci, Peter, *Introduction to the Philosophy of Religion* (New York: Prentice-Hall, 1951), Chapter 2.

Brightman, E. S., *A Philosophy of Religion* (New York: Prentice-Hall, 1940), Chapters 1 and 2.

Ducasse, C. J., *A Philosophical Scrutiny of Religion* (New York: Ronald Press, 1953), Chapter 1.

Garnett, A. C., *A Realistic Philosophy of Religion* (New York: Harper, 1942), Chapter 1.

MacGregor, Geddes, *Introduction to Religious Philosophy* (Boston: Houghton Mifflin, 1959), Chapter 2.

Patterson, R. L., *An Introduction to the Philosophy of Religion* (New York: Henry Holt, 1958), Chapter 3.

C H A P T E R   I I

The Definition of Religion

Brightman, E. S., *A Philosophy of Religion* (New York: Prentice-Hall, 1940), Chapter 1.

Drake, Durant, *The Problems of Religion* (Boston: Houghton Mifflin, 1916), Summaries of Parts I and II.

Feuerbach, Ludwig, *The Essence of Christianity* (New York: Frederick Ungar Publishing Co., Milestones of Thought Series, 1957).

Hocking, W. E., *The Meaning of God in Human Experience* (New Haven: Yale University Press, 1912), Chapters 1, 5, 6, 30, 31.

Kaufmann, Walter, *Critique of Religion and Philosophy* (New York: Harper, 1958), Chapter 4.

Man's Disorder and God's Design (New York: Harper, 1948). Reprints of speeches given at the World Council of Churches meetings at Amsterdam, 1948.

Niebuhr, H. R., *Radical Monotheism and Western Culture* (New York: Harper, 1960).

Otto, Rudolf, *The Idea of the Holy* (New York: Oxford University Press, 1950).

Royce, Josiah, *The Religious Aspect of Philosophy* (Boston: Houghton Mifflin, 1885), Chapters 1 and 12.

Schleiermacher, Friedrich, *On Religion* (New York: Harper, 1958), second speech on "The Nature of Religion."

C H A P T E R   I I I

Why Do We Have Religion?

Bergson, Henri, *The Two Sources of Morality and Religion* (New York: Doubleday, Anchor Books, 1954).

Berkeley, George, *Alciphron; Or, The Minute Philosopher* (Oxford: The Clarendon Press, 1901), Vol. II.

Calverton, V. F., *The Passing of the Gods* (New York: Charles Scribner's Sons, 1934).

Durkheim, Emile, *The Elementary Forms of the Religious Life* (London: George Allen and Unwin, 1915).

Feuerbach, Ludwig, *The Essence of Christianity* (New York: Frederick Ungar Publishing Co., Milestones of Thought Series, 1957).

Freud, Sigmund, *The Future of an Illusion* (New York: Doubleday, Anchor Books, 1957).

Heard, Gerald, *Social Substance of Religion* (New York: Harcourt, Brace, 1931).

Hobbes, Thomas, *Leviathan* (Oxford: The Clarendon Press, 1909).

Bibliography

Hocking, William E., *The Meaning of God in Human Experience* (New Haven: Yale University Press, 1912).

Jung, Carl H., *Modern Man in Search of a Soul* (New York: Harcourt, Brace, 1933).

Machiavelli, Niccolo, *The Prince and The Discourses* (New York: Random House, Modern Library, 1940).

Marx, Karl, *The Civil War In France* (New York: International Publishers, 1940).

———, *The Eighteenth Brumaire of Louis Bonaparte* (New York: International Publishers, 1940).

Otto, Rudolf, *The Idea of the Holy* (Oxford: Clarendon Press, 1926).

Santayana, George, *The Life of Reason: Reason in Science* (New York: Charles Scribner's Sons, 1906).

Schweitzer, Albert, *The Psychiatric Study of Jesus* (Boston: Beacon Press, 1958).

Tawney, Richard H., *Religion and the Rise of Capitalism* (New York: Penguin Books, 1950).

Wach, Joachim, *The Comparative Study of Religions* (New York: Columbia University Press, 1958).

Weber, Max, *The Protestant Ethic and the Spirit of Capitalism* (New York: Charles Scribner's Sons, 1958).

C H A P T E R   I V

The Idea of God: What Does the Term Mean?

Beckwith, Clarence A., *The Idea of God* (New York: Macmillan, 1924), Chapters 2 and 3.

Otto, Rudolf, *The Idea of the Holy* (New York: Oxford University Press, 1958), pp. 25–30, 179–185.

Tillich, Paul, *Systematic Theology* (Chicago: University of Chicago Press, 1951), Vol. I, pp. 221–289.

C H A P T E R   V

The Problem of the Existence of God

Saint Anselm, *Proslogium* (La Salle, Illinois: Open Court, 1939).

Aristotle, *Metaphysics* (Oxford: The Clarendon Press, 1942).

Berkeley, George, *Alciphron; Or, The Minute Philosopher* (Oxford: The Clarendon Press, 1901), Vol. II.

Bertocci, Peter, *The Empirical Arguments for God in Late British Thought* (Cambridge: Harvard University Press, 1938).

Bibliography

Saint Bonaventura, *The Mind's Road to God* (New York: Liberal Arts, 1953).

Calvin, John, *On the Christian Faith* (New York: Liberal Arts, 1957).

Descartes, René, *Meditations and Selections from the Principles of Philosophy* (La Salle, Illinois: Open Court, 1950).

Eddington, A. S., *The Nature of the Physical World* (New York: Macmillan, 1948).

Feuerbach, Ludwig, *The Essence of Christianity* (New York: Frederick Ungar Publishing Co., Milestones of Thought Series, 1957).

Gilson, Etienne, *God and Philosophy* (New Haven: Yale University Press, 1941).

Heidegger, Martin, *An Introduction to Metaphysics* (New Haven: Yale University Press, 1959).

Hume, David, *Dialogues Concerning Natural Religion* (New York: Hafner, 1951).

Huxley, Thomas, *Science and Christian Tradition* (New York: Appleton-Century-Crofts, 1896).

Kant, Immanuel, *The Critique of Pure Reason* (New York: P. F. Collier, 1901), Transcendental Dialectic, Book II.

Maimonides, Moses, *Guide for the Perplexed* (New York: Dover, 1956).

Plato, *Laws*, Book X.

Schleiermacher, Friedrich, *On Religion* (New York: Harper, 1958).

Spinoza, Benedict, *The Ethics* (New York: Tudor, 1936).

Saint Thomas, *Summa Theologica*, Part I.

Tillich, Paul, *Systematic Theology* (Chicago: University of Chicago Press, 1951), Vol. I.

Whittaker, Edmund, *Space and Spirit* (Chicago: Henry Regnery, 1948).

C H A P T E R   V I

The Problems of Religious Knowledge

Ayer, A. J., *Language, Truth and Logic* (New York: Dover, 1950), Chapter 6.

Feuerbach, Ludwig, *The Essence of Christianity* (New York: Frederick Ungar Publishing Co., Milestones of Thought Series, 1957), Chapters 2 and 3.

James, William, *Essays in Pragmatism* (New York: Hafner, 1948), "The Will to Believe," "Conclusions on Varieties of Religious Experience," and "Pragmatism's Conception of Truth."

Tillich, Paul, *Dynamics of Faith* (New York: Harper, 1958), Chapters 1 and 5.

Bibliography

C H A P T E R   V I I

The Problem of Natural Evil

Saint Augustine, *The Confessions* (New York: E. P. Dutton, 1886), Book VII, Chapter 5.

Hume, David, *Dialogues Concerning Natural Religion* (New York: Hafner, 1951), Parts X, XI.

Laird, John, *Mind and Deity* (New York: Philosophical Library, 1941).

Maimonides, Moses, *The Guide for the Perplexed* (New York: Dover, 1956), Part III, Chapters 10, 11, 12.

McTaggart, J. M., *Some Dogmas of Religion* (London: Edward Arnold, 1906).

Mill, John S., *Nature* (Eugene: University of Oregon Philosophical Reprints, No. 1).

Royce, Josiah, *The Religious Aspect of Philosophy* (Boston: Houghton Mifflin, 1885), Chapter 11.

Tagore, Rabindranath, "The Problem of Evil," *The Hibbert Journal*, Vol. II, 1913.

Tennant, F. R., *Philosophical Theology* (Cambridge: Cambridge University Press, 1928), Vol. II.

Tsanoff, Radoslav, *The Nature of Evil* (New York: Macmillan, 1931).

C H A P T E R   V I I I

The Problem of Immortality

Saint Augustine, *Concerning the Teacher and On the Immortality of the Soul* (New York: Appleton-Century-Crofts, 1938).

Bradley, F. H., *Ethical Studies* (Oxford: Clarendon Press, 1927).

Braham, Ernest G., *Personality and Immortality in Post-Kantian Thought* (London: George Allen and Unwin, 1926).

Broad, C. D., *The Mind and Its Place in Nature* (New York: Humanities Press, 1951).

Brown, W. A., *The Christian Hope* (New York: Charles Scribner's Sons, 1912).

Farnell, L. R., *Greek Hero Cults and Ideas of Immortality* (Oxford: Clarendon Press, 1921).

Frazer, J. G., *Man, God, and Immortality* (New York: Macmillan, 1927).

Hocking, W. E., *The Meaning of Immortality in Human Experience* (New York: Harper, 1957).

James, William, *Human Immortality* (Boston: Houghton Mifflin, 1899).

Montagu, Ashley, *Immortality* (New York: Grove Press, 1955).

Pringle-Pattison, A. Seth, *The Idea of God* (Oxford: The Clarendon Press, 1922).

Taylor, A. E., *The Christian Hope of Immortality* (New York: Macmillan, 1947).

Tsanoff, R., *The Problem of Immortality* (New York: Macmillan, 1924).

Unamuno, Miguel de, *The Tragic Sense of Life* (New York: Macmillan, 1926).

Weismann, August, *Essays upon Heredity* (Oxford: Clarendon Press, 1892).

C H A P T E R   I X

Is Religion a Matter of Knowledge?

Saint Anselm, *Proslogium* (New York: Open Court, 1944).

Saint Augustine, *Concerning the Teacher* (New York: Appleton-Century-Crofts, 1938).

Ayer, Alfred Jules, *Language, Truth, and Logic* (New York: Dover, 1950), Chapter 6.

Copleston, Frederick, *A History of Philosophy* (Westminster, Maryland: The Newman Press, 1955).

Freud, Sigmund, *The Future of an Illusion* (New York: Doubleday, 1957), Chapter 5.

Gilson, Etienne, *The Philosophy of Saint Thomas Aquinas* (London: B. Herder, 1937).

Jaspers, Karl, *Reason and Existenz* (New York: Noonday Press, 1957), pp. 77–106.

Kant, Immanuel, *Religion within the Limits of Reason Alone* (New York: Harper, 1960).

Tillich, Paul, *Systematic Theology* (Chicago: University of Chicago Press, 1951), pp. 204–210.

C H A P T E R   X

The Problem of Inerrant Scripture

Bewer, Julius A., *The Literature of the Old Testament* (New York: Columbia University Press, 1940).

Doane, William, *Bible Myths, Parallels in Other Religions* (New York: Somerby, 1892).

Frazer, James G., *Folklore in the Old Testament; Studies in Comparative Religion* (London: Macmillan, 1919).

Horne, Charles F., *The Great Rejected Books of the Biblical Apocrypha* (New York: Parke, Austin, and Lipscomb, 1917).

Bibliography

Loisy, Alfred, *The Origins of the New Testament* (London: George Allen and Unwin, 1950).

Munhall, L. W., *Anti-Higher Criticism* (New York: Hunt and Eaton, 1894).

Pfeiffer, Robert H., *Introduction to the Old Testament* (New York: Harper, 1941).

Prabhavananda, Swami, and Frederick Manchester, *The Upanishads* (New York: New American Library, 1954).

——, and Christopher Isherwood, *Bhagavad-Gita* (New York: New American Library, 1957).

Saunders, Daniel J., *Reason to Revelation* (London: B. Herder, 1949), Chapter 7.

Sparks, H. F., *The Formation of the New Testament* (London: SCM Press, Ltd., 1952).

Watts, Alan, *The Way of Zen* (New York: New American Library, 1959).

CHAPTER XI

The Problem of Fixed or Evolving Religions

Albright, W. F., *Archaeology and the Religion of Israel* (Baltimore: Johns Hopkins Press, 1953).

Buber, Martin, *Moses: The Revelation and the Covenant* (New York: Harper, 1958).

Burrows, Millar, *The Dead Sea Scrolls* (New York: The Viking Press, 1956).

Fosdick, H. E., *A Guide to Understanding the Bible* (New York: Harper, 1938).

Grant, Frederick C., *Early Christianity* (Greenwich, Conn.: The Seabury Press, 1954).

Harnack, Adolf, *Outlines of the History of Dogma* (Boston: Beacon Press, 1957).

Pfeiffer, Robert H., *Introduction to the Old Testament* (New York: Harper, 1941).

CHAPTER XII

The Problem of Fundamentalism

Calvin, John, *On God and Political Duty* (New York: Library of Liberal Arts, 1956).

——, *On the Christian Faith* (New York: Library of Liberal Arts, 1957).

Dillenberger, John and Claude Welch, *Protestant Christianity* (New York: Charles Scribner's Sons, 1954).

Furniss, Norman F., *The Fundamentalist Controversy, 1918–1931* (New Haven: Yale University Press, 1954).

Kerr, Hugh Thomson (ed.), *A Compend of Luther's Theology* (Philadelphia: Westminster Press, 1943).

Osborn, Henry F., *Evolution and Religion in Education* (New York: Charles Scribner's Sons, 1926).

Pratt, James B., *Can We Keep the Faith?* (New Haven: Yale University Press, 1941), Chapter 5.

Troeltsch, Ernst, *Protestantism and Progress* (Boston: Beacon Press, 1958).

Vanderlaan, Eldred C., *Fundamentalism versus Modernism* (New York: H. W. Wilson, 1925).

CHAPTER XIII

The Problem of Modernism

Booth, Edwin P. (ed.), *New Testament Studies* (Nashville: Abingdon-Cokesbury, 1942).

Bultmann, Rudolf, *History and Eschatology* (Edinburgh: Edinburgh University Press, 1957).

———, and Karl Jaspers, *Myth and Christianity* (New York: Noonday Press, 1958).

Gogarten, Friedrich, *Demythologizing and History* (New York: Charles Scribner's Sons, 1955).

Jones, G. V., *Christology and Myth in the New Testament* (London: George Allen and Unwin, 1956).

Knox, John, *Criticism and Faith* (Nashville: Abingdon-Cokesbury, 1952).

Loeppert, Adam J., *Modernism and the Vatican* (New York: Eaton and Mains, 1912).

Loisy, Alfred, *The Origins of the New Testament* (London: George Allen and Unwin, 1950).

Matthews, Shailer, *The Faith of Modernism* (New York: Macmillan, 1924).

Thorburn, Thomas J., *The Mythical Interpretation of the Gospels* (New York: Charles Scribner's Sons, 1916).

Torrey, David C., *Protestant Modernism* (New York: G. P. Putnam's Sons, 1910).

CHAPTER XIV

The Problem of Humanism

Cohen, Chapman, *A Grammar of Freethought* (London: The Pioneer Press, 1921).

Bibliography

"A Humanist Manifesto," in *The New Humanist*, Volume VI, No. 3.

Hume, David, "The Natural History of Religion" in *Essays Moral, Political and Literary* (New York: Longmans, Green, 1907), Volume II.

Huxley, T. H., *Science and Christian Tradition* (New York: D. Appleton, 1896).

Lamont, Corliss, *Humanism as a Philosophy* (New York: Philosophical Library, 1949).

Maritain, Jacques, *True Humanism* (London: Centenary Press, 1941).

Meslier, Jean, *Superstition in All Ages* (New York: Truth Seeker Company, 1950).

Potter, Charles F., *Humanism* (New York: Simon and Schuster, 1930).

Teller, Woolsey, *Essays of an Atheist* (New York: Truth Seeker Company, 1945).

CHAPTER XV

The Problem of Psychology and Religion

Allport, Gordon W., *The Individual and His Religion* (New York: Macmillan, 1951).

Boisen, Anton T., *The Exploration of the Inner World* (New York: Harper, 1936).

Freud, Sigmund, *The Future of an Illusion* (New York: Doubleday, 1957).

———, *Moses and Monotheism* (New York: Vintage, 1958).

———, *Totem and Taboo* (New York: Random House, 1946).

Fromm, Erich, *Psychoanalysis and Religion* (New Haven: Yale University Press, 1950).

James, William, *The Varieties of Religious Experience* (New York: New American Library, 1960).

Jung, Carl G., *Answer to Job* (New York: Meridian, 1960).

———, *Modern Man in Search of a Soul* (New York: Harcourt, Brace, 1933).

May, Rollo (ed.), *Existence* (New York: Basic Books, 1958).

Mowrer, O. Hobart, *The Crisis in Psychiatry and Religion* (Princeton: Van Nostrand, 1961).

Mullahy, Patrick, *Oedipus: Myth and Complex* (New York: Grove Press, 1955).

Stekel, Wilhelm, *Technique of Analytical Psychotherapy* (New York: Liveright, 1950).

C H A P T E R X V I

The Church and the State

Aristotle, *Politics* (New York: Random House, 1943).

Bacon, L. W., *An Inside View of the Vatican Council* (New York: American Tract Society, 1871).

Barker, Ernest, *The Political Thought of Plato and Aristotle* (New York: Dover, 1959).

——, *Church, State, and Education* (Ann Arbor: University of Michigan Press, 1957).

Beale, H. K., *Are American Teachers Free?* (New York: Charles Scribner's Sons, 1936).

Bigongiari, Dino (ed.), *The Political Ideas of St. Thomas* (New York: Hafner, 1960).

Blanshard, Paul, *American Freedom and Catholic Power* (Boston: Beacon Press, 1958).

Calvin, John, *On God and Political Duty* (New York: Liberal Arts Press, 1950).

Graham, Robert A., *Vatican Diplomacy* (Princeton: Princeton University Press, 1959).

Greene, Evarts B., *Religion and the State: The Making and Testing of an American Tradition* (New York: New York University Press, 1941).

Heering, G. J., *The Fall of Christianity* (New York: Fellowship Publications, 1943).

Houk, R. A. (ed.), *Hooker's Ecclesiastical Polity* (New York: Columbia University Press, 1931).

Kant, Immanuel, *Religion within the Limits of Reason Alone* (New York: Harper, 1960).

Moehlman, Conrad H., *The Catholic-Protestant Mind* (New York: Harper, 1929).

Rousseau, Jean Jacques, *The Social Contract* (New York: Hafner, 1947).

Stokes, Anson P., *Church and State in the United States* (New York: Harper, 1950).

C H A P T E R X V I I

The Problem of Science and Religion

Burtt, Edwin A., *Religion in an Age of Science* (New York: Frederick A. Stokes, 1929).

Eddington, Arthur S., *Science and the Unseen World* (New York: Macmillan, 1929).

Bibliography

Gillispie, Charles C., *Genesis and Geology* (Cambridge: Harvard University Press, 1951).

Thomson, J. Arthur, *Science and Religion* (New York: Charles Scribner's Sons, 1929).

Walsh, James J., *The Popes and Science* (New York: Fordham University Press, 1911).

White, A. D., *A History of the Warfare of Science with Theology* (New York: D. Appleton, 1903).

Wieman, Henry N., *Religious Experience and Scientific Method* (New York: Macmillan, 1926).

493

Index

Abelard, St., 199–200, 272.
Abraham, 230.
Adamic sin (see Original sin).
Adams, John, 398.
Actual vs. potential existence, 98–99.
Adler, Felix, 375.
Aesthetics and religion, 13, 56.
Agnosticism, 5, 111, 348–350.
Ahriman, 216.
Ahura-Mazda, 216.
Akkad, 159.
Albert, St.,
    cosmological argument, 101.
    faith and reason, 200–201.
Albigenses, 35.
Albright, William F., 255.
Alciphron, 105.
Alexander the Great, 228.
Alexander V, Pope, 289.
Alexander VI, Pope, 289.
Alexander, Samuel A., 74.
Alienation, man from God, 72–73.
Allport, Gordon W., 360–361.

Amalricians, 35.
Amentia, Meynert's, 363.
Analytic statements, 108, 115–137.
Anselm, St.,
    a posteriori arguments for God, 199.
    faith and reason, 114, 199.
    ontological argument, 85–89, 97, 199.
Anthropomorphic properties of God, 69.
Antichrist, 35.
Antinomies, 220.
Anti-Semitism, 58, 303.
Aphrodite, 265.
Apocrypha, 236–237.
Apollo, 228.
Apologetics, 6.
Apologists, New Testament, 262.
Apostles Creed, 289.
Apostolic succession, 48, 264, 268–269.

Index

Aquinas, St. Thomas,
  church and state, 384.
  cosmological argument, 97–103.
  faith vs. reason, 105–106, 114, 202, 374, 418.
  God, 97, 161.
  immortality, 184–185.
  ontological argument, 97.
  philosophy of religion, 8–9, 105–106.
Aristotelian method, 117, 147, 201.
Aristotle,
  church and state, 383.
  correspondence definition of truth, 121–122.
  cosmological argument, 100.
  law of excluded middle, 107, 154, 309–310.
  logic, 9, 198.
  nature of being, 84–85.
Ark of the covenant, 230, 256–257.
Ark, Noah's, 254.
Asceticism, 332–333, 338–339.
Assumption of Mary, 370–371.
Assyrian exile, 230–231.
Astruc, Jean, 254.
Athanasianism, 299.
Athanasius, St.,
  on scripture, 240.
  Trinity, 299.
Atheism, 109–114, 348–350.
Atman (see Brahma-Atman).
Atonement, 212, 224, 317.
Augsburg Confession, 294.
Augsburg, Peace of, 295.
Augustine, St.,
  Catholic Church, 384.
  Confessions, 19.
  creation, 242–243.
  faith, 105, 169, 195–197.
  God, 55, 105.
  immortality, 182–184.
  natural evil, 156, 159.
  reason, 105, 169, 195–197.
  scripture, 240–243, 254.
Autrecourt, Nicholas, 101–102.

Avicenna, 101.
Ayer, Alfred J.,
  immortality, 191.
  religious knowledge, 111, 113, 204–206, 214–215.

Baal, 66.
Babylonian exile, 230–231.
Baptism, 208, 264.
"Barking dog of capitalism," 51.
Barnard, Frederick, 193.
Bauer, Bruno, 321.
Beecher, Lyman, 405.
Being, 74–77, 84–85.
Belief, as a defining property of religion, 27–29.
Bennett, John, 37.
Bergson, Henri,
  God, 78.
  two sources of religion, 56–57.
Berkeley, George,
  on Christianity, 57–58, 274–275.
  immortality, 179–180.
  teleological argument, 93, 105.
Bernard, St.,
  on Abelard, 200.
  on Luther, 290.
Bernardo, Brother, 342–343.
Bertocci, Peter, 93.
Bhagavad-Gita, 229–230, 341.
Bible, inerrancy of, 226–249.
Bible Society, British and Foreign, 236–237.
Biblical parallels, 227–228, 254–255.
Bibliocracy, 296–299.
Birth control, 404, 406.
Bishops, role of, 268–269.
Black, Justice Hugo, 413–414.
Blavatsky, Madame H. P., 433, 435–436.
Boccaccio, 289.
Boehme, Jacob,
  God, 78.
  immortality, 188.
  mysticism, 120.
  natural evil, 153.
Boisen, Anton T., 375.

Index

Bonaventura, St.,
  definition of God, 74–75.
  ontological argument, 85, 97, 135.
  teleological argument, 93, 135.
Boniface III, Pope, 400.
Boniface VIII, Pope, 400.
Bowne, B. P., 78.
Bradley, F. H., 181, 190, 192.
Brahma-Atman, 167–168, 179, 340.
Brahmin caste, 170.
Brightman, Edgar S.,
  finite God, 162.
  personal God, 77.
  philosophy of religion, 7, 8.
Broad, C. D., 178, 189–190, 192.
Brothers of the Common Life, 288, 290.
Brothers and Sisters of the Free Spirit, 288.
Brunner, Emil,
  alienation of man, 72–73.
  encounter, 167.
  Kingdom of God, 428.
Bryan, William Jennings, 304.
Buber, Martin, 167, 260–261.
Buddha, Gautama, 138, 228, 331.
Buddhism,
  Hinayana, 28, 230, 334–335.
  immortality, 28, 171, 178–179.
  Mahayana, 334–335.
  scripture, 230.
  Ten Commandments, 333–334.
Bultmann, Rudolf, 214, 322–328.
Buridan, Jean, 102.
Burr, Aaron, 405.
Butler, Joseph, 92–93.

Cabalism, 233.
Calvin, John,
  Bible, 243, 272.
  Church and State, 296–299, 389–392.
  God, 106.
  immortality, 180.
  natural evil, 153.
  pantheism, 71.

Calvin, John (Continued)
  predestination, 297–298.
  Trinity, 299.
Calvinistic ethics, 298–299.
Cambridge Platform, 395.
Canaan, 230.
Canonization of scriptures,
  Old Testament, 233–237.
  New Testament, 237–240.
Capitalism and religion, 18, 37, 48, 298, 404.
Capital punishment, 58.
Carlyle, Thomas, 355.
Carroll, Charles, 398.
Carroll, Father John, 398.
Carthage, Synod of, 236, 240.
Caste system, 170–172.
Cause and effect, 99–103.
Cause, First, 201.
Cause, efficient, 99–100.
Caverne des Trois Frères, 63.
Celsus, 253, 267–268.
Celts, 227.
Certainty, 196.
Chaldean scripture, 227.
Champeaux, William of, 200.
Chaplaincy, 407–408.
Charlemagne, 399.
Charles V, 294.
Chinese religion, 227.
Christian Science, 156.
Church Fathers, 197, 199, 419–420.
Church and state, 296–299, 381–416.
Church, Christian
  first century, 264–266.
  second century, 266–268.
  Wyclif, 287.
Class struggle, 279.
Clement of Alexandria, 233, 235, 239.
Clement V, Pope, 400.
Clement VIII, Pope, 399.
Clement XIV, Pope, 399.
Cocheba, 236.
Codom, 228.
Coffin, H. S., 350.
Cogito argument, 118–119.

Cohen, Chapman, 109–110, 112.
Coherence method, 7, 8, 20, 186–187.
Communion (*see* Lord's Supper).
Communism and Christianity, 37–38, 59, 373.
Comte, Auguste, 17–18.
Concern, ultimate, 210–211, 377, 437.
Confucianism, 228.
Consistency, as a weak criterion, 90, 163.
Constance, Council of, 288.
Constantine, 48.
Constantinople, Council of, 267.
Consubstantiation (*see* Lord's Supper).
Contingency vs. necessity, 100, 103.
Contradiction, Principle of, 198.
Conversion, 213.
Copernican revolution, 422–425.
Copts, 267.
Cosmological argument for God, 97–103.
Cotton, John, 394–395.
Covenant, Ark of, 230, 256–257.
Creation, 140, 198, 242–243.
Creed, early Christian, 266–268.
Criticism, biblical, 16, 209, 252–285, 312–313, 319–322.
Cybele, 265.
Cyrus, 228.

Damien, St., 198–199.
Dante, 288.
Darwin, Charles, 62, 302.
Davis, Jerome, 36.
Dead Sea Scrolls, 259–260.
Decalogue, 33.
Declaration of Rights, Virginia, 397.
Deduction, 119, 129–137.
Deer Park, 332.
Definition,
  of definition, 23–27.
  nominal, 24.
  real, 23–24, 31.
  of religion, 22–40.

Definition (*Continued*)
  in religious argument, 26–28, 39–40.
  stipulative, 23, 25–26, 39.
Deistic supernaturalism, 8, 72–73, 81, 350.
Demythologizing, 214, 322–328.
Descartes, René,
  cogito, 118–119.
  ontological argument, 85–87, 114, 134.
  self-evidence, 118–119.
Devil, 149.
De Wette, W. M. L., 234.
Dewey, John, 351.
Dialectical logic, 198.
Dibelius, Martin, 322.
Dietary practices,
  Christian, 34.
  Jain, 341–342.
  Jewish, 266.
Dilemma of logic, the, 135–136.
Diocletian, 398.
Dionysius, 172, 265.
Divinity of Christ, 26–27, 314–315.
Divorce, 404.
Dodd, C. H., 322.
Dodds, Marcus, 313.
Doellinger, Professor, 400.
Dogmas, 279–280.
Donation of Constantine, 289, 399.
Doyle, Father, 403.
Donne, John, 172–173.
Drag, the, 161.
Drake, Durant, 31.
Dreadful freedom, 143.
Driver, S. R., 313.
Dromena, 52.
Dulles, John Foster, 37.
Dwight, Timothy, 405.
Dysteleology (*see* Natural evil).

Eckhart, Meister, 120, 188, 288.
Eddington, Arthur S., 91, 429–430.
Eddy, Mary Baker, 44, 71, 157.

Index

Eden, Garden of, 44, 390.

Education and religion, 215–217, 407, 410, 412–413.

Education, religious, 3, 411–412, 414–415.

Edwards, Jonathan, 18–19, 277.

Efficient cause, 99–100.

Eight-Fold Path, 333–334.

Elan vital, 57.

Election, 298.

Eleusinianism, 265.

Encounter, the, 283.

Encyclicals, 272–273.

England, Bishop, 402, 405.

Epicurus, 138, 265.

Epistemology, 120, 115–137.

Erasmus, 289, 343–344.

Erigena, John Scotus, 197–198.

Eschatology (see Millennialism).

Essence vs. existence, 84–85.

Essenes, 259, 262.

Ethics, and religion, 33–34, 57.

Etruscan creation story, 227.

Eucharist (see Lord's Supper).

Eusebius, 239, 269.

Everson Case, 412.

Evil (see Moral evil; Natural evil).

Evolution, biological, 62, 112, 374.

Evolution of religion, 250–285, 278–279.

Excluded Middle, Law of, 107, 154, 309–310.

Exile, Jewish, 230–231, 257–258.

Existence, actual vs. potential, 98–99.

Existence vs. essence, 84–85.

Existentialism,
  irreligious, 143.
  religious, 121, 169, 187, 207–214, 277, 326–327.

Ex nihilo, creation, 140, 198.

Experience, religious, 19, 354–380.

Extreme unction, 264.

Ezra, the determination of canonicity, 229, 236–237.

Faith,
  attack on, 204–206, 217–218.
  natural evil, 158–160.
  and reason, 105–106, 114, 195–217.
  and truth, 210–215.

Fall, the, 198.

fanaticism, 224.

Farrar, F. W., 313.

Fathers, Church (see Church Fathers).

Federal Council of Churches of Christ in America, 26.

Feeling, as a definition of religion, 29–33.

Feuerbach, Ludwig,
  definition of religion, 12, 32, 55–56, 108–109, 128.
  evolution of Christianity, 280–281, 322.
  God, 32, 79, 108–109, 114, 349.
  immortality, 176.

Fichte, Johann G., 73.

Fictions, religious, 12, 21, 87, 255.

Finite God,
  Brightman, 77–78, 162.
  Maimonides, 161.
  Mill, 162.
  Plato, 160–161.

First Cause, 97–103, 200, 439–440.

Flood, the, 227.

Forgiveness, 170.

Form, of religious arguments, 14, 90.

Forms, Platonic, 84.

Four Noble Truths, 332–333.

Fox, George, 355.

Francis, St., 35, 163, 342–343.

Frankfurter, Justice Felix, 413.

Franklin, Benjamin, 346, 397.

Frazer, Sir James G., 254–255.

Freedom of will,
  natural evil, 71, 141–145.
  salvation, 221, 277, 297–298.

Freud, Sigmund,
  anxiety, 32, 53, 54.
  God, 79–80.
  Immortality, 176.

Freud, Sigmund (*Continued*)
  religious knowledge, 54, 218.
  religion as a sign of neurosis, 5,
    19, 32, 217–218, 361–368.
Fromm, Erich, 376–377.
Fundamentalism, Protestant, 203,
    286–308, 443.

Gaunilon, 87–89.
Gelasius I, Pope, 398–399.
Genesis and biology, 92–93, 216–
    217, 424–425.
Genesis and geology, 203, 216–
    217, 227, 423–424.
Gentiles, 232.
Gibbons, Cardinal, 403.
Gilgamesh, epic of, 146, 159.
Gilson, Etienne, 75, 90–91.
Given, the, 77.
Gnosticism, 238–239.
God,
  anthropomorphic, 256–257.
  arguments, 15, 94–96, 113–
    114, 83–114.
  definition of, 4, 65, 63–82, 215,
    335, 372.
  deistic, 72–73, 81.
  finite, 160–165.
  ground of being, 74–77, 139.
  immanence, 81.
  as man, 33.
  negatively defined, 111–112.
  omnipropertied, 61, 86–89, 119,
    140, 142, 160–165, 186, 256.
  pantheism, 70–71, 81.
  and war, 256–257.
Gogarten, Friedrich, 323.
Gospels, 269, 280, 226–249.
Gosse, Philip Henry, 424.
Great Awakening, 18–19.
Greek religion, 67.
Gregory, St., 198.
Guilt, 4, 55, 224, 354–380.

Hadrian VI, Pope, 399–400.
Hagiographa, 235–236.
Harnack, Adolf, 279, 320.
Hawthorne, Nathaniel, 277.
Healing, divine, 4, 55.

Heard, Gerald, 52.
Hecker, Father, 318, 402.
Hedonism, 221.
Hegel, Georg W. F.,
  coherence, 7, 122–124.
  dialectic, 149, 175, 278–279,
    309–310.
  history of religion, 16.
  natural evil, 149, 156.
  ontological argument, 85.
  pantheism, 70–71.
Hegisippus, 269.
Hell, 398.
Henotheism, 67, 245, 260.
Hercules, 228.
Heresy, 16, 316, 398.
Heteronomy, 221.
Higher Criticism (*see* Biblical
    criticism).
Hilkiah, 233.
Hillel (*see* Pharisees, Hillel).
Hinayana (*see* Buddhism).
Hinduism,
  gods, 68, 164, 216.
  immortality, 28, 167–169.
  natural evil, 44, 146.
  scripture, 226–227, 229.
Hippo, Synod of, 236.
Hippolytus, 269.
History of religion, 5, 15–17, 27,
    278–279.
History of science, 16.
Hobbes, Thomas
  church and state 385.
  origin of religion, 46–48.
  scripture, 253.
Hocking, W. E.,
  God, 17, 78.
  immortality, 181.
  definition of religion, 31–32,
    58.
  role of will, 12, 136.
Holy Spirit, 372.
Hooker, Thomas, 393–394.
Horace, 172.
Horus, 228.
Hromadka, J. L., 37.
Hubbard, L. Ron, 433.
Humanism, 12, 278, 329–353.

Index

Humanist Manifesto, 350–351.
Hume, David
    cosmological argument, 95–96.
    natural religion, 16, 65, 69,
        344–345.
    teleological argument, 95–96.
Hus, John, 288.
Huxley, Thomas H., 109, 431.

Idolatry, 56.
Immaculate conception, 273, 371.
Immanence of God, 70, 81.
Immortality,
    arguments for: logical, 190–
        193, metaphysical, 182–188,
        pragmatic, 177–182, psychic,
        188–190.
    belief in, 4, 11, 167–177.
    concepts of: biological, 176,
        quality of life, 173–174, rein-
        carnation, 166–173.
    Judaism, 66–67, 166–167.
Incarnation, 170, 212, 274.
Index, the, 316.
Induction, 115–137, 119, 129–
    137.
Indra, 68.
Indulgences, 289–292.
Inerrancy, Bible, 4, 226–249, 421–
    422.
Infallibility, papal, 400.
Infinite regression, 99–100, 102.
Inherited religion, 41–43.
Innate ideas, 106.
Innocent I, Pope, 398.
Innocent II, Pope, 200.
Innocent III, Pope, 399.
Intuition, 116–118.
Ireland, Archbishop, 403.
Irenaeus,
    creed, 240, 267.
    Bible, 235, 240.
Isis, 216, 265.
Islam (see Moslem).

Jackson, Justice Robert, 413.
Jainism,
    gods, 28.
    immortality, 28, 171.

Jainism (Continued)
    Jina, 338.
    Jiva, 341.
    monasteries, 340–343.
    Nine Truths, 339–341.
    origin of, 337–338.
    Three Jewels, 339–340.
James, William,
    finite God, 77–78.
    immortality, 177, 180, 182, 191.
    natural evil, 153, 158.
    pragmatic truth, 18, 124–125.
    psychology of religion, 19, 354–
        360.
    religious knowledge, 9, 14, 114,
        219.
    role of the will, 10–12, 219.
Jamnia, Council of, 236, 252.
Jansenism, 107.
Jaspers, Karl, 169, 210, 214, 322–
    328.
Jefferson, Thomas, 346, 398.
Jerome, St., 234, 236, 398.
Jesus, historical, 309–328.
Jewels, Three, 339–340.
Jina, 338.
Jiva, 339.
Joan, St., 68.
Job, the problem of, 44, 141, 145,
    147, 369–373.
John, St., of Damascus, 101.
Jonah, 228, 257, 432.
Jones, Rufus, 114.
Josephus, 235, 263.
Judaism,
    evolution of, 231, 252–262.
    immortality, 166–167.
    scripture, 226–227.
Julius VI, Pope, 289.
Jung, Carl J.,
    psychotherapy and religion,
        54–55, 59, 368–372.
    religion and health, 219, 368–
        369, 379.
Juniper, Friar, 163.
Justinian, 399.

Kain, Archbishop, 403.
Kairos, 242.

Kant, Immanuel
  cosmological argument, 102–103.
  evolution of religion, 251–252.
  existence, 85, 186.
  freedom, 142, 143, 221, 415.
  God, 80–81, 104.
  immortality, 166–167, 180–181, 185, 187–188.
  infallibility of scriptures, 244.
  justification for religion, 121.
  moral argument, 104, 105, 121, 221.
  ontological argument, 104, 185.
  religious knowledge, 114, 134, 206–207, 219–221, 345.
  teleological argument, 93–94.
Karma, Law of, 170, 339–341.
Kathenotheism, 68, 260.
Keane, Archbishop, 402.
Kempis, Thomas a, 188.
Kenite hypothesis, 260.
Kennedy, John F., 403.
Kenrick, Archbishop, 400.
Kerygma, 323.
Kierkegaard, S.,
  deistic supernaturalism, 72.
  religious knowledge, 207–209, 214–215, 218.
  St. Paul, 232.
Kingsland, William, 435–436.
Kirkpatrick, A. F., 313.
Knowledge, religious, 7, 8, 14, 121, 209, 214–215.
Knowledge, absolute, 116–117.
Koch, Hugo, 318.
Koran, 229.
Krishna, 228.
Kshatriya caste, 170, 330.
Ku Klux Klan, 303, 409.
Kwan Yin, 337.

Laird, John, 148–149, 150.
Lamentabili, 316.
Lamont, Corliss, 175.
Lao-tsze, 228.
Law, the Jewish, 232–233, 234.
Lawes, Warden, 147.

Leib, Rabbi Mosh, 361–362.
Leibniz, G. W.,
  God, 76–77.
  natural evil, 145, 147, 157.
  ontological argument, 85.
Leo III, Pope, 399.
Leo IX, Pope, 289.
Leo XIII, Pope, 318, 403.
Lessing, G. E., 346.
Leuba, James, 22, 359–360.
Liber Pontificalis, 269.
Liberius, Pope, 398.
Lightfoot, J., 424.
Liturgy, 19, 272.
Locke, John, 403.
Loisy, Alfred, 247, 318, 347.
Lollards, 288.
Lombard, Peter, 101.
Lord's Supper, 201, 264, 287, 293–294.
Lotze, Hermann, 192.
Love, 120.
Luther, Martin
  Apocrypha, 236.
  church and state, 387–389.
  indulgences, 289–292.
  "tower experience," 290.
  Turks, 292–293.

Machiavelli, Niccolò,
  natural evil, 149.
  religion as a weapon, 45–46, 388.
Mahabharata, 330.
Mahavira, 338–343.
Mahayana (see Buddhism).
Maimonides, Moses,
  cosmological argument, 98, 101, 266.
  natural evil, 145–146, 152, 156–157, 161–162.
Magic, 53.
Mara, 332.
Marcellinus, Pope, 398.
Marcion, 238–239.
Maritain, Jacques, 347.
Martineau, James, 275.
Martyr, Justin, 239.
Marx, Karl, 48, 61, 279.

Index

Mary, Virgin, 273, 371.
Mass, the, 295.
Materialism, 191–192.
Maximus, 198.
May, Rollo, 219.
McCollum vs. Champaign, Illinois
    School Board, 413–414.
McTaggart, J. M.,
    immortality, 174.
    natural evil, 158, 164.
Meaning, of faith, 9, 11, 169,
    209–210, 214.
Mercury, 228.
Meslier, Jean, 111, 112, 113.
Messianic Hope, 233.
Metempsychosis, 172.
Methodism, 302–303.
Middle Ages, religious emphasis,
    16.
Mill, John Stuart,
    natural evil, 143–144.
    limited God, 162.
Millennialism, 248, 263, 274, 317,
    320–321.
Milton, John, 403.
Miracles, 8, 53, 228, 301.
Mithraism, 253, 265.
Modernism, 278, 309–328.
Moksa, 339.
Monadology, 76–77.
Monasticism, 35, 334–335, 341–
    343.
Monotheism, 66, 141, 255–256.
Montagu, Ashley, 178.
Moral argument for God, 103–
    105.
Moral argument for religion, 120–
    121, 221.
Moral evil, 233–234.
Moral Rearmament, 409.
Mortal sin, 287, 291–292.
Moses, 230, 362–368.
Moslem, 69, 200, 226.
Mowrer, O. Hobart, 375–376.
Mullahy, Patrick, 366.
Mundane theology, 202–203, 307.
Murray, Margaret, 68.
Mysterium tremendum, 30–31.
Mysticism, 19, 120.

Myth in religion, 12, 18, 21, 56–
    57, 214, 322–328.

National Council of Churches of
    Christ in America, 318.
Nationalism, 73–74, 296–297.
Natural evil,
    as a cause of religion, 43–44,
    65.
    problem of, Chap. VII.
    solutions, 141–171.
Naturalism, 73–74, 81.
Nazism, 37–38.
Necessity vs. contingency, 100,
    103.
Necromancy, 258.
Neo-orthodoxy, 74–75, 169 (see
    also Existentialism, reli-
    gious).
Neurosis and religion, 5, 19, 362–
    368.
Neutrality, an approach to philos-
    ophy of religion, 6.
Newton, Sir Isaac, 346.
Nicene Council, 267.
Nicene Creed, 27, 267.
Nicholas V, Pope, 289.
Niebuhr, H. Richard, 31, 37.
Niebuhr, Reinhold, 321.
Nietzsche, Friedrich, 232.
Nine Truths of Jainism, 339–341.
Ninety-five theses of Luther, 291–
    292.
Nirvana, 168–169, 179, 335.
Nott, Eliphalet, 405.
Numinous, 31, 219–220.

Occam, William of, 101, 290.
Oriental religion, 6, 330–343.
O'Connell, Cardinal, 403.
O'Gorman, Monsignor, 403.
Old Testament origins, 230–237.
Ontological argument, 84–91,
    103.
Opium of the people, 48.
Orderly events, 91–93, 127.
Origen, 253–254.
Original sin, 145, 146, 298, 307.
Origins, fallacy of, 60–62, 354.

Orphic mysteries, 172, 265.
Osiris, 216.
Otto, Rudolf, 30.

Pacifism, 58, 276, 408.
Paine, Thomas, 346.
Paley, William, 92–93.
Pantheism, 69–71, 81, 168.
Papacy, 269, 295, 389, 400.
"Parsonpower," 50.
Parsee, 227.
Parsvanatha, Rule of, 338.
Pascal, Blaise, 107–108.
Pascendi Dominici Gregis, 316, 318–319.
Patarenes, 35.
Patripassianism, 138.
Pauck, Wilhelm, 37.
Paul III, Pope, 399.
Paul, St., 198, 232–233, 269–270, 273.
Peirce, Charles S., 178.
Penance, 224.
Penn, William, 394.
Pentateuch, 232, 234, 253.
Persian religion, 227.
Personalism, 77–82.
Peter, St., 270–271.
Petrarch, 288, 343.
Pharisees, 259, 262–263.
Pherecydes, 172.
Philip of Hesse, 293.
Philo, 138, 254.
Pius VII, Pope, 399.
Pius IX, Pope, 406–407.
Pius X, Pope, 316, 318.
Plato,
    finite gods, 160–161.
    Forms, 115–116.
    immortality, 172, 177, 179, 182.
    moral argument, 84, 101, 103–104.
    religious knowledge, 15, 115–117.
    virgin birth, 228.
Plotinus, 101.
Polycarp, 263, 269, 349–350.
Polytheism, 65, 104, 255–256, 335.

Porphyry, 253.
Positivism, logical, 204–206.
Potential vs. actual existence, 98–99.
Potter, Charles F., 110–111, 113, 347, 348–349.
Pragmatic truth, 10, 18.
Praxeus, 138.
Predestination, 180, 277, 297–298.
Presbyterian Church, General Assembly of 1910, 304.
Priesthood of All Believers, 245, 294, 305–306.
Pringle-Pattison, A. Seth, 174.
Prohibition, 404.
Prometheus, 228.
Protagoras, 177, 343.
Protestantism and capitalism, 18, 37, 48, 298, 404.
Providentissimus, 318.
Pseudepigrapha, 237.
Psychic experience, 188–190.
Psychology, physiological, 206, 356.
Psychology of religion, 5, 18–19, 53–55, 354–380.
Pythagoras, 228.
Pythagoreans on immortality, 172.

Quaker Church, 36.

Ra, 228.
Radhakrishnan, S., 168.
Ramayana, 330.
Rank, Otto, 375.
Rauschenbusch, Walter, 36.
Reason and faith, 105–106, 114.
Reductio absurdum, 89.
Reincarnation, 166–173.
Religion,
    culturally determined, 6, 281–282.
    definition of, 22–40, 356–357.
    evolution of, 250–285.
    history of, 15–16, 27.
    inherited, 42–43.
    invented, 43–45.

Index

Religion (*Continued*)
Labor Foundation, 409.
political weapon, 45–51.
psychology of, 18–19, 53–55, 354–380.
sociology of, 17–18.
Religious experience, 19, 358.
Religious knowledge, 115–137, 194–225.
Religious values, 9, 20.
Reminiscence, in Plato, 115–116.
Resurrection, 173–174, 265, 317, 366.
Revealed theology, 273–274.
Revelation, 223, 282.
Ritual, 272.
Robertson, J. M., 322.
Roman Catholic,
authority of Church, 228–229, 271–272.
compared with Fundamentalism, 299–302.
search for truth, 9.
Welfare Council, 403.
Roman religion, 67, 265.
Roosevelt, Franklin D., 400–401.
Rousseau, Jean-Jacques, 385–387.
Royce, Josiah, 30, 152, 156, 159, 174–175.
Rudra, 44, 140–141.
Rush, Benjamin, 410.
Rutledge, Justice Wiley, 413.
Ruysbroeck, J., 288.

Sadducees, 234, 259.
Salvation Army, 276.
Samaritan schism, 234.
Sampson and Delilah, 228.
Samsara, 171.
Santayana, George,
definition of religion, 12, 14, 56.
function of religion, 12, 13, 206–207.
immortality, 175.
Sargant, William, 373.
Sartre, Jean-Paul, 343.
Scandinavian religion, 227.

Schleiermacher, Friedrich,
definition of religion, 12, 29, 105–106, 322.
evolution of Christianity, 281.
teleological argument, 94–95, 114.
Schlink, Edmund, 37, 325–326.
Schlick, Moritz, 191.
Schweitzer, Albert, 320–321.
Science and religion, 247–248, 304–305, Chap. XVII.
Scopes, John T., 302, 425.
Sects, multiplicity of, 22, 28.
Self-evidence, 118–119.
Sellars, R. W., 350.
Seng Ts'an, 336.
Sense experience, as a test of truth, 126–127.
Separation of church and state, Chap. XVI.
Septuagint, 242.
Sermon on the mount, 35, 50.
Sex, 198, 343, 364–365.
Sheldon, H., 274.
Siloam, Tower of, 141, 148.
Simon, Father Richard, 253–254.
Sin, 4, 145, 277, 292–293, 359–360, 376, 390 (*see also* Original sin; Moral sin).
Sira, Ben, 235.
Sixtus V, Pope, 399.
Skepticism, 5, 265, 329–353.
Smith, A. E., 403.
Smith, G. A., 313.
Social Gospel, 36, 303–304.
Sociology of religion, 5, 17–18.
Socrates, 57.
Soul,
Buddhism, 335.
Christianity, 4, 11, 177–193.
Hinduism, 171–172.
Spires, Diet of, 294.
Spinoza, Benedict,
definition of God, 70.
immortality, 167.
natural evil, 159–160.
ontological argument, 89–90.
role of reason, 195.
scripture, 253.

Index

Spiritual Mobilization, 409.

Stampitz, Joseph, 290–291.

State and church,
  Augustine, St., 384.
  Calvin, 389–392.
  Greek view, 382–383.
  Hobbes, 385.
  Luther, 387–389.
  Rousseau, 385.
  Thomas, St., 384.

Statute of Praemunire, 287.

Statutes of Provisos, 287.

Stekel, Wilhelm, 375.

Stephen III, Pope, 399.

Stoicism, 101, 265.

Strauss, David, 321.

Stuyvesant, Peter, 394.

Supremacy Act, 393.

Sylvester, Pope, 399.

Symbolic language, 211–215.

Symbols, religious, 118, 211–215.

Synagogue, 230–231, 257–258.

Synod,
  of Carthage, 236.
  of Constantinople, 236.
  of Hippo, 236.

Synoptic gospels, 268–270, 280.

Tagore, Rabindranath, 159, 168.

Tauler, J., 288.

Tauroboleum, 265.

Tawney, R. H., 18, 48–50, 61.

Taylor, A. E., 189.

Taylor, Myron, 400–401.

Teleological argument for God, 91–96, 123, 127.

Telepathy, 189–190.

Teller, W., 113.

Temple, Jewish, 230, 258, 263.

Tennant, F. R., 152–153.

Tertullian, St., 235, 267.

Tetzel, John, 291.

Theodicy, 138, 140–141, 145, 164–165.

Theological method, 6, 16, 201, 266, 353, 357.

Theology, mundane, 307.

Theology, revealed, 307.

Theology, systematic, 197.

Theosophy, 146.

Theresa, St., 355.

Thomas, Norman, 36.

Thomas, St. (see Aquinas, St. Thomas).

Thomson, J. A., 430.

Thoreau, Henry, 338.

Tillich, Paul,
  Christian uniqueness, 274, 282–283.
  faith, 169, 209–210, 214.
  God, 75–76, 129, 350.
  natural evil, 139.
  ontological argument, 90.
  religious knowledge, 118, 136, 284, 303.
  ultimate concern, 210–211, 377, 437–438.

Time, creation in, 242–243.

Tolstoy, Leo, 173–174.

Torrey, David C., 314.

Transmigration, 171–172.

Transubstantiation, 287.

Trent, Council of, 236, 398.

Trinitarianism, 27, 69, 78, 197, 299.

Troeltsch, E., 388.

Truth,
  coherence, 20, 122–124.
  correspondence, 121–122.
  definitions, 121–125.
  pragmatic, 10, 124–125.
  tests of, 125–129.

Turks, Luther on, 292–293.

Tychism (see Natural evil)

Tyrrell, Father, 318.

Ultimate concern, 210–211, 214.

Unamuno, Miguel de, 166.

Unitarian, 27.

Upanishads, 167–168, 229, 334.

Urban V, Pope, 287, 400.

Ussher, Bishop, 434.

Utility of religion, 13, 15, 18, 20–21.

Vaishya caste, 170.

Valla, Lorentius, 289.

Index

Values, religious, 9, 11, 120.
Vatican Council, 236.
Vatican diplomacy, 400–402.
Vatican library, 289.
Vedas, 140–141, 170–171.
Velikovsky, I., 433–434.
Venerable Company, 296.
Verifiability theory, 204–205.
Victor, Hugh of Saint, 200.
Virgil, 172.
Virgin Birth, 228, 398.
Voltaire, François, 147–148, 157, 346.
Vulgate, 289.

Wager, Pascal's, 107–108.
Waldo, Peter, 35.
Walker, R. L., 373.
War, 244, 256–257.
Ward, Harry, 36.
Weber, Max, 18, 61.

Weismann, August, 176.
Wells, H. G., 78.
Wesley, John, 303, 425.
Whitehead, Alfred North, 440.
"Wider teleological argument," 93.
Wieman, H. N., 73–74, 428–429.
Will, as a maker of truth, 10–11, 12.
Will to believe, 10.
Williams, Roger, 394–395.
Winthrop, John, 396.
Witchcraft, 69.
World Council of Churches, 37.
Wyclif, John, 286–288.

Zakkai, Johanan ben, 236, 259.
Zoroastrianism, 67, 228, 231.
Zen, 230.
Zend-Avesta, 227.
Zwingli, U., 293–294.

ABOUT THE AUTHOR

DONALD A. WELLS has been chairman of the Department of Philosophy at Washington State University since 1948. As an undergraduate at the University of Minnesota and Hamline University he majored in philosophy, and he later attended the Boston University School of Theology, from which he graduated *magna cum laude*. He received his Ph.D. from Boston University and did postdoctoral work at U.C.L.A. under Hans Reichenbach on a Ford grant. He is an ordained clergyman, a fellow of the National Council on Religion in Higher Education, past president of the Northwest Philosophical Association, a former member of the Executive Council of the American Philosophical Association, Pacific Division, and an active member of the National Ski Association, whose 1961 conference he attended as Western delegate. Dr. Wells is a frequent contributor to philosophical journals and, at Washington and as visiting professor elsewhere, has taught courses in the philosophy of religion every semester since 1946.